Lecture Notes in Computer Science 14518

Services Science

Subline of Lecture Notes in Computer Science

More information about this series at https://link.springer.com/bookseries/558

Flavia Monti · Pierluigi Plebani ·
Naouel Moha · Hye-young Paik ·
Johanna Barzen · Gowri Ramachandran ·
Devis Bianchini · Damian A. Tamburri ·
Massimo Mecella
Editors

Service-Oriented Computing – ICSOC 2023 Workshops

AI-PA, ASOCA, SAPD, SQS, SSCOPE, WESOACS and Satellite Events
Rome, Italy, November 28 – December 1, 2023
Revised Selected Papers

 Springer

Editors
Flavia Monti (iD)
Sapienza University of Rome
Rome, Italy

Naouel Moha (iD)
École de Technologie Supérieure
Montréal, QC, Canada

Johanna Barzen (iD)
University of Stuttgart
Stuttgart, Germany

Devis Bianchini (iD)
University of Brescia
Brescia, Italy

Massimo Mecella (iD)
Sapienza University of Rome
Rome, Italy

Pierluigi Plebani (iD)
Politecnico di Milano
Milan, Italy

Hye-young Paik (iD)
University of New South Wales
Sydney, NSW, Australia

Gowri Ramachandran (iD)
Queensland University of Technology
Brisbane, QLD, Australia

Damian A. Tamburri (iD)
TU/e – JADS, Politecnico di Milano
Milan, Italy

ISSN 0302-9743   ISSN 1611-3349   (electronic)
Lecture Notes in Computer Science
ISBN 978-981-97-0988-5   ISBN 978-981-97-0989-2   (eBook)
https://doi.org/10.1007/978-981-97-0989-2

This Springer imprint is published by the registered company Springer Nature Singapore Pte Ltd.
The registered company address is: 152 Beach Road, #21-01/04 Gateway East, Singapore 189721, Singapore

Paper in this product is recyclable.

Preface

This volume presents the proceedings of the scientific satellite events that were held in conjunction with the 21st International Conference on Service-Oriented Computing (ICSOC 2023), held from November 28 to December 1, 2023 in Rome (Italy). The satellite events provide an engaging space for specialist groups to meet, generating focused discussions on specific sub-areas within service-oriented computing, which contributes to ICSOC community building. These events significantly enrich the main conference by both expanding the scope of research topics and attracting participants from a wider community.

As is customary at ICSOC, this year's satellite events were organised around four tracks, a workshop track and a demonstration track, as well as a Ph.D. symposium and an invited tutorial track.

The ICSOC 2023 workshop track consisted of the following six workshops covering a wide range of topics that fall into the general area of service computing:

- The 7th Workshop on Adaptive Service-oriented and Cloud Applications (ASOCA 2023)
- The 3rd International Workshop on AI-enabled Process Automation (AI-PA 2023)
- The 19th International Workshop on Engineering Service-Oriented Applications and Cloud Services (WESOACS 2023)
- The 1st International Workshop on Secure, Accountable and Privacy-Preserving Data-Driven Service-Oriented Computing (SAPD 2023)
- The 1st Services and Quantum Software Workshop (SQS 2023)
- The 1st International Workshop on Sustainable Service-Oriented Computing: Addressing Environmental, Social, and Economic Dimensions (SSCOPE 2023)

This year in the workshop track, the themes of Internet of Things, artificial intelligence and quantum computing along with its applications in service computing were particularly noticeable. Workshops were selected based on the submission of a detailed description to the Conference Workshops Co-chairs. After a review of all the submissions, six workshops were selected by the Workshops Co-chairs, in consultation with the General Chair. All submitted papers to the workshops went through a heavy review process where each paper was single-blind reviewed by at least three members of the Program Committee of the workshop to which it was submitted. The Conference Workshops Co-chairs checked the assignments and the reviews before the final decisions were made. A total of 41 papers were submitted to the workshops and 21 were accepted. The workshops were held on November 28th, 2023, and included keynote talks from prominent speakers from industry and academia.

The demonstration track offers a highly interactive way to share practical research work in service-oriented computing and related areas. ICSOC 2023 Demo track received 8 submissions, of which 4 were accepted for publication and presentation. Demo authors had the chance to engage the audience's interest in a one-minute presentation per demo. Afterwards, all demos were successfully run in parallel and fruitful discussions between the authors and the other conference participants took place.

The Ph.D. Symposium received 5 submissions. Each submission was reviewed by three members of the Program Committee and after a thorough review process 2 submissions were accepted and 2 were invited to constitute the program of the Ph.D. symposium. The authors presented their work in front of a panel of experts, giving Ph. D. students an opportunity to showcase their research and providing them with feedback from both senior researchers and fellow Ph.D. students.

This volume contains 27 papers from the satellite events, selected from a total of 54 submissions. This represents an acceptance rate of 50%.

Finally, the volume also contains the extended abstracts of four tutorials that were invited by the General Chair and the Program Co-chairs on the basis of their relevance for the ICSOC community.

We would like to thank all the authors for submitting their work to the satellite events, as well as the various committee members, who together contributed to these important events of the conference. We hope that these proceedings will serve as a valuable reference for researchers and practitioners working in the service-oriented computing domain and its emerging applications.

November 2023

Pierluigi Plebani
Naouel Moha
Helen Paik
Johanna Barzen
Gowri Ramachandran
Devis Bianchini
Damian A. Tamburri
Massimo Mecella

Organization

Organizing Committee

General Chair

Massimo Mecella   Sapienza Università di Roma, Italy

Program Committee Co-chairs

Stefanie Rinderle-Ma   Technical University of Munich, Germany
Antonio Ruiz Cortés   Universidad de Sevilla, Spain
Zibin Zheng   Sun Yat-sen University, China

Focus Areas Chairs

Fabio Patrizi   Sapienza Università di Roma, Italy
Dan Li   Sun Yat-sen University, China
Francesco Leotta   Sapienza Università di Roma, Italy
Juan Manuel Murillo   University of Extremadura, Spain
  Rodríguez

Demo Co-chairs

Devis Bianchini   Università di Brescia, Italy
Damian A. Tamburri   TU/e – JADS, The Netherlands and Politecnico di
                              Milano, Italy

Workshop Co-chairs

Pierluigi Plebani   Politecnico di Milano, Italy
Naouel Moha   École de Technologie Supérieure de Montréal, Canada

Ph.D. Symposium Co-chairs

Helen Paik   University of New South Wales, Australia
Johanna Barzen   University of Stuttgart, Germany
Gowri Ramachandran   Queensland University of Technology, Australia

Proceedings and Conference Management System Chair

Flavia Monti   Sapienza Università di Roma, Italy

Local Organization, Finance and Sponsorship Chair

Massimo Mecella   Sapienza Università di Roma, Italy

Publicity, Web and Social Presence Co-chairs

Marco Calamo   Sapienza Università di Roma, Italy
Flavia Monti   Sapienza Università di Roma, Italy

Local Committee

Consulta Umbria   (organizing agency)
Filippo Bianchini   Sapienza Università di Roma, Italy
Marco Calamo   Sapienza Università di Roma, Italy
Mattia Macrí   Sapienza Università di Roma, Italy
Jerin George Mathew   Sapienza Università di Roma, Italy
Flavia Monti   Sapienza Università di Roma, Italy
Luciana Silo   Sapienza Università di Roma, Italy
Silvestro Veneruso   Sapienza Università di Roma, Italy

Steering Committee

Boualem Benatallah   Dublin City University, Ireland
Athman Bouguettaya   University of Sydney, Australia
Fabio Casati   University of Trento, Italy
Bernd J. Krämer   FernUniversität in Hagen, Germany
Winfried Lamersdorf   University of Hamburg, Germany
Heiko Ludwig   IBM, USA
Mike Papazoglou   Tilburg University, The Netherlands
Jian Yang   Macquarie University, Australia
Liang Zhang   Fudan University, China

International Workshop on AI-enabled Process Automation (AI-PA)

Amin Beheshti   Macquarie University, Australia
Boualem Benatallah   Dublin City University, Ireland
Hamid Motahari   UpBrains AI, Inc., USA

International Workshop on Adaptive Service-oriented and Cloud Applications (ASOCA)

Nesrine Khabou   University of Sfax, Tunisia
Ismael Bouassida Rodriguez University of Sfax, Tunisia
Khalil Drira   LAAS-CNRS, Univ. Toulouse, France

International Workshop on Secure, Accountable and Privacy-Preserving Data-Driven Service-Oriented Computing (SAPD)

Mattia Salnitri   Politecnico di Milano, Italy
Sebastian Werner   TU Berlin, Germany

Workshop on Services and Quantum Software (SQS)

Johanna Barzen	Institute of Architecture of Application Systems at the University of Stuttgart, Germany
Schahram Dustdar	TU Wien, Austria
Frank Leymann	Institute of Architecture of Application Systems at the University of Stuttgart, Germany
Juan M. Murillo	University of Extremadura, Spain

International Workshop on Sustainable Service-Oriented Computing: Addressing Environmental, Social, and Economic Dimensions (SSCOPE)

Roberta Capuano	University of L'Aquila, Italy
Daniele Di Pompeo	University of L'Aquila, Italy
Michele Tucci	University of L'Aquila, Italy

International Workshop on Engineering Service-Oriented Applications and Cloud Services (WESOACS)

Andreas S. Andreou	Cyprus University of Technology, Cyprus
George Feuerlicht	Unicorn University, Czech Republic
Willem Jan van den Heuvel	Tilburg University, The Netherlands
Winfried Lamersdorf	University of Hamburg, Germany
Guadalupe Ortiz Bellot	University of Cadiz, Puerto Real, Spain
Christian Zirpins	Karlsruhe University of Applied Sciences & STZ-SWE, Germany

Contents

AI-PA: AI-enabled Process Automation Introduction

Predictive Auto-scaling: LSTM-Based Multi-step Cloud Workload
Prediction.   5
    Basem Suleiman, Muhammad Johan Alibasa, Ya-Yuan Chang,
    and Ali Anaissi

Adapting LLMs for Efficient, Personalized Information Retrieval: Methods
and Implications   17
    Samira Ghodratnama and Mehrdad Zakershahrak

Towards Improving Insurance Processes: A Time Series Analysis of
Psychosocial Recovery After Workplace Injury Across Legislative
Environments   27
    John E. McMahon, Rasool Roozegar, Ashley Craig, and Ian Cameron

Uncovering LLMs for Service-Composition: Challenges and Opportunities. . . .   39
    Robin D. Pesl, Miles Stötzner, Ilche Georgievski, and Marco Aiello

Transformative Predictive Modelling in the Business of Health: Harnessing
Decision Trees for Strategic Insights and Enhanced Operational Efficiency. . . .   49
    John E. McMahon, Ashley Craig, and Ian Cameron

Breaking Boundaries: Can a Unified Hardware Abstraction Layer Simplify
Transformer Deployments on Edge Devices?   62
    Mehrdad Zakershahrak and Samira Ghodratnama

Improving Deep Learning Transparency: Leveraging the Power of LIME
Heatmap   72
    Helia Farhood, Mohammad Najafi, and Morteza Saberi

**ASOCA: Adaptive Service-oriented and Cloud Applications
Introduction**

Non-expert Level Analysis of Self-adaptive Systems   91
    Claudia Raibulet and Xiaojun Ling

**SAPD: Secure, Accountable and Privacy-Preserving Data-Driven
Service-Oriented Computing Introduction**

Federated Data Products: A Confluence of Data Mesh and Gaia-X for
Data Sharing 107
   Farouk Jeffar and Pierluigi Plebani

XPS++: A Publish/Subscribe System with Built-In Security and Privacy
by Design 119
   Noor Ahmed

SQS: Services and Quantum Software Introduction

On Rounding Errors in the Simulation of Quantum Circuits 137
   Jonas Klamroth and Bernhard Beckert

Linear Structure of Training Samples in Quantum Neural Network
Applications 150
   Alexander Mandl, Johanna Barzen, Marvin Bechtold,
   Michael Keckeisen, Frank Leymann, and Patrick K. S. Vaudrevange

Towards Higher Abstraction Levels in Quantum Computing 162
   Hermann Fürntratt, Paul Schnabl, Florian Krebs, Roland Unterberger,
   and Herwig Zeiner

Hybrid Data Management Architecture for Present Quantum Computing 174
   Markus Zajac and Uta Störl

Quantum Block-Matching Algorithm Using Dissimilarity Measure 185
   M. Martínez-Felipe, J. Montiel-Pérez, Victor Onofre,
   A. Maldonado-Romo, and Ricky Young

Some Initial Guidelines for Building Reusable Quantum Oracles 197
   Javier Sanchez-Rivero, Daniel Talaván, Jose Garcia-Alonso,
   Antonio Ruiz-Cortés, and Juan Manuel Murillo

**SSCOPE: Sustainable Service-Oriented Computing: Addressing
Environmental, Social, and Economic Dimensions Introduction**

Carbon-Awareness in CI/CD 213
   Henrik Claßen, Jonas Thierfeldt, Julian Tochman-Szewc,
   Philipp Wiesner, and Odej Kao

WESOACS: Workshop on Engineering Service-Oriented Applications and Cloud Services Introduction

Smart Public Transport with Be-in/Be-out System Supported by iBeacon
Devices 229
    Aneta Poniszewska-Marańda, Mateusz Kubiak, and Lukasz Chomątek

Towards a Systematic Comparison Framework for Cloud Services
Customer Agreements 241
    Elena Molino-Peña and José María García

Formalizing Microservices Patterns with Event-B: The Case of Service
Registry 253
    Sebastián Vergara, Laura González, and Raúl Ruggia

Privacy Engineering in the Data Mesh: Towards a Decentralized Data
Privacy Governance Framework 265
    Nemania Borovits, Indika Kumara, Damian A. Tamburri,
    and Willem-Jan Van Den Heuvel

Ph.D. Symposium

Towards a Taxonomy and Software Architecture for Data Processing and
Contextualization for the Internet of Things 279
    Adrian Bazan-Muñoz, Guadalupe Ortiz, and Alfonso Garcia-de-Prado

Advanced Serverless Edge Computing 285
    Inacio Gaspar Ticongolo, Luciano Baresi, and Giovanni Quattrocchi

Demos and Resources Introduction

Immersive 3D Simulator for Drone-as-a-Service 297
    Jiamin Lin, Balsam Alkouz, Athman Bouguettaya, and Amani Abusafia

SLA-Wizard - Automated Configuration of RESTful API Gateways Based
on SLAs 304
    Ignacio Peluaga Lozada, Pablo Fernandez, and José María García

The IDL Tool Suite: Inter-parameter Dependency Management in Web
APIs 311
    Saman Barakat, Alberto Martin-Lopez, Carlos Müller,
    and Sergio Segura

Smelling Homemade Crypto Code in Microservices, with KubeHound 317
   Thomas Howard-Grubb, Jacopo Soldani, Giorgio Dell'Immagine,
   Francesca Arcelli Fontana, and Antonio Brogi

Tutorials

What is Blockchain and How Can it Help My Business? (Extended Tutorial
Summary) 327
   Marco Comuzzi, Paul Grefen, and Giovanni Meroni

Quantum Services: A Tutorial on the Technology and the Process 335
   Javier Romero-Álvarez, Jaime Alvarado-Valiente, Enrique Moguel,
   José Garcia-Alonso, and Juan M. Murillo

Satellite Computing: From Space to Your Screen 343
   Qing Li and Daliang Xu

Services in Industry 4.0. Modeling and Composition for Agile Supply
Chains 350
   Francesco Leotta, Flavia Monti, and Luciana Silo

Author Index 359

AI-PA: AI-enabled Process Automation Introduction

Introduction to the 4th International Workshop on AI-enabled Process Automation (AI-PA 2023)

Amin Besheti[1] , Boualem Benatallah[2] , and Hamid Motahari[3]

[1] Macquarie University, Australia
amin.beheshti@mq.edu.au
[2] Dublin City University, Ireland
boualem.benatallah@dcu.ie
[3] UpBrains AI, Inc., USA
hamidreza.motaharinezhad@mq.edu.au

The 4th International Workshop on AI-enabled Process Automation (AI-PA) was held as one of the workshops of the 21th International Conference on Service-Oriented Computing (ICSOC 2023). The AI-PA workshop aimed to provide a forum for researchers and professionals interested in Artificial Intelligence (AI)-enabled Business Processes and Services; and in understanding, envisioning and discussing the opportunities and challenges of intelligent Process Automation, Process Data Analytics and providing Cognitive Assistants for knowledge workers. Recognizing the broad scope of the potential areas of interest, the workshop was organized into FOUR themes, as follows:

- Theme 1: Artificial Intelligence (AI), Services and Processes
- Theme 2: BigData, Services and Processes
- Theme 3: Smart Entities, Services and Processes
- Theme 4: AI in Industry

The papers selected for presentation and publication in this volume showcase fresh ideas from exciting and emerging topics in service-oriented computing and case studies in Artificial Intelligence (AI)-enabled Business Processes and Services. We selected 7 high-quality papers from the AI-PA 2023 submissions keeping the acceptance rate at around 43%. Each paper was single-blind reviewed by a team comprising a senior Program Committee member and at least two regular Program Committee members, who engaged in a discussion phase after the initial reviews were prepared. AI-PA 2023 workshop paid the Workshop Registration Fees for all accepted papers, and offered AUD$500.00 for the best paper award, thanks to AI-PA Workshop Sponsors:

- IBM Australia (https://www.ibm.com/au-en)
- SystemEthix (https://www.systemethix.com.au)
- NavigatorGroup (https://www.navigatorgroup.com.au)
- Centre for Applied Artificial Intelligence at Macquarie University
- (https://www.mq.edu.au/research/research-centres-groups-and-facilities/centres/centre-for-applied-artificial-intelligence)
- Google Australia (https://www.google.com.au)

We are grateful for the support of our authors, sponsors, program committees, and the ICSOC Organizing Committee. We very much hope you enjoy reading the papers in this volume.

November 2023   AI-PA 2023 Workshop Organizers

Organization

Workshop Organizers

Amin Beheshti — Macquarie University, Australia
Boualem Benatallah — Dublin City University, Ireland
Hamid Motahari — UpBrains AI, Inc., USA

Program Committee

Schahram Dustdar — Vienna University of Technology, Austria
Michael Sheng — Macquarie University, Australia
Fabio Casati — Servicenow, USA
Salil Kanhere — University of New South Wales, Australia
Jian Yang — Macquarie University, Australia
Qiang Qu — Shenzhen Institutes of Advanced Technology, China

Daniela Grigori — Paris-Dauphine University, France
Ashkan Sami — Edinburgh Napier University, UK
Azadeh Ghari Neiat — Deakin University, Australia
Mohammad Allahbakhsh — Ferdowsi University of Mashhad, Iran
Adrian Mos — Naver LABS, France
Samira Ghodratnama — Grainger, USA
Helia Farhood — Macquarie University, Australia
Marcos Baez — University of Trento, Italy

Predictive Auto-scaling: LSTM-Based Multi-step Cloud Workload Prediction

Basem Suleiman[1,2]([✉]), Muhammad Johan Alibasa[3], Ya-Yuan Chang[1], and Ali Anaissi[1]

[1] University of New South Wales, Sydney, Australia
b.suleiman@unsw.edu.au, ycha8280@uni.sydney.edu.au,
ali.anaissi@sydney.edu.au
[2] The University of Sydney, Sydney, Australia
basem.suleiman@sydney.edu.au
[3] Telkom University, Bandung, Indonesia
alibasa@telkomuniversity.ac.id

Abstract. Auto-scaling, also known as elasticity, provides the capacity to efficiently allocate computing resources on demand, rendering it beneficial for a wide array of applications, particularly web-based ones. However, the dynamic and unpredictable nature of workloads in web applications poses considerable challenges in designing effective strategies for cloud auto-scaling. Existing research primarily relies on single-step prediction methods or focuses solely on forecasting request arrival rates, thus overlooking the intricate nature of workload characteristics and system dynamics, which significantly affect resource demands in the cloud. In this study, we propose an innovative approach to address this limitation by introducing a multi-step workload prediction method using the Long Short-Term Memory (LSTM) model. By considering workload attributes over a specific time frame, our approach enables accurate predictions of future workloads over designated time intervals through multi-step forecasting. By utilising two real-world web workload datasets, our experiments aim to underscore the significance of using real-world data in delivering a comparative performance analysis between single-step and multi-step predictions. The results demonstrate that our proposed multi-step prediction model outperforms single-step predictions and other baseline models.

Keywords: cloud services · auto-scaling · workload prediction · machine learning

1 Introduction

Cloud computing has revolutionized the way users access and leverage computing resources by offering Web service APIs and adopting a pay-as-you-go model, where users pay only for the resources they consume. This transformation enables high-performance and cost-effective cloud services, emphasising the importance

F. Monti et al. (Eds.): ICSOC 2023 Workshops, LNCS 14518, pp. 5–16, 2024.
https://doi.org/10.1007/978-981-97-0989-2_1

of auto-scaling and cloud resource elasticity. These capabilities provide cost-efficient computing resources, avoiding the complexities of maintaining internal infrastructures. Cloud consumers can seamlessly request and adjust computing resources on-demand to accommodate the dynamic variations in their application workloads.

Proactively scaling applications based on accurate web workload predictions has long been a focal point in research, presenting two key challenges. First, precise workload predictions rely on effective workload characterization, considering the varying resource requirements of different application request types, as discussed in [11]. Second, in the context of auto-scaling, forecasting workloads multiple steps ahead, over an extended time period, holds significant value as it enhances resource preparation and acquisition. However, the literature analysis reveals the absence of datasets with predefined labels or observable patterns that could aid in workload classification and forecasting. For example, e-commerce web applications frequently experience increased workloads during weekends or holidays, underscoring the importance of scaling to avoid under-provisioning or over-provisioning during known events.

There are three primary auto-scaling methods: reactive, proactive, and predictive. The most widely adopted approach is reactive auto-scaling, as it enables responses based on pre-defined scaling rules or policies. Reactive and proactive auto-scaling both rely on reactive workload prediction, with the decision-maker pre-configured to adjust resources when the workload exceeds predefined thresholds, such as CPU or memory utilisation, and application performance measures [4]. However, these approaches can be ineffective due to factors such as the time required to detect workload changes, delays in requesting computing resources due to server booting, and sudden bursts of workload over short periods [12]. This may result in Service Level Agreement (SLA) violations until an appropriate autoscaling decision is made and executed. In contrast, predictive auto-scaling addresses these challenges by forecasting future workloads, identifying patterns, and provisioning the necessary resources.

Given the aforementioned challenges, the primary goal of this research is to propose an effective workload prediction model. The objective is to facilitate predictive autoscaling, allowing the seamless handling of fluctuating workloads from web applications by leveraging and adapting relevant machine learning algorithms. In comparison to previous studies, our approach emphasizes forecasting workloads multiple steps into the future. In summary, the key contributions of this study are as follows:

- We introduce pre-processing methods that employ various strategies to enhance the performance of multi-step workload predictions.
- We develop an LSTM-based model that leverages the pre-processed data to improve the accuracy of multi-step workload forecasting.
- We conduct a comparative analysis to assess the performance of single-step and multi-step workload predictions between our proposed LSTM-based model and a baseline model using Multi-layer Perceptron (MLP).

2   Related Work

According to the applied algorithm and forecasting process, the methods for predicting workload in cloud computing can be classified as either rule-based or machine learning prediction. Yang et al. [19] suggested a linear regression model to react to the changing resources configuration of cluster resources and to estimate the load of the application. They introduced a greedy method along with a user-defined threshold, which helps to lower the cost and to reduce SLA violations. Similar to Yang, Zang et al. [20] also provided a prediction-based scaling solution along with the collaborative filtering and pattern matching technique. This method slightly improved reactive rule-based scalability since it links SLA according to lower-level metrics from the infrastructure, yet more infrastructure metrics should be considered.

Many researchers have explored the comparison between the performances of ARIMA and other deep learning methods in different fields. Fu et al. [5] tried to forecast traffic flow and traffic speed. They found that RNN and LSTM performed better than the ARIMA models. Debashins et al. [15] also performed a comparison analysis between LSTM, MLP, and ARIMA for network load dataset. Their study also found that LSTM outperforms MLP at most of the time. Similarly, Cao et al. [2] have compared ARIMA and RNN in field of forecasting wind speed, and they found that RNN models have outperformed ARIMA models.

The majority of previous works focused on predicting single steps, as predicting multiple steps has presented a challenging problem. However, in recent years, numerous methods have been proposed in the literature across various engineering fields for multi-step prediction of time series variables. These methods have been applied to diverse domains, including stock price prediction, electric load forecasting, wind speed prediction, and weather forecasting. For predicting stock price, multi-step forecasting along with deep neural network have also been utilized in [14] and [16]. In the field of cloud computing, Zhu et al. [21] has used LSTM models to predict multiple steps ahead of the host load using the dataset from Alibaba and Dinda Traces. Another study by Gao et al. [6] also used Bi-LSTM to perform task failure prediction in cloud data centres.

Time series analysis is also applied to predict future workload and resource usage. Many existing time series problems comprise the works of forecasting a sequence of future values. However, time series workloads exhibit higher variability and larger noises [13], which in turn leads to very challenging issues and a lack of available studies for multi-step forecasting. Additionally, non-stationary workloads in the cloud environment continuously change their patterns, leading to increased overheads and constraints on prediction models [13]. Nevertheless, time series algorithms are widely utilised for estimating future workloads. Most of the existing studies and comparisons of the ARIMA and RNN models have been conducted for short-term prediction and specifically focused on single-step predictions. The existing state-of-the-art predictive auto-scaling methods for workload, which focus on request arrival rate or the number of requests per time step, often neglect the crucial and essential aspect of multi-step ahead predictions. Incorporating multi-step predictions is vital for achieving greater accuracy and cost reduction.

3   Method: Multi-step Workload Prediction

3.1   Data Collection

1998 World Cup Dataset: The 1998 World Cup took place from June 10, 1998, to July 12, 1998. The website for the 1998 World Cup was launched on May 6, 1997, providing live scores for soccer matches and other related information [1]. The trace logs of incoming requests to the website were collected from April 30, 1998, to July 26, 1998, spanning 88 days and in total 1,352,804,107 web requests. The ITA website [1] recorded 92 days of trace log data, with the initial 4 days left empty to serve as placeholders to identify the days of the week. To manage file size, each day's log data was further split into several files, each containing a maximum of 7 million requests. For instance, day 40 was divided into two files: `wc_day40_1.gz` with 6,999,999 requests and `wc_day40_2.gz` with 1,297,254 requests. A total of 249 binary files were generated, which required additional processing to read their contents.

The FIFA 1998 log site includes a recreate tool for converting binary logs back into Common Log Format. As we are only interested in the timestamp of the request, we have modified `recreate.c` file to ensure that the recreating file in common log format only returns the timestamp and ignores other variables such as ClientID, objectID, size, method, status, type, and server. In this way, it largely reduces the file size and the time to read and convert for each file. In our experimental setup, we focused on data extracted from June and July. To simplify the dataset and enhance its usability, we aggregated and processed all logs that occurred in the same minute but in different seconds. As a result, each record in the adapted dataset represents the total number of HTTP requests per minute. The minute interval spans from 0 (22:00:01 on May 31, 1998) to 80,639 (22:00:05 on July 26, 1998). The number of requests during this period ranges from 0 to 229,676, with an average of 15,890.92 requests per minute.

NASA Web Request Traces: The NASA website traces are utilized to assess the high accuracy of our model's predictions on different datasets. These traces encompass all HTTP requests made to the NASA Kennedy Space Center WWW server in Florida, spanning from July 1, 1995, to August 31, 1995. Notably, there is no access record from 14:52:01 on August 1, 1995, until 04:36:13 on August 3, 1995, due to Hurricane Erin. The dataset was split into two files, namely July and August, containing 1,891,715 and 1,569,898 web requests, respectively. Altogether, the dataset encompasses a total of 3,461,613 requests. These traces are employed to evaluate the model's predictive capabilities across different datasets. As we are only interested in the number of requests, only the timestamp variable will be kept in the data frame. We also combined all the logs that appeared in the same minute but in different seconds. Thus, the overall dataset is converted in such a way that each entry represents the number of HTTP requests per minute. The minute interval ranges from 0 (00:00:01 July 1, 1995) to 89,280 (23:59:53 August 31, 1995). To access the data, we obtained two files from the ITA website. Each log entry comprises host information, timestamp, HTTP request details, reply code, and reply size. As our focus is solely on the number of requests, we extracted only the timestamp variable, discarding the rest from the data frame. To streamline the dataset, we combined all the logs that occurred within the same minute, but had different seconds. Consequently, the entire dataset was transformed to represent the number of HTTP requests per minute. The minute interval spans from 0 (00:00:01 on July 1, 1995) to 89,280 (23:59:53 on August 31, 1995).

SHARCNet Cluster Traces: The SHARCNet traces encompass a year's worth of accounting records from the SHARCNet cluster, installed at various academic institutions across Ontario, Canada. Designed as a "cluster of clusters" that spans western, central, and northern Ontario, the SHARCNet infrastructure serves the computational needs of researchers across diverse research areas, facilitating cutting-edge tools for high-performance computing. The SHARCNet cluster traces consist of a total of 1,195,242 requests, recorded from 02:55:33 on December 21st to 11:41:00 on January 16, 2007, with a resolution of 1 s. We aggregated all entries occurring within the same minute but with different seconds into single minute intervals, presenting the dataset with the number of requests occurring in each minute. For file size reduction and comparability with other datasets, we specifically extracted data for two months, spanning from 00:00:01 on July 1, 2006, to 23:59:53 on August 31, 2006. Consequently, the resulting dataset comprises minute intervals ranging from 0 to 89,290.

3.2 LSTM-Based Multi-step Workload Prediction

Workload prediction can be categorized into two main approaches: single-step prediction and multi-step prediction. In single-step prediction, only one value is forecasted for the future, treating it as a singular input vector, with no feedback used for further predictions. On the other hand, multi-step prediction involves forecasting the next H values using historical time series, where $H > 1$ represents the forecasting horizon. There are three distinct strategies for multi-step prediction. Figure 1 demonstrates the use of historical data of size 4 to predict 3 steps ahead, illustrating various forms of multi-step predictions.

- *Direct Strategy*: A separated model is developed in each timestamp. It brings the benefit of not prone to any accumulated errors. However, it has some weakness as it requires a large computational cost since the number of models to learn is equal to the size of the horizon.
- *Recursive Strategy*: A single model is used multiple times for each prediction. The forecasted value from prior step fed into the model as an input for creating the prediction on next step [18]. A drawback of recursive method is its sensitivity to errors since it allows prediction errors to accumulate which degrades the performance as the forecasting horizons increase.

- *Multiple-Input-Multiple-Output (MIMO)*: Both direct and recursive methods are only capable of predicting single-output using multiple input where the output is respectively y_{t+1} for recursive case and y_{t+k} for direct case. However, single-output ignores the existence of stochastic dependencies between future values (y_{t+k} and y_{t+k+1}) with a very long term prediction, and therefore biases the prediction accuracy. Learning from a single multiple-output model, Multiple-Input-Multiple-Output prevents the conditional independence assumption made by Direct Strategy and Recursive Strategy [7,8].

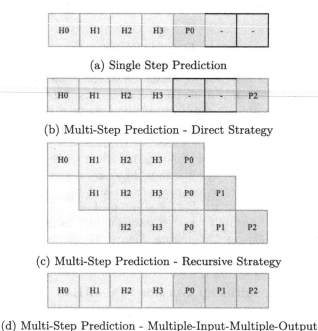

(a) Single Step Prediction

(b) Multi-Step Prediction - Direct Strategy

(c) Multi-Step Prediction - Recursive Strategy

(d) Multi-Step Prediction - Multiple-Input-Multiple-Output

Fig. 1. Single Step And Various Form of Multi-Step Prediction

Based on the strategies mentioned earlier, the selected dataset requires preprocessing before being fed into LSTM models. The transformation of the datasets can be described in four key steps:

1. The first step involves re-framing the sequence of time series data into supervised learning problems, forming pairs of input and output sequences. This enables the algorithm to learn how to predict output patterns based on input patterns. This can be achieved by employing a $shift()$ function where previous time steps $(t - n)$ used as inputs and a collection of current time steps (t) is used as output for the observed data.
2. The second step involves addressing trends and seasonality that may exist in the time series data. Trends can result in varying means over time, while seasonality can cause changing variances [9,17]. Both these factors contribute

to the non-stationarity of the time series data. To facilitate the model and improve forecasting accuracy, we transform the time series dataset into a stationary time series dataset. To achieve this, a few steps are followed. Firstly, the difference between the current observation and the previous observation is calculated. Then, to revert to the original scale, the difference value is added to the observation at the prior time step. This process effectively mitigates the impact of trends and seasonality, resulting in a stationary time series dataset.

3. The third step involves forcing the data points to be scaled within the range of -1 to 1. This scaling is necessary to ensure that the data falls within the appropriate range for the activation function used in the model. By scaling the data to this range, we facilitate the effective functioning of the neural network model during training and prediction processes.

4. Finally, the dataset is reshaped into a matrix form with a dimension of samples, timesteps, and features [17]. To achieve this, we fix the number of features to one and transform the original 2D array into a 3D array. This is accomplished by extracting the dimension value and the number of elements in each dimension from the original array. The dimension value is used as the value for the "sample" dimension in the matrix, while the number of elements in each dimension is used as the value for the "timesteps" dimension. This reshaping process prepares the data in a suitable format for input into the LSTM model.

Table 1. Data Partitioning

No.	Splitting Method	Train	Test
1	One week of June to train and the rest of June to test	10,079 min (23.33%)	33,120 min (76.66%)
2	One week of June to train and the rest of June and July to test	10,079 min (12.49%)	70,560 min (87.5%)
3	The whole June to train and the whole July to test	43,200 min (53.57%)	37,440 min (46.42%)

3.3 Prediction Models

After being pre-processed using the previous methods, the data were fed into LSTM (long short-term memory) model. LSTM models are good at persisting information for a long time and are suitable to predict the next sequence of the workload over time. The LSTM Model were developed using Python Ecosystem. Then $fit()$ function was called to train the model and $predict()$ function was called to make predictions. To perform the sample forecasting using LSTM models, the dataset were split into train and test to train the models and check the performance respectively. We have experimented with three different ways of splitting the dataset. Table 1 shows an overview of the split. After several experiments on testing out the number of input and outputs, the third way of splitting the dataset showed the best result of all. Therefore, we continued our experiments with the dataset split between June and July.

LSTM Model: The number of hidden nodes, the number of training epochs, and the number of samples to include in each mini-batch are fundamental architecture decisions for LSTM network. As there is no rule of thumb for selecting the right combination of parameters, to tune the hyper-parameters and select our network architecture, we perform a simple grid search on the above variables. To determine the number of hidden nodes, we conducted a grid search over n_node $\in$ {5, 10, 20, 50}. The one n_node = 50 achieves the best performance. For the number of epochs and samples to include in each batch, we also performed a grid search over epoch $\in$ {100, 200, 500, 1000, 2000} and batch $\in$ {4, 8, 12, 32, 64}. The value of epoch = 100, batch = 4 gives the best result. Simple LSTM network has been designed with single layer. To train our network, we used Adam optimization algorithm [10] and Root Mean Square Error as our loss function. The LSTM network used to configure our LSTM model was fitted with 50 hidden nodes, 100 epochs, and a batch size of 4.

Baseline Model: As a baseline to the LSTM model, we also build another model using Multiple Layer Perceptron (MLP). MLP is a feedforward artificial neural network which is often used for time series prediction. It follows supervised learning paradigm and is commonly trained with back propagation [15]. Each training pair consists of an input layer and an output layer. To evaluate it against our proposed model, we fed in the same configuration to our LSTM model, i.e., 50 hidden nodes were included with 100 epochs and a batch size of 4.

Different combinations of number of inputs and outputs are used to evaluate the performance. The sampling frequency of data was a minute. For example, if targeting one step ahead prediction with a history of five minutes, then single step prediction is used with the value of number of input is five and the value of number of outputs is one. On the other hand, using the past fifteen minutes to forecast ten minutes ahead will require multi step forecasting with the value of number of input is fifteen and the value of the number of output is ten. To forecast multiple steps ahead in the future, we are using Multiple-Input-Multiple-Output strategy in multiple step prediction as, rather than producing a single output, we are more interested in having multiple outputs. This can also avoid accumulating the errors in previous steps during the prediction. To measure the performance of the models, a frequently used quadratic evaluation in machine learning, root mean square error (RMSE) is used. The advantage of using RMSE is that it penalizes relatively large errors [3]. It is useful for companies who use predictions to make decisions that affect their profits because large individual errors entail more significant consequences [3].

4   Experiments and Results

Table 2 and 3 show the results of RMSE using different combination of the amount of historical values and steps ahead among World Cup, NASA and

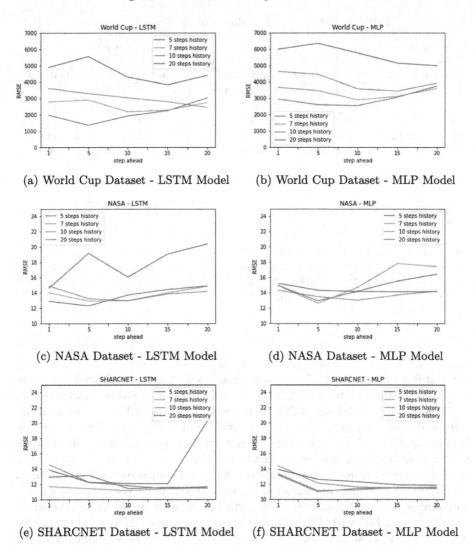

(a) World Cup Dataset - LSTM Model   (b) World Cup Dataset - MLP Model

(c) NASA Dataset - LSTM Model   (d) NASA Dataset - MLP Model

(e) SHARCNET Dataset - LSTM Model   (f) SHARCNET Dataset - MLP Model

Fig. 2. Visualize Results of Each Dataset with LSTM and MLP Models

SHARACNET dataset for LSTM and MLP model respectively. Furthermore, Fig. 2 illustrates the trend of RMSE in each datasets.

Based on Table 2 and Fig. 2, it is shown that multi-step prediction performance depends on the number of steps ahead. Some of the multi-steps prediction did perform better than single step prediction. Specifically, for both World Cup and NASA datasets, using 5 historical data points to predict 5 steps ahead showed the lowest RMSE. The RMSE of World Cup dataset and NASA dataset resulted in similar pattern, where the error increased as the output steps exceeded the number of input steps when using 5, 7, or 10 historical points. How-

Table 2. RMSE of LSTM Models With Three Datasets

Steps Ahead	WC				NASA				SHARCNET			
	H = 5	H = 7	H = 10	H = 20	H = 5	H = 7	H = 10	H = 20	H = 5	H = 7	H = 10	H = 20
1	1965.2	2777.7	3596.8	4888.9	12.9	14.0	14.9	14.6	12.9	12.7	14.6	13.9
5	1357.6	2896.9	3279.7	5547.8	12.3	12.9	13.2	19.2	13.1	11.4	12.3	12.2
10	1916.4	2168.7	3021.4	4291.6	13.7	13.0	12.9	16.1	11.4	11.2	11.8	12.1
15	2239.2	2272.2	2783.3	3807.0	14.4	14.0	13.8	19.1	11.6	11.4	11.4	12.1
20	3019.1	2731.5	2436.7	4396.5	14.9	14.8	14.2	20.4	11.5	11.5	11.7	20.2

Table 3. RMSE of MLP Models With Three Datasets

Steps Ahead	WC				NASA				SHARCNET			
	H = 5	H = 7	H = 10	H = 20	H = 5	H = 7	H = 10	H = 20	H = 5	H = 7	H = 10	H = 20
1	2945.2	3656.3	4641.7	5998.9	14.9	14.9	14.3	15.2	13.2	13.3	14.4	13.9
5	2595.0	3452.4	4459.0	6343.5	12.9	12.6	13.5	14.3	11.0	11.2	12.1	12.6
10	2544.9	2894.2	3556.8	5756.8	14.2	14.7	13.0	14.2	11.4	11.2	11.6	12.3
15	3061.2	3106.1	3428.0	5138.2	15.5	17.8	13.7	14.1	11.5	11.6	11.5	11.9
20	3729.4	3588.2	3909.5	4988.2	16.4	17.4	14.2	14.2	11.4	11.5	11.6	11.8

ever, using 20 historical data points did not produce a consistent result among any dataset. While World Cup dataset and NASA dataset showed a similar trend, the RMSE result of SHARCNET dataset was not consistent with others even though the model was still able to perform better in the case of multiple step prediction compared to single step prediction. The potential reason of not having aligned results was that there were many unexpected bursts. The average incoming requests per minute of SHARCNET dataset was 1.85, yet there were several bursts with over 800 requests per minute. Comparing to NASA dataset which had similar range of number of requests, it had an average request of 38.77 with only one burst that hits 400. Furthermore, based on our dataset exploration, the overall trend of SHARCNET dataset was much more bursty than the one in NASA dataset. Most data points in NASA dataset ranged between 0 to 200 with one burst at 400, while multiple spikes existed in SHARCNET dataset. Thus, the results of SHARCNET did not follow similar trend as other datasets.

To further evaluate our proposed model, we compare it with a baseline method using MLP algorithm. In Fig. 2(b), (d), and (f), MLP appeared to have worse results compare to the ones using LSTM on the left for all datasets. The RMSE range was between 1000 to 4000 for World Cup dataset when using LSTM while it was between 2500 to 5000 when using MLP. Nevertheless, even though it did not produce low error rate compare to using LSTM model, it was also able to perform better in multiple steps prediction for some cases. We found that it produced similar result as using LSTM while using 5 historical data points to predict 5 steps ahead. This set up was able produce the best result for both models. For SHARCNET, it did not appear to have a clear pattern and the differences between RMSE results of varied combinations of inputs and outputs were not obvious, which might due to the unsteady spikes among the dataset.

To summarize our evaluations in terms of the dataset, we found that, in general, using 5 historical data points to predict 5 steps ahead with LSTM model produced the best result when the data is relatively intensive such as World Cup dataset. While the proposed model also worked well on less intensive workload like SHARCNET, there was not a distinct difference between various combinations of inputs and outputs. Among all the datasets, it is worth noted that having too many historical data points (eg. 20) did not necessarily guarantee lower error rate.

5   Conclusion and Future Work

In this paper we proposed pre-processing methods for multi-step workload prediction. We conducted experimental analysis using real-world datasets to evaluate the accuracy of our multi-step LSTM-based workload prediction. The experiments involve various combinations of the number of historical data points and the number of prediction steps ahead. The results demonstrated that both our proposed LSTM-based model and MLP neural network model predicted multiple steps ahead with improved accuracy compared to single-step predictions. However, our LSTM-based multi-step prediction consistently outperformed MLP across all tested scenarios. Existing auto-scaling methods often rely on simplistic heuristics and struggle with the complexities of real-world workloads, leading to suboptimal performance. This research aims to address these limitations by developing a more versatile and adaptable auto-scaling approach to meet the evolving demands of modern cloud computing. LSTM models offer promise for real-world large-scale deployment due to their effectiveness in handling sequences, but their computational intensity and resource requirements can pose scalability challenges.

It would be valuable to expand this study by incorporating workload characterization to enhance decision-making in the auto-scaling process. Specifically, the dataset can be categorized into several clusters, and workload prediction for multiple steps ahead can be performed for each cluster. This approach enables the prediction of not only the number of requests but also the types of requests, enabling more precise scaling based on the required resources. Furthermore, extending this research to facilitate prediction in other contexts, such as CPU/memory usage or the number of containers, presents another promising research direction that merits further investigation.

References

1. Arlitt, M., Jin, T.: A workload characterization study of the 1998 world cup web site. IEEE Netw. **14**(3), 30–37 (2000). https://doi.org/10.1109/65.844498
2. Cao, Q., Ewing, B.T., Thompson, M.A.: Forecasting wind speed with recurrent neural networks. Eur. J. Oper. Res. **221**(1), 148–154 (2012)

3. Chai, T., Draxler, R.: Root mean square error (RMSE) or mean absolute error (MAE)? Geosci. Model Dev. **7**(3), 1247–1250 (2014). https://doi.org/10.5194/gmdd-7-1525-2014

4. Coutinho, E.F., de Carvalho Sousa, F.R., Rego, P.A.L., Gomes, D.G., de Souza, J.N.: Elasticity in cloud computing: a survey. Ann. Telecommun. **70**(7–8), 289–309 (2014). https://doi.org/10.1007/s12243-014-0450-7

5. Fu, Y., Hu, W., Tang, M., Yu, R., Liu, B.: Multi-step ahead wind power forecasting based on recurrent neural networks. In: 2018 IEEE PES Asia-Pacific Power and Energy Engineering Conference (APPEEC), pp. 217–222 (2018)

6. Gao, J., Wang, H., Shen, H.: Task failure prediction in cloud data centers using deep learning. IEEE Trans. Serv. Comput. **15**(3), 1411–1422 (2020)

7. Gomez-Perez, A., Fernández-López, M., Corcho, O.: Ontological Engineering: With Examples from the Areas of Knowledge Management, E-Commerce and the Semantic Web (2004)

8. Halpin, T.: Metaschemas for ER, ORM and UML data models: a comparison. J. Database Manag. **13**, 20–30 (2002). https://doi.org/10.4018/jdm.2002040102

9. Hyndman, R., Athanasopoulos, G.: Forecasting: Principles and Practice, 2nd edn. OTexts (2018)

10. Kingma, D.P., Ba, J.: Adam: a method for stochastic optimization (2017)

11. Kirchoff, D.F., Xavier, M., Mastella, J., De Rose, C.A.F.: A preliminary study of machine learning workload prediction techniques for cloud applications. In: 2019 27th Euromicro International Conference on Parallel, Distributed and Network-Based Processing (PDP) (2019)

12. Lorido-Botran, T., Miguel-Alonso, J., Lozano, J.A.: A review of auto-scaling techniques for elastic applications in cloud environments. J. Grid Comput. **12**(4), 559–592 (2014). https://doi.org/10.1007/s10723-014-9314-7

13. Masdari, M., Khoshnevis, A.: A survey and classification of the workload forecasting methods in cloud computing. Cluster Comput. **23**(4), 2399–2424 (2019). https://doi.org/10.1007/s10586-019-03010-3

14. Pan, Y., Xiao, Z., Wang, X., Yang, D.: A multiple support vector machine approach to stock index forecasting with mixed frequency sampling. KBS **122**, 90–102 (2017)

15. Sahoo, D., Sood, N., Rani, U., Abraham, G., Dutt, V., Dileep, A.: Comparative analysis of multi-step time-series forecasting for network load dataset (2020)

16. Samarawickrama, A., Fernando, T.: 2019 14th Conference on Industrial and Information Systems (ICIIS) (2019). https://doi.org/10.1109/iciis47346.2019.9063310

17. Sutcliffe, A.: Time-series forecasting using fractional differencing. J. Forecast. **13**(4), 383–393 (1994)

18. Taieb, S., Bontempi, G.: Recursive multi-step time series forecasting by perturbing data. In: Cook, D., Pei, J., Wang, W., Zaiane, O., Wu, X. (eds.) 11th IEEE International Conference on Data Mining, ICDM 2011, pp. 695–704. IEEE Computer Society (2011). https://doi.org/10.1109/ICDM.2011.123

19. Yang, J., Liu, C., Shang, Y., Mao, Z., Junliang, C.: Workload predicting-based automatic scaling in service clouds, pp. 810–815 (2013)

20. Zhang, L., Zhang, Y., Jamshidi, P., Xu, L., Pahl, C.: Workload patterns for quality-driven dynamic cloud service configuration and auto-scaling. In: 2014 IEEE/ACM 7th International Conference on Utility and Cloud Computing, UCC 2014, pp. 156–165. IEEE Computer Society (2014)

21. Zhu, Y., Zhang, W., Chen, Y., Gao, H.: A novel approach to workload prediction using attention-based LSTM encoder-decoder network in cloud environment. EURASIP J. Wirel. Commun. Netw. **2019**, 1–18 (2019). https://doi.org/10.1186/s13638-019-1605-z

Adapting LLMs for Efficient, Personalized Information Retrieval: Methods and Implications

Samira Ghodratnama$^{(\boxtimes)}$ and Mehrdad Zakershahrak

Macquaire University, Sydney, Australia
{samira.ghodratnama,mehrdad.zakershahrak}@mq.edu.au

Abstract. The advent of Large Language Models (LLMs) heralds a pivotal shift in online user interactions with information. Traditional Information Retrieval (IR) systems primarily relied on query-document matching, whereas LLMs excel in comprehending and generating human-like text, thereby enriching the IR experience significantly. While LLMs are often associated with chatbot functionalities, this paper extends the discussion to their explicit application in information retrieval. We explore methodologies to optimize the retrieval process, select optimal models, and effectively scale and orchestrate LLMs, aiming for cost-efficiency and enhanced result accuracy. A notable challenge, model hallucination-where the model yields inaccurate or misinterpreted data-is addressed alongside other model-specific hurdles. Our discourse extends to crucial considerations including user privacy, data optimization, and the necessity for system clarity and interpretability. Through a comprehensive examination, we unveil not only innovative strategies for integrating Language Models (LLMs) with Information Retrieval (IR) systems, but also the consequential considerations that underline the need for a balanced approach aligned with user-centric principles.

Keywords: Retrieval-Augmented Generation (RAG) · Scaling and Orchestrating LLM-based Applications · Examining Language Learning Model-Integrated Applications

1 Introduction

In the current digital landscape, there's a massive increase in data. This has intensified the need for systems that can effectively retrieve the right information. Information retrieval plays a crucial role in helping us navigate the vast amount of digital data, requiring methods that are both accurate and sensitive to context. The systems should not only be precise but also capable of understanding the context to provide users with the most relevant results. Additionally, they should be adept at summarization to condense information, thereby enabling users to quickly grasp the essence of the content and make well-informed decisions [1–3].

© The Author(s), under exclusive license to Springer Nature Singapore Pte Ltd. 2024
F. Monti et al. (Eds.): ICSOC 2023 Workshops, LNCS 14518, pp. 17–26, 2024.
https://doi.org/10.1007/978-981-97-0989-2_2

While traditional information retrieval systems have been helpful, they sometimes struggle to fully grasp the context of queries [4]. This can lead to results that don't quite match what the user was looking for [5]. Recent advances have brought forward neural network models, which have seen many improvements over the years [6]. Among these, Large Language Models (LLMs) stand out. They have exhibited notable capabilities in generating human-like language across various applications, from executing language tasks to creating content. They can understand and create text that's very similar to how humans write, due to the extensive data they've been trained on.

Despite their ability to produce seemingly fluent and authoritative responses, LLMs also present risks, making them principally advantageous for prototyping while often being limited in broader production contexts. One significant risk is the production of inaccurate or "hallucinated" information, in addition to confronting challenges related to bias, consent, and security. Secondly, their knowledge is confined to the information available up to the point of their last training, restricting their ability to utilize new data. Thirdly, their effectiveness in specialized tasks can be limited due to their generalized training background. Consequently, in a business context, granting excessive control to an LLM may yield unwelcome results, prompting it to generate irrelevant, harmful, or even dangerous content, all while exuding a misleadingly high level of confidence. Furthermore, the frequent refinement of these models can incur substantial costs. Given these risks, a pivotal question arises: How can we wisely employ the strengths of LLMs in our product development while minimizing potential drawbacks? It is imperative to acknowledge and navigate their inherent limitations, applying meticulous evaluation and probing techniques for specific applications, rather than solely relying on ideal-case interactions.

In this paper, we navigate through the extant challenges linked with Large Language Models (LLMs), addressing the pivotal question: 'Can integrating LLMs with current retrieval technologies engender a novel, enhanced strategy for information retrieval?' We explore potential solutions and scrutinize a variety of extant approaches. Our discourse is anchored steadfastly in the pragmatic aspects of the challenge, aiming to ensure that our findings and recommendations reverberate meaningfully across both academic and industrial domains. Our objective is to enrich the discourse in the field of information retrieval and delineate a trajectory for impending advancements in the field.

2 Related Work

The quest for better ways to extract information from large data repositories has been a constant theme in computational linguistics and computer science, especially with the complexity of the Internet's hyperlink networks [7]. Algorithms like PageRank [8] have tackled this challenge, navigating this network to evaluate the importance of web pages and bring some order to the vastness of the Internet. Early on, notable work by researchers like Salton and McGill introduced the Vector Space Model (VSM) [9] to the global academic and scientific community, setting the stage for many advancements to come. This model conceptualized text documents as vectors within a multi-dimensional space, igniting curiosity that subsequently catalyzed the advent of neural network-based language models [10–12]. The journey from early sequence modeling, represented by RNNs and LSTMs [13], to the transformative era brought about by transformer models [14], has been swift. Large Language Models (LLMs) like OpenAI's GPT series and Google's BERT have gone beyond just text retrieval or recognition, evolving to understand and generate text in a way that is much like human communication [15–17].

In the sections that follow, we delve into the crucial role of LLMs in enhancing information retrieval, with a special focus on employing Retrieval-Augmented Generation (RAG) [18] to address the prevalent challenges associated with language models. We outline the architecture of RAG models and discuss their applicability and efficacy in various settings. Furthermore, we explore the integration of knowledge bases with information retrieval systems to augment the richness of contextual understanding and provide a more comprehensive and accurate retrieval of information. This integration is pivotal in bridging the gap between structured and unstructured data, thereby facilitating a more informed and insightful interaction for users [19,20].

3   LLM as IR Enhancer: Methods and Implications

Despite the remarkable capabilities of foundation models, their utilization as direct information sources presents challenges. In this section, we expound upon key discussions related to employing language models within the context of information retrieval. We navigate through prevailing challenges, explore potential solutions applicable in varied situations. We particularly discuss the following considerations in context of information retrieval:

- Is fine-tuning a model advisable in an enterprise setting?
- What factors should be scrutinized before deploying large language models?
- How can different components be effectively integrated?
- What metrics should be in place for continuous performance evaluation?
- What security measures and privacy compliance standards need to be adhered to?

3.1   Enhancing the Information Retrieval Process

Foundation models, although powerful, encounter several limitations due to their intrinsic reliance on static, pre-trained knowledge, hampering their capability to stay abreast of contemporary developments and demonstrating difficulties in executing specialized, domain-specific tasks. Moreover, these models, while being vast reservoirs of general knowledge, sometimes fail to navigate the intricacies and depth required in specialized domains. This issue, paired with the risk of "hallucination" - generating plausible but incorrect or nonsensical information -

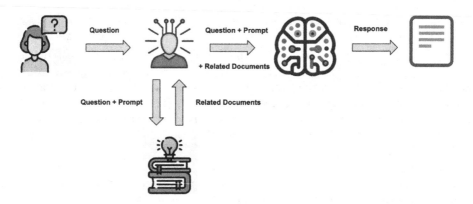

Fig. 1. An overview of the RAG architecture.

underscores the importance of seeking enhancements to leverage these models effectively and safely.

Retrieval-Augmented Generation (RAG) emerges as a pivotal technology to address some of these limitations, forging a connection between the foundational knowledge of large language models and the dynamic, up-to-date information contained in external repositories. Imagine a system that goes beyond just understanding a query, having the intelligence to know where to look for answers and the ability to form responses coherently and contextually. This vision, named Retrieval-Augmented Generation (RAG), was detailed by Lewis et al. [18], showing a close connection between retrieval systems and the generative capabilities of language models. An overview of teh RAG architecture id depicted in Fig. 1. This approach strengthens the model's ability to find relevant information and present it in a useful and contextually relevant way, enhancing the usefulness of machine learning models in real-world information query scenarios. By facilitating real-time retrieval of relevant information during the inference process, RAG circumvents the static knowledge limitation, providing outputs that are not only rich and contextually relevant but also verifiable against a known dataset.

Navigating the practical implementation of RAG brings several key advantages to the forefront. The potential for cost and computational savings is evident, as the need for frequent, exhaustive retraining of the model is mitigated, supplanted by updates to the retrieval database. Interestingly, the approach of RAG also lends a hand in addressing privacy concerns. Since RAG pulls from an external retrieval database, instead of integrating data into the model, it aids in keeping sensitive information more secure. This characteristic ensures that the responses generated are current and relevant, while also providing a structured way to handle sensitive or private information within the retrieval data. This setup aims at striking a careful balance between dynamism and privacy.

A question that often arises is whether RAG can be replaced by fine-tuning. The distinction between RAG and fine-tuning becomes apparent when considering the dynamic nature of the information involved, the computational resources available for retraining, and the specific requirements of the task at hand. While both methodologies aim at enhancing the performance and applicability of Large Language Models (LLMs), they cater to different aspects and scenarios. Fine-tuning is a well-suited approach for tailoring a model to a specific domain or set of long-term tasks, especially when the underlying challenges are relatively static. It involves adjusting the model parameters on a new dataset to make the model's behavior more aligned with the desired task or domain. On the other hand, RAG is designed to tackle scenarios where the model needs to stay updated with rapidly evolving or expansive information without requiring continuous retraining. By leveraging an external retrieval database, RAG enables the model to interact dynamically with the latest data, ensuring its responses are current and relevant. While fine-tuning demands substantial computational resources for retraining with new data, RAG offers a cost-effective alternative by minimizing the need for exhaustive retraining. In summary, the choice between RAG and fine-tuning is not a matter of simple replacement, but rather a strategic decision based on the particular demands of the task, the nature of the data, and the available resources. Each approach has its own set of advantages and is suited to different use cases, necessitating a careful consideration of the project's requirements to determine the most appropriate strategy.

3.2 Determining the Optimal Model: Criteria and Considerations

Selecting a suitable Large Language Model (LLM) requires a careful look at different factors. Domain specificity is crucial. Specialized models often perform better than general-purpose ones in specific areas. Given the variety in their training datasets, different models may be more suitable, each aligning well with different scenarios in their own way.

Scalability is a key feature when selecting an LLM. This refers to the model's ability to effectively manage increased demands, handle a growing number of requests without a significant drop in performance. Computational costs, infrastructure needs, the possible need for distributed processing, and a smooth transition to updated models or versions are factors that highlight an LLM's scalable nature. A truly scalable LLM should not only meet immediate needs but also anticipate and accommodate future growth, ensuring continued relevance and performance in a rapidly changing environment.

Addressing bias and fairness is critical when deploying LLMs. LLMs, trained on vast web-based data, may unintentionally reflect and spread societal biases present in their training data, potentially producing outputs that reinforce stereotypes or marginalize groups. Moreover, how a model deals with biases and possibly produces inappropriate content, as well as its ease of integration and availability of support, tools, and community resources, all play a role in its usefulness and upkeep in practical situations. Ensuring fairness requires that outputs are unbiased and don't unfairly favor or disadvantage any group, needing ongoing, use-case-specific testing, tuning, and validation.

Data privacy is also a major concern, requiring measures to ensure that LLMs neither retain nor disclose sensitive data and comply with global data protection standards. Moreover, transparency and interpretability, although challenging due to the 'black-box' nature of LLMs, are essential for trust and understanding the reasoning behind the model's outputs, requiring methods that reveal its workings to users and stakeholders.

3.3   Orchestrating and Deploying LLM-Based Applications

Solving advanced tasks with language models and retrieval models require frameworks to unify techniques for prompting and fine-tuning LMs - and approaches for reasoning, self-improvement, and augmentation with retrieval and tools. Langchain[1] serves as a pioneering framework tailored for crafting applications that harness the power of language models. At its heart, it operates on the principle that multiple components can be seamlessly chained together, enabling the design of sophisticated use cases centered around LLMs. While Langchain offers a robust solution, the ecosystem is enriched by the presence of other notable frameworks. LlamaIndex[2] and DSPy[3], for instance, also bring unique capabilities to the table, each contributing to the expansive landscape of language model application development. Navigating through the domain of sophisticated language model application frameworks, it is pivotal to delve into the strengths and capabilities of the emerging libraries like Langchain, LlamaIndex, and DSPy. These libraries proffer unique functionalities and methodologies, each converging on the development and deployment of Large Language Models (LLMs) but diverging in the nuances of their application and usability.

Langchain emerges as a front-runner, providing a pioneering framework that meticulously blends various components and tools to harness the might of LLMs, thereby establishing itself as a versatile framework, especially for developers seeking a flexible and extensible interface for a general-purpose application. Its principle revolves around the seamless chaining of multiple components, creating a vibrant ecosystem that is not only adaptable but can synergistically integrate with numerous external models, which in turn, pave the path for the deployment of innovative and versatile solutions. The inherent flexibility of Langchain enables the realization of varied use-cases, thus broadening the horizons for developers engrossed in crafting applications anchored on LLMs.

On the flip side, LlamaIndex, while maintaining some functional overlap with Langchain, prioritizes efficiency and simplicity in search and retrieval applications, particularly via its conversational interface. It's not merely a tool but an intuitive facilitator that empowers developers to efficiently manage, search, and summarize documents by utilizing LLMs and inventive indexing techniques, with graph indexes being a cornerstone feature. It is interesting to observe how LlamaIndex and Langchain, while overlapping in functionalities such as data-augmented summarization and question answering, distinguish themselves in their approach and utility. LlamaIndex's intensive utilization of prompting and

---

[1] https://www.langchain.com.

[2] https://www.llamaindex.ai.

[3] https://github.com/stanfordnlp/dspy.

its prowess in creating hierarchical indexes for efficient data organization carve its unique niche in the landscape of language model application development. However, Langchain offers a more granular control and caters to an expansive array of use-cases.

On a slightly divergent trajectory, DSPy maneuvers the pathway by emphasizing programming, complemented by an encompassing approach that unifies techniques for not only prompting and fine-tuning LMs but also enhancing them through reasoning and tool/retrieval augmentation. Its distinctive facet lies in its ability to provide composable and declarative modules for instructing LMs in a syntax familiar to developers acquainted with Python. Moreover, DSPy's automatic compiler, which traces programs and crafts premium prompts or trains automatic finetunes, exemplifies a nuanced approach to instructing LMs in task steps, thus presenting an alternative methodology compared to Langchain and LlamaIndex.

Although LlamaIndex and Langchain boast frequent updates and a steadfast evolution, posing a potential for amalgamation in the future, and DSPy treads its own unique path with a definitive emphasis on programming and a Pythonic approach, all three libraries together enrich the developer's toolkit, each offering varied approaches and functionalities catering to diverse application needs in the realm of language model application development and the choice between them would pivot on the specific requisites of the project.

3.4 Examining Language Learning Model-Integrated Applications

In traditional machine learning problems, 'Ground Truths' are pivotal for model building as they measure the quality of the model's predictions. They are crucial for determining which model experiment should be deployed in production and help teams sample and annotate production data to identify and improve cohorts of low model performance. Before the advent of Large Language Models, which excel in custom use-cases right out of the box, model evaluation followed a fairly straightforward protocol: data was split into training, test, and dev sets, with the model being trained on the training set and evaluated on the test/dev set. This category also includes transfer learning and fine-tuning of models. LLMs, however, navigate scenarios where establishing a clear Ground Truth is arduous.

Given the multi-dimensional nature of the problem, a comprehensive performance evaluation framework is necessitated. Proper evaluation metrics should encompass all aspects of an application. Key engineering aspects required for model performance evaluation during development include:

- Prompt Tuning: Framing the prompt differently can yield considerably varied results.
- Embeddings Model: Connecting custom data with LLMs provides the necessary context. The choice of embeddings and similarity metrics is crucial.
- Model Parameters: Parameters like temperature, top-k, and repeat penalty in LLMs are noteworthy.

- Data Storage: For advanced retrieval augmented generation (RAG) solutions, considerations on how to store and retrieve data, such as storing document keywords alongside embeddings, are important.

There are some other aspects that need to be evaluated post-development, which include:

- Accuracy: Are the answers relevant to the query?
- Speed/Response time: Is the answer generated within a reasonable time-frame?
- Completeness: Are all relevant items retrieved?
- Error rate: Frequency of errors or incorrect information.
- Prompt quality: The number of interactions needed to attain the desired result.
- Output structure: The quality of the presented answer.

With evaluation parameters in place, deciding on the evaluation metrics and model performance evaluation becomes feasible. Generating evaluation datasets from representative user inputs might pose a challenge; however, benchmark datasets like MTBench, MMLU, and TruthfulQA can serve as guidelines. Recent developments like RAGAS[4] and LangSmith[5] have attempted to streamline LLM evaluation based on various metrics such as faithfulness, relevancy, and harmfulness which provide a framework to debug, test, evaluate, and monitor LLM applications respectively. The shift from employing Generative AI as personal search engines to integrating them into production underscores the exciting prospects in deploying, monitoring, and evaluating LLMs.

There is also a new line of research on how to evaluate LLM-based applications. A recent paper by Zheng et al. [21] proposed employing robust LLMs as judges to evaluate applications on nuanced, open-ended questions. By introducing two benchmarks, MT-bench and Chatbot Arena, it aims to bridge the conventional evaluation metrics and human preferences gap. The paper explores the potential of using state-of-the-art LLMs like GPT-4 as a surrogate for human judges, termedc "LLM-as-a-judge," to automate the evaluation process. A systematic study revealed that the LLM-as-a-judge approach could achieve over 80% agreement with human evaluations, matching the level of human-human agreement. This suggests a scalable and swift method to evaluate human preference in LLM-based applications, presenting a promising alternative to traditionally slow and costly human evaluations. The study also emphasizes the importance of a hybrid evaluation framework, amalgamating existing capability-based benchmarks and new preference-based benchmarks with the LLM-as-a-judge approach, for a more comprehensive evaluation of both core capabilities and human alignment of models.

---

[4] https://github.com/explodinggradients/ragas.
[5] https://www.langchain.com/langsmith.

4   Conclusion

In conclusion, this paper sheds light on the nuanced advantages and challenges tied to employing Large Language Models (LLMs) in refining Information Retrieval (IR) systems. Emphasizing personalized and efficient information retrieval, we investigated various strategies to bolster the retrieval process, choose suitable models, scale and manage LLMs effectively, and thoroughly assess their performance and impacts. LLMs, with their capacity for human-like text comprehension and generation, extend beyond traditional query-document matching, paving the way for a richer, personalized IR experience.

Nevertheless, the path to fully unlocking LLMs' potential in IR systems is laden with obstacles. Notable challenges include model hallucination, ensuring user privacy, optimizing data usage, and maintaining system clarity and interpretability. These issues underscore the necessity for a balanced approach encompassing technical innovations, ethical considerations, and user-centric design.

The dialogue advanced in this paper advocates for a harmonious fusion of LLMs and IR systems, inviting a collective effort among researchers, practitioners, and policymakers to tackle model-centric challenges and broader ramifications. As the lines between human and machine interaction blur further, the collaborative intelligence of this human-machine amalgam is instrumental in nurturing an IR ecosystem that is efficient, personalized, and accountable. Through relentless exploration and iterative improvements, the potential of LLMs in substantially elevating the IR domain is not only conceivable but also promising.

References

1. Ghodratnama, S., Beheshti, A., Zakershahrak, M., Sobhanmanesh, F.: Extractive document summarization based on dynamic feature space mapping. IEEE Access **8**, 139084–139095 (2020)
2. Ghodratnama, S., Zakershahrak, M., Sobhanmanesh, F.: Am i rare? An intelligent summarization approach for identifying hidden anomalies. In: Hacid, H., et al. (eds.) ICSOC 2020. LNCS, vol. 12632, pp. 309–323. Springer, Cham (2020). https://doi.org/10.1007/978-3-030-76352-7_31
3. Ghodratnama, S., Zakershahrak, M., Sobhanmanesh, F.: Adaptive summaries: a personalized concept-based summarization approach by learning from users' feedback. In: Hacid, H., et al. (eds.) ICSOC 2020. LNCS, vol. 12632, pp. 281–293. Springer, Cham (2020). https://doi.org/10.1007/978-3-030-76352-7_29
4. Beheshti, A., Benatallah, B., Motahari-Nezhad, H.R., Ghodratnama, S., Amouzgar, F.: A query language for summarizing and analyzing business process data. arXiv preprint arXiv:2105.10911 (2021)
5. Ghodratnama, S., Zakershahrak, M., Beheshti, A.: Summary2vec: learning semantic representation of summaries for healthcare analytics. In: 2021 International Joint Conference on Neural Networks (IJCNN), pp. 1–8. IEEE (2021)
6. Khanna, U., Ghodratnama, S., Beheshti, A., et al.: Transformer-based models for long document summarisation in financial domain. In: Proceedings of the 4th Financial Narrative Processing Workshop@ LREC2022, pp. 73–78 (2022)

7. Beheshti, A., Ghodratnama, S., Elahi, M., Farhood, H.: Social Data Analytics. CRC Press, Boca Raton (2022)

8. Duhan, N., Sharma, A., Bhatia, K.K.: Page ranking algorithms: a survey. In: 2009 IEEE International Advance Computing Conference, pp. 1530–1537. IEEE (2009)

9. Salton, G., Wong, A., Yang, C.-S.: A vector space model for automatic indexing. Commun. ACM **18**(11), 613–620 (1975)

10. Ghodratnama, S.: Towards personalized and human-in-the-loop document summarization. arXiv preprint arXiv:2108.09443 (2021)

11. Ghodratnama, S., Behehsti, A., Zakershahrak, M.: A personalized reinforcement learning summarization service for learning structure from unstructured data. In: 2023 IEEE International Conference on Web Services (ICWS), pp. 206–213. IEEE (2023)

12. Ghodratnama, S., Beheshti, A., Zakershahrak, M., Sobhanmanesh, F.: Intelligent narrative summaries: from indicative to informative summarization. Big Data Res. **26**, 100257 (2021)

13. Hochreiter, S., Schmidhuber, J.: Long short-term memory. Neural Comput. **9**(8), 1735–1780 (1997)

14. Vaswani, A., et al.: Attention is all you need. In: Advances in Neural Information Processing Systems, vol. 30 (2017)

15. Radford, A., Wu, J., Child, R., Luan, D., Amodei, D., Sutskever, I., et al.: Language models are unsupervised multitask learners. OpenAI Blog **1**(8), 9 (2019)

16. Devlin, J., Chang, M.-W., Lee, K., Toutanova, K.: BERT: pre-training of deep bidirectional transformers for language understanding. arXiv preprint arXiv:1810.04805 (2018)

17. Zakershahrak, M., Ghodratnama, S.: Are we on the same page? Hierarchical explanation generation for planning tasks in human-robot teaming using reinforcement learning. arXiv preprint arXiv:2012.11792 (2020)

18. Lewis, P., et al.: Retrieval-augmented generation for knowledge-intensive NLP tasks. In: Advances in Neural Information Processing Systems, vol. 33, pp. 9459–9474 (2020)

19. Beheshti, A., et al.: ProcessGPT: transforming business process management with generative artificial intelligence. In: 2023 IEEE International Conference on Web Services (ICWS), pp. 731–739 (2023)

20. Beheshti, A.: Empowering generative AI with knowledge base 4.0: towards linking analytical, cognitive, and generative intelligence. In: 2023 IEEE International Conference on Web Services (ICWS), pp. 763–771 (2023)

21. Zheng, L., et al.: Judging LLM-as-a-judge with MT-bench and chatbot arena. arXiv preprint arXiv:2306.05685 (2023)

Towards Improving Insurance Processes: A Time Series Analysis of Psychosocial Recovery After Workplace Injury Across Legislative Environments

John E. McMahon[1]([⊠]) [iD], Rasool Roozegar[2] [iD], Ashley Craig[1] [iD], and Ian Cameron[1]

[1] John Walsh Centre for Rehabilitation Research, Kolling Institute for Medical Research, Sydney Medical School-Northern, The University of Sydney, St. Leonard's, NSW, Australia
johnm@navigatorgroup.com.au, {a.craig,ian.cameron}@sydney.edu.au
[2] Navigator Group, Suite 1, Level 3, 66 Clarence Street, Sydney, NSW, Australia
rasoolr@navigatorgroup.com.au

Abstract. Enhancing insurance processes when workers grapple with physical injuries necessitates a deep dive into the cognitive science facets to optimize recovery. Time series analysis emerges as an instrumental tool within this framework, offering profound insights and data-driven analysis, ultimately paving the way for a more refined and efficient insurance process. This paper uses time series analysis, a machine learning approach, to enhance insurance business processes by understanding the cognitive aspects of post-injury workers. We delve into the intertwined roles of legislative environments, administrative processes, and their impacts on recovery outcomes, gauged through psychometric measures. By distinguishing between "state" (changeable) and "trait" (constant) psychological variables, we ascertain how legislative measures influence these variables, especially under adverse impacts leading to discernible patterns in claims. Our study compares time series models across various legislative environments in Australia, examining the claims managed by multiple insurers to discern any variability due to legislation. This analysis is enriched by the data from the Navigator Support Program, which screens claimants through psychometric tests, providing insights into the effects of legislation and insurer behaviour on recovery from workplace injuries. The ultimate aim is to harness these insights to improve insurance business processes.

Keywords: Workers Compensation · prognosis · OMSPQ-FS · PSS · SES · DES · HWS · ARIMA · Facebook™ Prophet

1 Introduction

Enhancing insurance processes when workers grapple with physical injuries requires a deep dive into the psychological and social components to recovery. Recovery from insured injuries involves not only the physical injury itself, but a complex social environment with multiple stake holders, legislative and administrative processes. Suffering

F. Monti et al. (Eds.): ICSOC 2023 Workshops, LNCS 14518, pp. 27–38, 2024.
https://doi.org/10.1007/978-981-97-0989-2_3

an injury can be stressful, but so too the repercussions on lifestyle, finances, the demands of rehabilitation and return to work are also stressful. These cognitive aspects intertwine with the physical, often influencing the duration and quality of recovery, the perception of pain, and return-to-work timeline. The bureaucratic and legislative environment can exacerbate or relieve stress. Within these multifaceted environments, the need for nuanced, data-driving insights becomes evident. Time series analysis offers a method of deriving insights by analysing data points over time to identify patterns, predict outcomes, and understand the interplay between psychological and administrative factors on recovery, paving the way for more refined and efficient insurance processes.

Psychometric measurement of recovery, being correlates of recovery, allow the comparison of different injuries over time. Psychologists distinguish between "state" and "trait" variables, with state variables being changeable, and trait variables being resistant to change or immutable. It would be expected that legislative environments may affect state but not trait variables. Stress is a state variable, changing in response to perceived adversity. At times when legislation or administration has greatest adverse impact, then stress would be expected to increase, producing identifiable seasonality in claims. Comparing the results of times series analyses of psychometric measures in different legislative environments, could inform on the effects of legislation on recovery from work related injury. In Australia each state or territory has its own legislation. Comparing a single insurer between different locations within the same state and between different state's legislative environments would contribute to identifying the effect of an insurers administrative style.

Set against Australia's diverse legislative environments, this paper harnesses the power of time series analysis and psychometric evaluations. We aim to develop a more responsive insurance process that not only acknowledges but actively addresses the psychological complexities experienced by injured workers. To achieve this goal, we compare various time series models of state and trait psycho-metric measures for claims managed by multiple insurers across different states and a single insurer between other regions within states and between states to see if there was variability attributable to legislation. The population was screened successively across their claims with psychometric measures by an independent support service known as the Navigator Support Program.

The rest of the paper is organized as follows: In Sect. 2 we provide the background and related work. We present the Curve Fitting and Forecasting Models in Sect. 3. In Sect. 4, we present the experimental work for states, before concluding the paper with discussion and remarks for future directions in Sect. 5. Table 1 is a table of the abbreviations and terms used throughout the paper.

2   Related Work

2.1   Time Series Analysis in Healthcare and Insurance

Time series forecasting has been applied to many different problems in health care including expenditure and medication consumption [1], survival rates and emergence rates for medical conditions, and patterns of expression for different medical conditions over time [2, 3]. Methods for determining future states of people within healthcare

Table 1. Abbreviations and terms used throughout the manuscript.

Abbreviation	Term	Manuscript Location
OMSPQ-SF	Orebro Musculoskeletal Pain Questionnaire-Short Form	2.2
PSS-4	Perceived Stress Scale-4 Item	2.2
SES	Single Exponential Smoothing	3.1
DES	Double Exponential Smoothing	3.2
HWS	Holt Winters Seasonal	3.3
ARIMA	Autoregressive Integrated Moving Average	3.4
Prophet	Facebook™ Prophet Model	3.5
MAE	Mean Absolute Error	2.1
MAPE	Mean Absolute Percentage Error	2.1
MSE	Mean Squared Error	2.1
ACT	Australian Capital Territory	
NSW	New South Wales	
QLD	Queensland	
WA	Western Australia	
NT	Northern Territory	
SA	South Australia	
TAS	Tasmania	

systems on the basis of current features of their condition can assist policy makers to optimes health care systems. Systematically searching for predictors of outcomes and expenses is a meaningful enterprise. For example, Harly et al. demonstrated that the best method for determining medical expenditure within a health fund was not the degree of comorbidity or various complex risk measures, rather it was a simple count of prescriptions which lead to the most accurate predication of future medical expenses [4]. In Australia there are multiple workers' compensation schemes with different legal, procedural and medical funding dynamics. It would be meaningful to policy makers to see if these insurance environments effected injured people differently or if there are some universal psychosocial variables that predict recovery. Time series analyses of the prediction of recovery outcomes across these different insurance environments is a practical application of this statistical method, unique from its use in reserving [9].

There are many ways to fit and forecast curves in general in times series analysis and with variations within a class of models [7]. Approaches such as Simple Exponential Smoothing (SES), Double Exponential Smoothing (DES), Holt-Winters' seasonal (HWS), Auto-Regressive Integrated Moving Average (ARIMA), the Facebook™ Prophet Model and other models have been applied in diverse health contexts from predicting outpatient attendances, medication consumption patterns, to the spread of COVID19 and as alternate approach in general insurance reserving [3, 6–9]. Systematic application of time series forecasting has shown differences between performance on different types of data. Pinho et al. found ARIMA outperformed Prophet models in most cases on telecommunications data [10], qualifying the models with Root Mean Squared Error (RMSE) and Mean Absolute Percentage Error (MAPE). Time series models can also be compared using Mean Squared Error (MSE) and Mean Absolute Error (MAE). The present study will systematically review the accuracy of time series models for state and trait measurements between compensable environments and evaluate the goodness of forecast using MAPE, MAE and MSE.

2.2 Psychometric Testing

The Orebro Musculoskeletal Pain Questionnaire-Short Form (OMPQ-SF) is a 10-item questionnaire, based on a longer scale [11], which has been demonstrated to identify people at risk of developing persistent pain. Such a trait measurement should be predictable over time and remain relatively unchanged over the course of a claim, regardless of the number of times it is administrated; a feature referred to in psychometry as test-retest reliability. The OMPQ-SF has good test-retest reliability in chronic lower back pain and across languages [12] suggesting that these questions are assessing some universal constructs that transcend language and time.

The Perceived Stress Scale-4 (PSS-4 [13]) is a 4-item version of a longer questionnaire of the same name which measures the self-assessed state of being stressed. While internally consistent, such a state is expected to be variable over time and to increase at times of stress such as when adverse administrative thresholds are crossed such as wage payment reductions. These would be expected to cause predictable spikes of scores, or seasonality, coinciding with these thresholds in similar legislative environments. Like the OMPQ-SF, the PSS-4 has been translated and validated across languages, such as German and Chinese, suggesting that the questions are assessing some universal construct.

3 Curve Fitting and Forecasting Models

Exponential smoothing (ES) is a time series forecasting method for univariate data. Exponential smoothing forecasting methods are similar in that a prediction is a weighted sum of past observations, but the model explicitly uses an exponentially decreasing weight for past observations. Specifically, past observations are weighted with a geometrically decreasing ratio. Exponential smoothing methods may be considered as peers and alternative to the Box-Jenkins ARIMA class of methods for time series forecasting. There are three main types of exponential smoothing time series forecasting methods. A simple method that assumes no systematic structure (SES), an extension that explicitly handles trends (DES), and the most advanced approach that adds support for seasonality (HWS). If m_t is a trend component, s_t is a seasonal component, and Y_t is zero-mean error, a time series model (X_t) over time (t) described as:

$$X_t = m_t + s_t + Y_t$$

The Dicky-Fuller Test is a statistical test of stationarity, which is the property of a time series that the mean of the series should be independent of the effect of time.

Secondly the amplitude of variance in a time series should not be a function of time, that is the series should have homoscedasticity across time. Time series methods are differentiated in how they accommodate stationarity and homoscedasticity. The Dickey-Fuller test compares the mean and amplitude of variance to a series generated by a random walk, which will have no stationarity or homoscedasticity. The null hypothesis being that the time series is non-stationarity. For a detailed treatment see [14].

3.1 Single Exponential Smoothing (SES)

The simplest time series model is one with no trend or seasonal component. In SES each observation is used to forecast the next value in succession. A single forecast, with α is a given *weighting* value to be selected with limits $0 < \alpha < 1$, is defined as:

$$F_{t+1} = \alpha Y_t + (1 - \alpha)F_t$$

So, F_{t+1} is the weighted average of the current observation Y_t with the forecasted value F the retrospective value at time point t-1. Iterating this process, the formula becomes:

$$F_{t+1} = (1 - \alpha)^t F_1 + \alpha \sum_{j=0}^{t-1} (1 - \alpha)^j Y_{t-j}$$

This causes the dependency of the current forecast for successive forecasts to fall away in an exponential way controlled by the weighting value α.

3.2 Double Exponential Smoothing (DES)

DES extends SES by controlling the decay of the influence of change in trend. This beta factor (β) is a weighting, with limits $\beta < 1$, to mitigate this decay or dampen in a linear way, so called "additive trend", or exponentially, "multiplicative trend". In multistep forecasting a trend may continue unrealistically, and it can be useful to dampen or reduce the size of the trend over time, again this can occur linearly in "additive dampening" or exponentially in "multiplicative dampening". This permits a damping coefficient ϕ. As such DES offers more controls and descriptors for curve estimation being the hyperparameters:

$\alpha =$ Smoothing factor for the level
$\beta =$ Smoothing factor for the trend
Trend Type $=$ additive or multiplicative
Dampen Tye $=$ additive or multiplicative
$\phi =$ Damping coefficient
The resulting equations are:

$$L_t = \alpha Y_t + (1 - \alpha)(L_{t-1} + b_{t-1}),$$
$$B_t = \beta(L_t - L_{t-1}) + (1 - \beta)b_{t-1}$$
$$F_{t+m} = L_t + b_t m$$

where L_t and b_t are exponentially smoothed estimates of the level and linear trend of the series at time t respectively, while F_{t+m} is the linear forecast from t onwards.

3.3 Holt-Winters Seasonal (HWS)

HWS is an extension of the DES taking into account seasonality denoted as S_t. It engages three smoothing equations, one for the level L_t, one for the trend b_t, and one for the seasonal component S_t. There are two variants with additive seasonality and multiplicative seasonality, treating seasonality as either a linear or exponential effect respectively. The HWS additive seasonality method equations are:

$$L_t = \alpha(Y_t - Y_{t-s}) + (1 - \alpha)(L_{t-1} + b_{t-1})$$
$$b_t = \beta(L_t - L_{t-1}) + (1 - \beta)b_{t-1}$$
$$S_t = \gamma(Y_t - L_t) + (1 - \gamma)St_{-s}$$
$$F_{t+m} = L_t + b_t m + S_{t-s+m}$$

where s is the number of periods in one cycle, the initial values of L_s and b_s can be as in the multiplicative case. The initial seasonal indices are:

$$S_k = Y_k - L_s, k = 1, 2, \ldots, s.$$

where α, β, γ are values within the interval of $(0, 1)$ selected to minimize MAE, MSE or MAPE.

The HWS Multiplicative Seasonality equations are:

$$L_t = \alpha(Y_1/S_{t-s}) + (1 - \alpha)(L_{t-1} + b_{t-1})$$
$$b_t = \beta(L_t - L_{t-1}) + (1 - \beta)b_{t-1}$$
$$S_t = \gamma(Y_1/L_t) + (1 - \gamma)St_{-s}$$
$$F_{t+m} = (L_t + b_t m)S_{t-s+m}$$

To initialise the computation a single cycle of data, (i.e. s values) must be completed and set:

$$L_s = (1/S) * (Y_1 + Y_2 + \ldots + Y_s)$$

And to initialise trend $s + k$ time periods:

$$b_s = (1/k) * ((Y_{s+1} - Y_1)/s + (Y_{s+2} - Y_2)/s + \ldots + (Y_{s+k} - Y_k)/s))$$

where α, β, and γ are values within the interval of $(0, 1)$ selected to minimize MAE, MSE or MAPE.

3.4 Autoregressive Integrated Moving Average (ARIMA)

ARIMA models combine autoregression (AR) with moving average (MA), and in general AR models are classified by the number of time lags, p. Generally, an AR model is defined by the pth order of time lags, and termed an AR(p) model written as:

$$Y_t = c + \phi Y_{t-1} + \phi Y_{t-2} + \ldots + \phi_p Y_{t-p} + e_t$$

where c is constant, ϕ_j are parameters to be determined and e_t is the error term with four constraints on allowable values of ϕ_j:

- For $p = 1, - < \phi < 1$
- For $p = 2, -1 < \phi < 1, \phi_2 + \phi_1 < 1$ and $\phi_2 - \phi_1 < 1$
- For $p > 2$, more complex conditions are applied.

Moving average models (MA) are regressions on error terms at previous time lags. As with AR, MA are defined by the number of time lags, q, used in the regression. A general model is defined MA(q) and written:

$$Y_t = c + e_t - \theta e_{t-1} - \ldots - \theta_q e_{t-q}$$

where c is constant, θ_j are parameters to be determined and e_t are the error terms. There are restrictions on the allowable values of θ_j:

- For $q = 1, -1 < \theta < 1$
- For $q = 2, -1 < \theta_2 < 1, \theta_2 + \theta_1 < 1$ and $\theta_2 - \theta_1 < 1$
- For $q > 2$, more complex conditions are applied.

An ARIMA models combines AR and MA with seasonal differences of order s, and the models are defined:

$$\text{ARMIA}(p, d, q)(P, D, Q)s$$

where s is the number of time periods per season, with:

- AR (p) at time lag p.
- Integrated (I) difference of order d.
- MA(q) regression on errors to lag q.
- seasonal autoregression to time lag P
- seasonal differences of order D
- seasonal regression on errors to lag Q

This results in seasonal and non-seasonal variants of equations. ARIMA addresses correlation between observations which are not accommodated by simpler models. The above components are combined in the following linear equation:

$$Y_t = c + \phi_1 Y_{dt-1} + \ldots + \phi_p Y_{dt-p} + e_t + \theta_1 e_{t-1} - \ldots - \theta_q e_{t-q}$$

Our approach to ARIMA model selection was to determine stationarity using the Augmented Dickey-Fuller test, then use difference or logarithmic transformation to convert nonstationary times series into stationary time series. Determine the p, d, and q values, with d determined by the number of differentials. From autocorrelation function (ACF) and partial autocorrelation function (PACF) plots against lag length to identify potential models, then the AR and MA parameters were selected. Comparing Akaike information criterion (AIC) and Bayesian information criterion (BIC), the optimal model was chosen on the basis of the smallest AIC and BIC values. An estimation of the fitted model was made using the appropriate p and q values using the maximum likelihood estimation method and checked using Ljung-Box Q test to see if the residual series is white noise, and if so the model was accepted. The Ljung-Box Q statistic is:

$$Q = n(n+2) \sum_{k=1}^{h} (n-k)^{-l} r_k^2$$

Where n is the number of observations and h is the maximum time lags considered. If the residuals of the model are white noise, Q has a chi-square (X^2) distribution with (h-m) degrees of freedom where m is the number of parameters in the model. If the Q lies in the right-hand 5% tail of the X^2 distribution (with a p-value of < 0.05), it is concluded that the data are not white noise. If the estimated residuals were white noise we moved to forecasting and if not, then there was a return to the model identification phase.

3.5 Facebook™ Prophet

Time series forecasting with Facebook™ Prophet model is more machine driven with automatic identification of inflexion points in the data originated in changes in trend on varying scales from hourly to weekly to monthly. A disadvantage of such machine driven approaches is there is little transparency into the action of the equation. A novel feature is the possibility of accommodating the existence of seasonal features e.g. festive periods or events like the Superbowl in modeling such as conducted by Facebook™. It combines three components: the trend (a logistic function), the seasonality (Fourier function) and the festive periods modeled by some function as follows:

$$Y(t) = g(t) + s(t) + h(t) + (t)$$

where g(t) describes a piecewise-linear trend or "growth term", s(t) describes the various seasonal patterns, h(t) captures the seasonal features or "holiday effects", and ϵ(t) is a white noise error term.

4   Experimental work for States

The data used for modeling was deidentified OMSPQ-SF and PSS-4 test scores recorded from 2500 workers compensation claimants who were screened by the Navigator Support Program across the time of their claims, and whose claims had closed. The claimants were distributed across all states Australia. There were 10139 telephone screening calls made, with 6482 administrations of the OMSPQ-SF and 3874 administrations of the PSS. All data was cleaned, loaded and transformed using MINITAB and R (version 4.2.1) and the test of stationarity was conducted using the 'tseries_0.10–54', ARIMA model was fitted using 'forecast' package and Prophet with the 'prophet' package. For each State SES, DES, HWS, ARIMA, and Facebook™ Prophet Models were generated.

4.1 Inferential Statistics

We first generated histograms plotted against the normal curve for basic demographics, levels of support provided by the service, different levels of certification, and states and insurance environments which visual inspection showed generally normal frequency distributions by state and insurance environment, and skewness for support level, which reflects the psychometric properties of the OMPQ-SF and PSS-4. There were no significant differences between genders (OMPSQ-SF mean = 43.93 (SD = 16.41), PSS-4 mean = 4.28 (SD = 2.90)). ANOVA comparing states on the OMSPQ-SF approached significance (sig. 0.05) and Tukey's Simultaneous 95% confidences intervals revealed greatest difference between NSW (mean = 45.97 (SD = 17.47) and VIC (mean = 36.25 (SD = 15.15) accounting for 0.14% adjusted variance. Similar analysis for PSS-4 showed a significant (p = 0.028) difference between states with VIC having significantly less stress than other states and this accounted for 0.23% of adjusted variance.

4.2   Time Series Analysis Between States

In this section we will report the results of the application of the time series analysis methods as outlined in 3.1–3.5 comparing the states and the accuracy of methods were compared using MAE, MAPE and MSE. Data was divided 90% training and 10% testing data. Augmented DFS results showed all states had stationarity except for SA and VIC which had very small sample size. The ARIMA values for models forecasting OMSPQ-SF and PSS showed that non-seasonal differences for stationarity are immaterial, and where there was sufficient data ARIMA usually produced few forecast errors in the prediction equation.

Where data was sufficient long-term forecasts can be made. Table 2 shows the number of days of successful forecast for each state for the best model.As can be seen in Table 3, the more sophisticated Prophet models have better prognostic value. However, in the largest data set, WA, ARIMA had better forecasting capacity. There was little predictability to PSS stress levels at the state level with successful models being generated in only QLD and SA, with both states having small and very small data sets.

Table 2. Number of Days Forecast for each Measure by State.

	ACT	NSW	NT	QLD	SA	TAS	VIC	WA
OMSPQ-SF	63	20	44	8	4	48	3	346
PSS-4	37	12	37	5	1	36	1	150

Table 3. Best Models by MAE, with MAPE and MSE reported by State.

		OMSPQ-SF			PSS-4		
State		MAE	MAPE	MSE	MAE	MAPE	MSE
ACT	Prophet	50.500	14.181	300.154	Inf	2.4523	2.8107
NSW	Prophet	36.136	13.930	298.77	Inf	2.0943	2.5484
NT	Prophet	46.579	13.202	264.206	Inf	2.6374	2.9248
QLD	ARIMA	26.555	13.475	247.951	166.9253	2.5319	2.6138
SA	Prophet	33.703	16.971	643.436	21.3874	3.4376	3.4376
TAS	Prophet	51.982	13.766	291.527	Inf	2.5587	2.8901
WA	ARIMA (4, 0, 3)	35.772	13.300	267.709	Inf	2.7356	2.6950

4.3 Inferential Findings by Insurance Environment: Regions Held by One Insurer Across Administrative Regions Within and Between States

Comparing the scores of a single insurer across 6-insurance environments with two locations in two states and cases from two other states using ANOVA showed that workers in the region of Launceston Region of Tasmania (mean = 38.3, SD = 18.43) had significantly (p = 0.003) lower scores on the OMSPQ-SF than workers from the state of ACT (mean = 43.960, SD = 17.397) and in the Bunbury Region of WA (mean = 44.215, SD = 17.121) with location accounting for 0.25% adjusted variance. No significant difference was found between these insurance environments in terms of PSS.

4.4 Time Series Analysis Between Insurance Environments: Regions Held by One Insurer Across Administrative Regions Within and Between States

Augmented DFS showed that all-time series were stationary. The most successful ARIMA Models for each region again showed non-seasonal differences for stationarity were immaterial, and where there was sufficient data ARIMA usually produced few forecast errors in the prediction equation. The number of days' forecast can be seen in Table 4. The MAE, MAPE and MSE for the best models can be seen in Table 5.

Table 4. Number of Days Forecast for each Measure by Administrative Region

	ACT	Bunbury	Hobart	Launceston	NT	Perth
OMSPQ-SF	58	58	41	14	58	291
PSS-4	46	42	28	8	43	150

The ARIMA model for Perth was the most successful predictive model, with MAE of 12.3723, given the OMSPQ-SF has a total score of 100, at 291-days represents good accuracy of forecast. Nevertheless, overall, Prophet tended to be better than other models.

Table 5. Best Model MAE, MAP and MSE by each region for one insurer.

Region	OMSPQ-SF				PSS-4		
		MAE	MAPE	MSE	MAE	MAPE	MSE
ACT	Prophet	47.6194	14.1577	17.2791	Inf	2.4719	2.8307
Bunbury	HWS	31.7209	12.9082	15.2747	Inf	2.6519	2.9522
Hobart	Prophet	50.6491	13.5935	16.9218	Inf	2.5133	2.8947
Launceton	HWS	38.8256	13.4987	18.2019	171.0107	3.2004	3.3077
NT	Prophet	44.1650	12.8793	16.0591	Inf	2.5938	2.9073
Perth	ARIMA (2, 0, 0)	12.3723	4.4703	9.4361	Inf	2.7169	2.9646

5 Discussion

The main purpose of this study was to use time series analysis to make inferences about different insurance environments across states within Australia. Unlike telecommunications data, where ARIMA models predominated [10] for this type of data, Facebook™ Prophet models tended to have better capacity to predict than other models, especially as the subject data set increased in size. With that said, the best model was an ARIMA (2, 0, 0) model for the Perth region which was able to predict OMSPQ-SF scores within 12.37/100 points of accuracy out to 291-days. This suggests a sinusoidal oscillation of scores over time with random changes, "like the motion of a mass on a spring that is subject to random shocks" [15].

The predictability of scores over time contributes the construct validity of the OMSPQ-SF, that it measures a trait type construct permitting prediction of future scores due to the stability of the measure over time. Nevertheless, that it is not similarly predicable across administrative environments reveals the impact of the insurer on the claim. Similarly, the poor predictability of the PSS-4 shows it to be a state construct, and the absence of successful prediction at time points across claims in state-wide jurisdiction, infers that administrative thresholds do not cause predictable stress. The accuracy with which trait scores can be predicted within a specific administrative region, versus across a state, suggests that it is the local behaviour of insurers rather than simply the jurisdictional environment, that influences claims. The upshot is that there are discrete insurance environments within which predictions can be made, rather than gross legislative regions producing predictable psychosocial and claims outcomes. Timeseries has been proposed for use as an alternative to standard actuarial practice to predict claims costs [9]. The present paper represents a unique use of time series to predict psychosocial outcomes from insurance processes, and will permit the evaluation of future interventions to improve psychosocial outcomes in insured injury. Future research will also address the relationship between psychosocial outcomes and claims costs.

References

1. Kaushink, S., et al.: AI in healthcare: time-series forecasting using statistical, neural, and ensemble architectures. Front Big Data. **3**(4), 1–17 (2020). https://doi.org/10.3389/fdata.2020.00004
2. Crabtree, B.F., Ray, S.C., Schmidt, P.M., O'Çonnor, P.T., Schmidt, D.D.: The individual over time: time series applications in health care research. J. Clin. Epidemiol. **43**, 241–260 (1990). https://doi.org/10.1016/0895-4356(90)90005-A
3. Furtado, P.: Epidemiology SIR with regression, arima, and prophet in forecasting Covid-19. Eng. Proc. **5**(1), 52 (2021). https://doi.org/10.3390/engproc2021005052
4. Farley, J.F., Harley, C.R., and Devine, J.V.: A comparison of comorbidity measurements to predict healthcare expenditures. Am. J. Manag. Care, **12**, 110–118 (2006). https://pubmed.ncbi.nlm.nih.gov/16464140
5. Brockwell, P.J., Davis, R.A.: Time Series: Theory and Methods, 2nd Ed. Springer: New York (2009). ISBN 9781441903198
6. Luo, L., Luo, L., Zhang, X., He, X.: Hospital daily outpatient visits forecasting using a combinatorial model based on ARIMA and SES Models. BMC Health Serv. Res. **17**, 469 (2017). https://doi.org/10.1186/s12913-017-2407-9
7. Burinskiene, A.: Forecasting model: the case of the pharmaceutical retail. Front. Med. **9**, 582186 (2022). https://doi.org/10.3389/fmed.2022.582186
8. Prophet Forecasting at Scale. https://facebook.github.io/prophet/.Accessed 26 Sept 2023
9. Kartikasari, M.D., Imani, N.: Time series analysis of claims reservice in general insurance industry. In: The Proceedings of The 8th Annual Basic Science International Conference. https://repository.unesa.ac.id/sysop/files/2020-06-30_conference%20or%20workshop%20Harun%2016.pdf
10. Pinho, A., Costa, R., Silva, H., Furtado, P.: Comparing time series prediction approaches for telecom analysis. In: Valenzuela, O., Rojas, F., Pomares, H., Rojas, I. (eds.) ITISE 2018. CS, pp. 331–345. Springer, Cham (2019). https://doi.org/10.1007/978-3-030-26036-1_23
11. Linton, S.J., Nicholas, M., Macdonald, S.: Development of a short form of the orebro musculoskeletal pain screening questionnaire. Spine **36**(22), 1892–1895 (2011). https://doi.org/10.1097/BRS.0b013e3181f8f775
12. Opsommer, E., Hilfiker, R., Raval-Roland, B., Crombez, G., River, G.: Test-retest reliability of the Orebro Musculoskeletal pain screening questionnaire and the situational pain scale in patients with chronic low back pain. Eur. J Med Sci. **143**, 13903 (2013). https://doi.org/10.4414/smw.2013.13903
13. Cohen, S., Karmarck, T., Mermelstein, R.: A global measure of perceived stress. J. Health Soc. Behav. **24**, 385–396 (1983). https://doi.org/10.2307/2136404
14. Srivastava, T.: A Complete Tutorial on Time Series Modelling in R. Analytica Vidhya (2023). https://www.analyticsvidhya.com/blog/2015/12/complete-tutorial-time-series-modeling
15. Duke University: Introduction to ARIMA: Non-Seasonal Models https://people.duke.edu/~rnau/411arim.htm.Accessed 13 Oct 202

Uncovering LLMs for Service-Composition: Challenges and Opportunities

Robin D. Pesl[1]([✉])[iD], Miles Stötzner[2][iD], Ilche Georgievski[1][iD],
and Marco Aiello[1][iD]

[1] Institute of Architecture of Application Systems, University of Stuttgart,
Stuttgart, Germany
{robin.pesl,ilche.georgievski,marco.aiello}@iaas.uni-stuttgart.de
[2] Institute of Software Engineering, University of Stuttgart, Stuttgart, Germany
miles.stoetzner@iste.uni-stuttgart.de

Abstract. Large Language Models (LLMs) have gained significant
attention for using natural language to generate program code without
direct programming efforts, e.g., by using ChatGPT in a dialog-based
interaction. In the field of Service-Oriented Computing, the potential of
using LLMs' capabilities is yet to be explored. LLMs may solve significant service composition challenges like automated service discovery or
automated service composition by filling the gap between the availability of suitable services, e.g., in a registry, and their actual composition
without explicit semantic annotations or modeling. We analyze the classical way of service composition and how LLMs are recently employed
in code generation and service composition. As a result, we show that
classical solution approaches usually require extensive domain modeling and computationally expensive planning processes, resulting in a
long time needed to create the composition. To ground the research on
LLMs for service compositions, we identify six representative scenarios of
service compositions from the literature and perform experiments with
ChatGPT and GPT-4 as a notable, representative application of LLMs.
Finally, we frame open research challenges for service composition in the
context of LLMs. With this position paper, we emphasize the importance
of researching LLMs as the next step of automated service composition.

Keywords: Automated Service Composition · Large Language
Models · Code Generation · Automatic Programming · ChatGPT ·
GPT-4 · Service-Oriented Architecture

1 Introduction

Service composition is about the automatic discovery of remote services and their
coordinated invocation to solve a complex business goal. While the service composition problem has been identified and addressed extensively over the years,
there is no final solution to the problem as of now [1]. Large Language Models (LLMs) are a recent technology based on natural language inputs that can

© The Author(s), under exclusive license to Springer Nature Singapore Pte Ltd. 2024
F. Monti et al. (Eds.): ICSOC 2023 Workshops, LNCS 14518, pp. 39–48, 2024.
https://doi.org/10.1007/978-981-97-0989-2_4

be applied for code generation. Their abilities in Service-Oriented Computing (SOC) and the service composition challenge are yet unknown but can impact the field of automated service composition by not requiring semantic annotations, explicit modeling, or long composition times. With the present work, we provide an initial investigation on the potential of using LLMs for service composition. Our investigation consists of identifying a set of representative examples from the literature on service composition and using them to experimentally evaluate the performance of LLM for service composition. For our experiments, we select ChatGPT with GPT-4 as an application of a state-of-the-art LLM and identify six representative examples from the literature on service composition. In particular, we focus on the subproblems of service discovery and service composition design.

Multiple "classical" approaches are trying to solve the service-composition challenge, such as using semantic Web technologies or AI planning. These, though, may suffer from issues such as the time and effort necessary for annotating the services, the long composition times, or the need to transform generated compositions into executable code. The shortcomings are especially apparent when putting these systems to work on real-world services and their implementations.

1.1 Classical Approaches to Service Composition

From the early days of SOC, the service composition challenge is considered a search into an immense space of possible combinations of online services. The search is often modeled as an AI planning problem solved using various planning techniques, e.g., with a domain-specific planner [28] or a domain-independent planner [19]. Advanced planning techniques can cope with more complex scenarios, e.g., continual planning [24] or hierarchical planning [13]. Another approach is to use the situation calculus by describing a set of user objectives as a sufficiently generic Golog program [20,29]. Further, the "Roman model" abstracts services to transition systems, resulting in the use of finite state machines to describe the execution of the available services [6,12]. All of these methods need modeling of the problem in some specific format, e.g., as a planning problem or with semantic annotations. These models are rare and laborious to create, which leads to a low level of dissemination in practice.

1.2 LLMs for Code Generation

While the research on LLM-based service composition is at the beginning, a considerable body of work on code generation is already available. Within software engineering, Gu et al. use LLMs to elicit and process natural language requirements to generate the program code [14]. Huo et al. use LLMs to extract program explanations or APIs [15]. Researchers and practitioners have shown that LLMs are capable of code generation, and several systems have been built based on LLMs that can generate code, such as Google's Bard, ChatGPT, CODEX, CodeGen, GitHub Copilot, INCODER, and PolyCoder [8]. While such tools can support the programmer in generating code and reduce production times, several authors remark that the generated code is far from perfect. For example, Khoury et al. notice that the code generated by ChatGPT is not secure, and even with multi-shot prompting, one cannot achieve strongly secure code [16]. Others show how to improve the quality of the results by appropriately prompting the system using the recent technique of chain-of-thought prompting with multi-step optimizations [18]. In the SOC domain, Alizadehsani et al. captured service usage in open-source projects and trained a GPT-2 model using this data. The model is then used to perform auto-completion [4]. Another recent significant advance is the integration of LLMs with chat interaction in the GitHub Copilot [25]. Aiello and Georgievski introduce the idea of LLM to generate a service composition using a single demonstrative example, which showed promise but lacks statistical validity [2].

1.3   Service-Composition Benchmarks

To fairly compare service composition approaches, a standardized benchmark is needed. Unfortunately, such a widely accepted benchmark does not exist. A keyword-based search on Google Scholar to determine suitable service-composition benchmarks and our experience confirm this. In our search, we use the keywords *web*, *service-composition*, *benchmark*, and *service-computing* and their combinations. A popular benchmarking framework is "WSBen," consisting of synthetic web services in WSDL [22]. The services do not possess any semantic meaning but are composable syntactically. Later versions of similar benchmarking approaches add Quality of Service (QoS) capabilities but stick to synthetic services [3, 31]. These benchmarks are limited to composition abilities without semantic meaning and, therefore, have difficulties representing realistic service-composition challenges.

For service discovery challenges, service registries like "ProgrammableWeb" are resorted to [17, 32]. Cremaschi et al. perform experiments using JSON-LD annotations for OpenAPI specifications to achieve ontological compatibility [9]. Serbout et al. use GitHub to create a dataset with 106,873 APIs based on their OpenAPI specifications to analyze compatibility by matching property names and data types [27]. These approaches usually stick to tasks like service classification and do not expose complete service compositions.

Meanwhile, other researchers also identify the lack of holistic service-composition benchmarks with semantic details and look for representative examples in the literature that can be used for comparison studies [11, 26, 30]. There are lists with ten composition examples [11], eighteen [26], and six [30].

Using the Google Scholar results, the listed examples, and snowballing, we identify 57 examples[1], of which we select six representative service composition examples for our experiments. The selection is based on (i) how common the described scenario is, (ii) how complex it is, i.e., how many services interact, and (iii) how detailed the description of the services and parameters is. Table 1

---

[1] https://doi.org/10.18419/darus-3767.

Table 1. Representative Examples of Service Composition from the Literature.

ID	Author	Reference	Application Domain	Number of Services
S1	Pautasso	[23]	Online shop	3
S2	Zhang et al.	[33]	Context awareness	5
S3	Cremaschi et al.	[10]	Book info retrieval	2
S4	Netedu et al.	[21]	Transport	6
S5	Bultan et al.	[7]	Online shop	4
S6	Benatallah et al.	[5]	Travel agency	7

lists the six papers, the application domain of the example, and the number of services involved in the composition. The other papers found in our search have very similar examples to the selected six. Often, the described services cannot be used for papers using real services because the services no longer exist.

In particular, we select the example S1 because it is representative of service composition describing RESTful web services and defining a comprehensive set of operations for all services. S1 is about an online shop of RESTful web services described in detail with all operations, endpoints, parameters, etc. [23]. We select examples S2 and S3 because they allow us to evaluate whether ChatGPT can compose existing services. In S2, Zhang et al. present a context-aware service mashup of real services to discover relevant and physically close services [33]. In S3, Cremaschi et al. describe a book information system consisting of real services [10]. We rely on the first described composition of *Google Books API* for information about the book and the *Amazon Market API* for its availability. We selected S4, S5, and S6 because their application domains are typical for service composition, and the described set of services is relatively complex and described in detail with operations, parameters, and an invocation order. S4 represents the transport domain expressed with all input and output parameters, data types, and how they can be composed [21]. In S5, Bultan et al. show an online shop of a store, a bank, and two warehouse services. They describe each interaction, including parameters, in detail [7]. S6 presents a complex composition example from Benatallah et al. in the travel domain, consisting of seven services, including conditional service invocations depending on the location and destination of the traveler. It involves flight and accommodation booking, attraction search, car rental, and travel insurance. All invocations and conditions are present in detail [5].

2   Experiment

We conduct three experiments by choosing ChatGPT as a tool with GPT-4 as a contemporary representative of LLMs and take the six representative composition examples from Table 1. Our prompting strategy is to (i) ask for the service composition, (ii) check for any error, and then, for each error, (iii) request a fix until we have a fully functional service composition. For each composition example, we perform three experiments each in a separate chat to avoid the contextual effects of the prompts. We define the following experiments to analyze ChatGPT's capabilities. The full chats are available online (see Footnote 1).

Experiment 1: Service Discovery. To examine the service discovery abilities, we ask ChatGPT for existing real services matching the functionality described in the composition example from the literature.

Experiment 2: Service Composition. Given the list of services from Experiment 1 and the task specified in the composition example, we ask to create a composition in Python matching the task.

Experiment 3: Combined Service Discovery and Composition. We ask to make the composition purely based on the natural language description of the task without providing a list of available services.

2.1 Service Discovery

We evaluate the ability of ChatGPT to discover actual existing services on the Internet. We prompt an OpenAPI specification matching to a service of the composition example and ask for matching real services. Each specification of the composition example is entered as its own prompt. We measure the results by counting how many of the proposed services are valid, i.e., real and reachable. For all composition examples and services, our experiments reveal that 82% are valid services. In addition to providing the APIs, ChatGPT always summarizes what the service does in natural language. The experiment shows that, in general, the stated services are valid but often do not offer a public API. The lists of proposed services vary between queries and are incomplete. E.g., for S3, it also states "Library-specific APIs," which is not a valid service.

2.2 Automated Service Composition

To assess ChatGPT's service composition capabilities for real services, we take the services from Experiment 1, i.e., their names and the natural language composition task, and ask for a service composition in Python. Then, we check the used API against its specification, and if the API is publicly available, we execute the code. We prompt for a correction in case of coding errors, code omissions, or an invalid API.

We can generate valid service compositions for all composition examples after a few prompts. Especially for map, routing, and payment services, ChatGPT can generate valid code without extensive user interactions. Often, we get incomplete snippets, mock code, or excuses that the code cannot be generated, which can be fixed with additional prompts. One issue that emerges is that ChatGPT does not know the APIs for the services of Experiment 1. We can alleviate this by prompting ChatGPT until it states a known API. Especially in such cases, hallucinations are a problem. E.g., for S1, the system states the non-existent URL "https://stripeapi.com/process-payment." Likewise, the remainder of the APIs include hallucinations, such as headers, request data, attributes, parameters, or even endpoints. By stating the errors in further prompts, ChatGPT can correct these. Another problem is outdated data, e.g., in S2, ChatGPT tried using an old Foursquare API version. We then described the new endpoint in natural language within five prompts and got a current functioning version. Sometimes, we must be very explicit, e.g., by putting the Shopify Python package in the prompt. Then, ChatGPT can use it in the composition correctly. These problems seem minor and fixable, but they require further research to be eliminated.

2.3 Combined Service Discovery and Composition

The final test is about generating compositions without providing a list of available services but simply stating the goal of the composition in natural language. We do this by rephrasing the prompts used in Experiment 2 and removing the list of discovered services, e.g., *"Create a service composition in Python that searches for cinemas and the route to them. For the cinemas, combine multiple services. Combine the location information with the movie schedule. Find and use real services."* For the validation, we adopt the same approach as in Experiment 2, analyzing the API specifications and executing the code, if possible. In case of errors or omissions, we prompt for fixes.

The service compositions are generally correct but use fewer services than in the previous cases, e.g., in S4, the number of used services decreased from six to one. ChatGPT often has difficulties discovering the services, even if it can find this information in Experiment 1. In comparison to Experiment 2, the number of prompts needed to get a proper composition is lower. On the other hand, in S6, ChatGPT cannot determine a service for travel insurance booking. For the car rental service, it needs to be persuaded to search for real services with three prompts.

3 Open Research Challenges

In accordance with very recent literature on LLMs for code generation, our preliminary experiments reveal the potential of LLMs to solve or at least alleviate the service-composition challenge. While the research in this area is in its infancy, we notice the potential of LLMs to revolutionize the field of automated service composition as a novel approach that does not rely on semantic annotations or modeling and allows for fast composition to be generated. We synthesize the following open research challenges from our results and lessons learned as a guide for future research.

Analysis of LLMs. LLMs are a probabilistic approach. In comparison to, e.g., AI planning, correctness cannot be guaranteed without further efforts. To further analyze its capabilities, we need to determine to which degree LLMs can automatically compose services by specifying appropriate measures and quantitatively identifying limitations.

Full Automation. Our preliminary experiments are based on ChatGPT as a dialog-based application of LLMs. It requires a user to manually design and input the prompts and manually interpret the output. Future research must automate the process by measuring the presented solutions' quality, determining deficits, and reacting to the answers automatically. The analysis outputs can then be input for the following query to enhance the composition. Using the APIs of the LLMs, we can create a fully automated approach that steadily improves itself and solves the service composition challenge.

Prompt Engineering. A further finding of our experiments is the need to appropriately specify the prompts to the LLMs as we often experience excuses and abbreviated code snippets. Consequently, it is crucial to investigate and define guidelines for prompting to improve the answer quality. This research involves concise "system" and "user" messages.

Informed Machine Learning. Service compositions with LLMs can be enriched with other technologies like AI planning or workflow languages like BPMN or BPEL to incorporate the benefits of all involved technologies. The LLM is applied to the natural language parts, whereas the other technologies are involved in the formal composition modeling and execution. It is necessary to analyze how and if this approach is beneficial compared to solely using LLMs. They might affect the quality of the result or the composition time.

Integration with Tooling. To enhance the integration of LLMs in the automated service composition workflow, there is the demand for sophisticated tool support, e.g., as Alizadehsani et al. propose by enabling auto-completion for available services [4]. Such approaches need to be further investigated and improved to allow practitioners to easily create service compositions, reducing development effort and eliminating manual work errors.

4 Concluding Remarks

LLMs are a contemporary technology useful for code generation, which are based on natural language prompts and do not require any formal modeling. Their application in the SOC domain is in its infancy. Our preliminary experiments show that LLMs have the potential to alleviate the drawbacks of current solutions to service composition. We state open research challenges to guide future research to exploit this promising technology in SOC. If these research attempts are successful, LLMs can revolutionize SOC and should be, therefore, further researched.

Acknowledgements. This work was partially funded by the German Federal Ministry for Economic Affairs and Climate Action (BMWK) project Software-Defined Car (SofDCar) (19S21002).

References

1. Aiello, M.: A challenge for the next 50 years of automated service composition. In: Troya, J., Medjahed, B., Piattini, M., Yao, L., Fernández, P., Ruiz-Cortés, A.

(eds.) Service-Oriented Computing, pp. 635–643. Springer, Cham (2022). https://doi.org/10.1007/978-3-031-20984-0_45

2. Aiello, M., Georgievski, I.: Service composition in the ChatGPT era. SOCA **17**(4), 233–238 (2023). https://doi.org/10.1007/s11761-023-00367-7

3. Al-Masri, E., Mahmoud, Q.H.: Investigating web services on the world wide web. In: Proceedings of the 17th International Conference on World Wide Web, WWW 2008, pp. 795–804. Association for Computing Machinery, New York (2008). https://doi.org/10.1145/1367497.1367605

4. Alizadehsani, Z., Ghaemi, H., Shahraki, A., Gonzalez-Briones, A., Corchado, J.M.: DCServCG: a data-centric service code generation using deep learning. Eng. Appl. Artif. Intell. **123**, 106304 (2023). https://doi.org/10.1016/j.engappai.2023.106304

5. Benatallah, B., Dumas, M., Sheng, Q., Ngu, A.: Declarative composition and peer-to-peer provisioning of dynamic web services. In: Proceedings 18th International Conference on Data Engineering, pp. 297–308 (2002). https://doi.org/10.1109/ICDE.2002.994738

6. Berardi, D., Calvanese, D., De Giacomo, G., Lenzerini, M., Mecella, M.: Automatic composition of *E*-services that export their behavior. In: Orlowska, M.E., Weerawarana, S., Papazoglou, M.P., Yang, J. (eds.) ICSOC 2003. LNCS, vol. 2910, pp. 43–58. Springer, Heidelberg (2003). https://doi.org/10.1007/978-3-540-24593-3_4

7. Bultan, T., Fu, X., Hull, R., Su, J.: Conversation specification: a new approach to design and analysis of e-service composition. In: Proceedings of the 12th International Conference on World Wide Web, WWW 2003, pp. 403–410. Association for Computing Machinery, New York (2003). https://doi.org/10.1145/775152.775210

8. Chen, M., et al.: Evaluating large language models trained on code (2021). https://doi.org/10.48550/arXiv.2107.03374

9. Cremaschi, M., De Paoli, F.: Toward automatic semantic API descriptions to support services composition. In: De Paoli, F., Schulte, S., Broch Johnsen, E. (eds.) ESOCC 2017. LNCS, vol. 10465, pp. 159–167. Springer, Cham (2017). https://doi.org/10.1007/978-3-319-67262-5_12

10. Cremaschi, M., De Paoli, F.: A practical approach to services composition through light semantic descriptions. In: Kritikos, K., Plebani, P., de Paoli, F. (eds.) ESOCC 2018. LNCS, vol. 11116, pp. 130–145. Springer, Cham (2018). https://doi.org/10.1007/978-3-319-99819-0_10

11. Dai, F., Mo, Q., Qiang, Z., Huang, B., Kou, W., Yang, H.: A choreography analysis approach for microservice composition in cyber-physical-social systems. IEEE Access **8**, 53215–53222 (2020). https://doi.org/10.1109/ACCESS.2020.2980891

12. De Giacomo, G., Patrizi, F., Sardiña, S.: Automatic behavior composition synthesis. Artif. Intell. **196**, 106–142 (2013). https://doi.org/10.1016/j.artint.2012.12.001

13. Georgievski, I., Aiello, M.: HTN planning: overview, comparison, and beyond. Artif. Intell. **222**, 124–156 (2015). https://doi.org/10.1016/j.artint.2015.02.002

14. Gu, X., Zhang, H., Zhang, D., Kim, S.: Deep API learning. In: Proceedings of the 2016 24th ACM SIGSOFT International Symposium on Foundations of Software Engineering, FSE 2016, pp. 631–642. Association for Computing Machinery, New York (2016). https://doi.org/10.1145/2950290.2950334

15. Huo, S., Mukherjee, K., Bandlamudi, J., Isahagian, V., Muthusamy, V., Rizk, Y.: Natural language sentence generation from API specifications (2022). https://doi.org/10.48550/arXiv.2206.06868

16. Khoury, R., Avila, A.R., Brunelle, J., Camara, B.M.: How secure is code generated by ChatGPT? (2023). https://doi.org/10.48550/arXiv.2304.09655

17. Li, S., Luo, H., Zhao, G., Tang, M., Liu, X.: Bi-directional Bayesian probabilistic model based hybrid grained semantic matchmaking for Web service discovery. World Wide Web **25**(2), 445–470 (2022). https://doi.org/10.1007/s11280-022-01004-7
18. Liu, C., et al.: Improving ChatGPT prompt for code generation (2023). https://doi.org/10.48550/arXiv.2305.08360
19. McDermott, D.V.: Estimated-regression planning for interactions with Web services. In: AIPS, pp. 204–211. AAAI Press (2002)
20. McIlraith, S., Son, T.C.: Adapting Golog for composition of semantic web-services. In: International Conference on Principles of Knowledge Representation and Reasoning, pp. 482–496 (2002)
21. Netedu, A., Buraga, S.C., Diac, P., Ţucăr, L.: A web service composition method based on OpenAPI semantic annotations. In: Chao, K.-M., Jiang, L., Hussain, O.K., Ma, S.-P., Fei, X. (eds.) ICEBE 2019. LNDECT, vol. 41, pp. 342–357. Springer, Cham (2020). https://doi.org/10.1007/978-3-030-34986-8_25
22. Oh, S.C., Kil, H., Lee, D., Kumara, S.R.: WSBen: a web services discovery and composition benchmark. In: 2006 IEEE International Conference on Web Services (ICWS 2006), pp. 239–248 (2006). https://doi.org/10.1109/ICWS.2006.148
23. Pautasso, C.: RESTful Web service composition with BPEL for REST. Data Knowl. Eng. **68**(9), 851–866 (2009). https://doi.org/10.1016/j.datak.2009.02.016. Sixth International Conference on Business Process Management (BPM 2008) - Five selected and extended papers
24. Peer, J.: A POP-based replanning agent for automatic web service composition. In: Gómez-Pérez, A., Euzenat, J. (eds.) ESWC 2005. LNCS, vol. 3532, pp. 47–61. Springer, Heidelberg (2005). https://doi.org/10.1007/11431053_4
25. Rodriguez, M.: GitHub copilot chat beta now available for every organization (2023). https://github.blog/2023-07-20-github-copilot-chat-beta-now-available-for-every-organization/. Accessed 24 July 2023
26. Sangsanit, K., Kurutach, W., Phoomvuthisarn, S.: REST web service composition: a survey of automation and techniques. In: 2018 International Conference on Information Networking (ICOIN), pp. 116–121 (2018). https://doi.org/10.1109/ICOIN.2018.8343096
27. Serbout, S., Pautasso, C., Zdun, U.: How composable is the web? An empirical study on OpenAPI data model compatibility. In: 2022 IEEE International Conference on Web Services (ICWS), pp. 415–424 (2022). https://doi.org/10.1109/ICWS55610.2022.00068
28. Sheshagiri, M., DesJardins, M., Finin, T.: A planner for composing services described in DAML-S. In: Proceedings of the AAMAS Workshop on Web Services and Agent-Based Engineering (2003)
29. Sohrabi, S., Prokoshyna, N., McIlraith, S.A.: Web service composition via the customization of Golog programs with user preferences. In: Borgida, A.T., Chaudhri, V.K., Giorgini, P., Yu, E.S. (eds.) Conceptual Modeling: Foundations and Applications. LNCS, vol. 5600, pp. 319–334. Springer, Heidelberg (2009). https://doi.org/10.1007/978-3-642-02463-4_17
30. Toubal, E.B., Belkhir, A., Kheldoun, A., Rahim, M.: A model driven approach for web service composition. In: 2022 International Conference on Advanced Aspects of Software Engineering (ICAASE), pp. 1–8 (2022). https://doi.org/10.1109/ICAASE56196.2022.9931566
31. Wang, X., Xu, H., Wang, X., Xu, X., Wang, Z.: A graph neural network and pointer network-based approach for QoS-aware service composition. IEEE Trans. Serv. Comput. **16**(3), 1589–1603 (2023). https://doi.org/10.1109/TSC.2022.3196915

32. Wu, S., et al.: Popularity-aware and diverse Web APIs recommendation based on correlation graph. IEEE Trans. Comput. Soc. Syst. **10**(2), 771–782 (2023). https://doi.org/10.1109/TCSS.2022.3168595

33. Zhang, Y., Wang, J., Yan, Y.: Context-aware generic service discovery and service composition. In: 2014 IEEE International Conference on Mobile Services, pp. 132–139 (2014). https://doi.org/10.1109/MobServ.2014.27

Transformative Predictive Modelling in the Business of Health: Harnessing Decision Trees for Strategic Insights and Enhanced Operational Efficiency

John E. McMahon(✉) [ID], Ashley Craig [ID], and Ian Cameron

John Walsh Centre for Rehabilitation Research, Kolling Institute for Medical Research, Sydney Medical School-Northern, The University of Sydney, St. Leonard's, NSW, Australia
johnm@navigatorgroup.com.au, {a.craig,ian.cameron}@sydney.edu.au

Abstract. Predictive modelling has emerged as an indispensable tool in the dynamic business realm, shaping strategies and driving impactful decisions. This study provides a framework to transform raw data (customer behaviours, employee responses) into actionable insights, emphasizing the importance of data-driven decision-making. This research aims to harness Decision Tree (DT) Analysis to develop a robust predictive modelling system suitable for regular application in business decision-making processes. Data from two customer types (350 versus 267) were analyzed to predict process outcomes categorized as Successful (S), Needing Further Intervention (NFI), or Non-Compliant (NC) with standard processes. Various predictive models, including Classification and Regression Tree (CRT), Chi-squared Automatic Interaction Detection (CHAID), Exhaustive Chi-Squared Automatic Interaction Detection (Ex-CHAID), and Quick Unbiased Efficient Statistical Tree (QUEST) were employed, with systematic tweaks in their hierarchical structures. Through this method, 324 DTs were generated, adjusting structural parameters. Upon consolidating both datasets, a CRT model yielded a correct classification rate of 71.6%. Specific indicators and interview data pinpointed the Ex-CHAID model as the most predictive for the first dataset at 70.1% accuracy, while the CRT model for the second dataset was most accurate at 74.5%. When diving deeper into specific indicators, the first dataset best aligned with a CHAID model, predicting 74.3% of outcomes, whereas the second dataset favoured a CRT model with a 77.7% prediction accuracy. A CRT model with specific structural parameters achieved the pinnacle of performance, registering an 88.6% accuracy. However, its intricate 15-leaf, 6-level structure suggests potential overfitting, and the complexity rendering it less practical for routine business applications. The ability to predict how consumers or clients might respond to a product or service after their first interaction can provide valuable feedback for product and program development teams. The unique outcome of this paper will result in service refinement, risk management, and improved operational efficiency.

Keywords: Business Process · Predictive Modelling · Decision Trees · Prognosis · Whiplash Associated Disorder · Shoulder Injury

F. Monti et al. (Eds.): ICSOC 2023 Workshops, LNCS 14518, pp. 49–61, 2024.
https://doi.org/10.1007/978-981-97-0989-2_5

1 Introduction

In the age of digitalization and information abundance, businesses face the challenge of sifting through vast amounts of data to make well-informed decisions. This deluge of data, when leveraged appropriately, can act as a powerful catalyst for transformative change within organizations. Over recent years, predictive modelling has evolved from a niche analytical tool to a cornerstone of strategic business initiatives. It is a testament to the union of technology and business acumen, creating pathways for companies to anticipate market trends, customer behaviours, and even internal employee dynamics.

The power of predictive modelling lies not just in forecasting future occurrences but in shaping present strategies to align with anticipated outcomes. In this context, Decision Tree (DT) Analysis has gained prominence. DTs, with their hierarchical structure and ability to handle multifaceted datasets, offer businesses a structured methodology to transform raw, often overwhelming, data into actionable insights. These insights are potential game-changers that can steer a business towards unprecedented growth, mitigate risks, and create competitive advantages. However, the effectiveness of these models hinges on their adaptability and accuracy. A delicate balance must be struck between model complexity and practicality. Overly intricate models, while potentially accurate, may not be feasible for regular business applications due to their inherent complexity and the time required to interpret them.

This paper delves into the intricacies of DT Analysis applied to two distinct datasets—representing markedly different customer types. Both datasets, though different, carry significant business implications. Understanding customer reactions can inform product development teams, optimize marketing strategies, and ensure a higher return on investment. Concurrently, grasping employee responses post-task can improve training programs, better human resource management, and enhance operational efficiency. In our exhaustive research, we ventured into various predictive models, continuously tweaking their structures to achieve optimal results.

The onboarding data of 350-clients with Whiplash Associated Disorder (WAD) after a motor vehicle crash and of 267-clients with work-related Shoulder Injuries (SI) were used to predict the discharge status as Successfully treated (S), suffering chronic pain and Needing Further Intervention (NFI), or Non-Compliant (NC) with standard processes or treatment. WAD is the most common injury after motor vehicle accident and known to have inflated expenses due to excessive imaging, inappropriate treatment, and delays in appropriate treatment. SI are the third most common workplace injury presenting for treatment and prone to the same injury management inefficiencies as WAD, with the addition of excessive surgical costs. These injuries are high value targets for motor vehicle accident and workers compensation insurance companies respectively. Classification and Regression Tree (CRT), Chi-squared Automatic Interaction Detection, Exhaustive Chi-Squared Automatic Interaction Detection (Ex-CHAID), and Quick Unbiased Efficient Statistical Tree (QUEST) models were used with systematic variation of the parent and child node values to predict discharge status. 324-DTs were generated systematically varying parent and child nodes sizes. Using combined WAD and SI data a CRT model with 6-levels and 9-leaves correctly classified 71.6% of outcomes. Using psychometric test total scores and interview variables, the best model for WAD was an Ex-CHAID model that predicted 70.1% and for SI a CRT model that predicted 74.5%.

Using psychometric test item-level data the best model for WAD was a CHAID model that predicted 74.3% of outcomes correctly and for SI was a CRT model that predicted 77.7% of outcomes. The best-performing tree was a CRT for SI with a minimum parent node of 10 and minimum child node of 2 and had 88.6%, but with 15-leaves and 6 levels, this likely represented overfitting and was too complex for everyday use by clinicians and will not be deployed to clinical practice.

Our findings, as outlined in the forthcoming sections, underscore the transformative potential of predictive modelling, primarily when powered by DT Analysis. The insights derived from this study will serve as a beacon for health businesses aiming to harness the full potential of their data, ensuring they remain agile, proactive, and poised for success in a rapidly evolving marketplace.

The rest of the paper is organized as follows: In Sect. 2 we provide the background of related work. We discuss the acquisition of data including psychometric testing and the coding of the outcome of treatment in Sect. 3. In Sect. 4 we discuss the systematic generation and comparison of effectiveness of decision tree model types. Section 5 comprises the probabilistic narratives generated for clinical use in the process of prognosis by the multidisciplinary teams, and in Sect. 6 we discuss future validation and research applications of these models. Table 1 contains abbreviations used repeatedly in this manuscript.

Table 1. Abbreviations used repeatedly in this manuscript.

Abbreviation	Term
DT	Decision Tree
WAD	Whiplash Associated Disorder
SI	Shoulder Injury
S	Successfully Treated
NC	Non-Complaint
NFI	Need Further Intervention
CRT	Classification and Regression Tree
CHAID	Chi-squared Automatic Interaction Detection
Ex-CHAID	Exhaustive Chi-squared Automatic Interaction Detection
QUEST	Quick Unbiased Efficient Statistical Tree
ML	Machine Learning
ARC	Active Recovery Clinics
VAS	Visual Analogue pain Scale
IES	Impact of Events Scale
NDI	Neck Disability Index
SPADI	Shoulder Pain and Disability Index
TOMM 1/2	Test of Memory Malingering trial 1 or trial 2
ACE	Adverse Childhood Experiences
AAE	Adverse Adult Experiences

2 Background and Related Work

2.1 Machine Learning in Health Care

There are a multitude of ML models that have been applied in healthcare with varying risks and challenges, with a central challenge being the ethical and practical application of these methods [1]. There have been attempts to identify predictors of recovery at a meta-analytic level, using logistic regression [2] in the primary care environment, however there is an absence of systematic prognostic indicators for compensable injuries like Whiplash Associated Disorder (WAD) and Shoulder Injury (SI) at the specialist clinic level. Machine learning (ML) methods have been used in predicting outcomes to diverse problems in health such as employment outcomes of people with orthopaedic disabilities [3, 4], outcomes of traumatic brain injuries, [5–7], improvement in aphasia [8], the effects of COVID on the heart [9], antibody incompatible kidney transplantation [10], and youth mental health status from psychosocial antecedents [11] with successful DT having prediction accuracy between 70% and 86% for medical conditions. In another study related to health insurance claim data, a machine learning predictive regression model Least Absolute Shrinkage and Selection Operator (LASSO) was developed to formulate a population health management in Japan [12]. In other fields ML has been used on datasets looking at defects in the construction industry [13] and have systematically compared different DT models to determine which model is best for practical application in construction. For predicting accidental claims using telematics data, the logistic regression showed better prediction than the eXtreme Gradient Boosting (XGBoost) machine learning algorithm [14]. There are no successful systematic comparisons of different DTs for prediction on biomedical data [15], although there are some papers comparing other machine learning models to DTs [10, 16]. The present study aims to compare different DT models appropriate for relatively small data sets including Chi-square Automatic Interaction Detector (CHAID [17]), Classification and Regression Tree (CRT [18]) analysis, Quick Unbiased Efficient Statistical Tree (QUEST [19]) algorithms to predict the discharge status of clients of an interdisciplinary clinic from data collected at onboarding.

2.2 Ethics and Reporting Requirements in Healthcare

Non-malfeasance is a primary concern for the deployment of machine learning in healthcare [20] with threats coming from clinical relevance, data governance, model relevance, and utilization safety. Luo et al. provide guidelines for reporting ML predictive models in biomedical research (JMIR) [21]. The Transparent Reporting of a multivariate prediction model for Individual Prognosis or Diagnosis (TRIPOD) statement is a 22-item checklist to improve the reporting of predictive models [22]. The ML/Artificial Intelligence Transparent Replicable Ethical and Effective (AI-TREE) framework sets 20-questions to identify issues and facilitate project planning for ML/AI projects and Vollmer et al. take a similar approach [23, 24]. The present paper aims to satisfy these requirements.

2.3 Interpretability and Utility

Comparing DT predictive models for motor vehicle crash-related WAD and work-related SI and the combined data, can show if there are uniform factors at play in recovery from these insured injuries, or if different psychosocial factors affect these injuries. Ultimately, these DT models will generate clinical narratives for prognosis that are easily interpreted by working clinicians and permit valid prognostic statements [24, 25]. The immediate benefits to the insured injury environment, in which the specialist interdisciplinary clinics are embedded, is that the insurers can have realistic expectations of the response of injured people to the interdisciplinary programs and secondly strategies to address negative prognostic factors can be tailored to try and improve recovery rates in the future.

3 Data Acquisition and Outcome Coding

3.1 Multidisciplinary Clinics

The specialist interdisciplinary clinics, known as the Active Recovery Clinics (ARC), treat only high frequency compensable injuries in an outpatient clinical setting or via telehealth. The research period was from January 2018 until November 2021 and 350 WAD and 267 SI were onboarded during this period. Each clinic visit comprises of 30-min reviews by either an orthopaedic surgeon or sports medicine physician, a psychologist, and either a physiotherapist or exercise physiologist. The client then completes a tailored exercise program on a digital platform with motion sensors. The client may also have psychological therapy if required which was usually delivered remotely via telehealth. The clinicians reviewed WAD clients at a physical clinic or remotely every 6-weeks until discharged at a maximum of 12-weeks. The clinicians reviewed SI clients at a physical clinic or remotely every 4-weeks until discharged at a maximum of 12-weeks. All health data recorded in the course of these clinics and treatment is retained on specifically configured Sales Force Health Cloud on a secure server within Australia and using systems that are compliant with ISO 27000 and deidentified and exported for statistical processing purposes, a process considered of negligible risk by Sydney University Human Ethics Committee.

3.2 Psychometric Testing

Along with various historical information including number of adverse childhood and adult experiences, pre-existing mental disorder, and medical disorder, at attendance to the ARC injured people completed a brief battery of screening tests recommended by various guidelines which constitute the predictors in the DT models. These included the 25-Item Impact of Events Scale-Revised (IES [26]) to assess for current traumatic symptoms and the Visual Analogue Scale (VAS [27]) for pain. WAD completed the 10-item Neck Disability Index (NDI [28]) and SI completed the 13-item Shoulder Pain and Disability Index (SPADI [29]) to measure injury related pain and disability. The medical review included a general history, assessment of collateral medical disorders and formal assessment of the WAD or SI. The psychologist administered a semi-structured clinical interview inquiring about history of mental disorder, adverse/traumatic experiences in childhood (ACE) or adulthood (AAE), and assessment of the presenting issue. The psychologist then administered standardized measures at initial assessment including the Test of Memory Malingering (TOMM [30]) to assess feigning spectrum behaviour; with the second trial not administered if TOMM Trial 1 was over 45 [31].

3.3 Treatment and Outcomes

The psychological treatment was in the form of structured Eye Movement Desensitization and Reprocessing Therapy protocol and assumed moderate structural dissociation of personality [32–34]. The physiotherapy program was a curated a personalized program using the SWORD Phoenix system and when there were significant barriers to the use of SWORD Phoenix, such as supply issues or technical limitations, a Physitrack program was developed [35]. The catalogue of exercise for WAD were taken from the SIRA guides [36] and for SI from a systematic review of evidenced-based rehabilitation for rotator-cuff impingement [37].

Clients were discharged either recovered with Successful (S) treatment, having chronic pain (CP) and Needing Further Intervention (NFI), or being non-compliant with the process of treatment (NC). S was defined as a substantial reduction in pain, subclinical psychometric scores, and a return to pre-morbid function. NFI was defined as persistence of pain and physical disability that produces a clinically significant reduction in function and clinical elevations on psychometric measures. NC was defined as engaging in less than 1-h of treatment, either physical or psychological, or that the individual was lost to follow-up with less than 1-h of digitally recorded exercise engagement.

4 DT Generation

4.1 Inferential Work: Statistical Comparison of WAD and SI Groups

There were significant differences in the onboarding characteristics of the WAD and SI groups which may be antecedents for different DTs predicting recovery. Table 2 shows these comparisons between WAD and SI.

The pattern of medical determinations at onboarding and psychometric results reflect different factors at play in recovery, however the general results appear equivalent between WAD and SI when there was treatment compliance. Table 3 shows the onboarding, psychometric and recovery differences between WAD and SI.

Table 2. Comparison of WAD and SI Onboarding Characteristics

	WAD (N = 350)	SI (N = 267)
Gender (female), n, %	205, 58.57%	158, 59.17%
*Age (years), Mean (SD), [Range]	40.54 (13.850) [16–80]	49.21 (11.49) [18–72]

(continued)

Table 2. (*continued*)

	WAD (N = 350)	SI (N = 267)
Unemployed/Retired/DSP %	15.43%	0%
Home Duties/Carer's Pension %	3.71%	0%
Student %	3.43%	0%
Unskilled %	20.86%	39.1%
Skilled %	28.57%	54.24%
White Collar %	28%	6.64%
Frontline Worker n, %	14, 4%	95, 35.58%
*Interval Date of Injury to Onboard Mean weeks (SD) [Range]	7.13 (6.50) [1–68]	25.5 (38.60) [2–663]
Reported ACEs, n, Mean (SD) [Range], % > 0	322, 0.165 (0.475) [0–4] 13.62%	241, 0.115 (0.343) [0–3] 14.94%
*Reported AAEs, n, % > 0	322, 0.394 (0.81) [0–3] 30.74%	241, 0.811 (1.085) [0–11] 49.37%
Pre-Existing Psychopathology, n, Mean (SD), %	322, 0.375 (0.485) 40.0%	241, 0.424 (0.496) 44.81%

* Indicates significant differences calculated by MANOVA and T-test at the $p < 0.000$ level.

Table 3. Differences between WAD and SI

	WAD (total N = 350)	SI (total N = 267)
Administrative Withdrawals, *n*, %	14, 4%	12, 4.4%
*Not Suitable for Clinic, n, %	1, 0.29%	13, 4.8%
*Surgical Withdrawal, *n*, %	1, 0.2%	34, 12.5%
*Lost To Follow Up, *n* %	16, 4.68%	1, 0.41%
*Non-Compliant (NC), *n*, %	52, 15.2%	13, 5.35%
*SWORD Mean Minutes, (SD)	266, (375)	332, (333)
Optimistic About Recovery, *n*, %	342, 52.33%	243, 51.44%
*TOMM Trial 1, n, Mean (SD)	266, 43.96 (7.35)	170, 47.42 (3.49)
*TOMM Trial 2, *n*, Mean (SD)	264, 47.59 (5.94)	170, 49.68 (1.68)

(*continued*)

Table 3. (*continued*)

	WAD (total N = 350)	SI (total N = 267)
*VAS OB, *n*, Mean (SD)	349, 59.96 (21.93)	256, 49.51 (24.97)
*IES OB *n*, Mean (SD)	332, 34.56 (19.42)	243, 19.74 (16.93)
NDI OB *n*, Mean (SD)	339, 23.15 (9.03)	N/A
SPADI OB, *n*; Mean (SD)	N/A	249: 63.49 (27.67)
Recovered/Onboarded, X/*n*, %	213/342, 62.28%,	135/243, 55.55%
Recovered/Onboarded-NC, X/*n*, %	213/259, 82.24%	135/170, 79.41%
Chronic Pain Needing Further Intervention	46, 17.76%	35, 20.588%

* indicates significant differences calculated by MANOVA and T-test at the $p < 0.000$ level.

4.2 DT Pooled Common WAD and SI

Pooling the data common to WAD and SI, CHAID, Ex-CHAID, CRT and QUEST models were generated classifying outcome using onboard data Age, Injury to Onboard Interval, Optimistic About Recovery, VAS, IES, TOMM1, TOMM2, ACE, AAE, and Pre-existing psychopathology varying minimum parent node [100, 75, 50, 25] and child node [50, 25, 10, 5, 2] sizes, 60-models were generated. The top 10 models on pooled data were 6-CRT models which correctly classified 75%, 73.2%, 72.6% (x2), 71.6% (x2) and 4-QUEST models that correctly identified 71% (x4).

4.3 DT WAD and SI Using Common Variables

The process in Sect. 4.2 was replicated for WAD and SI for the data in the common variable fields. The top 10 WAD models were all CHAID or Ex-CHAID but for one CRT and correctly classified 76.6% (CRT), 71.1% (CHAID), 70.7% (Ex-CHAID), 70.4% (x2 CHAID), and 70.1% (x5 Ex-CHAID). The top 10 SI models were all CRT models but one and correctly classified 79.3% (CRT), 77.2% (CRT), 75% (Ex-CHAID) and 74.5% (x6 CRT).

4.4 DT WAD Using WAD Specific Variables

28-DT Models were calculated for WAD using the scale total scores of psychometric measures and demographic variables, with parent nodes at 50, 25, 10 and child nodes 25, 10, 5, and 2. The top 5 total score models for WAD classified 77% (CRT), 75.7% (CHAID), and 74.3% (CHAID x 3). 28- DT Models were calculated for WAD using the item level responses with parents at 50, 25, 10 and child nodes 25, 10, 5, and 2. The top 5 item level models for WAD classified 75.35% (Ex-CHAID), 74.7% (Ex-CHAID), 74% (CRT), 72.7% (CHAID), and 72% (5 x CHAID).

4.5 DT SI Using SI Specific Variables

28-DT Models were calculated for SI using the scale total scores of psychometric measures and demographic variables, with parent nodes at 50, 25, 10 and child nodes 25, 10, 5, and 2. The top 5 total score models for SI classified 88.6% (CRT), 80.4% (Ex-CHAID), 79.3% (CHAID), and 77.7% (CHAID x 3). 28- DT Models were calculated for WAD using the item level responses with parents at 50, 25, 10 and child nodes 25, 10, 5, and 2. The top 5 Item level models for SI classified 85.3 (CRT), 82.6% (CRT x 2), 80.4% (Ex-CHAID) and 79.3% (CHAID).

4.6 Statistical Comparison of DT Types for Identifying S, NFI, and NC

Overall, we conducted an extensive analysis involving a total of 324 models. To assess the accuracy of DT model type, we employed a Multivariate Analysis of Variance (MANOVA) comparing the accuracy of the classes of DTs. The results of this analysis, characterized by Wilks' Lambda ($p = 0.001$) and significance (Sig $= 0.000$), indicated highly significant differences in the performance of the DT Models under consideration. Following the MANOVA, we conducted Post Hoc testing using the Scheffe method to delve deeper into these differences. Notably, our findings revealed that CRT models outperformed the QUEST models in overall accuracy, and this difference was statistically significant. However, CRT was not significantly better than the other models under consideration. Further analysis revealed that all models significantly outperformed QUEST in identifying the S.

Additionally, our results indicated significant variations in the classification of NC instances among different models. QUEST identified significantly more NC instances compared to the CHAID model. The Ex-CHAID model identified significantly more NC instances than the CHAID model. But otherwise, there were no significant differences.

Lastly, both CRT and CHAID models were significantly better than QUEST in identifying NFI.

5 Recovery Narratives or Prognostic Statements from DTs

5.1 Narrative for Combined SI and WAD Data

Narrative 1 (71.6% accuracy): Injured people scoring at or below 41 on T1 of the TOMM and being younger than 30-years of age are likely to be NC. For people scoring above 41 on T1 of the TOMM with pain greater than 69.5mm on the VAS, who have an injury-onboard interval of less than 7.5-weeks and who are male are as likely as not to be NC, and those with greater than 7.5-weeks onboard to injury who have more than three adverse childhood experiences are as likely as not to NFI if the VAS is less than 89.5mm or NC if the VAS is greater than 89.5mm. Otherwise, the prognosis is S.

5.2 Narratives for WAD

Narrative 2 (70.1% accuracy) Common variables with SI: For injured people who were not optimistic about their recovery, if Trial 2 on the TOMM was less than or equal to 42 then there was a risk of chronic pain, if Trial 2 on the TOMM was between 42 and 49 then there is a risk of NC, and if Trial 2 on the TOMM was 49 or 50 the person is likely to recover. Otherwise, the prognosis is S.

Narrative 3 (74.3% accuracy) Assessment and Psychometric Total Scores: If the NDI is less than or equal to 25 the prognosis is for recovery. If the NDI was not completed or between 25 and 34, and the TOMM Trial 2 was less than or equal to 48 then the prognosis is NC. If the NDI is greater than 34 and the injury to onboard interval is less than 5-weeks then the prognosis is for S, if it is greater than 5-weeks then the prognosis is likely NC. Otherwise, the prognosis is S.

Narrative 4 (72% accuracy) Assessment and Psychometric Item Scores: If the person is pessimistic about recovery and they endorse Item 6 of the NDI as "I have a 'fair degree' (2) or 'a lot of' (3) difficulty concentrating or do not respond to the question and endorse Item 10 of the NDI as "I cannot do any recreation activities at all" then the prognosis is NC. If on NDI Item 6 they have "no difficulty concentrating" (0), have "slight difficulty concentrating when needed" (1) or "cannot concentrate at all" (5) and on item 14 of the IES endorsed that "any reminder brought back feelings about it" as 'sometimes' (3) then the prognosis is as likely as not to be NC. If on Item 6 of the NDI, they endorsed "I have a great deal of difficulty in concentrating when I want to" (4) then the prognosis is NC. Otherwise the prognosis is S.

5.3 Narratives for SI

Narrative 5 (74.5% accuracy) Common variables with WAD: If the VAS at onboard greater than 79mm it is as likely as not the prognosis is to NFI. Otherwise, the prognosis is S.

Narrative 6 (77.2% accuracy) Assessment and Psychometric Total Scores: If the SPADI is less than or equal to 57 there will be S and if the score is greater than 57 then the prognosis is likely to be NFI.

Narrative 7 (77.7% accuracy) Assessment and Psychometric Item Scores: If on Item 9 of the SPADI the injured person scored 6 or greater, but not 9, for difficulty "putting on a shirt with buttons down the front", but not eight or less on Item 13 for difficulty "removing something from your back pocket" then they are likely to NFI. Otherwise the prognosis is S.

6 Conclusion

Recovery outcomes from a multidisciplinary clinic treating high frequency insured injuries can be effectively predicted from measurements at onboarding using CHAID, Ex-CHAID and CRT modelling with comparable accuracy to predictors of other problems in health. As in Lin and Fan's [13] research in construction QUEST produced poorer predictions in comparison to other models. Unlike the other methods tested here QUEST involves "post-pruning", as opposed to "pre-pruning", and does not interrogate all nodal splits, just highly weighted ones i.e., the "Quick" in QUEST. In problems like medical prognostication, it appears breadth of variable consideration may be more important than depth of calculation or specificity. The predictive accuracy of the DTs generated in this paper were adequate compared to other DTs used in health to predict likely outcomes of interventions, and comparable to unrelated fields such as predicting faults in building construction.

Easily interpretable injury narratives can be generated from DTs that assist clinicians to make probabilistically informed prognostic statements rather than relying on clinical judgment alone. Machine learning, such as DTs, can augment clinical practice by generating ethical and utilisable insights especially for frequent injuries like WAD and SI which have high unnecessary cost burdens such as unnecessary imaging and surgical costs, and overservicing with inappropriate interventions. For those clients likely to NFI, the accurate prediction of this requirement overcomes common issues and treatment inefficiencies associated with delays due to waiting lists, funding approval delays, and perseveration of ineffective treatment at the clinic level. Research like the present paper can improve both the customer journey for the injured person and the cost efficiency of treating insured injury. Generation of similar modelling across other injuries and services would reduce the costly inefficiencies in systems of injury management through more accurate prognostic processes, thus improving the business of healthcare.

The current paper has focused on the development of these DTs on a suitably sized data set. Future research will involve systematic validation and refinement of these models on a larger clinical data set. These validated models will then be used to inform clinical practice and evaluate new interventions for the variables identified as critical to recovery. Systematically addressing these variables with interventions will show the mutability of these factors, and further DTs can be generated to see if further treatment is valid or moot. This future research will possibly demonstrate the value of the interplay between ML insights and clinical practice with compensable injuries and the contribution this can make to the business of healthcare.

References

1. Habehh, H., Gohel, S.: Machine learning in healthcare. Curr. Genomics **22**, 291–300 (2021). https://doi.org/10.2174/1389202922666210705124359
2. Kuijpers, T., van der Windt, D.A.W.M., Boeke, J.P.A., et al.: Clinical prediction rules for the prognosis of shoulder pain in general practice. Pain **120**, 276–285 (2006). https://doi.org/10.1016/j.pain.2005.11.004
3. Chan, F., Cheing, G., Chan, J.Y.C., Rosenthal, D.A., Chronister, J.: Predicting employment outcomes of rehabilitation clients with orthopaedic disabilities: a CHAID analysis. Disabil. Rahabil. **28**, 257–270 (2006). https://doi.org/10.1080/09638280500158307
4. Anan, T., Kajiki, S., Oka, H., et al.: Effects of an artificial intelligence-assisted health program on workers with neck/shoulder pain/stiffness and low back pain: randomized controlled trial. JMIR Mhealth Uhealth **9** (2021). https://doi.org/10.2196/27535
5. Oh, H.S., Seo, W.S.: Development of a decision tree analysis model that predicts recovery from acute brain injury. Jpn. J. Nurs. Sci. **10**, 89–97 (2013). https://doi.org/10.1111/j.1742-7924.2012.00215.x
6. Andrews, P.J., Sleeman, D.H., Statham, P.F., et al.: Predicting recovery in patients suffering from traumatic brain injury by using admission variables and physiological data: a comparison between decision tree analysis and logistic regression. J. Neurosurg. **97**, 326–336 (2002). https://doi.org/10.3171/jns.2002.97.2.0326

7. Temkin, N.R., Holubkov, R., Machamer, J.E.: Classification and regression trees (CART) for prediction of functioning at 1 year following head trauma. J. Neurosurg. **82**, 764–771 (2016). https://doi.org/10.3171/jns.1995.82.5.0764

8. Lahiri, D., Dubey, S., Ardila, A., Sanyal, D., Ray, B.K.: Determinants of aphasia recovery: exploratory decision tree analysis. Lang. Cogn. Neurosci. 109–115 (2020). https://doi.org/10.1080/23273798.2020.1777314

9. Lu, J.Q., Lu, J.Y., Wang, W., et al.: Clinical predictors of acute cardiac injury and normalization of troponin after hospital discharge from COVID-19. EBioMedicine **76** (2022). https://doi.org/10.1016/j.eiom.2022.103821

10. Shaikhina, T., Lowe, D., Daga, S., Briggs, D., Hggins, R., Khovanova, N.A.: Decision tree and random forest models for outcome prediction in antibody incompatible kidney transplantation. Biomed. Signal Process. Control **52**, 456–462 (2017). https://doi.org/10.1016/j.bspc.2017.01.012

11. Battista, K., Diao, L., Patte, K.A., Dublin, J.A., Leatherdale, S.T.: Examining the use of decision trees in population health surveillance research: an application to youth mental health survey data in the COMPASS study. Health Promot. Chronic Dis. Prev. Can. **43**, 73–86 (2023). https://doi.org/10.24095/hpcdp.43.2.03

12. Takeshima, T., Keino, S., Aoki, R., Matsui, T., Iwasaki, K.: Development of medical cost prediction model based on statistical machine learning using health insurance claims data. Value Health **21** (2018). https://doi.org/10.1016/j.jval.2018.07.738

13. Lin, C.-L., Fan, C.-L.: Evaluation of CART, CHAID, and QUEST algorithms: a case study of construction defects in Taiwan. J. Asian Archit. Build. Eng. **18**, 539–553 (2019). https://doi.org/10.1080/13467581.2019.1696203

14. Pesantez-Narvaez, J., Guillen, M., Alcaniz, M.: Predicting motor insurance claims using telematics data - XGBoost versus logistic regression. Risks **7** (2019). https://doi.org/10.3390/risks7020070

15. Hajjej, F., Alohali, M., Badr, M., Rahman, M.A.: Retracted: a comparison of decision tree algorithms in the assessment of biomedical data. BioMed. Res. Int. (2022). https://doi.org/10.1155/2023/9810245

16. Long, W.J., Griffith, J.L., Selker, H.P., D'Agostino, R.B.: A comparison of logistic regression to decision-tree induction in a medical domain. Comput. Biomed. Res. **26**, 74–97 (1993). https://doi.org/10.1006/cbmr.1993

17. Kass, G.V.: An exploratory technique for investigating large quantities of categorical data. J. R. Stat. Soc. (Appl. Stat.) **29**, 119–127 (1980). https://doi.org/10.2307/2986296

18. Brieman, L., Friedman, J.H., Olshen, R.A., Stone, C.J.: Classification and Regression Trees. Wodsworth & Brooks/Cole Advanced Books & Software, Monterey (1987)

19. Loh, W., Shin, Y.: Split selection methods for classification trees. Stat. Sin. **7**, 815–840 (1997)

20. Weins, J., Saria, S., Sendak, M., et al.: Do no harm: a roadmap for responsible machine learning for health care. Nat. Med. **25**, 1337–2140 (2019). https://doi.org/10.1038/s41591-019-0548-6

21. Luo, W., Phung, D., Tran, T., et al.: Guidelines for developing and reporting machine learning predictive models in biomedical research: a multidisciplinary view. J. Med. Internet Res. **18**, e323 (2016). https://doi.org/10.2196/jmir.5870

22. Collins, G.S., Reitsma, J.B., Altman, D.G., et al.: Transparent reporting of a multivariable prediction model for individual prognosis or diagnosis (TRIPOD): the TRIPOD Statement. BMC Med. **13** (2015). https://doi.org/10.1186/s12916-014-0241-z

23. Vollmer, S., Mateen, B.A., Bohner, G., et al.: Machine learning and AI research for Patient Benefit: 20 critical questions on transparency, replicability, ethics and effectiveness. BMJ (2020). https://doi.org/10.1136/bmj.l6927

24. Batra, M., Agrawal, R.: Comparative analysis of decision tree algorithms. In: Nature Inspired Computing: Proceedings of CSI, pp. 31–36 (2018)

25. Windeler, J.: Prognosis-what does the clinician associate with this notion? Stat. Med. **19**, 425–430 (2000). https://doi.org/10.1002/(sici)1097-0258(20000229)

26. Chistianson, S., Marren, J.: The impact of events scale-revised (IES-R). Medsurg. Nurs. **21**, 321-322 (2012)

27. Kelly, A.M.: The minimum clinically significant difference in visual analogue scale pain score does not differ with severity of pain. Emerg. Med. J. **18**, 205–207 (2001). https://doi.org/10.1136/emj.18.3.205

28. Vernon, H., Mior, S.: The Neck Disability Index: a study of reliability and validity. J. Manipulative Physiol. Ther. **14**, 409–415 (1991)

29. Roach, K.E., Budiman-Mak, E., Songsiridej, N., Lertrantanakul, Y.: Development of a shoulder pain and disability index. Arthritis Care Res. **4**, 143–149 (1991)

30. Tombaugh, T.N.: The Test of Memory Malingering (TOMM) Normative data from cognitively intact and cognitively impaired individuals. Psych. Assess. **9**, 260–268. https://doi.org/10.1037/1040-3590.9.3.260

31. O'Bryant, S.E., Engel, L.R., Kleiner, J.S., Vasterling, J.J., Black, F.W.: Test of Memory Malingering (TOMM) trial 1 as a screening measure for insufficient effort. The Clin Neuropsycho. **21**, 511–521 (2007). https://doi.org/10.1080/13854040600611368

32. Shapiro, F.: EMDR Institute Basic Training Course Weekend 2 Training of the Two-Part EMDR Therapy Basic Training. EMDR Institute Inc. (1990–2022)

33. van der Hart: Dissociation of the personality in complex trauma-related disorders and EMDR: theoretical considerations. J. EMDR Pract. Res. **49**, 76-92 (2010)

34. Steele, K., van der Hart, O., Nijenhuis, E.R.: Phase-oriented treatment of structural dissociation in complex traumatization: overcoming trauma-related phobias. J. Trauma Dissociation **6**, 11–53 (2005). https://doi.org/10.1300/J229v06n03_02. PMID: 16172081

35. Bennell, K.L., Marshall, C.J., Dobson, F., Kasza, J., Lonsdale, C., Hinman, R.S.: Does a web-based exercise programming system improve home exercise adherence for people with musculoskeletal conditions? A randomized controlled trial. Am. J. Phys. Med. Rehabil. **98**, 850–858 (2019). https://doi.org/10.1097/PHM.0000000000001204

36. State Insurance Regulatory Authority. Guidelines for the management of acute whiplash associated disorders for health professionals. Sydney: third edition (2014)

37. Kuhn, J.E.: Exercise in the treatment of rotator cuff impingement: a systematic review and a synthesized evidence-based rehabilitation protocol. J. Shoulder Elbow Surg. **18**, 138–160 (2009). https://doi.org/10.1016/j.jse.2008.06.004

Breaking Boundaries: Can a Unified Hardware Abstraction Layer Simplify Transformer Deployments on Edge Devices?

Mehrdad Zakershahrak[✉] and Samira Ghodratnama

Macquaire University, Sydney, Australia
{mehrdad.zakershahrak,samira.ghodratnama}@mq.edu.au

Abstract. The deployment of transformer models on edge devices like smartphones and tablets is pivotal for leveraging machine learning benefits in real-world scenarios. However, it brings forth challenges including hardware compatibility, memory efficiency, energy efficiency, and real-time performance. We introduce a versatile Hardware Abstraction Layer (HAL) to (1) bridge pre-trained transformer models with the target hardware for optimized deployment, and (2) incorporate intermediate representations (IR) as a crucial element. The IR facilitates seamless execution of models across diverse hardware backends, ensuring enhanced privacy, security, and functionality, especially in regions with limited internet connectivity. Our HAL, endowed with configurable parameters, dynamic model optimizations, and a modular design, caters to varied performance objectives, offering a unified layer that eases the deployment of IR while focusing on user-specified performance priorities. The main contribution of this work is the introduction of IR within the HAL framework, pushing the frontier in edge-device machine learning deployments to focus on latency, energy efficiency, or memory usage. Our results exhibit that the proposed HAL, with its IR component, significantly trims down deployment time and boosts inference efficiency, without compromising model accuracy on iPhone devices.

Keywords: Hardware Abstraction Layer (HAL) · Deep Learning Model Optimization · Ultra-low edge-device inference · Performance Optimization · Real-Time Performance Monitoring

1 Introduction and Related Work

The drive to deploy machine learning models, particularly transformer models, on-edge devices has escalated due to the proliferation of smart devices and the increasing demand for on-device intelligence. However, the heterogeneity in hardware platforms and the distinct performance requirements in edge scenarios necessitate a robust mechanism to bridge the gap between high-level model representations and low-level hardware intricacies. Previous works have delved into various aspects of this domain, albeit with a narrower focus.

F. Monti et al. (Eds.): ICSOC 2023 Workshops, LNCS 14518, pp. 62–71, 2024.
https://doi.org/10.1007/978-981-97-0989-2_6

1.1 Model Optimization Techniques

Numerous studies Numerous studies have explored model optimization techniques such as quantization, pruning, and knowledge distillation to reduce the computational footprint of models for edge deployment. These techniques are crucial for fitting large transformer models into the resource constraints of edge devices [1].

Model Optimization Techniques

- **Quantization:** Quantization is a technique that reduces the precision of the numerical representations in models, thereby reducing the required memory and computational resources. Techniques like weight quantization and activation quantization have been explored to achieve significant model size reduction and speedup in inference time, with minimal impact on model accuracy.
- **Pruning:** Pruning involves removing certain elements of the model such as weights, neurons, or even entire layers that contribute less to the model's output. Various pruning strategies like weight pruning, neuron pruning, and structured pruning have been employed to create sparser models that require less computational resources while retaining a comparable level of accuracy.
- **Knowledge Distillation:** Knowledge distillation is a technique where a smaller model (student) is trained to mimic the behavior of a larger, more accurate model (teacher). Through this process, the student model learns to generalize the knowledge encapsulated in the teacher model, enabling the deployment of smaller, more efficient models on edge devices while maintaining a high level of accuracy.

These optimization techniques are particularly pivotal for the deployment of large transformer models on edge devices, where computational resources and memory are at a premium. They provide a pathway to compress models while maintaining acceptable levels of performance, thereby facilitating the practical deployment of advanced machine learning models in resource-constrained edge environments.

Despite the advances in model optimization techniques, there remains a pressing need for a robust Hardware Abstraction Layer (HAL) that can further streamline the deployment process, ensure hardware compatibility, and provide a user-centric interface for performance tuning based on specific user-defined criteria [2]. Our proposed HAL aims to address these challenges by offering a unified, configurable interface for optimized deployment of transformer models on diverse edge devices.

1.2 Hardware-Specific Deployments

Efforts have been channeled towards hardware-specific deployments, a paradigm where machine learning models, especially transformer models, are meticulously optimized to exploit the full potential of particular hardware platforms. These optimizations could range from leveraging hardware accelerators, tuning model parameters to align with hardware specifications, to employing hardware-specific libraries and frameworks [3,4].

1. **Hardware Accelerators:** Certain hardware platforms come equipped with dedicated accelerators for machine learning tasks. Tailoring models to leverage these accelerators can significantly boost performance. For instance, utilizing Apple's Neural Engine on iOS devices or exploiting the capabilities of GPUs on other platforms.
2. **Hardware-Specific Libraries and Frameworks:** Libraries and frameworks such as Apple's Core ML for iOS, or Qualcomm's Neural Processing SDK for Snapdragon platforms, offer a suite of tools and optimizations for deploying models on specific hardware.
3. **Parameter Tuning:** Adjusting model parameters like batch size, precision, and others in accordance with the hardware capabilities can also contribute to enhanced performance.

While hardware-specific deployments often yield high performance, they inherently lack the flexibility to adapt to different hardware platforms without substantial re-optimization. This model-to-hardware tight coupling can be resource-intensive and might hinder the broad adoption of models across a diverse range of devices. Moreover, the rapid evolution of hardware technologies necessitates a continual adaptation of models to new or updated hardware platforms, further exacerbating the challenge.

1.3   Benchmarking and Evaluation Frameworks

Benchmarking frameworks such as MLPerf have emerged as standard tools for evaluating and comparing the performance of machine learning models across a variety of hardware platforms. These frameworks typically provide a set of benchmarks that assess various performance metrics like throughput, latency, and energy efficiency under different operational conditions. They aim to provide a standardized environment for fair comparisons among different models and hardware configurations, thereby aiding developers and researchers in understanding the performance characteristics of their models [5].

1. **Performance Metrics:** MLPerf and similar frameworks define a suite of performance metrics that provide insights into how well models perform across different hardware setups. These metrics are essential for understanding the trade-offs involved in deploying models on edge devices.
2. **Standardized Benchmarks:** By offering standardized benchmarks, these frameworks ensure a level playing field for comparing different models and hardware configurations, which is crucial for the community to measure and drive progress in machine learning efficiency and effectiveness.
3. **Cross-Platform Comparisons:** Benchmarking frameworks facilitate cross-platform comparisons, enabling a better understanding of how different hardware architectures impact model performance.

However, while these benchmarking frameworks are invaluable for performance evaluation, they often do not delve into the intricacies involved in deploying models on diverse hardware platforms. Deployment intricacies could include hardware-software compatibility issues, optimization for specific hardware features, and the ease of deployment and maintenance over time.

- **Hardware-Software Compatibility:** Different hardware platforms may support different sets of operations, data types, and runtime environments [6]. Ensuring compatibility between the model and the target hardware is a non-trivial task that goes beyond performance benchmarking.
- **Hardware-Specific Optimizations:** Achieving optimal performance may require hardware-specific optimizations that are not captured by standard benchmarks. These optimizations might include leveraging hardware accelerators, tuning model parameters, or employing hardware-specific libraries and frameworks.
- **Ease of Deployment and Maintenance:** Ease of Deployment and Maintenance: The process of deploying, updating, and maintaining models on edge devices poses challenges that are not addressed by benchmarking frameworks. These challenges include but are not limited to, model versioning, update rollout, and real-time monitoring of model performance.

These gaps underline the necessity for a more comprehensive solution that not only evaluates model performance across different hardware platforms but also addresses the deployment intricacies and hardware compatibility issues. Our proposed Hardware Abstraction Layer (HAL) aims to bridge these gaps by providing a unified, configurable interface for deploying transformer models on various edge devices, thus addressing the challenges associated with hardware-specific deployments and ensuring a seamless deployment experience.

1.4 Runtime Environments

Runtime environments like TensorFlow Lite and ONNX Runtime have emerged to facilitate model deployment on edge devices. These runtimes provide some level of hardware abstraction, but often fall short in providing a configurable and user-centric interface for optimizing model deployment based on specific performance focuses.

TensorFlow Lite and ONNX Runtime handle the allocation and deallocation of hardware resources required for model execution, such as memory and computation resources. They manage memory buffers, schedule operations, and orchestrate the execution flow of the model. These runtimes map the high-level operations in a model to the low-level operations supported by the target hardware. For instance, they map matrix multiplications or convolution operations to the respective hardware-accelerated operations if available. They may apply some optimizations to improve execution efficiency, like operation fusion, where multiple operations are combined into a single operation to reduce the computational overhead.

While TensorFlow Lite and ONNX Runtime provide a level of hardware abstraction, they often lack the configurability to tailor the deployment based on specific performance focuses like latency, energy efficiency, or memory usage. The settings are usually static and may not cater to diverse user requirements. These runtimes generally don't provide a user-centric interface that allows end-users to define and adjust performance thresholds, select optimization profiles, or monitor model performance in real time. Although they facilitate generic optimizations, they might not fully exploit the hardware-specific features or optimizations that could significantly enhance performance on a particular device. They do not inherently provide tools for continuous monitoring and analysis of model performance and hardware resource utilization, which are crucial for understanding and optimizing the deployment.

2   Need for Hardware Abstraction Layer (HAL)

The proposed Hardware Abstraction Layer (HAL) addresses the limitations of the existing solutions by providing a unified, configurable interface for deploying transformer models on various edge devices. The HAL encapsulates the hardware-specific details, offering a standardized interface for model deployment and execution while allowing for user-defined configurations to meet diverse performance goals. The need for a Hardware Abstraction Layer (HAL) stems from several factors:

- **Hardware Heterogeneity**: The diverse range of hardware platforms with varying computational capabilities, memory sizes, and energy constraints requires a flexible interface that can cater to these differences while ensuring optimized model deployment.
- **User-Centric Optimization:** End-users may have different performance priorities such as latency, energy efficiency, or memory efficiency. A configurable HAL empowers users to tailor the deployment to meet their designated performance goals.
- **Ease of Deployment:** Simplifying the deployment process by abstracting the hardware intricacies facilitates a smoother transition from model development to deployment, accelerating the realization of on-device intelligence.
- **Performance Monitoring and Adaptability:** A HAL can provide tools for monitoring and analyzing the performance of deployed models, enabling dynamic adjustments to meet the desired performance criteria.

3   Benefits of Hardware Abstraction Layer (HAL)

- **Cross-Platform Deployment:** A HAL facilitates the deployment of transformer models across different hardware platforms without necessitating hardware-specific optimizations, thereby promoting a more streamlined and scalable deployment process.

- **Performance Tune-ability:** By allowing for user-defined performance focuses, a HAL enables fine-grained control over the trade-offs between accuracy, latency, energy consumption, and other critical metrics.
- **Reduced Development Effort:** Developers can focus more on model development rather than the nuances of hardware compatibility and optimization, thus reducing the development effort and time to deployment.
- **Enhanced User Experience:** Providing users with the ability to define and adjust performance thresholds ensures a better alignment with their expectations and use case requirements, enhancing the overall user experience.

The envisioned HAL is not merely a tool for model deployment, but a comprehensive solution aimed at simplifying, optimizing, and personalizing the deployment of transformer models on edge devices to meet the real-world demands of diverse application scenarios.

4 Methodology

The following is an outline of how the HAL can interconnect with pre-trained models to facilitate optimized deployment on edge devices. Through this methodology, the HAL facilitates a streamlined, user-centric, and optimized process for deploying pre-trained models on edge devices. It ensures that the deployment is tailored to both the capabilities of the hardware and the performance goals defined by the user, enabling a more effective and efficient utilization of edge computing resources in machine learning applications.

4.1 Model Preparation and Deployment

The Model Preparation outlines the systematic conversion and optimization of pre-trained models into a standardized format, along with the generation of a user-defined deployment configuration profile in Table 1.

Table 1. Model Preparation Stages

Stage	Input	Process	Output
Conversion	Pre-trained model files (TensorFlow, PyTorch, etc.)	Conversion to a standardized IR compatible with HAL	Standardized model IR for optimization and deployment
Optimization	Standardized model IR	Optimization techniques application (quantization, pruning, knowledge distillation) based on configurations	Optimized model IR with reduced size and demands
Configuration	User-defined performance goals (latency, energy efficiency, etc.)	Generation of a configuration profile for deployment	Deployment configuration profile

4.2   HAL Interface

The HAL Interface in Table 2 delineates the process of hardware profiling, dynamic mapping of model operations to hardware instructions, and efficient resource allocation guided by the deployment configuration profile.

Table 2. HAL Interface Stages

Stage	Input	Process	Output
Hardware Profiling	Target hardware specifications	Profiling to ascertain hardware capabilities, including memory, computational power, and accelerators	Hardware capability profile
Dynamic Mapping	Optimized model IR, hardware profile, deployment configuration	Dynamic mapping of model operations to hardware instructions, utilizing hardware acceleration if available	Execution blueprint for deployment
Resource Allocation	Execution blueprint, hardware profile	Allocation and management of memory and computational resources based on the execution blueprint	Resource allocation blueprint

4.3   Deployment

The Deployment stages explained in Table 3 encapsulate the execution and real-time monitoring of the deployed model on the target hardware, ensuring adherence to the specified performance parameters.

Table 3. Deployment Stages

Stage	Input	Process	Output
Execution	Execution and resource allocation blueprints	Model deployment and execution on target hardware, adhering to specified performance parameters	Inference results, performance metrics
Monitoring	Inference results, performance metrics	Continuous monitoring and analysis of performance and resource utilization	Performance analysis report
Feedback Loop Performance Analysis	Performance analysis report, user-defined performance goals	Comparative analysis for alignment between actual performance and goals	Insights for optimization
Iterative Optimization	Insights from performance analysis, optimized model IR	Iterative optimizations and HAL configuration adjustments for improved performance	Updated model IR, updated deployment configuration

5   Evaluation

The essence of the proposed Hardware Abstraction Layer (HAL) unfolds a new paradigm in easing the deployment of transformer models on edge devices, addressing the quintessential challenges of hardware compatibility, memory efficiency, energy efficiency, and real-time performance. By encapsulating the hardware intricacies and furnishing a unified, configurable interface, HAL mitigates the tedious and often error-prone manual optimizations typically required for model deployment on diverse hardware platforms.

A thorough review of the existing literature and industry practices revealed a distinct lack of frameworks similar to our proposed HAL, specifically tailored for transformer models. The unique challenges posed by transformer models, due to their inherent complexity and the high computational resources they demand, necessitate a dedicated abstraction layer like HAL for optimized deployment on edge devices.

6   Results

Our empirical evaluation of HAL on ARM processors within iPhone 14 device, leveraging the Apple Neural Engine Transformers and utilizing insights from the Xcode Core ML Performance Report, demonstrated significant enhancements in latency and memory efficiency for ML tasks like face recognition and image segmentation, while preserving high accuracy levels as illustrated in Table 4. These findings emphasize HAL's prowess in optimizing transformer model deployments on edge devices. HAL's unified interface notably diminished the development effort and deployment time, aligning well with user-specified performance objectives. The simplified deployment process, real-time performance feedback, and user-centric configurability of HAL were instrumental in achieving these encouraging results, showcasing its potential as an essential tool for enabling optimized, user-centric model deployments on edge devices.

Our results, albeit promising, are preliminary and could vary under different conditions or hardware configurations. The numbers presented are derived from a controlled set of experiments and further comprehensive testing is warranted to validate the robustness and effectiveness of HAL across a broader spectrum of

Table 4. Performance Metrics of Various Tasks on iPhone 14 using HAL

Task	Model	Latency (ms)	Memory Usage (MB)	Model Size (MB)	Accuracy (%)
Face Recognition	MobileFaceNet	10	14	40	95.0
Object Detection	Tiny YOLOv4	30	28	23.1	90.0
Image Segmentation	DeepLabV3+	50	56	105	88.0
Speech Recognition	DeepSpeech2	60	84	180	92.0
Language Translation	DistillBERT	40	28	77	85.0

scenarios and hardware platforms. This underscores the necessity for extended experimentation to solidify our understanding and optimization of HAL for real-world, diverse deployment landscapes.

7   Conclusion

Our crafted Hardware Abstraction Layer (HAL) emerges as a potent bridge, adeptly navigating the nuances between transformer models and the hardware terrain of edge devices. It unfolds an intuitive, user-tailored deployment arena, significantly dialing down the developmental grind and launch lag. As the clamor for on-device acumen escalates, HAL is well-positioned to expedite machine learning model deployments on edge devices, delivering the machine learning marvels directly into the everyday user's ambit across a spectrum of real-world endeavors.

The empirical validations and gleaned insights from this venture solidify the groundwork for the continual refinement and expansion of HAL's horizon. Venturing forth, the spotlight will focus on amplifying HAL's functionality, delving into avant-garde optimization avenues, and widening its embrace to accommodate a diverse spectrum of hardware ecosystems and machine learning models, making strides towards a more inclusive and optimized machine learning deployment landscape on the edge. For instance, efficient summarization techniques can be employed within the HAL to compress the models without significant loss of accuracy, facilitating smoother deployments on hardware with limited resources [7–9]. Additionally, intelligent planning algorithms can be integrated to manage the computational resources dynamically, ensuring real-time performance while adhering to the energy constraints inherent in edge deployments [10–12].

References

1. Rahman, M.W.U., et al.: Quantized transformer language model implementations on edge devices, arXiv preprint arXiv:2310.03971 (2023)
2. Beheshti, A., et al.: ProcessGPT: transforming business process management with generative artificial intelligence, arXiv preprint arXiv:2306.01771 (2023)
3. Reidy, B., Mohammadi, M., Elbtity, M., Smith, H., Ramtin, Z.: Work in progress: real-time transformer inference on edge AI accelerators. In: IEEE 29th Real-Time and Embedded Technology and Applications Symposium (RTAS), pp. 341–344. IEEE (2023)
4. Reidy, B.C., Mohammadi, M., Elbtity, M.E., Zand, R.: Efficient deployment of transformer models on edge TPU accelerators: a real system evaluation. In: Architecture and System Support for Transformer Models (ASSYST@ ISCA 2023) (2023)
5. Nag, S., Datta, G., Kundu, S., Chandrachoodan, N., Beerel, P.A.: ViTA: a vision transformer inference accelerator for edge applications, arXiv preprint arXiv:2302.09108 (2023)

6. Yang, C., et al.: Lite vision transformer with enhanced self-attention. In: Proceedings of the IEEE/CVF Conference on Computer Vision and Pattern Recognition, pp. 11998–12008 (2022)
7. Ghodratnama, S., Beheshti, A., Zakershahrak, M., Sobhanmanesh, F.: Intelligent narrative summaries: from indicative to informative summarization. Big Data Res. **26**, 100257 (2021)
8. Ghodratnama, S., Zakershahrak, M., Beheshti, A.: Summary2vec: learning semantic representation of summaries for healthcare analytics. In: 2021 International Joint Conference on Neural Networks (IJCNN), pp. 1–8. IEEE (2021)
9. Ghodratnama, S., Behehsti, A., Zakershahrak, M.: A personalized reinforcement learning summarization service for learning structure from unstructured data. In: 2023 IEEE International Conference on Web Services (ICWS), pp. 206–213. IEEE (2023)
10. Zakershahrak, M., Gong, Z., Sadassivam, N., Zhang, Y.: Online explanation generation for planning tasks in human-robot teaming. In: 2020 IEEE/RSJ International Conference on Intelligent Robots and Systems (IROS), pp. 6304–6310. IEEE (2020)
11. Zakershahrak, M., Ghodratnama, S.: Are we on the same page? Hierarchical explanation generation for planning tasks in human-robot teaming using reinforcement learning, arXiv preprint arXiv:2012.11792 (2020)
12. Zakershahrak, M., Sonawane, A., Gong, Z., Zhang, Y.: Interactive plan explicability in human-robot teaming. In: 27th IEEE International Symposium on Robot and Human Interactive Communication (RO-MAN), pp. 1012–1017. IEEE (2018)

Improving Deep Learning Transparency: Leveraging the Power of LIME Heatmap

Helia Farhood[1]([⊠]), Mohammad Najafi[2], and Morteza Saberi[2]

[1] Faculty of Science and Engineering, Macquarie University, Sydney, Australia
helia.farhood@mq.edu.au
[2] Faculty of Engineering and IT, University of Technology Sydney, Sydney, Australia
{mohammad.najafi,morteza.saberi}@uts.edu.au

Abstract. Deep learning techniques have recently demonstrated remarkable precision in executing tasks, particularly in image classification. However, their intricate structures make them mysterious even to knowledgeable users, obscuring the rationale behind their decision-making procedures. Therefore, interpreter methodologies have emerged to introduce clarity into these techniques. Among these approaches is the Local Interpretable Model-Agnostic Explanations (LIME), which stands out as a means to enhance comprehensibility. We believe that interpretable deep learning methods have unrealised potential in a variety of application domains, an aspect that has been largely neglected in the existing literature. This research aims to demonstrate the utility of features like the LIME heatmap in advancing classification accuracy within a designated decision-support framework. Real-world contexts take centre stage as we illustrate how the heatmap determines the image segments playing the greatest influence on class scoring. This critical insight empowers users to formulate sensitivity analyses and discover how manipulation of the identified feature could potentially mislead the deep learning classifier. As a second significant contribution, we examine the LIME heatmap data of GoogLeNet and SqueezeNet, two prevalent network models, in an effort to improve the comprehension of these models. Furthermore, we compare LIME with another recognised interpretive method known as Gradient-weighted Class Activation Mapping (Grad-CAM), evaluating their performance comprehensively. Experiments and evaluations conducted on real-world datasets containing images of fish readily demonstrate the superiority of the method, thereby validating our hypothesis.

Keywords: Deep learning classification · Visual explanation · LIME · Image classification · Interpretable deep learning methods · Local Interpretable Model-Agnostic Explanations

1 Introduction

From the business world to the intelligence community, machine learning has significantly advanced in many fields [1]. Increasingly, researchers and scientists

F. Monti et al. (Eds.): ICSOC 2023 Workshops, LNCS 14518, pp. 72–83, 2024.
https://doi.org/10.1007/978-981-97-0989-2_7

rely on machine learning models to improve decision-making in a variety of contexts [2]. Neural networks, especially deep learning models such as convolutional neural networks (CNNs), are renowned for their ability to perform complex tasks competently [3].

However, using deep learning in high-stakes situations such as healthcare and security presents a significant challenge [4]. In these circumstances, a strong partnership between human experts and artificial intelligence (AI) systems is required to prevent or mitigate potential deep learning-related issues. The mysterious nature of deep learning models, also known as "black boxes", makes it difficult to explain their decisions. Explainability becomes crucial for machine learning in order to develop trust and comprehension [5]. While some applications may tolerate errors with minimal repercussions, errors in high-risk situations can cause severe damage or even death. Therefore, it is essential to comprehend how these models make decisions. Explaining a system's decision can help unearth biases and encourage users to trust and understand the model's suggestions [3]. So, given the potential challenge technology might pose [6], and deep learning tries to address several security and safety issues [7], providing humans with a transparent and interpretable model can be beneficial.

Innovative approaches such as LIME [8] have been created to resolve the issue of transparency. LIME provides crucial insights into the image and text decision-making processes. The primary objective of this study is to investigate LIME's application in image classification models and evaluate its consistency in explaining image data [5,9]. This method seeks to establish a more efficient connection between humans and deep learning models by revealing which features are essential for decision-making and which parts of a test image have the greatest impact on the model's classification. There have been numerous proposed solutions to the interpretability problem in deep neural networks. This study focuses on the interpretability of the LIME framework's most valuable features. In this study, we evaluate the accuracy of a convolutional neural network's judgements and validate the significance of input data. We accomplish this by extracting the most important features from the LIME heatmap, which indicates which portions of the test image are essential for the classification decision. Figure 1 illustrates the most important characteristics identified by the LIME heatmap. We also demonstrate how removing specific features from the test image affects the classification accuracy. We have captured the image of the fish shown in Fig. 1. The following are the primary contributions of this work:

- Analysing the LIME heatmap to investigate potential failure scenarios in deep learning models.
- Using LIME, evaluating the reliability and precision of two advanced, pre-trained networks (GoogleNet [10] and SqueezeNet [11]).
- A comparison of LIME's effectiveness and Grad-CAM's [12] performance.

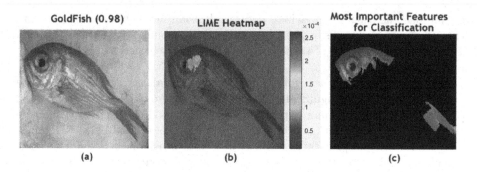

Fig. 1. (a) After applying CNN model to the test image, the image classified the object as a "goldfish", with 98% accuracy (b) LIME heatmap shows which features have been used to make that decision. The red part is the most critical part, which by removing this part, the ccuracy of the neural network will be decreased. (c) Shows the most important features. (Color figure online)

2   Related Work

This section describes similar methods for visual explanations of neural networks, including Layer-wise Relevance Propagation (LRP), Grad-CAM, and LIME.

- Layer-wise Relevance Propagation (LRP) is an explanation technique proposed by Bach et al. [13]. LRP explains the decisions of deep neural networks by allocating a relevance score to every neuron of the network. The relevance allocation is attained by propagating the relevance score of a target prediction from the outputs back to the inputs [14]. LRP can be used for both text and image explanations. Eitel et al. [15] used LRP to uncover the decision of neural networks for diagnosing multiple sclerosis on conventional MRI images. They assumed that utilising LRP could enable them to transparent relevant image features that a trained network uses for decision-making. Sun et al. [16] extended the LRP technique to design an LRP-inference fine-tuning method that can reduce the object visualisation of image captioning models. They employed LRP to create an explanation-weighted context representation.
- The Gradient-weighted Class Activation Mapping (Grad-CAM) approach can be used to reveal why a deep neural network makes its classification decisions. Grad-CAM generates a localisation map by including the gradients of any target feature into the last convolutional layer, emphasising critical locations in the photo that may be used to anticipate the effect's consequences. Grad-CAM, introduced by Selvaraju et al. [12], generalises the class activation mapping (CAM) method. Gorski et al. [17] used Grad-CAM in the domain of law to indicate the explainability concept for legal texts. Using adapted Grad-CAM metrics showed the interaction between the choice of embedding, its attention to contextual data, and its effect on downstream processing. Chattopadhay et al. [18] extended the Grad-CAM method to Grad-CAM++, which utilised a weighted combination of the last layer of convolutional neural

network feature maps about a particular class score as weights to create a visual description for the class label under observation.

- Local Interpretable Model-Agnostic Explanations(LIME), introduced by Ribeiro et al. [8], describe the classification behaviour of a machine learning model (classification or regression) for a single data point by finding important features and fitting a simple, explainable model, such as a regression tree. Chen. et al. [19] used LIME to create an interpretable neural text classifier. They adopted LIME to propose the variation word mask (VMASK) method to automatically learn task-specific important words and reduce irrelevant information on classification, which ultimately refines the model prediction's interpretability. Magesh et al. [9] utilised the LIME framework to prepare superpixel markings for brain scans focusing on the most effective features. They used the LIME explanation to distinguish Parkinson's Disease from non-Parkinson's Disease, using visual superpixels on the scans of the brain images. Mohseni et al. [20] contrasted the results of LIME and GradCAM explanations against human judgement to discover possible biases. Some other research works have employed LIME to enhance the detection and identification of objects, as seen in references [21,22].

As far as we are aware, there have been few efforts to implement and employ interpretable deep learning methods in order to facilitate better communication between deep learning systems and human experts. This work contributes to bridging this divide by facilitating a more efficient exchange of data for a more comprehensive evaluation of deep learning performance.

3   The Research Approach

This study aims to investigate and evaluate the factors underlying the complex decisions made by LIME in convolutional neural network image classification, with a particular emphasis on determining the dependability of these decisions. Numerous visual explanation techniques for image classification have been developed. However, a substantial portion of these current approaches for interpretation require previous understanding or human annotations as additional data inputs during the training phase of the network [19]. When interpreting CNN decisions, LRP has difficulty distinguishing between valid (true-positive) and incorrect (false-positive) terms, whereas LIME is capable of providing explanations for a wide variety of CNN models. Grad-CAM has difficulty accurately localising objects in a test image, particularly when the image contains multiple instances [18].

We demonstrate how LIME can be utilised to improve the collaboration between individuals and deep learning networks. In addition, we demonstrate how the accuracy of image classification can be improved by concentrating on key aspects of an input image during photo capture. We suggest, for instance, that the presence of a fish's eyes, which plays a crucial role in identifying fish species, is one of the most influential factors in the result of classification. Therefore, when capturing the input image, it is essential to capture the fish's eye in order to achieve higher classification accuracy, a fact that can be derived from LIME's heatmap. A knowledge worker or data scientist may be involved in this situation. While there are numerous techniques for enhancing the interaction between deep learning networks and individuals, we provide two LIME-based approaches.

1) We conduct an analysis of the feature map to evaluate test images and validate the network's input by identifying the most important features on which classification relies. Any alteration of these essential characteristics can result in inaccurate or inappropriate categorisation. In simplified terms, the visual feature of LIME enables any average user to evaluate the dependability of a particular deep learning algorithm. Using real-world examples, we demonstrate that the omission of these critical features substantially affects classification accuracy. In order to facilitate this, following MathWorks [23], we generate a LIME heatmap in Matlab that enables regular users to quickly identify the most important features in any given instance.

2) Furthermore, we explain how LIME's heatmap can explain the fundamental causes of errors made by various deep learning methods in particular cases. This feature-based comparison is especially advantageous for non-technical users with extensive domain expertise who may not be familiar with deep learning models' complex and opaque structures. This capability is demonstrated by comparing the performance of two well-known deep learning methods: GoogLeNet [10] and SqueezeNet [11].

3.1 Deep Learning Performance Sensitivity Analysis

The first section offers a framework designed to aid data scientists and knowledge workers in evaluating the efficacy of deep learning using a LIME-based methodology. This framework improves the utility of a specific deep-learning network. The proposed and illustrated structure is depicted in Fig. 2, and the captured image is referred to as the Human Intelligence Task (HIT). When the knowledge worker is already familiar with the image's label, this is referred to as a "golden HIT". Figure 2 depicts how the LIME heatmap can be utilised to increase the practical dependability of deep learning systems. This suggests that three different situations are possible when the red portion is eliminated. In extreme circumstances, deleting the red area may fail categorisation, functioning as a form of error mitigation for regular users. In a second scenario, the categorisation score will decrease, and the outcome will not change in exceedingly rare instances.

3.2 Feature-Based Comparison of Deep Learning

We utilise LIME to identify the regions in a test image that substantially impact the output of the classifier. The segmentation of the input image is a crucial stage in the process of generating explanations in LIME. LIME accomplishes this by segmenting the input image into distinct features using a variety of techniques. The superpixels paradigm has been used, which typically produces superior results, particularly for photographic image data. In contrast to prior segmentation algorithms, LIME's superpixels model is adept at identifying important regions within the input image and extracting features based on pixel values [8]. This implies that features are selected based on the content of the image, effectively dividing the input image into sections based on pixel values. Our research employs the LIME framework, using different fish images and classifying them with a deep neural network. To generate a heatmap, the significance of these features is translated into a map that emphasises the image regions with the greatest influence on the model. This heatmap is a valuable resource for illustrating which aspects of an image are crucial to the classification decision. This information can assist users in comprehending how deep learning reacts to the sensitivity of these particular features.

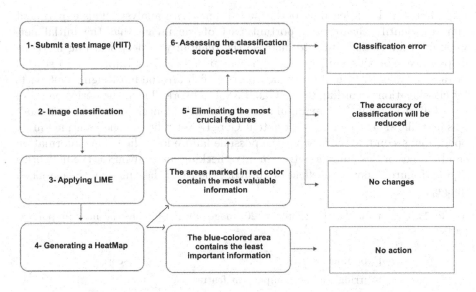

Fig. 2. LIME-based framework for deep learning models.

4   Experimental Result and Evaluation

This section presents three different types of experiments as running examples of our proposed framework, demonstrating how the LIME heatmap's supplied capabilities could be utilised to analyse and enhance a given decision-support system.

4.1   Database

Two different datasets are utilised for our experiments: 1) The first dataset contains a collection of fish images for classification, gathered from publicly available images on Wikipedia. 2) The second one is a custom database in which the fish images are chaptered by the authors of this research work with a phone camera (Samsung note8).

4.2   Deep Learning Structure

In this work, we have chosen a convolutional neural network as a classifier for our experiments because CNN is adaptable and performs well with image data but lacks transparency. We use GoogLeNet as a pre-trained network [10]. This network has 22 deep layers, and the overall number of layers utilised for the construction of this network is about 100 [10].

4.3   Experiments

Experiment 1: Deep learning performance sensitivity analysis: This experiment aims to identify the most important part of the image that the initial network used for classification to increase the reliability of deep learning methods in practice. For this aim, we use a heatmap of LIME and apply it to several instances (images) to find out which parts of fish are the most significant parts for classification according to the GoogLeNet network. Then, the performance of GoogLeNet is studied by manipulating the input's identified feature. This analysis first allows us to see to what extent GoogLeNet relies on the identified in its operation; second, it shows what the possible failure looks like. This information can be used for designing a better quality-checking mechanism for the network's inputs. Figure 3 shows the effect of applying the LIME heatmap on the classified image.

Table 1. The amount of F1 score for 20 images after blurring the most important parts.

Experiment	F1-score
Blurring the most important feature	63%
Blurring the two most significant features	41%
Blurring the three most important features	29%

It is clear from the figures that by removing the eyes of the fish (red parts), the classification results will be changed. Therefore, we can investigate that the network focuses on the eye of fish to make the prediction, which, without using the LIME heatmap, makes it hard for an ordinary user to find this critical information. Figure 3.1 and 3.2 are captured by ourselves (belong to the custom database). To obtain the overall statistics based on all pictures used in this experiment and to draw inferences regarding diminishing accuracy, we employed the F1-score, which considers both precision and recall when determining the model's accuracy. We calculated the F1 score using 20 photographs from both databases in this experiment. The F1 score is shown in Table 1 for three distinct

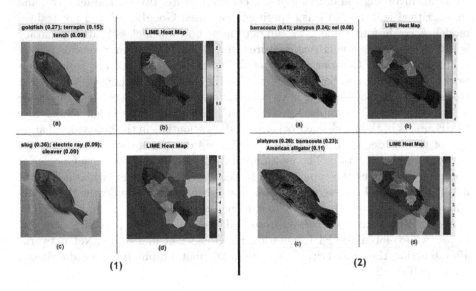

Fig. 3. (a) Shows the original test image and the result of the classification score. (b) Shows the LIME heatmap; the features have been used to make that decision. The red part (fish eye) is the most critical. (c) We removed the fish eye and tested the accuracy of the edited image again; (d) Shows the most important features after editing the image. (Color figure online)

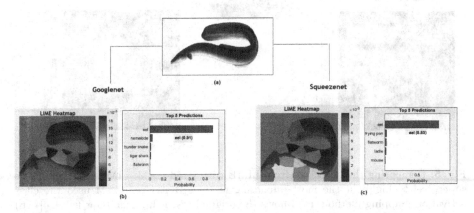

Fig. 4. Comparing two networks of GoogLeNet and SqueezeNet via LIME. (a) Shows the original test fish image (Eel fish [24]). (b) Displays how GoogleNet accurately identifies the test image with a 91% accuracy rate; the LIME heatmap helps us to clearly understand how GoogleNet works properly to detect important parts of the fish (c) In the case of Squeeznet, it achieved a lower accuracy rate of 83%. The LIME heatmap shows that Squeeznet focused on specific parts of the fish for object identification.

scenarios involving the blurring of one critical feature, two critical features, and three critical features. In this experiment, we used GoogLeNet as a pre-trained model. According to Table 1, we can determine how much classification accuracy is lost by obscuring the critical features that the LIME heatmap reveals.

Experiment 2: Comparing the reliability of two states of art trained networks (GoogLeNet and SqueezeNet) via LIME The two well-known CNN models, GoogLeNet and SqueezeNet, have been validated in the ImageNet Large Scale Visual Recognition Competition (ILSVRC) [25]. This experiment shows how LIME assists both knowledge workers and data scientists in the behavioural analysis of various deep learning networks. Figure 4 compares the features of every network for classification. The heatmap of LIME in Fig. 4 shows how GoogLeNet accurately identifies the type of fish. In the case of Squeeznet, while it did not fail, it achieved a lower accuracy rate. The LIME heatmap indicates the particular parts of the fish that Squeeznet focus on for recognizing the object. The image for Fig. 4 has been chosen from Wikipedia [24]. As a part of this experiment, we explored the F1 calculation for GoogLeNet and SqueezNet networks after blurring the most critical regions of 20 photographs from the databases, shown in Table 2.

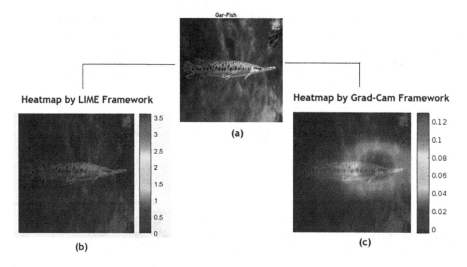

Fig. 5. Comparing the heatmaps from LIME with Grad-CAM. LIME is based on the superpixel to highlight the most impacting features, but Grad-CAM used the class activation mapping method. (a) Shows the original test fish image (Gar fish [26]) (b) displays LIME heatmap (c) Shows Grad-CAM heatmap.

Experiment 3: Comparing LIME with Grad-CAM. This experiment compares the obtained heatmap from LIME and Grad-CAM. The idea behind LIME is to provide superpixel markings on images to highlight the most impacting features; however, the Grad-CAM framework achieves a similar goal by using the gradient

Table 2. Comparing the F1 score for networks of GoogleNet and Squeeznet after blurring the most important parts.

Experiment	F1-score (GoogLeNet)	F1-score (SqueezeNet)
Blurring the most crucial feature	63%	55%
Blurring the two most significant features	41%	36%
Blurring the three most critical features	29%	19%

of the score of the classification. It is clear from Fig. 5, which compared the two heatmaps, that LIME can identify the most important feature more accurately and clearly. This image has been selected from Wikipedia [26]. To compare the accuracy of the heatmap acquired with LIME and Grad-CAM, we analysed several images and calculated the F1 score for each one after blurring the red portions. Table 3 summarises the output of the two heatmap models. As shown in Table 3, LIME is more effective than Grad-CAM at highlighting the most significant area (red part) in this scenario.

Table 3. Comparing the amount of F1 score from heatmap of LIME and Grad-CAM after blurring the red part

Experiment	F1-score (LIME)	F1-score (Grad-CAM)
Blurring the red part	68%	59%

5   Conclusions and Future Work

The visual explanations created by the LIME heatmap approach are employed in an innovative way in this study to promote communication between deep learning networks and humans. It was presented in three instances how the interaction between deep learning networks and people may be enhanced further by utilising the visual explanation of LIME. Two distinct datasets of fish categorisation were utilised to demonstrate the proposed framework's applicability and usefulness. The three situations demonstrated how the LIME's acquired heatmap might be utilised for fish image categorisation as a decision-support system to detect fish more reliably. In the first scenario, we demonstrated how manipulating the specified critical attributes of individual fish instances might result in network failure. The second experiment further examines the GoogleNet and SqueezNet CNN models by examining their LIME heatmaps. In the third experiment, we compare the evaluation of LIME with Grad-CAM. We expect that as the area of explainable machine learning grows, our analysis of the obtained heatmap will be applicable to a greater range of machine learning challenges. In future studies, in order to contribute more theoretically, the dependability of the trained model can be increased further by adjusting the learning mechanising.

References

1. Stiffler, M., Hudler, A., Lee, E., Braines, D., Mott, D., Harborne, D.: An analysis of reliability using lime with deep learning models. In: Annual Fall Meeting of the Distributed Analytics and Information Science International Technology Alliance, AFM DAIS ITA (2018)
2. Shah, S.S., Sheppard, J.W.: Evaluating explanations of convolutional neural network image classifications. In: 2020 International Joint Conference on Neural Networks (IJCNN), pp. 1–8. IEEE (2020)
3. Schallner, L., Rabold, J., Scholz, O., Schmid, U.: Effect of superpixel aggregation on explanations in LIME – a case study with biological data. In: Cellier, P., Driessens, K. (eds.) ECML PKDD 2019. CCIS, vol. 1167, pp. 147–158. Springer, Cham (2020). https://doi.org/10.1007/978-3-030-43823-4_13
4. Cian, D., van Gemert, J., Lengyel, A.: Evaluating the performance of the lime and grad-cam explanation methods on a lego multi-label image classification task. arXiv preprint arXiv:2008.01584 (2020)
5. Lee, E., Braines, D., Stiffler, M., Hudler, A., Harborne, D.: Developing the sensitivity of lime for better machine learning explanation. In: Artificial Intelligence and Machine Learning for Multi-Domain Operations Applications, vol. 11006, pp. 349–356. SPIE (2019)
6. Hessari, H., Nategh, T.: The role of co-worker support for tackling techno stress along with these influences on need for recovery and work motivation. Int. J. Intell. Property Manage. **12**(2), 233–259 (2022)
7. Ashraf, J., Bakhshi, A.D., Moustafa, N., Khurshid, H., Javed, A., Beheshti, A.: Novel deep learning-enabled LSTM autoencoder architecture for discovering anomalous events from intelligent transportation systems. IEEE Trans. Intell. Transp. Syst. **22**(7), 4507–4518 (2020)
8. Ribeiro, M.T., Singh, S., Guestrin, C.: "Why should i trust you?" Explaining the predictions of any classifier. In: Proceedings of the 22nd ACM SIGKDD International Conference on Knowledge Discovery and Data Mining, pp. 1135–1144 (2016)
9. Magesh, P.R., Myloth, R.D., Tom, R.J.: An explainable machine learning model for early detection of Parakinson's disease using LIME on DaTSCAN imagery. Comput. Biol. Med. **126**, 104041 (2020)
10. Szegedy, C., et al.: Going deeper with convolutions. In: Proceedings of the IEEE Conference on Computer Vision and Pattern Recognition, pp. 1–9 (2015)
11. Iandola, F.N., Han, S., Moskewicz, M.W., Ashraf, K., Dally, W.J., Keutzer, K.: SqueezeNet: AlexNet-level accuracy with 50x fewer parameters and <0.5 mb model size. arXiv preprint arXiv:1602.07360 (2016)
12. Selvaraju, R.R., Cogswell, M., Das, A., Vedantam, R., Parikh, D., Batra, D.: Grad-CAM: visual explanations from deep networks via gradient-based localization. In: Proceedings of the IEEE International Conference on Computer Vision, pp. 618–626 (2017)
13. Bach, S., Binder, A., Montavon, G., Klauschen, F., Müller, K.-R., Samek, W.: On pixel-wise explanations for non-linear classifier decisions by layer-wise relevance propagation. PLoS ONE **10**(7), e0130140 (2015)
14. Montavon, G., Binder, A., Lapuschkin, S., Samek, W., Müller, K.-R.: Layer-wise relevance propagation: an overview. In: Samek, W., Montavon, G., Vedaldi, A., Hansen, L.K., Müller, K.-R. (eds.) Explainable AI: Interpreting, Explaining and Visualizing Deep Learning. LNCS (LNAI), vol. 11700, pp. 193–209. Springer, Cham (2019). https://doi.org/10.1007/978-3-030-28954-6_10

15. Eitel, F., et al.: Uncovering convolutional neural network decisions for diagnosing multiple sclerosis on conventional MRI using layer-wise relevance propagation. NeuroImage: Clin. **24**, 102003 (2019)

16. Sun, J., Lapuschkin, S., Samek, W., Binder, A.: Explain and improve: LRP-inference fine-tuning for image captioning models. Inf. Fusion **77**, 233–246 (2022)

17. Gorski, L., Ramakrishna, S., Nowosielski, J.M.: Towards grad-cam based explainability in a legal text processing pipeline. arXiv preprint arXiv:2012.09603 (2020)

18. Chattopadhay, A., Sarkar, A., Howlader, P., Balasubramanian, V.N.: Grad-CAM++: generalized gradient-based visual explanations for deep convolutional networks. In: 2018 IEEE Winter Conference on Applications of Computer Vision (WACV), pp. 839–847. IEEE (2018)

19. Chen, H., Ji, Y.: Learning variational word masks to improve the interpretability of neural text classifiers. arXiv preprint arXiv:2010.00667 (2020)

20. Mohseni, S., Block, J.E., Ragan, E.D.: A human-grounded evaluation benchmark for local explanations of machine learning. arXiv preprint arXiv:1801.05075 (2018)

21. Farhood, H., Saberi, M., Najafi, M.: Improving object recognition in crime scenes via local interpretable model-agnostic explanations. In: 2021 IEEE 25th International Enterprise Distributed Object Computing Workshop (EDOCW), pp. 90–94. IEEE (2021)

22. Farhood, H., Saberi, M., Najafi, M.: Human-in-the-loop optimization for artificial intelligence algorithms. In: Hacid, H., et al. (eds.) ICSOC 2021. LNCS, vol. 13236, pp. 92–102. Springer, Cham (2022). https://doi.org/10.1007/978-3-031-14135-5_7

23. Matlab-heatmap. https://au.mathworks.com/help/deeplearning/ug/understand-network-predictions-using-lime.html. Accessed 9 Dec 2023

24. Wikipedia-eel-fish. https://en.wikipedia.org/wiki/American_eel. Accessed 9 Dec 2023

25. Oh, H.M., Lee, H., Kim, M.Y.: Comparing convolutional neural network (CNN) models for machine learning-based drone and bird classification of anti-drone system. In: 2019 19th International Conference on Control, Automation and Systems (ICCAS), pp. 87–90. IEEE (2019)

26. Wikipedia-gar-fish. https://en.wikipedia.org/wiki/Gar. Accessed 9 Dec 2023

ASOCA: Adaptive Service-oriented and Cloud Applications Introduction

Introduction to the 8th International Workshop on Adaptive Service-oriented and Cloud Applications

Nesrine Khabou[1], Ismael Bouassida Rodriguez[1] ⓘ, and Khalil Drira[2] ⓘ

[1]ReDCAD, University of Sfax, Tunisia
bouassida@redcad.org
[2]LAAS-CNRS, Univ. Toulouse, France
drira@laas.fr

The ASOCA 2023 workshop addressed the adaptation and reconfiguration issues of Service-oriented and cloud applications and architectures.

An adaptive and reconfigurable service-oriented application can repair itself if any execution problems occur, in order to successfully complete its own execution, while respecting functional and non-functional agreements. In the design of an adaptive and reconfigurable software system, several aspects have to be considered. For instance, the system should be able to predict or detect degradations and failures as soon as possible and enact suitable recovery actions.

The main topics of the ASOCA 2023 workshop were devoted to the design and implementation of adaptive and reconfigurable service-oriented and cloud applications and architectures. Specifically, the relevant topics included, but were not limited to:

– Distributed and centralized solutions for the diagnosis and repair of service-oriented and cloud applications
– Design for diagnosability and repairability
– Monitoring simple and composite architectures, components and services
– Semantic (or analytic) architectural and behavioral models for monitoring of software systems
– Dynamic reconfiguration of service-oriented and cloud applications
– Planning and decision-making technologies for ensuring autonomic properties
– Predictive management of adaptability
– Management of autonomic properties
– Experiences in practical adaptive and reconfigurable service-oriented and cloud applications
– Tools and prototypes for managing adaptability

After reviewing the submitted papers, the program committee selected one paper based on the originality, quality, and relevance to the topics of the workshop, keeping the acceptance rate at 50%. Each submission was single-blind reviewed by at least two reviewers.

– Claudia Raibulet, Xiaojun Ling. *Non-Expert Level Analysis of Self-Adaptive Systems.*

Acknowledgement

We are grateful to all program committee members and the external reviewers for their effort to read and discuss the papers in their area of expertise. We would also like to thank the authors for their submissions and for ensuring the success of this track.

November 2023   ASOCA 2023 Workshop Organizers

Organization

Workshop Organizers

Nesrine Khabou	University of Sfax, Tunisia
Ismael Bouassida Rodriguez	University of Sfax, Tunisia
Khalil Drira	LAAS-CNRS, Univ. Toulouse, France

Program Committee

Wafa Gabsi	Laboratory, University of Sfax, Tunisia
Chouki Tibermacine	University of Montpellier, France
Cinzia Cappiello	Politecnico di Milano, Italy
Mohad-Said Hacid	Univ. Lyon 1, France
Philippe Roose	Université de Pau et des Pays de l'Adour, France
Marcos Da Silveira	Luxembourg Institute of Science and Technology, Luxembourg
Carlos E. Cuesta	Rey Juan Carlos University, Spain
Volker Gruhn	Universität Duisburg-Essen, Germany
Djamal Benslimane	Lyon 1 University, France
Abdulatif Alabdulatif	Qassim University, Saudi Arabia
Sami Yangui	INSA Toulouse, LAAS-CNRS and Univ. Toulouse, France
Takoua Abdellatif	University of Sousse, Tunisia
Henry Muccini	University of L'Aquila, Italy
Mohamed Mosbah	University of Bordeaux, France
Uwe Zdun	University of Vienna, Austria
Fairouz Fakhfakh	University of Sfax, Tunisia
Mouna Rekik	University of Sousse, Tunisia
Claudia Raibulet	University of Milano-Bicocca, Italy
Mehmet Aksit	University of Twente, The Netherlands
Karim Guennoun	Hassania School of Public Works, Morocco
Federico Bergenti	Università degli Studi di Parma, Italy
Dimka Karastoyanova	University of Groningen, The Netherlands
Grzegorz Kolaczek	Wroclaw University of Technology, Poland
Francisco Moo-Mena	Universidad Autónoma de Yucatán, Mexico

Rodrigo Bonacin   CTI Renato Archer and UNIFACCAMP,
                                    Brazil
Miriam Capretz   Western University, Canada
Leila Hadded   University of Tunis El Manar, Tunisia
Mehdi Khouja   University of Gabes, Tunisia
Imen Abdennadher   University of Sfax, Tunisia

Non-expert Level Analysis of Self-adaptive Systems

Claudia Raibulet[1,2](✉) ⓘ and Xiaojun Ling[1]

[1] Computer Science Department, Vrije Universiteit Amsterdam, Amsterdam, The Netherlands
c.raibulet@vu.nl
[2] DISCo-Dipartimento di Informatica, Sistemistica e Comunicazione, Universita' degli Studi di Milano-Bicocca, Viale Sarca 336, Edificio 14, Milan, Italy
claudia.raibulet@unimib.it

Abstract. Self-adaptivity is mainly used to address uncertainties, unpredicted events, as well as to automate administration tasks. It allows systems to change themselves while executing in order to address expected or unexpected changes and to adapt as much as possible to the current execution context. Self-adaptivity is particularly meaningful for dynamic application domains such as Internet of Things (IoT), Cyber-Physical Systems (CPS), service oriented based solutions (SOA), cloud computing, robotics, among many others. There are various available solutions in these domains that exploit self-adaptivity. The question is how can we analyze them to understand how self-adaptivity is implemented and exploited in order to use and re-use, as well as to adapt existing solutions to new or other systems? In this paper, we propose a first step in this direction, by analyzing available self-adaptive systems (and especially their self-adaptive mechanisms) in various application domains using the Understand tool - widely used for software development, analysis, and quality assessment.

Keywords: Self-Adaptation · Self-Adaptive Systems · Static Analysis · Understand tool · Software Quality Assessment

1 Introduction

In the last two decades, several self-adaptive systems (SAS) [1, 2, 7] have been developed in various application domains both in industry [2] and academia [1] – as those provided by the Software Engineering on Adaptive and Self-Managing Systems[1] (SEAMS) community. All of them propose interesting and meaningful self-adaptive mechanisms that may be potentially adopted or extended for other systems in the same or in different application domains. The self-adaptive mechanisms are usually documented in a related scientific paper. Also, the related code implementation is made available by the authors. However, to deeply understand the self-adaptation mechanisms, a software engineer non-expert (with no or limited experience) in SAS may need tool support to analyze an implemented solution, zoom in into its self-adaptive mechanisms, and identify the parts suitable to be reused or adapted for the current system.

---

[1] SEAMS Artifacts: https://www.hpi.uni-potsdam.de/giese/public/selfadapt/exemplars/.

© The Author(s), under exclusive license to Springer Nature Singapore Pte Ltd. 2024
F. Monti et al. (Eds.): ICSOC 2023 Workshops, LNCS 14518, pp. 91–102, 2024.
https://doi.org/10.1007/978-981-97-0989-2_8

Considering these premises, the main idea of this paper is to analyze SAS solutions through available tools, e.g., Understand[2], and provide a preliminary guide for the analysis and understanding of self-adaptive artifacts for software engineers without a relevant background on SAS. Specifically, this paper presents: (1) overviews of self-adaptive artifacts considered as case studies (Sect. 2), (2) analysis of the self-adaptive artifacts through tool support (Sect. 3) by focusing on their architectures, entities, and features (Sect. 4), (3) comparisons of self-adaptive exemplars in terms of their self-adaptivity (Sect. 4), and (4) a guideline on analyzing self-adaptive artifacts for software engineers with limited knowledge of self-adaptation (Sect. 4).

In our previous work, we analyzed SAS for the assessment of their quality (e.g., [3, 5, 6]). For example, we have considered the code smells present in SAS or the most frequent design patterns [5, 6]. We have analyzed their adaptive mechanisms theoretically, approach that does not scale for large SAS [11]. In this paper, we propose guidelines to approach SAS for non-experts in the domain (e.g., students or developers with software engineering background but no knowledge on SAS).

2 Self-adaptive Artifacts

Self-adaptive systems (SAS) are *self-aware* (i.e., have explicit representation of themselves) and *context-aware* (i.e., have explicit representation of their execution environment) [4, 7, 12, 13]. These features allow SAS to ensure the quality of their functionality even in the presence of variations, faults, or other expected or unexpected changes. To achieve this, SAS have to implement a MAPE-K loop through which to Monitor their execution environment, Analyze their current execution conditions and, if necessary, Plan the adaptation to be applied, and finally, Execute the adaptation (see Fig. 1). The loop uses common Knowledge accessible during all the adaptation steps. The functionality of a SAS is provided by the managed part, while self-adaptation is implemented by the managing part. Every SAS has its own self-adaptive mechanisms suitable for the application domain and for the actual system. Even if SAS solutions are different, conceptually they also have various common features. In this section we provide a brief overview of three available SAS artifacts from different application domains, with the objective of further analyzing them and extracting common steps in their analysis from a non-expert point of view. This will help software engineers not familiar with SAS to know how to approach SAS artifacts to understand and use them.

2.1 Platooning LEGOs

Platooning LEGOs [9] is an artifact that allows independent vehicles to form a platoon and drive together by applying self-adaptive mechanisms. Unlike most self-adaptive artifacts, it uses LEGO Mindstorms EV3 vehicles to provide a real physical experimental environment rather than relying entirely on software data simulations to inject the uncertainty that can exist in a real environment. Its implementation consists of two parts, the physical and the software implementations. The former consists of physical components such as LEGO robots, which are used to perform the functionality of the managed

---

[2] Understand Tool - https://scitools.com/.

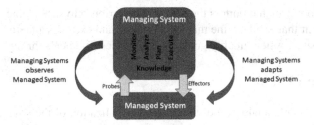

Fig. 1. SAS - Managing and Managed Parts

part, and the latter consists of user-written programs that invoke physical components through the LEGO API to perform the functionality of the managing part.

Adaptation is achieved through the activities of the vehicles organized as a MAPE-K loop. Each vehicle operates an independent loop. By monitoring the distance to obstacles ahead and receiving information about the vehicle ahead, as well as receiving manual commands from the driver, an independent vehicle obtains all the information for adaptive decision-making. This information is analyzed according to adaptation goals, adaptation decisions are made, and the corresponding decisions to change the driving speed or driving path are executed.

2.2 TAS: Tele Assistance System

Tele Assistance System (TAS) [10] is a reference implementation of a healthcare service-based system using the Research Service Platform (ReSeP). Its intended use case is providing healthcare services to patients with chronic diseases. Assuming that a patient is recuperating at home, TAS monitors and analyzes the patient's vital parameters and, based on the results, changes the dosage or type of medication to be delivered, or triggers an alarm so that the patient can be treated appropriately. TAS is build based on the service oriented paradigm.

To achieve self-adaptation, TAS has an adaptation engine and implements the MAPE-K loop. The adaptation engine uses workflow probes for monitoring the failures and costs of service calls. Based on the monitored conditions, different adaptive policies customized by the user are applied to the workflow via effectors.

2.3 RDMSim

RDMSim [8] is a Remote Data Mirroring Environment (RDM) simulator. Its objective is to provide a customizable RDM experimental environment and multiple configurable experimental scenarios with varying uncertainties to test the performance of the designed adaptation logic, to confirm whether the applied adaptation strategies result in a system that achieves the desired quality objectives, and to allow comparison with other decision-making techniques. It primarily aims at self-adaptive decision-making in the RDM domain but can also be utilized more generally to test decision-making logic applicable to other domains. It provides a cloud-based approach.

This artifact achieves self-adaptation through a two-layered architecture, which consists of a managing system and a managed system. The managing system implements the MAPE-K loop which monitors through probes various physical elements of the network component that reside in the managed system, and executes adaptive decisions to achieve the desired system quality goals by setting these elements through effectors.

3   Understand Tool

Understand is a static analysis tool that allows visualization of the source code using graphs, charts, metrics, and reports. It can function as an integrated development environment (IDE). In addition, it is capable of standard testing, instant search and has plug-in support. It generates hierarchy graphs, cluster graphs, structure graphs, UML diagrams (e.g., class, sequence), dependency graphs, metrics treemaps, comparison graphs. It computes various metrics including complexity metrics (e.g., McCabe Cyclomatic Complexity, Path Count, Knots), count metrics (e.g., SLOC, Number of Functions, Statements), object oriented metrics (e.g., Coupling, Depth of Inheritance Tree, Lack of Cohesion). The types of graphs and metrics available for generation are dependent on the programming language. Understand supports various languages such as Ada, Assembly, C/C++, C#, Cobol, Java, JavaScript, PHP, Python, .NET], and XML.

4   Guidelines for SAS Analysis Using Understand

In this section, we compile a guideline containing the main steps in analyzing SAS artifacts and the support in which Understand can facilitate these steps, building on the analysis experienced. The resulting guideline can be of general use to studies of SAS in both academic research and industrial environments. It shows that when new to conducting analysis on self-adaptive based solutions, it is possible to understand the specifics of SAS by following the guidelines as indicated in Fig. 2. The left-hand side of this flowchart shows the specific steps of SAS analysis, while the right-hand side reflects the means by which Understand can provide insights into the analysis at each step. The Understand user interface and a summary of the features involved in the process are shown in Fig. 3. In the following, each step in the guideline, the motivation for that step, the relevance to the conducted analysis, and the support provided by Understand for that step are elaborated upon.

1. **Identify the components/classes/entities and the relationships among them.** In this step, it is necessary to identify which entities are present in the artifact, how they relate to each other, and how they are divided; in more specific terms, if there are inclusion and interaction relationships among entities, and if the entities are functional or non-functional, i.e., meaningful for adaptation. Typically, entities in SAS are architecturally divided into a managed part and a managing part. The managed part contains the functional entities that are deployed to implement system functionalities, such as a drivable LEGO robot with a series of sensors for detecting road conditions in the Platooning LEGOs artifact, a combination of sensors for monitoring different vital signs of patients in TAS, and all the entities for simulating an RDM network in the RDMSim. The managing part contains the entities required to make the system self-adaptive. Some entities that provide other services to the system, may also be present. For instance, most SAS experimental environments use

software simulations rather than real physical experimental environments, such as TAS and RDMSim, so simulation-related entities are needed to enable data generation from functional entities and uncertainties that may exist in real environments. Furthermore, communications between the managed part and the managing part need to be achieved through interfaces. For example, the software implementation part of Platooning LEGOs uses the Python API provided by LEGO to manipulate the movements of the LEGO robots and adjustments to the traveling status, while both TAS and RDMSim apply probes and effectors as interfaces to the managed part. There are also knowledge base components that store system logs, formulas, and other data inputs for adaptation managers.

To summarize, this step is intended to provide a comprehensive understanding of the composition of a SAS and to understand the artifact's architecture. In this step, software engineers may use Understand to import the artifact source code and identify all the entities in the artifact and the relationships among them by a view of code, the directory structure of the artifact, the UML class diagrams, and the butterfly diagrams showing the include tree of all entities.

2. **Obtain the architectural view of the SAS with the managed and managing parts.** Based on the information observed in the previous step, we draw the architecture of a SAS representing the main entities and the relationships among them. The focus is to show the division between the managed and managing parts, the composition of each part, and the interaction among the two parts.

    To summarize, this step is intended to identify the functional, i.e., managed part and the adaptive, i.e., managing part of a SAS. Understand can help identify these two parts and can provide an overall visual view of the SAS architecture. Further, it can help software engineers to further zoom-in for details.

3. **Analyze the managed part – identify the functionalities of SAS and how they were designed.** By examining the functionalities of the identified entities in the managed part, software engineers can gain awareness of SAS goals. For Platooning LEGOs, LEGO robots equipped with sensors are used to carry out driving tasks, so it is about driving multiple LEGO vehicles while sensing road conditions; for TAS it is about sensors and central hubs to observe and analyze the health status of patients; for RDMSim, multiple network properties and simulation properties are implemented for RDM network construction, so it is about building RDM networks as an experimental environment.

    To summarize, this step is intended to understand the details in the managed part. Understand enriches the knowledge about the functionalities with direct code display of the relevant entities, function descriptions of the classes in UML class diagrams, Calls & Called By diagrams describing the invocation relationships between entities, and control flow diagrams showing how entities operate.

4. **Analyze the managing part – identify the self-adaptive mechanisms of SAS and how they were designed.** By examining the functionalities of the identified entities in the managing part, software engineers can gain awareness of the self-adaptivity. We identified the following sub-steps in the guideline:

    a. **Identify feedback control loops.** For instance, the MAPE-K loop is frequently used for implementing SAS. The goal of this step is to clarify the process of self-adaptive mechanisms in SAS. The identification of a control feedback process

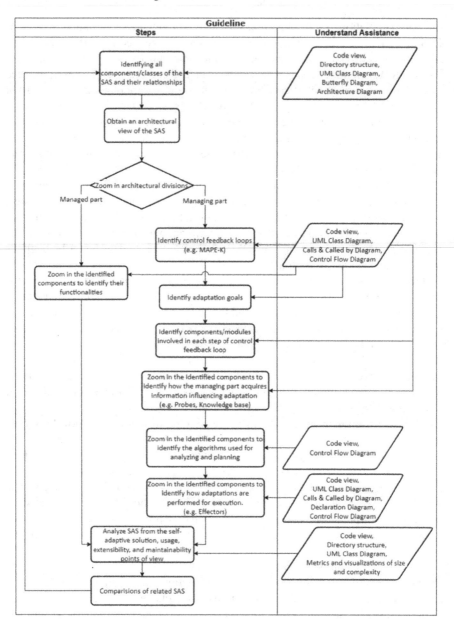

Fig. 2. SAS Analysis Guidelines

provides a starting point for the subsequent analysis of the specific steps in the process. In the analysis conducted, the control flows that manipulate the operations of the three vehicles in Platooning LEGO show that self-adaptation follows the MAPE loop; the series of functions monitor, analyze, plan and execute that TAS applies corroborate the existence of the MAPE-K loop; RDMSim has also

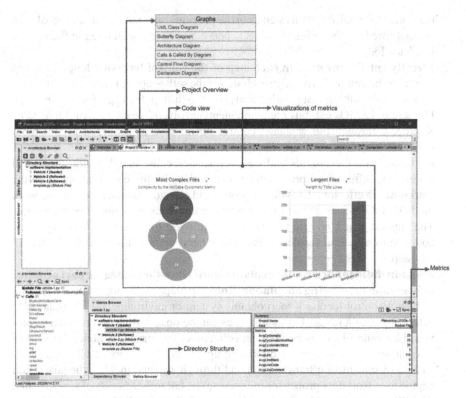

Fig. 3. Understand User Interface and Features Meaningful for SAS Analysis

implemented an explicit MAPE-K loop. In this step, Understand aids the analysis by providing a view of code, UML class diagrams of classes implementing the MAPE-K loop, Calls & Called By diagrams describing invocation relationships of entities, and control flow diagrams that show operations of self-adaptive mechanisms.

b. **Identify adaptation goals.** Before analyzing the details of self-adaptive processes, a good point to start with is the discovery of adaptation goals. This is because, in general, adaptation goals are related to the information that an adaptation manager obtains from a system or environment in a control feedback process, and also reflect the adaptations that are ultimately executed. For example, Platooning LEGOs' adaptation goals are keeping vehicles in a platoon and avoiding collisions, while the objects monitored by the artifact in the MAPE-K process include the driving lane and the speed of the vehicle in front of it, and finally adapts by adjusting the driving lane and speed. TAS balances the two interplaying QoS attributes of reliability and cost through adaptation, while the system attributes and self-adaptive policies monitored and produced are QoS attributes and set points of QoS attributes respectively; RDMSim's adaptation goal also lies in the QoS attributes of cost and reliability, while it monitors and executes on the network properties related to cost and reliability in the self-adaptive process. Understand can provide the same observations in this step as in the previous one since adaptation goals can be confirmed by observing the objects being monitored or adapted in the control feedback loop.

c. **Identify entities involved in each step of the control feedback loop.** This step identifies the entities involved in each step of the self-adaptive process and provides a basis for the subsequent detailed analysis of each step. In the performed analysis, Platooning LEGOs exhibits the components involved in each step of the MAPE-K process through the vehicles' control flows, such as sensors and Bluetooth mailboxes involved in monitoring the environment; TAS uses workflow probes for monitoring the failures and costs of service calls; based on the monitored conditions, different adaptive policies customized by the user are applied to the workflow via effectors; RDMSim's probes and effectors interact with the network module in the managed part to participate in the monitoring and execution steps. The support that Understand was able to provide for the prior two steps may continue to be useful for deepening researchers' understanding of the artifact in this step.

d. **Zoom-in the identified components to identify how the managing part acquires information influencing adaptation.** This step helps to develop an understanding of how a control feedback loop obtains system or environmental information to detect adaptation needs. For example, as can be observed in the conducted analysis, Platooning LEGOs ensures the collection of information about the vehicle in front and the environment by setting up Bluetooth servers or clients to form a chain of information transmission and through sensors; in TAS, the adaptation engine uses workflow probes for monitoring the failures and costs of service calls; RDMSim also uses probes to learn the properties of the RDM network. This step can still be achieved with the help of relevant code views provided by Understand, class diagrams of the identified entities, Calls & Called By diagrams between the identified entities, and control flow diagrams containing the process of obtaining information about the environment or system affecting adaptation. Examples of diagrams generated through Understand for the RDMSim artifact are shown in Fig. 4 and Fig. 5.

e. **Zoom-in the identified components to identify the algorithms used for analyzing and planning.** This step focuses on the analyzing and planning steps of a control feedback loop. The analysis performed in this step can further refine the understanding of the artifact's self-adaptive process. As in Platooning LEGOs, the control flows of the three vehicles show in detail the logic of self-adaptive decisions formation; TAS monitors and analyzes the invocation of pre-defined services in the workflow, while the object of its analyzing and planning of self-adaptive policies is also the services that make up the workflow; e.g., the self-adaptive policy may be to retry if the service invocation fails or to invoke other services with the same utility but with a higher commitment to provide the service in terms of cost or other QoS attributes; RDMSim is used as an artifact for evaluating decision-making techniques, and the analyzing and planning steps are where users can apply their designed decision-making logic. Understand helps with specific code views and control flow graphs for the self-adaptive algorithms.

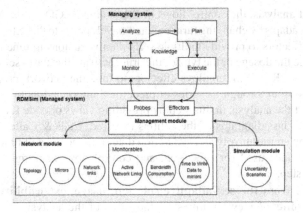

Fig. 4. RDMSim Architecture

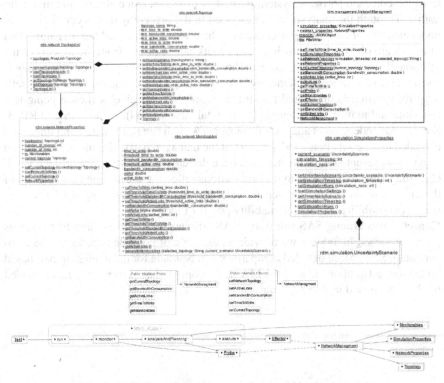

Fig. 5. RDMSim: UML Diagrams Generated by Understand

f. **Zoom-in the identified components to identify how adaptations are performed for execution.** The focus here is on the last step in a control feedback process, namely the execution of self-adaptive decisions. The analysis performed in this step reveals how SAS applies adaptive changes to reach adaptation goals. In the carried out analysis, the control flows of Platooning LEGOs' vehicles reveal that the artifact adapts by changing turn rates and travel speeds to the vehicles; TAS uses ReSeP's effectors to provide multiple self-adaptive actions to tune the workflow, e.g., change the dosage or the type of the drug, activate the alarm service, press the alarm button; RDMSim employs effectors to tune the network properties of the managed system through its series of predefined interface functions. Understand can support the analysis in this step by providing views of code for the execution step, UML class diagrams of the entities involved, Calls & Called By diagrams between the entities involved, Declaration diagrams showing all functions defined by the interface used for execution, and control flow diagrams describing the execution step.

5. **Analyze SAS from the self-adaptive solution, usage, extensibility, and maintainability points of view.** In this step, the focus of the analysis reverts from the implementation details back to the self-adaptive artifact as a whole. We can arrive at a holistic view of the self-adaptive solutions and a range of observations on SAS from the common software system properties of usage, extensibility, and maintainability. Through the analysis steps described in the preceding text, a certain level of understanding of the general architecture, the managed part, and the managing part of a SAS are obtained. Meanwhile, some facts can be drawn from the aspects of the self-adaptive solution, usage, extensibility, and maintainability. For example, how is a self-adaptive solution implemented in a SAS? E.g., in Platooning LEGOs the self-adaptive solution is integrated into the code for driving vehicles (hence being less re-usable and maybe more complex to maintain and extend), while TAS and RDM-Sim employ independent adaptation managers (which can be reused, maintained, and extended more easily being independent of the managed part). Moreover, Understand provides a presentation of the actual code, a directory structure of the artifact, UML class diagrams, and metrics and visualizations reflecting the size and complexity of the entities in the artifact, which provide arguments for evaluating SAS from the usage, extensibility, and maintainability points of view.

6. **Comparisons among SAS solutions.** SAS artifacts may be compared from various points of views. In Table 1 we provide an example of possible criteria for the comparison of SAS. More detailed comparison can be made for the managing part based on the four adaptation steps of the MAPE-K loop. Or, based on the metrics provided by the Understand tool (e.g., complexity).

Table 1. SAS artifacts comparison from various points of view

SAS	Application Domain	Domain Dependency	Architecture Model	Self-Adaptive Model	Self-Adaptive Strategies
Platooning LEGOs	CPS	Dependent	Client Server	MAPE-K	Ad-hoc strategies
TAS	IoT	Dependent	Service Oriented	MAPE-K	Ad-hoc strategies
RDMSim	Remote Data Mirroring	Dependent	Cloud based	MAPE-K	Ad-hoc strategies

5 Conclusions and Further Work

This paper presents how non-experts in self-adaptive domain may approach available SAS with the objective to understand, use, or extend them. We provide a starting point for the analysis and comparison of SAS with the aid of a well-known static code analysis tool, i.e., Understand. Three SAS exemplars, Platooning LEGOs, BSN, and RDMSim from various application domains and using different adaptation mechanisms have been analyzed in a multidimensional way, from an architectural, functional, overall, and comparative perspective. This paper intends to provide insights and methodological references for non-expert software engineers in SAS. Therefore, we have considered the three exemplars to demonstrate the feasibility of our analysis approach. We summarized the output of our approach in a guideline consisting of various key steps for the analysis of SAS and their comparison. The steps follow the self-adaptation MAPE-K loop.

Further work may focus on refining the guideline by considering additional SAS artifacts to identify potential variations. Another direction may consider the specification of more precise guidelines for a particular domain (e.g., cloud computing, service-oriented systems, IoT). Application domains may have specific characteristics driving their adaptation needs, and hence, they may also need specific guidelines.

Acknowledgement. This research is partially supported by ExtremeXP, a project co-funded by the European Union Horizon Programme under Grant Agreement No. 101093164.

References

1. Weyns, D.: An Introduction to Self-adaptive Systems: A Contemporary Software Engineering Perspective. Wiley, IEEE Press (2020)
2. Weyns, D., et al.: Self-adaptation in industry: a survey. ACM Trans. Auton. Adapt. Syst. **18**(2), 5:1–5:44 (2023). https://doi.org/10.1145/3589227
3. Masciadri, L., Raibulet, C.: Frameworks for the development of adaptive systems: evaluation of their adaptability feature through software metrics. In: Fourth International Conference on Software Engineering Advances, pp. 309–312 (2009). https://doi.org/10.1109/ICSEA.2009.51

4. Raibulet, C., Drira, K., Fornaro, C., Fugini, M.: Software architectures for smart and adaptive systems (SASAS). Inf. Softw. Technol. J. **157** (2023). https://doi.org/10.1016/j.infsof.2023. 107158

5. Raibulet, C., Arcelli Fontana, F., Capilla, R., Carrillo, C.: Chapter 13 - An overview on quality evaluation of self-adaptive systems. Mistrik, I., Ali, N., Kazman, R., Grundy, J., Schmerl, B. (eds.) Managing Trade-Offs in Adaptable Software Architectures, pp. 325–352. Morgan Kaufmann (2017). https://doi.org/10.1016/B978-0-12-802855-1.00013-7. ISBN 9780128028551

6. Raibulet, C., Arcelli Fontana, F., Carettoni, S.: A preliminary analysis of self-adaptive systems according to different issues. Softw. Qual. J. **28**(3), 1213–1243 (2020). https://doi.org/10. 1007/s11219-020-09502-5

7. Salehie, M., Tahvildari, L.: Self-adaptive software: landscape and research challenges. ACM Trans. Auton. Adapt. Syst. **4**(2), 14:1–14:42 (2009). https://doi.org/10.1145/1516533.151 6538

8. Samin, H., Paucar, L. H. G., Bencomo, N., Hurtado, C. M. C., and Fredericks, E. M.: RDMSim: an exemplar for evaluation and comparison of decision-making techniques for self-adaptation. In: 2021 International Symposium on Software Engineering for Adaptive and Self-Managing Systems (SEAMS), pp. 238–244 (2021). https://doi.org/10.1109/SEAMS51251.2021.00039

9. Shin, Y. -J., Liu, L., Hyun, S. and Bae, D.-H.: Platooning LEGOs: an open physical exemplar for engineering self-adaptive cyber-physical systems-of-systems. In: International Symposium on Software Engineering for Adaptive and Self-Managing Systems (SEAMS), pp. 231–237 (2021). https://doi.org/10.1109/SEAMS51251.2021.00038

10. Weyns, D., Calinescu, C.: Tele assistance: a self-adaptive service-based system examplar, software engineering for adaptive and self-managing systems. In: International Symposium on Software Engineering for Adaptive and Self-Managing Systems (SEAMS), pp. 88–92 (2015). https://doi.org/10.1109/SEAMS.2015.27

11. Oh, J.-Y., Raibulet, C., Leest, J.: Analysis of MAPE-K loop in self-adaptive systems for cloud, IoT and CPS. In: Troya, J., et al. (eds.) ICSOC 2022. LNCS, vol. 13821, pp. 130–141. Springer, Cham (2022). https://doi.org/10.1007/978-3-031-26507-5_11

12. Arcelli Fontana, F., Raibulet, C., Tisato, F., Adorni, M.: Architectural reflection in adaptive systems. In: Sixteenth International Conference on Software Engineering Knowledge Engineering (SEKE 2004), pp. 74–79 (2004)

13. Raibulet, C., Arcelli Fontana, F., Mussino, S., Riva, M., Tisato, T., Ubezio, L.: Components in an adaptive and QoS-based architecture. In: International Workshop on Self-Adaptation and Self-Managing Systems (SEAMS 2006), pp. 65–71 (2006)

SAPD: Secure, Accountable and Privacy-Preserving Data-Driven Service-Oriented Computing Introduction

Introduction to the 1st International Workshop on Secure, Accountable and Privacy-Preserving Data-Driven Service-Oriented Computing (SAPD 2023)

Mattia Salnitri[1] [ID] and Sebastian Werner[2] [ID]

[1]Politecnico di Milano, Italy
mattia.salnitri@polimi.it
[2]TU Berlin, Germany
werner@tu-berlin.de

The 1st International Workshop on Secure, Accountable and Privacy-Preserving Data-Driven Service-Oriented Computing (SAPD 2023) was held as one of the workshops of the 21st International Conference on Service-Oriented Computing (ICSOC 2023). The workshop focused on exploring cutting-edge approaches to addressing security, privacy, and accountability concerns in data-driven systems. It delved into topics such as federated data governance and new security approaches in distributed service-oriented systems. With the increase in data and the need to share and incorporate it to build emerging machine learning models or increase data space value, it becomes crucial to explore new approaches for privacy, accountability, and security and ensure that these practices can be easily modeled into policies attached to services. Therefore, the workshop invited submissions on the following topics:

- Adaptive Approaches in Security Governance for Service-Oriented Computing
- Privacy and Data Protection in Service-Oriented and Cloud Computing
- Trust and Accountability in Data Sharing Systems
- Application of Machine Learning (ML) in securing, optimizing, and protecting Service-Oriented Computing

Accepted Papers

After carefully reviewing the five submitted papers, the program committee selected two that showcased originality, high-quality research, and strong relevance to the workshop's objectives. Each submission was single-blind reviewed by at least two reviewers and received at least one meta-review.

Acknowledgements

We thank the authors, program committees, and the ICSOC Organizing Committee for their support and contribution during the event. Moreover, the workshop was supported by the EU Project TEADAL (101070186).

November 2023   SAPD Organizers

Organization

Workshop Organizers

Mattia Salnitri	Politecnico di Milano, Italy
Sebastian Werner	TU Berlin, Germany

Program Committee

Frank Pallas	TU Berlin, Germany
Andre Ostrak	Cybernetica, Estonia
Victor Casamayor-Pujol	TU Wien, Austria
Boris Sedlak	TU Wien, Austria
Duncan Ki-Aries	University of Bournemouth, UK
Michele Carminati	Politecnico di Milano, Italy
Achim Brucker	University of Exeter, UK

Federated Data Products: A Confluence of Data Mesh and Gaia-X for Data Sharing

Farouk Jeffar and Pierluigi Plebani[✉][iD]

Politecnico di Milano, Piazza Leonardo da Vinci 32, 20133 Milan, Italy
farouk.jeffar@mail.polimi.it, pierluigi.plebani@polimi.it

Abstract. The goal of this paper is to investigate to which extent the principles defined by the Data Mesh paradigm can find a valuable support in Gaia-X. In particular, an alignment between the Data Mesh self-serve platform and the Gaia-X federated services has been analyzed to understand if the concept of data product, which is central in data mesh, it can evolve into a federated data mesh, serving as the architectural element that supports data sharing in a federated setting.

Keywords: Data sharing · Data sovereignty · Data spaces

1 Introduction

Regardless of the domain and the market in which a company operates, digitalization has increased the amount, and at the same time also the value, of data. As a consequence, data has been recognized as one of the most fundamental assets in a company and a lot of effort has been dedicated to increase the effectiveness and the efficiency of data internally managed.

Recently, it has become increasingly clear that the value of data can be enhanced through sharing it with other companies [11]. While data sharing is a common practice among organizations to support supply chains, organizations themselves see an opportunity in sharing complementary data assets. For example, for those who produce sensorized products, the data linked to what is collected by these sensors. We then move from sharing transactional data to sharing analytical data [14] but, at the same time, it is important to protect one's data so that the value of the asset is not lost. In other words, once the data has been shared, it must be clear that ownership of the asset is not transferred, but, on the contrary, must be safeguarded. It is therefore important that an organization has full control of the data and thus has assurance that the data is used according to its instructions.

In this context, the European Commission, in line with its data strategy [3], is promoting the creation of data spaces [7]: federated architectures enabling the data sharing while preserving data sovereignty that, among the several definitions offered in the literature [9], it is considered in this paper as the ability for the data owner to have a complete control on their data, where control includes,

F. Monti et al. (Eds.): ICSOC 2023 Workshops, LNCS 14518, pp. 107–118, 2024.
https://doi.org/10.1007/978-981-97-0989-2_9

among the others, the decisions on where to store the data, who has the right to access them, according to which purpose.

From a technical standpoint, Gaia-X[1] has been proposed to create a safe and reliable environment for data sharing in a federated context. Gaia-X promotes data ownership by providing data owners with the tools to have complete control over their data, i.e., to ensure data sovereignty. While Gaia-X is mainly focused on the architectural aspect, less interest is given to the data management practices that must be put in place to use the provided toolset.

To fill this gap, this paper analyses to which extent Gaia-X can take advantage of the principles indicated in Data Mesh: a decentralized socio-technical approach to share, access, and manage analytical data in complex and large-scale environments, within or across organizations [2]. Data Mesh advocates for a self-serve data platform that empowers data consumers to discover, access, and use data autonomously without relying on centralized teams. A key element of the Data Mesh proposal is represented by the *data product*: the architectural unit with high functional cohesion and that can be independently deployable and managed.

Considering that, on the one side, the concept of data product seems to be aligned with the Gaia-X approach setting and, on the other side, the data sovereignty has not explicitly covered by Data Mesh, the primary objective of this paper is to assess the compatibility of Data Mesh and Gaia-X, identify areas of convergence, and see whether they can interplay to support the definition of mechanisms enabling sovereignty-aware data sharing among organizations.

The rest of the paper is organized as follows. Section 2 contextualizes the topic discussed in the paper in the existing literature. Section 3 and Sect. 4 introduces Data Mesh and Gaia-X limiting itself to the basic notions considered essential to understand the proposed approach. Section 5.1 discusses the proposed alignment between the Data Mesh self-serve platform and the Gaia-X federated services toolbox. Finally, Sect. 6 concludes the document with a discussion on the limitations and potential development of the proposed approach.

2   Related Work

Organizations are finding the need to share data with other organizations increasingly pressing. Data that does not only concern the performance of operational processes, but data resulting from analysis processes that can provide greater insights into one's processes [11].

To enable an effective data sharing, as discussed in [10], infrastructural, technological, and legal concerns must be taken into account to support an articulated process. Such process includes activities related to the preparation of the data to be shared, the definition of an agreement among the involved parties, the actual data exchange, and the monitoring of what have been done.

Especially in the European Union there is a strong push towards the creation of solutions capable of facilitating data sharing. In this context, the definition of

---

[1] https://Gaia-X.eu.

data spaces are holding a central role [7] where, as pointed in [5], different levels of governance may be required as part of a governance continuum. Broader governance regulates the federation, while narrower governance regulates the single data exchange also involving the technical aspects related to the platform supporting such exchange. Data mesh [2] is emerging as an approach able to support a governance in line with this vision [13] but, at the same time, other initiatives have been started in the recent years: IDSA[2] and Gaia-X to name the most relevant ones. As far as we know, no one in the literature has considered analyzing the overlaps, contiguity and oppositions in these approaches. This contribution therefore aims to start a discussion in this direction.

3 Data Mesh

As Data Mesh is an articulated proposal [8], this section introduces the minimum set of concepts useful to understand the rest of the paper. Notably, this section discusses the four main principles, the data product as the basic architectural element and the main functionalities of the self-serve platform.[3]

3.1 Data Mesh Principles

The logical architecture and operating model of Data Mesh can be summed up in four straightforward principles [2]:

- *Domain ownership.* Inspired by the domain-driven software design [4], the responsibilities of the data are given to the people that are closer to them. Talking about people and not technology implies a distribution of responsibilities that does not depend on the way in which the platform used to manage data is organized, but is aligned with the business.
- *Data as a product.* Like in the service oriented solutions, data sets need to be managed having in mind the final consumer which can be also seen as a customer. For this reason, data need to be curated, properly described, made visible, and easily and efficiently accessible.
- *Self-service data platform.* To avoid situations where the different teams involved in managing their own data products independently develop platforms and applications for this purpose, a common platform offering a set of capabilities to support the data life-cycle managed is offered.
- *Federated computational governance.* Having different teams that independently manage their data products could lead to a chaotic scenario where every team decides to govern their products according to policies which could clash with each other. This call for a common data governance based on policies that enactment needs to be automated as much as possible.

These guidelines are intended to move us closer to the goals of Data Mesh: maximizing the value of data at scale, maintaining agility as a company expands, and embracing change in a challenging and unstable business environment.

---

[2] https://internationaldataspaces.org.

[3] For a complete introduction to this topic, we suggest the readers to refer to [2].

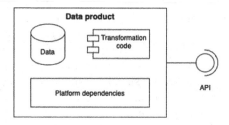

Fig. 1. Overview of Data Mesh Data product with the minimum viable components

3.2   Data Product

An architectural quantum [6] pertains to the most compact architectural entity capable of standalone deployment. It boasts significant functional unity and encompasses all necessary structural aspects for its operation.

In the context of the Data Mesh concept, a data product embodies an architectural quantum. It signifies the tiniest autonomous deployable and manageable architectural component [13]. Demonstrating strong functional coherence, it executes a precise analytical transformation and securely disseminates domain-specific analytical data. It encompasses all essential constituents for its function: the transformation algorithms, the dataset, governing data regulations, as well as metadata for comprehension, discovery, and monitoring. Additionally, it includes its interconnections with the underlying platform.

While data is a very important aspect of a data product, it is not its sole component (see Fig. 1). Since a data product needs to be autonomously discoverable and understandable, it also needs to contain the structural components needed to sustain such requirements. This means that the data product would also contain a set of APIs and software (code) in order to enable it to autonomously oversee the lifecycle of data-handling the creation of business logic, overseeing revisions, regulating access, and facilitating content sharing.

3.3   Self-serve Data Platform

The essential purpose of a self-service data platform is to provide the means for diverse cross-functional domain teams to independently manage their respective data products. It also enables data users to securely explore, understand, and utilize an array of interconnected data products, all in compliance with established mesh policies. This approach involves dividing a sophisticated platform into distinct capabilities, accessible through APIs, each featuring open interfaces designed to seamlessly integrate with other collaborating capabilities.

The Data Mesh self-serve data platform is operationally summarized in five fundamental components (see Fig. 2) that constitute the minimum viable components needed to operate the data platform:

- Data queries unification: Facilitates and unifies the data exchange protocols and standards between domains via providing a unified querying language adapted to the mesh.

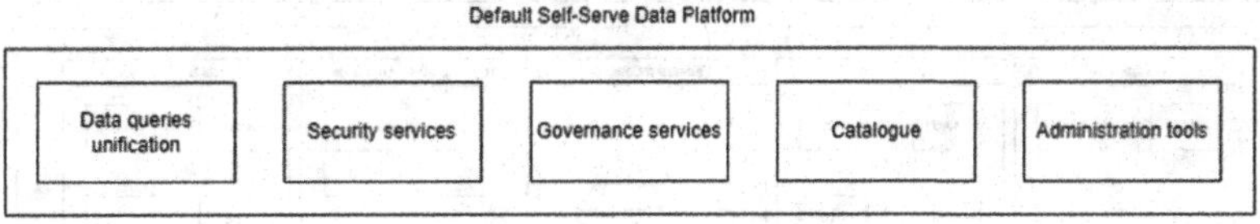

Fig. 2. Data Mesh Self-serve platform overview

- security services: These services ensure that the data and information exchange within the mesh are secure while also ensuring the authentication of users and identity systems.
- governance services: This component implements the Data Mesh principle of automated governance, meaning that governance policies are encoded and automatically enforced in an effort to overcome any issues that may result from decentralization.
- Catalogue: The data products shared on the mesh need to be discoverable and reachable, the catalogue publishes the data products and constitutes the entry point before engaging in data sharing.
- Administration tools: The tools range from monitoring data sharing, continuous integration and deployment engine, and enabling infrastructure support for any centralized services .

4 GAIA-X

The objective of Gaia-X involves creating a structure for sharing data, encompassing shared norms, effective methods, tools, and governance systems. It also establishes a collaborative network of cloud platforms and data utilities anchored within the European Union, with commitment from all 27 EU member nations [1].

Similarly to what have been done for Data Mesh, due to the complexity of Gaia-X, we here focus only on the toolbox offered by this platform to support the data sharing in a federated setting (see Fig. 3) [12].

Identity and Trust

- Authentication and Authorization (AAU): Authenticate users and systems in a reliable and distributed self-sovereign fashion.
- Organization Credential Manager (OCM): Builds trust among diverse Participants in the Gaia-X ecosystem through the issuance of credentials to corporate Participants and the management of organizational credentials.
- Personal Credential Manager (PCM): Supplies the necessary technological tools to selectively reveal attributes for authentication and utilizing services.
- Trust Services (TRU): The Trust Services serve as the technological realization for upholding policies governing the usage of Gaia-X's decentralized and self-sovereign elements.

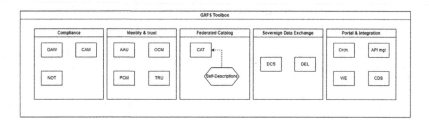

Fig. 3. Gaia-X Federated Service Toolbox

Federated Catalogue

– Catalog (CAT): A Catalog houses Self-Descriptions, both individually and in an aggregated form using a graph data structure. The Storage of Self-Descriptions contains the original Self-Description files in the JSON-LD (JavaScript Object Notation for Linked Data) format, accompanied by supplementary lifecycle metadata. Once published a Self-Description cannot be altered.
– Self-Descriptions: Gaia-X Self-Descriptions convey attributes of Resources, Service Offerings, and Participants, all tied to their respective Identifiers. Providers bear the responsibility of generating Self-Descriptions for their Resources. Self-Descriptions serve various purposes including: (i) identifying and assembling Service Offerings found within a Catalog; (ii) Facilitating the assessment, selection, incorporation, and orchestration of Service instances and Resources with the help of tools; (iii) enforcing adherence to Usage Policies, while maintaining continuous validation and trust monitoring; (iv) supporting negotiations related to contractual terms concerning Resources of a Service Offering and the Participants involved.

Sovereign Data Exchange. Preserving the right to informational self-determination for all Participants encompasses two essential facets within the data ecosystem, i.e., transparency and control over data usage, offered via two tools:

– Data Contract Service (DCS) which role is to (i) enables contract negotiation; (ii) initiates the initial interaction between the data provider and consumer; and (iii) verifies, authenticates, and disseminates the contract
– Data Exchange Logging (DEL) that is in charge of logs exchanged data and enforces rules and records violations.

Compliance. The primary goal of the Compliance Federation Service is to provide Gaia-X users with confirmation of compliance to the specified attributes for each individual Service Offering.

– Onboarding and Accreditation Workflow (OAW): ensures that all Participants, Resources, and Service Offerings undergo a validation procedure before inclusion in a Catalog.

- Continuous Automated Monitoring (CAM): facilitates ongoing compliance oversight based on the previously mentioned Self-Descriptions within the context of the Federated Catalog. CAM operates by engaging with the service being tested in an automated manner, employing standardized protocols and interfaces to gather technical evidence.
- Notarization Service (NOT): manages requests for notarization, issuing digital, legally binding, and dependable credentials.

Portal and Integration. The Gaia-X Portal functions as an illustrative integration layer, displaying the Federation Services and offering user-friendly access to these services.

- Orchestration: Through the orchestration service, Gaia-X consumers can swiftly initiate service instances from the catalog search results using the portal. The orchestration service incorporates a Life Cycle Management Engine (LCM Engine) and a standardized API dedicated to LCM services.
- API Management: Facilitating the coordination of different Gaia-X services along with their respective APIs.
- Workflow Engine: Predominantly operates in alignment with the onboarding and accreditation process, granting approval and maintaining records of service provisioning.
- Compliance Documentation Service: To demonstrate that a Federation Service meets all specified requirements, this provides relevant evidence.

5   A Confluence of Data Mesh and Gaia-X

5.1   Comparative Analysis of Data Mesh and Gaia-X

Looking at the short description of Data Mesh and Gaia-X, it is evident that Data Mesh paradigm has a rather conceptual approach compared to Gaia-X which is a more technical approach that aims at providing not only a technical architecture but also software and tools to implement the architecture.

Nevertheless, there are different points of contact. They are both focused on decentralization with small form of centralization that rests in the self-serve platform. Moreover, governance and automated governance are also similar in both cases, the only difference is that while Data Mesh keeps it purely conceptual, Gaia-X provides tools embedded in the trust framework that enables the federator to execute and automate governance tasks within the federation. One very similar aspect of both is the self-serve data platform as they both emphasize some centralized party in a mainly decentralized structure. Therefore, it is safe to say that the core paradigm of Data Mesh is preserved in the Gaia-X approach.

Architecturally speaking, the concept of a data product is not present in Gaia-X, it is simply referred to as service offering/dataset, whereas in Data Mesh some guidelines have been proposed such as the embedding of APIs for data management. This means that in order to fusion the two approaches it is needed to propose a technical design for the data product as it is a core element of the Data Mesh, and it does also enable domain-ownership and data quality monitoring which are core principles of Data Mesh that cannot be overlooked nor disregarded like it is in Gaia-X. However, this does not mean that the principle of data as product from Data Mesh is completely overlooked, in fact, discoverability, security, and policies as code, which are Data Mesh sub-principles within data as a product, are present in Gaia-X via the catalogue, the Trust Framework, and the data exchange services respectively.

The notion of data contract is present in the Gaia-X architecture but while it is introduced, it is clearly stated that it is out of scope Gaia-X when it comes to terms and negotiations. While the negotiations' part is normal not be in the scope of Gaia-X, the contract terms not being taken into consideration is an issue and diverts from Data Mesh which considers contracts an enabler of domain-ownership and control over data. At this stage, we note the data contract concern, but it will be further explored in the following chapters. It is also important to remember that while nothing blocks the Data Mesh from being a federation it is designed primarily and targeted towards use within a single organization, whereas Gaia-X is purely federation oriented, making the use Gaia-X a solid foundation for the extension of Data Mesh as a federation but also in improving gaps that Gaia-X has left unattended such as data quality, data products, and contract management between participants.

Fundamentally, there is a noticeable resemblance and convergence between the concepts employed in the contexts of Data Meshes and Gaia-X. Conversely, the divergences exhibited by Gaia-X in relation to the previously mentioned Data Mesh paradigm can be seen as a kind of concept simplification, it means that while Data Meshes mainly focus on overseeing the management of diverse data types, including analytical data, within a solitary entity (even if it's sizeable and intricate, legally defined), Gaia-X introduces standardized organizational principles and technological elements aimed at actualizing interconnected ecosystems comprising numerous distinct entities.

5.2 Gaia-X as an Enabler of Federation Capabilities

While the Data Mesh has a strong foundation for federation purposes, it lacks the infrastructure, security, and sovereignty standards that are the core focus of Gaia-X. While Gaia-X has many tools in the Gaia-X federation services, the focus would be on the following:

- Federated Catalogue: Ensures discoverability of services using a self-description system.
- CDCS: Modified version of Data contract services that manages participants agreements on a federal level while taking into account their veracity.
- Gaia-X Trust Framework: Responsible for safety, security and policy enforcing for the federation.
- Authorization and Authentication: Secure authentication for participants into the federation.

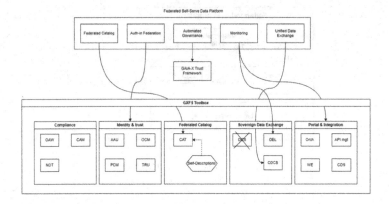

Fig. 4. Connection between Data Mesh and Gaia-X

On these basis, Fig. 4 presents a possible alignment between the self-serve platform of Data Mesh and the toolset offered by Gaia-X, which can be seen as an initial step to achieve a federated mesh.

5.3 Federated Data Product

In addition to the alignment between Data Mesh and Gaia-X from a functionalities standpoint, a Federated Data Product can be also proposed. This results from the connection of data product with the facilities offered by Gaia-X. A Federated Data Product is as an enhanced component of the typical data product defined in Data mesh, which is able to communicate with the federation and also adds another layer of access control to preserve sovereignty for each provider on the federation (see Fig. 5). Each federated data product must have self-description and thus must interface with the Federated Catalogue to create and manage the self-description. Moreover, one major part of the federated data product is handling the data contracts. The data contracts are part of the data product, they are used to automate the application of the agreements during the data/service exchange as the data contracts are computable and machine readable. Because the CDCS provides a set of services, the data product can directly exchange with the self-serve platform for any process related to contract making or validation.

The federated data product should also be linked to the infrastructure of its original domain in order to enforce terms that are linked to the Quality of Service aspect of the data contract, in this case it is up to the domain owner to either include this capability as part of the data exchange protocol or to have these terms enforced outside the data product but with ability to log proof that these terms have been respected, these proofs should be available not only to the data product but also to the self-serve platform since it encapsulates audit components responsible of verifying that the terms have been respected and this is part of the monitoring component of the self-serve data platform.

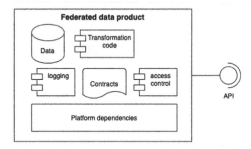

Fig. 5. Federated Data Product

Evidently, since providers are proposing advanced form of data (high quality, queries, QoS) and even services(computations for example), it is up the domain to pick the appropriate infrastructure to host its data products but they are required to follow the principles described in this section so that data quality is kept at a good threshold, automate governance and sovereignty, enable monitoring of data transactions, and allow discoverability and accessibility of the data and services shared on the federation.

5.4 Key Insights

The exploration of the Data Mesh concept and its principles showed not only the potential it has to implement a data federation but also its limitations when it comes to sovereignty and governance as the Data Mesh was initially designed and conceived to solve scalability issues facing organizations. This means that Data Mesh was made primarily for use within an internal organization and not within a mesh of nodes having different laws and policies. On the other hand, Gaia-X made its sole purpose focused on the federated services and most importantly the security, sovereignty, and governance behind it.

However, Gaia-X was not a perfect solution either since it lacked the concept of a proper data product which is necessary for fulfilling data quality objectives that Data Mesh mandates in its principles. Moreover, Gaia-X omitted certain aspects from its scope such as the data contract which breaks the self-serve data platform principle from Data Mesh. This necessitated a custom solution to replace and enhance the contract mechanisms that were implemented in Gaia-X contract services in order to not only add custom terms and policies to the data contract but also connect it to the Federated Catalogue which lead to the design and implementation of the Custom Data Contract Services which interfaces not only with the catalogue but also with the data product in order to allow it to control access and monitor its data.

In our framework, the data product is not only raw data but a combination of component (APIs and scripts) that enable the data product to control its quality, automate data processing and querying, and preserve domain ownership by enabling each federated data product to have full sovereignty on its data through the CDCS, for example, during data exchange. In summary, the idea behind the data product is to modernize the data and code combination. Traditionally, the code always lived outside the data, which often lead to silos and bottlenecks due to centralization, but in the federated data product the code lives with the data enabling not only decentralization but also contributing to enhance data quality due to services being made-to-measure and not generically made without taking into account the data itself, its type, and its characteristics. Furthermore, another pivotal aspect of the federation is the discoverability and reachability of the data products. The implementation of these two concepts was facilitated by the self-description notion within Gaia-X, which enabled the data product to group its terms, policies, type of data, provider, and other fundamental information such as how it can be accessed or previewed. This self-description would then be listed in a federated catalogue where every participant could see it, interact with it, or start negotiations in relation to the data contract.

Consequently, by putting this together we achieve a federated Data Mesh that is focused on sovereignty, security, governance, data quality, and decentralization; thus, answering the research questions by affirming that a Data Mesh can be extended into a federation through Gaia-X and also by proposing an architecture that englobes all the major and necessary components of such Federated Data Mesh extended via Gaia-X.

6   Concluding Remarks

In this paper, we have delved into the concepts and paradigms of Data Mesh and Gaia-X in order to design and introduce a decentralized Federated Data Mesh based on Gaia-X Federation Services.

While the designed architecture and solution of the federated Data Mesh depict the minimum viable product and the backbone of a federation, more research and development are needed in the implementation side. It is necessary to work on implementing common software solutions to facilitate the operating of the data product to encourage software reusability and avoid reinventing the wheel as long as generalizing these services within a data product would not negatively impact the data quality. Moreover, the contract services need to be more integrated and automated with both the federation and the data product to provide more features and possibilities for both the consumer and provider.

The big portion required next is the self-serve data platform, implementing and designing a profound architecture for the self-serve data platform which requires many considerations such as integrating well with decentralized aspects of the federation, provide a unified data exchange (queries, exchange protocols) that preserve performance and unifies the data transfer lexicology within the federation and should allow for easy integration with data products. The concept of unified exchange should be tied to the catalogue as the idea is to transition from the self-description listed in the catalogue to a data transfer given that an agreement has been reached. Additionally, the self-serve data platform also plays a monitoring role since it is the central piece in a decentralized ecosystem. The portal, which is also part of the platform should be addressed in a software engineering approach because it needs accurate and calculated requirements in order to craft a federation portal that operates for all users no matter what their role within the federation is (Federator, provider, consumer) and enable easy-to-use tools to manage their presence in the federation.

Finally, one aspect of the self-serve data platform that is crucial to a federation is governance, while data products enable sovereignty and governance at the level of the domain, the self-serve data platform enables governance and sovereignty for the entire federation. Finally, the platform should enable through code and computable terms (machine readable policies) the possibility to automatically enforce these terms and conditions and monitor whether they are being respected and followed adequately.

Acknowledgements. This research was supported by EU Horizon Framework grant agreement 101070186 (TEADAL).

References

1. Autolitano, S., Pawlowska, A.: Europe's quest for digital sovereignty: Gaia-x as a case study. IAI Pap. **21**(14), 1–22 (2021)
2. Dehghani, Z.: Data Mesh: Delivering Data-Driven Value at Scale. O'Reilly Media, Incorporated (2022)
3. European Commission: A European strategy for data (2020)
4. Evans, E.: Domain-Driven Design: Tackling Complexity in the Heart of Software. Addison-Wesley (2004)
5. Farrell, E., et al.: European data spaces - scientific insights into data sharing and utilisation at scale (2023). https://doi.org/10.2760/400188
6. Ford, N., Parsons, R., Kua, P.: Building Evolutionary Architectures Support Constant Change. O'Reilly (2019)
7. Gieß, A., Möller, F., Schoormann, T., Otto, B.: Design options for data spaces. In: ECIS 2023 (2023). https://aisel.aisnet.org/ecis2023_rp/287
8. Goedegebuure, A., et al.: Data mesh: a systematic gray literature review (2023)
9. Hummel, P., Braun, M., Tretter, M., Dabrock, P.: Data sovereignty: a review. Big Data Soc. **8**(1), 2053951720982012 (2021)
10. Jussen, I., Schweihoff, J., Dahms, V., Möller, F., Otto, B.: Data sharing fundamentals: characteristics and definition. In: Proceedings of the 56th Hawaii International Conference on System Sciences (HICSS), Maui, Hawaii, USA (2023)
11. Lefebvre, H., Flourac, G., Krasikov, P., Legner, C.: Toward cross-company value generation from data: design principles for developing and operating data sharing communities. In: Gerber, A., Baskerville, R. (eds.) DESRIST 2023. LNCS, vol. 13873, pp. 33–49. Springer, Cham (2023). https://doi.org/10.1007/978-3-031-32808-4_3
12. Otto, B.: A federated infrastructure for European data spaces. Commun. ACM **65**(4), 44–45 (2022)
13. Wider, A., Verma, S., Akhtar, A.: Decentralized data governance as part of a data mesh platform: concepts and approaches. In: 2023 IEEE International Conference on Web Services (ICWS), pp. 746–754 (2023)
14. Wixom, B.H., Sebastian, I.M., Gregory, R.W.: Data sharing 2.0: new data sharing, new value creation (2020). https://cisr.mit.edu/publication/2020_1001_DataSharing_WixomSebastianGregory

XPS++: A Publish/Subscribe System with Built-In Security and Privacy by Design

Noor Ahmed[✉][iD]

U.S Air Force Research Laboratory/RIS, Rome, NY 13441, USA
norman.ahmed@us.af.mil

Abstract. This paper presents a content-based publish/subscribe (pub-/sub) middleware system designed to securely broker/filter XML events over insecure computing platforms without the complexities of the traditional cryptographic approaches (i.e., homomorphic encryption). We adopt a combination of *Micro-services* based pub/sub service implementation, and XML predicate/filter and the metadata hashing scheme to simultaneously achieve security and privacy objectives by design. To illustrate the practicality of the proposed system, we discuss the design and implementation details with system demonstration of a prototype, dubbed *XPS++*. Then, show a preliminary performance results.

Keywords: Micro-services · Publish/Subscribe · Security & Privacy

1 Introduction

Publish/Subscribe (pub/sub) is a dissemination paradigm that has emerged as a popular means of disseminating time-sensitive filtered messages across large number of clients. There are two types of pub/sub: *topic*-based where the events are filtered and routed based on the topic/name, and *content*-based where the metadata content is filtered against registered predicate/filter. This paper focuses on both types of pub/sub.

Typically, in pub/sub, a broker(s) mediates the exchange of the events/messages between loosely coupled producers (publishers) and consumers (subscribers) to prevent the publishers flooding the network with information that are not of interest to the subscribers. The loosely coupled abstraction nature of pub/sub requires both the predicate filters and the metadata in clear-text to be brokered efficiently. This poses security and privacy challenges for many applications, especially when deployed in public cloud platforms.

There have been several solutions addressing this issue as in [13,22], and [19], to name a few. However, the common denominator of the existing solutions

DISTRIBUTION STATEMENT A: Approved for Public Release, Distribution Unlimited: PA CLEARANCE NUMBER - AFRL-2023-2422.

is their underlying crypto primitives such as *Identity/Attribute Based Encryption (IBE/ABE)* [18], *Predicate/Policy Based Encryption (PBE)* [7], *Ciphertext Policy-ABE (CP-ABE)* [6], and homomorphic *Paillier* [14] or ElGmal [10]. Most importantly, these protocol primitives are mathematically proven to be secure. However, the construction of the cryptographic key parameters of these primitives does not align well with pub/sub due to its conflicting requirements; performance in terms of predicate registration and filtering efficiency, scaleability and loose coupling (space/time coupling) due to required crypto handshakes.

On the other hand, Message Queuing Telemetry Transport (MQTT) [4], a widely adopted standardized messaging protocol, supports security and privacy through TLS and OAuth protocols, however, it lacks fine-grained privacy support (i.e., query/filter and topic name). With wide adoption on cloud computing, we believe shifting from over-emphasis on cryptographic protocol-centric solutions to a design-based security and privacy solutions. In this paper, we introduce a content-based XML pub/sub system prototype, dubbed *[X]ML [P]ublish [S]ubscribe (XPS) plus Security* and *plus Privacy (XPS++)*, that simultaneously addresses the integrity (*security*) of the published contents/payload, and the subscribers predicate filters along the published metadata *privacy* by design. Thus, we make the following key contribution:

> We introduce a design-based privacy-preserving scheme for XML pub/sub middleware system that preserves the privacy of the predicate filters and data from suspicious brokers without the complexities of cryptographic schemes.

We organized the paper as follows: First we present *XPS++* system model in Sect. 2, followed by the threat model in Sect. 3. In Sect. 4, we describe the algorithms, then, discuss the implementation details in Sect. 5. We report a preliminary performance evaluations in Sect. 6. Finally, highlight the related work in Sect. 7 and the conclusion in Sect. 8.

2   XPS++ System Design

Inspired by *Software Defined Networking* (SDN) design concept, the separation of network functionality into a *control* and *data* plane for the program-ability of the network functions. We decompose the pub/sub system into *control* and *data* planes and assign two groups of services in each plane. As the name implies, we assign *Controller* micro services (CS) group to the *control plane* to perform the pub/sub control functions such as; subscription and topic registration management, providing brokering/routing service endpoints (url's) to clients. In addition, it enables service discovery, access control, and enforcing security policies (beyond the scope of this work). On the other hand, we assign *Broker* (BS) and *Notifier* (NS) micro services to the *data plane* to match the registered predicates/filters against the incoming events/data from the publishers then route the matched event to the subscribers.

Figure 1 illustrates a high-level architecture of the proposed system model, dubbed XPS++. In Fig. 1, the pub/sub clients connect to a *Trusted Authority*

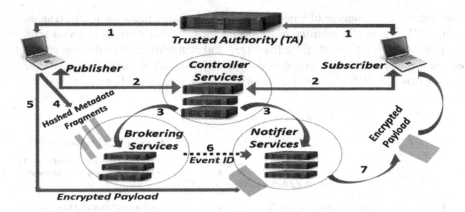

Fig. 1. High-level XPS++ System Architecture.

(TA), beyond the scope of this work, via a secure channel. The TA provides the public (for publishers) and private keys (for subscribers) with a Unique User ID (*UUID*), security tokens for service access authorization, and the *Controller* endpoint (url) (arrows labeled 1). Then, clients connect to the *CS* to register their hashed interests (subscription predicates and publishers' topics) using only their security token and *UUID* (arrows labeled 2) where the *CS* provides them the *data* plane (*BS/NS*) service endpoints and injects their interests into these services (arrows labeled 3), specifically, the predicates/filters to the *BS* and the publication topic ID to the *NS*. Thus, the information flow of our pub/sub system model is as follows:

1. The publishers send hashed event metadata fragments (discussed next) to the *Brokers* as shown in Fig. 1 arrow 4, and an encrypted content (payload) to the *Notifiers* (arrow 5).
2. The *Brokers* filter the hashed metadata fragments against the registered hashed subscription predicates and send only the ID of the metadata fragment to the *Notifiers* if there's a match (arrow 6).
3. The *Notifiers* route the encrypted payload of the given event ID to the subscribers (arrow 7).

Note that the *Broker* operation is *content*-based pub/sub since it compares the fragmented hashes of the metadata against the hashed predicates/filters, and the *Notifiers* are *topic-based* since they match the ID of the metadata with the ID of the encrypted payload.

2.1 XML Data and XPath Predicate Model

One of the common data format for machine-to-machine communication is eXtensible Markup Language (*XML*). XML is a standardized markup language created by the World Wide Web Consortium (W3C) which defines a syntax for encoding documents readable for humans and machines through the use of tags that define the structure of the data in a tree form for processing and transmission. XML is a widely adopted data format for pub/sub systems in an enterprise environments due to its standardized text and rich content distribution support. For example, events/data in pub/sub typically consists of an XML metadata file to describe the rich content file, referred to as a payload (i.e., XML payload, blob, images/video).

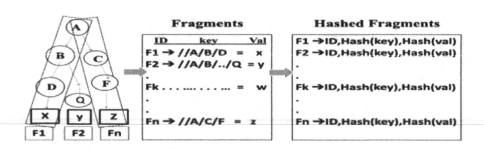

Fig. 2. An illustration of XML Event Fragmentation into Hashed Key/Values

On the other hand, *XPath* is the query/predicate filtering language for XML data that defines operations for checking the existence of a given path (i.e., attributes k_i, k_j) in the tree with a specific leaf value (i.e., $x, y \ldots z$). For example, subscription filters are in the form of //stocks/company/IBM = 500, //stocks/company/IBM $\geq$ 500, and //stocks/company/IBM > 500 < 700. This is analogous to our notional XML event tree depicted in Fig. 2 (left quadrant), //A/B/D = x where A is the branch of the tree name stocks, B represents companies, and D which is the last node in the tree is a specific company like IBM with stock value x, where x = 500, for instance.

With this XML tree representation, we fragment/slice each event into attribute *key* and *value* pairs where the branches of the tree are the attribute keys ($k_1 \ldots k_n$) and the leaf nodes are the values ($v_1 \ldots v_n$). To illustrate, Fig. 2 shows a simple *XML* metadata represented as a tree (left), then, fragmented/sliced into key/value pairs where the fragments $F_1 \leftarrow //A/B/D = x$ (left branch) and another $F_n \leftarrow //A/C/F = y$ (right branch) form the *key/value* pairs as shown in the middle quadrant. Finally, hashing the key and the value pairs separately and assigning each of the fragments to an ID as shown in right quadrant. Note that the encrypted payload of this metadata is also assigned to this exact ID (discussed in Sect. 5) to ensure correct routing of the fragments.

Furthermore, *XPath* subscription predicates/filters can be expressed as attribute *key/value* pairs with *conjunction* and *dis-junction* forms such as attribute J = x AND attribute K = y AND/OR attribute M = z(...). These logical operations can be evaluated in clear since they don't leak any information about the hashed key/value pairs. With this *XPath* predicate and *XML* metadata slicing techniques, we enable the brokers to preserve the privacy of both the *Xpath* predicates and the metadata by design. It is intuitive to see that a hashed predicate attribute key/value comparing it to a hashed XML metadata key/value is a simple string comparison, however, this implies that the system only supports exact string matching filters (equality matching).

To deal with the range XPath predicates (<and>) with numerical values, only the attribute k is hashed and the numerical value v is processed in clear text. This is because, it is mathematically proven (with some probability) for finding a pre-image of a hash of an attribute key k *(i.e., //stocks/company/IBM)* from a given numerical value v ($500), especially, when the clients' real ID's are masked with *UUID* and a collusion-resistant hash (i.e., SHA-256) is used.

2.2   Limitations

The key limitation of the proposed system lies in the XPath predicate filter model. Specifically, XPath supports predicate expressions with a *star* * where the attribute *key* can occur in any path within the XML data tree. For example, `//*/IBM = 500` or `//*/disease = "diabetes"` where the *star* * represents the stock info from any provider/publisher or disease info from any hospital. Since we hash the *key/value* pairs separately, such expression will require breaking the *key* into multiple parts that are hashed independently, hence, imposes performance cost. A workaround for this problem is for the subscribers construct full XPath predicate filters from the XML schema.

3   Threat Model

We consider the semi-trusted threat model where the pub/sub services, the *Controller*, *Broker* and *Notifier* services are trusted but curious. However, they should not know neither the published events nor the subscription predicate filters. We further assume the publishers are trusted to send "good" data and the subscribers are trusted to send "good" subscription predicates/filters and cannot collude.

The *Controller* services could intercept subscription predicates registration requests from the subscribers and topic registration requests from the publishers. This is to inject the registrations into the *broker* and *notifier* services and provide service endpoints to them. Note that the *controllers* neither store the hashed predicates/filters nor the topic names from the publishers.

The *Broker* services could intercept the fragmented metadata from the publishers to apply arbitrary functions (matching the predicate filters with the metadata fragments) in order to route the fragment IDs to the *Notifiers* when there is a match. Similarly, the *Notifiers* could intercept the encrypted events from the publishers and the matched fragment event IDs from the *Brokers* to perform arbitrary functions (matching two IDs) in order to route the encrypted event to the subscribers.

4   Algorithms

Algorithm 1 illustrates the *Controller* (CS) micro service function. In Algorithm 1, the clients send their registration request to the *Controller* service through the REQUEST/RESPONSE channel in line 4 and 7. Note that the `accesToken` used for the registration is issued by the *TA* as illustrated in Fig. 1. (omitted). The CS injects the subscription predicates to the *Brokers* (BS) in the data plane then returns the *Notification* (NS) endpoint to the subscribers in line 5, and the *BS* and the *NS* service endpoints to the publishers in line 9.

Algorithm 1. Controller Micro Service (CS)

1: **procedure** CONTROLLER
2: require: *Predicate, Topic*   ▷ subscription predicate, publisher topic
3:     **repeat**
4:         **if** $(REQ/RES_{sub,accessToken})$ **then**
5:             $BS_{[list]} \leftarrow Predicate$ **return** $NS_{endpoints}$
6:         **end if**
7:         **if** $(REQ/RES_{pub,accessToken})$ **then**
8:             $NS_{[list]} \leftarrow Topic$
9:             $BS_{[list]} \leftarrow Topic$ **return** $BS_{endpoints}, NS_{endpoints}$
10:         **end if**
11:     **until** *terminate*
12: **end procedure**

Algorithm 2 illustrates the *Broker* (BS) micro service function. In Algorithm 2, the *Broker* checks if there is data in the PULL channel (from *CS*) and adds the predicate in its list in line 4. Also, it checks the SUB channel (fragmented hashed events from the publishers) and compares the fragment with the registered hashed predicates injected by the *CS*, then it forwards the ID of the matched fragments to the *NS* in line 7. On the other hand, the *NS* Algorithm (omitted due to space limitations) is similar to the *BS* Algorithm as it checks the SUB channel (fully encrypted event from the publishers) and compares the event ID with the ID the *BS* sent when matched/brokered, then, publishes/routes it to the subscribers if it is a match.

Algorithm 2. Broker Micro Service (BS)

1: **procedure** BROKER
2: require: *Predicate P, Fragments F*   ▷ P from *CS*, F from publishers
3:     **repeat**
4:         **if** $(DEVICE_{control})$ **then** $Preds_{list} \leftarrow P$
5:         **end if**   ▷ from Controller
6:         **if** $(SUB_{publisher}^{F})$ **then**   ▷ from Publishers
7:             **if** $(F - in - Preds_{list})$ **then** $PUSH \leftarrow F_{ID}$
8:             **end if**   ▷ to Notifiers
9:         **end if**
10:     **until** *terminate*
11: **end procedure**

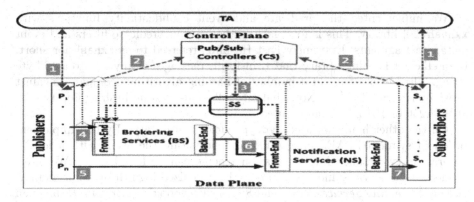

Fig. 3. XPS++ Building Blocks and Information Flow labeled 1–7.

For the client Algorithms (omitted due to space limitations), the publishers publish the hashed key/value pair fragments F to *Broker'* SUB channel as shown in line 6 in Alg. 2 using *0MQ's* `broker_socket.send_multipart` (`[part1,,..n]`) and the encrypted payload to the *NS* using the PUSH channel. Similarly, the subscriber micro service function is to simply connect to the *Notifier* endpoint given by the *Controller* as shown in line 5 in Algorithm 1 for the matched events.

5   Implementation

Figure 3 illustrates the building blocks of the system. The *Trusted Authority* (TA) shown in the top cylinder box handles service access control and crypto key distribution for the clients depicted in arrows labeled 1. Building upon our previous code base [3], we compose three micro-services; a *Controller Service (CS)*, *Brokering Services (BS)*, and *Notification Services (NS)* where the CS operates in the *control* plane and both the BS and NS services in the *data* plane. They are interconnected with *Stream Service (SS)* (depicted as a cylinder), and *Monitoring Service* (MS) depicted as triangles on the arrows for logging.

We built our pub/sub services on top of *ZeroMQ* (commonly written as 0MQ or zmq), an open source message brokering library. Specifically, we used *pyzmq*, a *Python* implementation of the *zmq* message brokering library. The algorithms are implemented also with the *Python* programming language with 20 lines of code (LOC). *0MQ* was selected from a number of other libraries analyzed in [5].

We implemented PULL/PUSH messaging patterns for inter-services and PUB/SUB between the publishers and the *data plane* services. The PUSH/PULL pattern is used because it requires the service to be active and bound together in order to pull/push data to and from a channel. With this, the *Controllers*, *Brokers*, and the *Notifier* services have to be active and work together at all times given that they are deployed independently.

We implemented the predicate and event confidentiality functions with xxhash [20] library. This is for **hashing** the key/val predicate filters and event metadata fragments. Extremely Fast Hashing, referred to as **xxhash** for short, is an efficient hashing library that transforms messages of any size to a 16 byte string. The performance of a number of hashing algorithms compared against *xxash* is elaborated in [20]. Note that any collusion-resistant hashing library such as SHA256 or RIPEMD can be used.

On the other hand, we used **pycryptodome** [15] library– Python implementation of symmetric AES encryption for encrypting the event with a locally generated key, detailed implementation scheme can be found in [3]. We interconnected the services and the clients with specialized high throughput and low latency *Streaming Services* (SS). The *SS* uses Facebook's *Tornado IOLoop* open source library [11], highly efficient message routing library for native sockets. This is to allow the formation of different service topology and service plugability without code changes.

We packaged the services as *Docker* container images [2], then deployed and managed in a Kubernetes. Kubernetes is a cloud agnostic service orchestration engine for ease of deployment and load-balancing for high availability (HA) with unprecedented scale. It supports upto 5,000 nodes with 300,000 containers on each cluster [1], thus, the proposed system is highly scaleable by design.

5.1 Proof-of-Concept Demonstration

Figure 4 shows the publisher screen output. Highlighted is the hashed key/value pairs of an event that will match the subscribers' predicate (shown in Fig. 7).

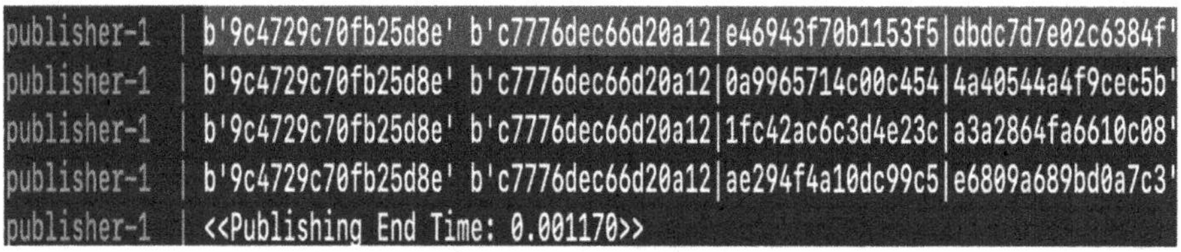

```
publisher-1 | b'9c4729c70fb25d8e' b'c7776dec66d20a12|e46943f70b1153f5|dbdc7d7e02c6384f'
publisher-1 | b'9c4729c70fb25d8e' b'c7776dec66d20a12|0a9965714c00c454|4a40544a4f9cec5b'
publisher-1 | b'9c4729c70fb25d8e' b'c7776dec66d20a12|1fc42ac6c3d4e23c|a3a2864fa6610c08'
publisher-1 | b'9c4729c70fb25d8e' b'c7776dec66d20a12|ae294f4a10dc99c5|e6809a689bd0a7c3'
publisher-1 | <<Publishing End Time: 0.001170>>
```

Fig. 4. Publisher screen shot showing fragmented and hashed slices of an event metadata [EventID, topic|key|value] with published time stamp.

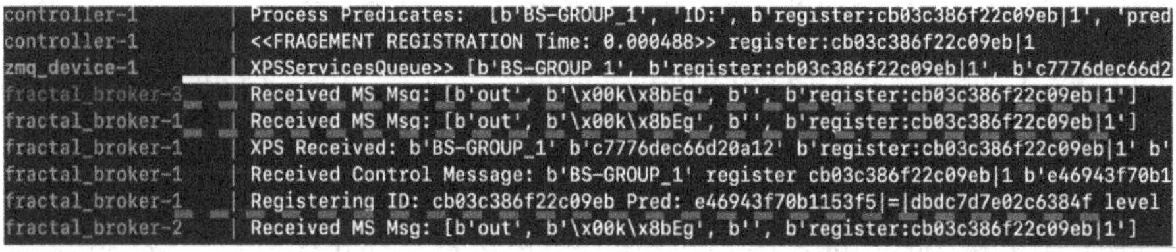

```
controller-1  | Process Predicates: [b'BS-GROUP_1', 'ID:', b'register:cb03c386f22c09eb|1', 'pred
controller-1  | <<FRAGEMENT REGISTRATION Time: 0.000488>> register:cb03c386f22c09eb|1
zmq_device-1  | XPSServicesQueue>> [b'BS-GROUP_1', b'register:cb03c386f22c09eb|1', b'c7776dec66d2
fractal_broker-3 | Received MS Msg: [b'out', b'\x00k\x8bEg', b''. b'register:cb03c386f22c09eb|1']
fractal_broker-1 | Received MS Msg: [b'out', b'\x00k\x8bEg', b''. b'register:cb03c386f22c09eb|1']
fractal_broker-1 | XPS Received: b'BS-GROUP_1' b'c7776dec66d20a12' b'register:cb03c386f22c09eb|1' b'
fractal_broker-1 | Received Control Message: b'BS-GROUP_1' register cb03c386f22c09eb|1 b'e46943f70b1
fractal_broker-1 | Registering ID: cb03c386f22c09eb Pred: e46943f70b1153f5|=|dbdc7d7e02c6384f level
fractal_broker-2 | Received MS Msg: [b'out', b'\x00k\x8bEg', b''. b'register:cb03c386f22c09eb|1']
```

Fig. 5. The subscription registration processed by the *Controller* shown in the first two lines and passing to the *Stream Service* named **zmq_device-1** (underlined) to be injected to the *Brokers* to register the predicate filter (dotted lines).

```
fractal_broker-2   | MATCHED >>> b'c7776dec66d20a12' c7776dec66d20a12*e46943f70b1153f5=dbdc7d7e02c6384f
fractal_broker-2   | Match->Notifier: NS-GROUP_1 b'c7776dec66d20a12' cb03c386f22c09eb b'c7776dec66d20a12
zmq_device-1       | XPSServicesQueue>> [b'NS-GROUP_1', b'c7776dec66d20a12', b'cb03c386f22c09eb']
fractal_notifier-1 | RECEIVED TX: c7776dec66d20a12 cb03c386f22c09eb
                     SENDING>> b'cb03c386f22c09eb' b'\x98\x96\n?F\x1a\xa7\xb4\x18t\xce\xc1\x9f\xef\xa4\
6N5bMfZrF75cRgV8iRxtnCMQsDNzz/FHEfnouw573/IbpWHlnDd0k9w8Z+xEZ9Q51GQpxJvEg7NwF+I55h2cd235ModKVcOpZkfuNQDy
fractal_notifier-1 | EVENT NOTIFICATION TIME: 0.000062
```

Fig. 6. Hashed key/value brokering–Underlined is the published hashed metadata fragment matched by the *Broker* with the registered hash predicate which is then its ID is matched with the encrypted event by the *Notifier* and routed to the subscriber (dotted lines).

```
clients-subscriber-1 | Registering pred to  tcp://zmq_device:5557
clients-subscriber-1 | sent: b'c7776dec66d20a12*e46943f70b1153f5|=|dbdc7d7e02c6384f'
clients-subscriber-1 | Rcvd PredTX ID: b'cb03c386f22c09eb'
clients-subscriber-1 | RCVD TIME: 1685466294.144623 Cypher Event: b'cb03c386f22c09eb' b'
QI6rQQaFZzpYVq065Vk6ok6N5bMfZrF75cRgV8iRxtnCMQsDNzz/FHEfnouw573/IbpWHlnDd0k9w8Z+xEZ9Q51GQ
x1swD8E9dQqntdRZcmAmDmH9tW42kg='
clients-subscriber-1 | XML Event: <?xml version="1.0" encoding="utf-8"?>
clients-subscriber-1 | <root><node_a>trigonelline</node_a><node_b>takyr</node_b><node_c>
d></root>
```

Fig. 7. Subscriber screen shot–Underlined is the hashed registered predicate [topic* key = value] sent to the *Controller*. Dotted line is the transaction ID `cb03c386f22c09eb` assigned to the predicate by the *Controller*. The last three rows are the XML payload cipher and the decrypted version of the event.

Figure 5 above shows how the subscribers' predicate filter is injected to the *Broker* by the *Controller* service through the *Stream Service*. Then, blindly brokered by the *Broker* and routed to the subscriber by the *Notifier* as shown in Fig. 6. Finally, Fig. 7 shows the subscriber receiving the encrypted event and displaying the decrypted form (see details in the Figure captions).

6 Performance Evaluations

Figures 4, 5, 6 and 7 above shows the practicality of a privacy-preservation in pub/sub without the complexity of the traditional cryptographic protocols. To assess the efficacy, we evaluated the performance impact on blindly brokering events vs. the traditional pub/sub system brokering in plain-text.

6.1 Experimental Setup

We run the experiments on an 8 core MacOS machine with 32 GB of memory. For the experimental data, we developed a tool that generates variable XML metadata sizes from an English dictionary data set with random words for the XML attribute keys, and a combination of strings, integers and floating point data types for the values. We use variable XML and jpeg image sizes for the payload. We took the delta between the event publication time and the received time by the subscriber. We run one *Controller (CS)*, a *Broker (BS)* and a *Notifier (NS)* services on docker container with one subscriber and a publisher with mixed metadata and payload sizes. Each experiment is run 10 times and averaged the results.

6.2 Experimental Results

Figure 8(a) shows the results for a variable XML metadata with fixed encrypted payload. We used a *primitive predicates* (single attribute key/value) to show the performance impacts on brokering plain XML *(PRIVACY OFF)* vs. brokering hashed key/val XML fragments *(PRIVACY ON)*. Figure 8(b) shows the results for a fixed metadata size (200 Bytes) with variable payload size to evaluate the inherent performance impact of the *(NS)*. We found the variable encrypted payload sizes has no performance impact because the *NS* only compares two ID's and routes the encrypted payload if there is a match regardless of its size.

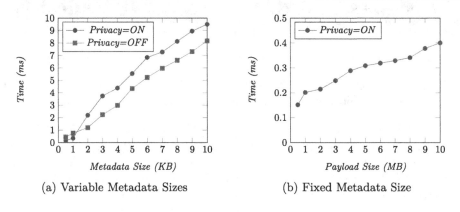

(a) Variable Metadata Sizes   (b) Fixed Metadata Size

Fig. 8. Key/Value Hash Brokering vs. Plaintext XML

Note that a 200 Bytes long of XML metadata is four branches that can represent 4 distinctive key/value pairs. This is common data format for several pub/sub application domains such as; IoT, stocks, health, and weather. For example, a metadata with stock prices can be blindly filtered and also routed as encrypted payload or a metadata with longitude and latitude for a location where the payload is an image/video of that location. Similarly, for health applications where the metadata specifies certain types of a disease and an X-ray image is the payload.

We found that *XPS++* performs better on small metadata (≤ 1 KB) and with negligible performance impact on larger metadata sizes. This is credited to the combination of *ZeroMQ*'s efficiency in handling small messages, and the XML transformation to key/val pairs that reduced the metadata 40% to 60%. Furthermore, we observed memory usage increases 0.5% linearly as the XML metadata size increases. This is due to the XML DOM parsers loading the entire XML object into the memory vs. our key/value hash string matching.

7   Related Work

There have been a wide range of solution schemes that addressed pub/sub security and privacy. Early studies such as k-anonymity [17] and l-diversity [23], were based on ad-hoc techniques that either supports subscription privacy or event integrity. With the advances in cryptographic protocols, authors of [16] introduced a secure pub/sub system that preserves confidentiality and integrity, and another approach is introduced that extended these techniques with Paillier homomorphic for full privacy [13]. Due to the computational overhead of the cryptographic protocol primitives, these solutions suffered performance issues.

Authors of [13] introduced a technique to guarantee performance in which a trusted third party performing a second layer of encryption with *Paillier* homomorphic for the attribute filters and *ABE* for the payload. A dual-policy ABE scheme for efficient and secure pub/sub content brokering is introduced in [21]. Authors of [12] completely shifted the filtering role from the brokers to the subscribers and combined *PBE* for encrypting the meta data and *CP-ABE* for the content (payload) with *Paillier* primitives where the key is shared between clients to improve performance, hence, broke pub/subs loose coupling requirements. Similarly, in [22] authors shifted the key exchanges to the brokers for loose coupling but suffer scaleability issue due to the explosion of the number of messages exchanged in relation to the broker hops.

From middleware messaging protocol solutions, authors of [8] proposed VIR-TUS, a middleware built on XMPP protocol to provide secure event-driven communications with both authentication through TLS protocol and encryption through SASL protocol mechanisms. Similarly, a combination of MQTT, CoAP, and HTTP as application-layer protocols for security is introduced in [9]. Due to their dependency on transport-level security for privacy (i.e., TLS), they lack predicate/filter and topic-level privacy support. To the best of our knowledge, this work is the first design-based security and privacy for XML pub/sub built on *ZeroMQ*. Given that we did not employ any complex cryptographic primitives which are computationally intensive or specialized vendor specific hardware, *XPS++* is different from above systems in terms of the simplicity of the *SDN*-based design concepts with the internet-scale deployment using cloud-native tools to simultaneously address pub/subs' conflicting requirements. Most importantly, our approach explores a new area that have not been sufficiently explored, thus, complementing these works.

8   Conclusion

We introduced a pub/sub system that preserves subscription predicate filters and metadata privacy by design. We discussed the implementation details of a prototype, dubbed *XPS++*, and presented preliminary experimental results. For future work, we plan for a more formal approach to defining the security properties associated with XPS++, and consider experiments with a realistic use cases and distributed network settings to assess; throughput and scaleability.

References

1. kubernates: Considerations for large clusters. https://docs.oasis-open.org/mqtt/mqtt/v5.0/os/mqtt-v5.0-os.html
2. Docker containers (2020). https://docker.io/. Accessed 19 Apr 2023
3. Ahmed, N.: TinyZMQ++: a privacy preserving content-based publish/subscribe IoT middleware (best paper). In: 2023 6th Conference on Cloud and Internet of Things (CIoT), pp. 40–46 (2023). https://doi.org/10.1109/CIoT57267.2023.10084896
4. Banks, A., et al.: MQTT version 5.0 (2019). https://docs.oasis-open.org/mqtt/mqtt/v5.0/os/mqtt-v5.0-os.html. Accessed 23 Oct 2023
5. Bayer, T.: Broker Wars: ActiveMQ, Qpid, HornetQ and RabbitMQ in comparison (2013)
6. Bethencourt, J., Sahai, A., Waters, B.: Ciphertext-policy attribute-based encryption. In: IEEE Symposium on Security and Privacy, SP 2007, vol. 50, pp. 321–334 (2007)
7. Boneh, D., Waters, B.: Conjunctive, subset, and range queries on encrypted data. In: Vadhan, S.P. (ed.) TCC 2007. LNCS, vol. 4392, pp. 535–554. Springer, Heidelberg (2007). https://doi.org/10.1007/978-3-540-70936-7_29
8. Conzon, D., et al.: The VIRTUS middleware: an XMPP based architecture for secure IoT communications and networks. Inf. Sci. **387**, 1–6 (2012)
9. da Cruz, M.A.A., et al.: The VIRTUS middleware: an XMPP based architecture for secure IoT communications and networks (ICCCN). In: IoT-A New Middleware for Internet of Things, vol. 8, p. 7902 (2021)
10. Golle, P., Jakobsson, M., Juels, A., Syverson, P.: Universal re-encryption for mixnets. In: Okamoto, T. (ed.) CT-RSA 2004. LNCS, vol. 2964, pp. 163–178. Springer, Heidelberg (2004). https://doi.org/10.1007/978-3-540-24660-2_14
11. IOLoop: Eventloops and PyZMQ. Accessed 19 Mar 2023
12. Khoury, J., et al.: Efficient private publish-subscribe systems. In: 17th International Symposium on Object/Component-Oriented Real-Time Distributed Computing, pp. 64–71 (2014)
13. Nabeel, M., Appel, S., Bertino, E., Buchmann, A.: Privacy preserving context aware publish subscribe systems. In: Lopez, J., Huang, X., Sandhu, R. (eds.) NSS 2013. LNCS, vol. 7873, pp. 465–478. Springer, Heidelberg (2013). https://doi.org/10.1007/978-3-642-38631-2_34
14. Paillier, P.: Public-key cryptosystems based on composite degree residuosity classes. In: Proceedings of the 41st Annual ACM Symposium on Theory of Computing on Librarians and Computers, Middleware 2012, pp. 223–238 (1999)
15. pycryptodome. https://pycryptodome-master.readthedocs.io/en/latest/
16. Raiciu, C., Rosenblum, D.S.: Enabling confidentiality in content-based publish/-subscribe infrastructures. In: In Securecomm and Workshops, pp. 1–11 (2006)
17. Sweeney, L.: Achieving k-anonymity privacy protection using generalization and suppression. Int. J. Uncertain. Fuzziness Knowl.-Based Syst. **10**, 571–588 (2002)
18. Goyal, V., Pandey, O., Sahai, A., Waters, B.: Attribute-based encryption for fine-grained access control of encrypted data. In: 13th ACM conference on Computer and communications security, ACN 2006, New York, NY, pp. 89–98 (2006)
19. Chen, W., Jiang, J., Skocik, N.: On the privacy protection in publish/subscribe systems. In: Wireless Communications, Networking and Information Security. WCNIS, vol. 50, pp. 597–601 (2010)
20. xxHash: xxhsh 1.4.3 (2020). https://pypi.org/project/xxhash

21. Yang, K., et al.: Privacy-preserving attribute-keyword based data publish-subscribe service on cloud platforms. Inf. Sci. **387**, 116–131 (2017)
22. Yoon, Y., Kim, B.H.: Secret forwarding of events over distributed publish/subscribe overlay network. PLOS One 1–23 (2016)
23. Zhou, Y., et al.: Dissemination of anonymized streaming data. In: Proceedings of the 9th ACM International Conference on Distributed Event-Based Systems, pp. 104–115 (2015)

SQS: Services and Quantum Software Introduction

Introduction to the 1st Workshop on Services and Quantum Software - SQS 2023

Johanna Barzen[1] (iD), Schahram Dustdar[2] (iD), Frank Leymann[1] (iD),
and Juan M. Murillo[3] (iD)

[1] Institute of Architecture of Application Systems at the University of Stuttgart, Germany
frank.leymann@iaas.uni-stuttgart.de
[2] TU Wien, Austria
dustdar@dsg.tuwien.ac.at
[3] University of Extremadura, Spain
juanmamu@unex.es

The 1st Workshop on Quantum Software and Services was held on 20 November 2023 in Rome, co-located with ICSOC 2023. The workshop was organised on the basis of the evidence that quantum software is already a reality. It is commonly accepted that future software will be hybrid, integrating both classical and quantum pieces. With this, interest in Quantum Software is also beginning to appear from researchers in the field of Software Engineering. In this scenario, it is necessary to start designing the way in which the integration between the classical and quantum parts of systems will take place. This is where Service-Oriented Computing can provide techniques for this. The aim of SQS was to bring together experienced participants interested in discussing different techniques for building information systems by composing classical services with hybrid services. SQS topics of interest included Quantum Program Models, Quantum Program Styles, Quantum Hybrid Computing, Quantum in the Compute Continuum and Execution Environments for Hybrid Quantum Services.

SQS received twelve high-quality submissions. Each paper received at least three single-blind by members of the Program Committee. After the review process six papers were accepted, with an acceptance rate of 50%. The number of workshop attendees was 22.

SQS was held as a full-day event. The scientific programme during the morning consisted of two industrial keynotes, each of which was followed by a discussion session. The first keynote was given by **Vincent van Wingerden**, Business Development Manager Europe at **CLASSIQ** (https://www.classiq.io/), which is a leading company devoted to quantum software development. The talk was entitled *"Create large-scale quantum programs using Classiq"*. The capabilities of the tool developed by the company were demonstrated and the attendees were even able to practice with it.

The second keynote was given by **Iraitz Montalbán**, Lead Software Developer at **Kipu Quantum GmbH** (https://kipu-quantum.com/), a German startup aiming to provide quantum advantage to industry in the near future. He is also co-author of the book "Financial Modeling Using Quantum Computing". In his talk titled *"Making quantum computing an industry grade solution for the near future"* Iraitz explored the past, present and future of Quantum Computing and how Kipu Quantum is merging its cutting-edge technology with the latest advances in the field to make quantum computing an industry-grade solution in the near future.

The afternoon programme was devoted to the presentation of the accepted papers in two sessions. The titles of the papers and their authors are listed below.

1. *Linear Structure of Training Samples in Quantum Neural Network Applications* by Mandl, Alexander; Barzen, Johanna; Bechtold, Marvin; Keckeisen, Michael; Leymann, Frank; Vaudrevange, Patrick K.S.
2. *Hybrid Data Management Architecture for Present Quantum Computing* by Zajac, Markus; Störl, Uta
3. *Quantum Block-Matching Algorithm using Dissimilarity Measure* by Martínez Felipe, Miguel de Jesús; Montiel Pérez, Jesús Yaljá; Onofre, Víctor; Maldonado Romo, Alberto; Young, Ricky
4. *On Rounding Errors in The Simulation of Quantum Circuits* by Klamroth, Jonas; Beckert, Bernhard
5. *Towards higher abstraction levels in quantum computing* by Fürntratt, Hermann; Schnabl, Paul; Krebs, Florian; Unterberger, Roland; Zeiner, Herwig
6. *Some Initial Guidelines for Building Reusable Quantum Oracles* by Sanchez-Rivero, Javier; Talavan, Daniel; Garcia-Alonso, Jose; Ruiz-Cortés, Antonio; Murillo, Juan M.

Detailed information about the workshop, the keynotes and the accepted papers can be found at the url https://sqs2023.spilab.es/.

The SQS organisers would like to thank the keynote speakers and their companies for their full availability, the authors of both accepted and unsuccessful papers for their contributions, the attendees for their interest in the event, the members of the Programme Committee for their selfless contribution as well as the ICSOC 2023 Organising Committee for hosting the event.

November 2023   The SQS 2023 Organising Committee

Organization

Organizing Team

Johanna Barzen	Institute of Architecture of Application Systems at the University of Stuttgart, Germany
Schahram Dustdar	TU Wien, Austria
Frank Leymann	Institute of Architecture of Application Systems at the University of Stuttgart, Germany
Juan M. Murillo	University of Extremadura, Spain

Program Committee

Shaukat Ali	Simula Research Laboratory, Norway
Johanna Barzen	University of Stuttgart, Germany
Antonio Brogi	University of Pisa, Italy
Schahram Dustdar	TU Wien, Austria
Michael Falkenthal	Anaqor AG, Germany
Sebastian Feld	Delft University of Technology, The Netherlands
Ignacio García	University of Castilla-La Mancha, Spain
Jose Garcia-Alonso	University of Extremadura, Spain
Beatriz C. Hiesmayr	University of Vienna, Austria
Frank Leymann	University of Stuttgart, Germany
Kostas Magoutis	University of Crete and FORTH-ICS, Greece
Wolfgang Mauerer	Ostbayerische Technische Hochschule, Germany
Tommi Mikkonen	University of Jyväskylä, Finland
Juan M. Murillo	University of Extremadura, Spain
Ricardo Perez-Castillo	University of Castilla-La Mancha, Spain
Aritra Sarkar	Delft University of Technology, The Netherlands
Benjamin Weder	University of Stuttgart, Germany
Indika Weerasingha	Tilburg University, The Netherlands
Manuel Wimmer	JKU Linz, Austria

On Rounding Errors in the Simulation of Quantum Circuits

Jonas Klamroth[1]([✉]) and Bernhard Beckert[2]

[1] FZI Research Center for Information Technology, Karlsruhe, Germany
klamroth@fzi.de
[2] Institute of Information Security and Dependability, Karlsruhe Institute of
Technology, Karlsruhe, Germany
beckert@kit.edu

Abstract. The realm of quantum computing is inherently tied to real numbers. However, quantum simulators nearly always rely on floating-point arithmetic and thus may introduce rounding errors in their calculations. In this work, we show how we can nevertheless trust the computations of simulators under certain conditions where we can rule out that floating-point errors disturb the obtained measurement results. We derive theoretical bounds for the errors of floating-point computations in quantum simulations and use these bounds to extend the implementation of an existing verification tool to show the soundness of the tool's analysis for a number of well-established quantum algorithms.

Keywords: quantum simulation · floating-point arithmetic · software verification

1 Introduction

Motivation. Quantum computers have undeniable potential, allowing for a super-polynomial speedup compared to classical solutions. Providing insight into this new field of computation is thus more important than ever. However, implementing quantum programs cannot be compared to that of their conventional counterparts, since quantum computers constitute a completely new paradigm. Additionally, current quantum computers are not able to provide logical (error-free) qubits. To both these challenges simulators for quantum circuits provide a solution as they allow for the logical execution of quantum circuits and provide means to debug and test quantum circuits in ways an actual quantum computer cannot. Thus simulation of quantum circuits is a very relevant topic in the realm of quantum computing. However, since simulators are written in classical programming languages they normally rely on classical data types as well. The use of floating-point numbers instead of reals famously introduces rounding errors.

This work is part of the SEQUOIA End-to-End project funded by the Ministry of Economic Affairs Baden-Württemberg, Germany.

If these rounding errors get too big they could potentially introduce mismatches between the theoretical result and the simulation. In this work, we will take a deeper look at these disparities and try to provide practical solutions on how to avoid them or at least rule out that they are indeed problematic.

Contribution. Our contribution is twofold. We first examine the use of floating-point arithmetic in quantum simulators or similar programs. We show that, due to the nature of how quantum computation works, several unique properties hold in the realm of floating-point arithmetic. In particular, we are able to derive a bound for the maximum possible rounding error that can occur during the simulation of a given quantum circuit assuming the standard matrix semantics. We then use this bound to provide conditions under which the most likely measurement computed by a simulator is indeed the correct result even accounting for all possible rounding errors.

As a second contribution, we use this theory to extend an existing verification tool for hybrid quantum circuits which relies on the translation of quantum circuits into equivalent Java programs. Due to the use of floats in Java rather than reals, this translation may introduce rounding errors and, thus, may not be a faithful simulation, which could render the translation-based verification approach unsound. With the presented extension of the tool (based on our theoretical findings) this soundness gap can be ruled out. We show that with the presented approach we can prove the soundness of the verification for several practical examples including implementations of Shor, Grover and Deutsch-Josza. We also show that the additional verification effort is very limited for most of the examples.

Outline. This article is structured as follows. We start by introducing some fundamentals of floating-point arithmetic and make first observations about their nature regarding rounding errors. We then characterize these errors in more detail which results in the main theoretical contribution. In the following section, we present how we implemented the theoretical contributions into an existing verification tool and show its effectiveness. We conclude with related work and some final remarks.

2   Considerations on the Use of Floating-Point Numbers

In the following sections, we will use the following notation: variables or literals with a subscript f are assumed to be calculated in floating-point arithmetic whereas a subscript r indicates that calculations are assumed to be carried out with real values. Variables that only differ in subscript refer to the same calculations only differing in the type (float/real) in which they were executed. E.g. $var_r = 0.1_r + 0.2_r$ would be a real-valued assignment. Then var_f refers to the same calculation carried out with floats instead of reals and introduces rounding errors (which results in $var_f = 0.30000000000000004$, if calculated as IEE 754 float). If the type is clear from context we may leave out subscripts. Furthermore, we will use the terms floating-point numbers or floats interchangeably and will use those terms to refer to the general format of floating-point numbers rather than the 32-bit precision as defined in several typical programming languages.

2.1 Floating-Point Format

Floating-point numbers are widely used as a means to represent real numbers with finite precision. The format most commonly used is the following: Floats are represented as a triple (s, m, e) where s is the sign of the number, m is the mantissa and e is an exponent (basically moving the "point" around, hence the name). The value of such a triple is $s \times (1.m) \times b^e$, where b is a predefined basis (commonly 2 or 10). In this work, we consider the floating-point standard IEEE 754, which is the most commonly used standard. It defines two main versions for floating-point numbers with different precision: 23 resp. 52 bits for the mantissa and 8 resp. 11 bits for the exponent (and 1 sign bit). These are commonly known as float resp. double types in programming languages such as Java or C. The IEEE standard defines several properties that implementations have to satisfy. The most important property for this work is that certain operations have to be rounded to the nearest representable floating-point number [6]. These operations include addition, subtraction, multiplication, division and taking the square root among others. In the remainder of this paper, we will call these operations *base operations*.

The IEEE standard also defines several special values including NANs ("not a number") as well as positive and negative infinity. However, for this work, these special values can be ignored as they never occur in the relevant calculations (which is important for the following considerations).

2.2 Some Fundamental Observations About Floating-Point Numbers

In this section, we will make two very fundamental observations about the nature of floating-point numbers which will allow us to find more interesting properties later on regarding the use of floating-point numbers in the context of quantum computations.

Observation 1 (Distance between floats). *The distance between two consecutive floats is increasing (or equal) for increasing absolute values. More formally: If FP is the set of all floats, then, for all $x, y \in FP$, $|x| > |y|$ implies $|nf(x)| - |x| \geq |nf(y)| - |y|$ (where $nf(\cdot)$ is the floating-point number with the next biggest absolute value).*

Proof Sketch: As the sign bit does not change the absolute values we can ignore it here. If the exponent of two floating-points is identical, then the difference between the two values just depends on the position of the mantissa bit that is changed. Thus changing a bit with higher significance also increases the difference. Since changing the exponent is essentially just shifting the bits around the "point", this is true for different exponents as well. Note that changing a mantissa bit will always result in a smaller value change than changing the exponent as the exponent changes the value by exactly one order of magnitude while the mantissa only changes the value within one magnitude.

Using this observation, we can bound the error of each floating-point operation given a bound on the size of the result of the operation.

Observation 2 (Error bounds for floats). *If the result of some base operation is known to be in some interval $[-b_f, b_f]$, then the maximum rounding error associated with this operation is $(|b_f - pf(b_f)|/2)_r$ (where $pf(\cdot)$ is the floating-point number with the next smaller absolute value).*

Proof Sketch: A direct consequence of Observation 1 is that the largest rounding error occurs when the result is right between the largest and second-largest absolute values in the interval. Thus the resulting error would be half the distance between those two values.

Consider the following example: The addition of two floating-point values, each taken from the interval $[0.0, 10.0]$, is known to result in a value in the interval $[0.0, 20.0]$. We can simply look up the biggest floating-point value smaller than 20.0 to be 19.999998 and, thus, know that the maximum error for this kind of operation is $(20.0 - 19.999998)/2.0 = 0.000001$. Similarly, for the same operation with double precision, we get a maximum error of $(20.0 - 19.999999999999996)/2.0 = 2 \times 10^{-15}$.

2.3   Charaterizing Floating-Point Errors for the Simulation of Quantum Circuits

In this section, we make further observations leading to the possibility to bound the maximum rounding errors occurring during a simulation of a given quantum circuit. We start by realizing that any floating-point computation occurring in the simulation of a quantum circuit is restricted to a very small subset of all possible floating-point values.

Observation 3 (Value of range for quantum circuits). *All real numbers (complex numbers are considered to be two real numbers) occurring in a quantum computation are in the interval $[-1.0, 1.0]$.*

This can be seen by the fact that every quantum state $|\phi\rangle$ is normalized and, thus, $\||\phi\rangle\| = \sum_{i=0}^{n} |\phi[i]|^2 = 1$, which implies $|\phi[i]|^2 \leq 1$. Let $\phi[i] = x + yi$ where $x, y \in \mathbb{R}$. By the definition $|\phi[i]| = \sqrt{x^2 + y^2}$ of the absolute value of a complex number, we know that $|\phi[i]|^2 = x^2 + y^2 \leq 1$, which leads to the aforementioned observation that $|x| \leq 1$ and $|y| \leq 1$ or equivalently $-1 \leq x \leq 1$ and $-1 \leq y \leq 1$.

The same is true for any value that occurs in a unitary matrix. An easy way to see this is by the fact that one property of unitary matrices is that their rows are orthonormal. Thus any row has length 1 and the same argument as above can be applied. Notice that the property observed above does not rely on the strict normalization constraint. Rather we can relax this constraint to be $\|\phi\rangle\| \leq 1$. The arguments are identical to the ones used above. Thus, any quantum state (normalized or not) with a length less or equal to 1 can be represented with real values only from $[-1, 1]$. Using Observation 2 and 1 we can see that if all occurring values are in the interval $[-1, 1]$ the maximum possible rounding error per operation during the simulation of quantum circuits is 3×10^{-8} for single precision and 5×10^{-17} for double precision (assuming only base operations are needed). We will call this maximum error ϵ and use ϵ as a placeholder for the value corresponding to whichever precision we are talking about. Note that this is a very coarse overapproximation of the error that the use of floating-point arithmetic may introduce. We will later discuss one possibility to improve that approximation. For now, however, we will be content with a generic ϵ as the upper bound for the error introduced per operation.

Now that we have found an upper bound for rounding errors in quantum circuits we want to characterize the maximum error of simulating a circuit. To do so, we need to compute a limit on the number of operations needed to do so. In the following when we talk about simulation of quantum circuits we will consider the approach where quantum states are vectors in an n-dimensional complex-valued Hilbert space and quantum gates are simulated as matrix multiplications. We will call this approach a standard simulation (although we are aware that other methods exist). We start by computing the number of base operations needed to calculate the effect of a single gate on an arbitrary quantum state.

Observation 4 (Number of operations to simulate a gate). *Computing the effects of the application of a gate described by a unitary matrix to a given quantum state can be done with $n \times (6n + 2(n - 1)) = n \times (8n - 2) = 8n^2 - 2n$ float/real-operations where n is the size of the quantum state.*

A matrix multiplication can be considered as computing each element of the resulting vector separately. Each of these computations consists of n multiplication and $n - 1$ additions (multiplying the row of the matrix with n elements with the elements of the vector and then adding those up). However, in the general case, all those elements are complex values which means addition and multiplication have to be done with complex values. Adding up two complex values requires the addition of 2 real values and multiplying two complex values requires 4 multiplications as well as 2 additions. This leaves us with a total of 2 operations per complex addition and 6 operations per complex multiplication. Thus, for n complex multiplications, we need $6n$ real operations and equivalently for $n - 1$ complex additions we need $2(n - 1)$ operations. Since there are n elements in the vector and the operations have to be done for each of them we get a total number of operations of $n \times (6n + 2(n - 1)) = n \times (8n - 2) = 8n^2 - 2n$.

Observation 5 (Number of operations to simulate a measurement). *Computing the effects of a measurement of one qubit given a quantum state can be done with $5 \times \frac{n}{2} + \frac{n}{2} - 1 + \frac{n}{2} = 7\frac{n}{2} - 1$ float/real-operations where n is the size of the quantum state.*

A measurement consists of two parts. Calculating the probabilities with which each outcome will occur and adapting the state according to the measurement. Calculating the probability of measuring 0 for a certain bit in a given quantum state is done by adding up all squared absolute values of half of the elements of that state (the other half constitutes the probability of measuring 1). Since computing the absolute value of a complex number $|c| = |a + bi| = \sqrt{a^2 + b^2}$ can be done with 2 multiplications, 1 addition and 1 square root a total of 5 operations is needed. Adding up all those $\frac{n}{2}$ values takes $\frac{n}{2} - 1$ operations thus computing the probability takes $5 \times \frac{n}{2} - 1$. Normalizing the state can be done with $\frac{n}{2}$ operations as normalizing is effectively just multiplying the state vector with a scalar. However, we know that after a measurement at least half of the elements of that vector are equal to 0 thus leaving only $\frac{n}{2}$ operations. This results in the final number of operations of $7 \times \frac{n}{2} - 1$ per measurement.

Using the last two Observations we can now compute the total number of operations needed for the standard simulation of a quantum circuit.

Observation 6 (Number of operations for quantum circuits). *The final state of a quantum circuit with q qubits, g gates and m measurements can be computed using $g \times (8 \times 2^{2q} - 2 \times 2^q) + m \times (7 \times 2^{q-1} - 1)$ real/float operations.*

This is basically a direct result from Observation 4 and 5. Since the state size of a quantum state with q qubits is 2^q and each application of a gate is equivalent to one matrix multiplication, the given number of operations follows directly.

As we have characterized the amounts of operations needed to simulate a quantum circuit and the maximum error each operation can carry, we can now quantify the maximum error that can occur when simulating a quantum circuit in the way we depicted.

Theorem 1 (Maximum error of quantum circuit). *Given a quantum circuit with q qubits, g gates and m measurements, the maximum error for each element of the final state resulting from a standard simulation is: $(g \times (8 \times 2^{2q} - 2^q) + m \times (7 \times 2^{q-1} - 1)) \times \epsilon$.*

This follows directly from our previous Observations 6 and 2 with one small adaptation. Due to the fact that each element of a unitary matrix may be subject to rounding errors, we additionally account for a maximum error of $n \times \epsilon = 2^q \times \epsilon$ this may introduce. The reason why this is not quadratic but only linear in the size of the vector will become evident in Sect. 2.4. Theorem 1 allows us to bound the error on the calculated probability distribution for a given circuit.

We have now characterized the maximum rounding error possible in the simulation of quantum circuits. To reason about how this might affect the observed measurement results we realize the following: For a lot of quantum algorithms, the full probability distribution is not of interest. In fact, for major quantum algorithms, it suffices to know which state is measured with the highest probability. Neither the exact probability nor the total order of all possible states is relevant as the most likely result encodes the solution to the problem at hand.

Examples of such algorithms include the Deutsch-Josza [3], the Shor [11], and the Grover [7] algorithm. Assuming this property of an algorithm we can use our analysis of floating-point rounding errors to reason about whether such rounding errors could possibly affect the outcome of an algorithm. Or put differently: if the most likely observed bit sequence obtained by measurements could be different for simulations and real quantum computations. This is the case if the most likely and second most likely measurements differ by less than the rounding error that can at most occur. We state the following theorem capturing the relation between the errors possibly occurring and the possibility that the observed result is not the actually correct one.

Theorem 2 (Perturbance of most likely measurement).
Given

- *the probabilities $p1_f$ and $p0_f$ to measure 1 and 0 for some qubit in some quantum state*
- *and the number of floating point operations k necessary to compute $p0_f$*

$|p1_f - p0_f| > (k + 4) \times \epsilon_f$ *implies* $p0_f < p1_f \leftrightarrow p0_r < p1_r$.

Proof Sketch: If $p0_f$ is computed using k floating-point operations and each of these operations can (by Observation 2) introduce a rounding error of at most ϵ. The computed value of $p0_f$ can be off by at most $k \times e$. The value of $p1_f$ can then be computed with one operation $p1_f = 1.0_f - p0_f$. The total rounding error can thus at most be $(k+1) \times \epsilon$. So if the difference between the two probabilities is greater than the maximum possible rounding error then the order of them can not be affected by rounding errors. As the inequality $|p1_f - p0_f| > (k + 4) \times \epsilon_f$ introduces three floating-point operations itself we use $k + 4$ instead of $k + 1$ operations and thus allow this expression to be evaluated as floats rather than reals. This allows us to show the irrelevance of floating-point errors purely in the domain of floats.

Using the same logic, we can also derive the maximum rounding error for which the most likely observed measurement is guaranteed to be unchanged by rounding errors.

Observation 7 (Maximum allowed rounding error). *The most likely observed result of a circuit and its simulation do not differ as long as the maximum error ϵ per operation in the simulation is bound as follows:*

$$\epsilon_r < \frac{p_f - (1 - p_f)}{k}$$

where k is the number of operations to calculate the final state and p_f is the probability of observing the most likely result in the simulation.

This is obtained by rewriting the inequality derived in Theorem 2.

Instead of using k as a given number of operations, we can again calculate the number of operations necessary for a circuit with q qubits, g operations and

m measurements: $g \times (8 \times 2^{2q} - 2 \times 2^q) + m \times (6 \times 2^{q-1} - 1)$. Using this we can rewrite the bound for the maximum error in Observation 7 as:

$$\epsilon_r < \frac{p_f - (1 - p_f)}{g \times (8 \times 2^{2q} - 2^q) + m \times (6 \times 2^{q-1} - 1)}$$

As an example let us consider the Deutsch-Josza Algorithm for a function with 3 bits. The circuit to solve this problem has 4 qubits and 9 gates (assuming a given oracle as one gate). Additionally, we know that the algorithm returns the correct result with 100% probability. Using this information we can determine the maximum allowed rounding error:

$$\epsilon < \frac{1 - (1 - 1)}{9 \times (8 \times 2^{2 \times 4} - 2^4) + 3 \times (6 \times 2^{4-1} - 1)} = \frac{1}{18429} \approx 5,4 \times 10^{-5}$$

Notice how despite that being a 100% theoretical success the probability of the allowed error gets quite small as we consider a very coarse overapproximation of the error here. On the other hand, even for single precision floating-points, this is still magnitudes away from the actual maximum error which we showed to be 3×10^{-8}. However, due to the exponential scaling in the number of qubits for the same amount of gates at 9 or more qubits this threshold gets broken. On the other hand, the same logic applied to a circuit with 10000 gates and 15 qubits but using doubles instead of floats still allows us to show the absence of relevant floating point errors. As a final example consider a circuit with 1000000 gates and 50 qubits (which is around what current HPCs can simulate) and the most likely result being observed with a probability of 70%. The resulting maximum allowed error would be approximately 6.9×10^{-38}. This is beyond the scope even of double precision however we could use this to determine the necessary precision for such a circuit.

2.4   Improve the Error Bound

We already talked about the fact that we can do much better than the coarse overapproximation introduced in Observation 7. This has to do with the fact that by multiplying unitary matrices and normalized vectors we basically calculate the dot product of two unit vectors multiple times. But a unit vector has the obvious property that increasing one of its elements always has to come with the decrease of another element. Thus, the maximum error can not occur for each operation (because this would imply that all operations have a result very close to 1). Using this intuition we arrive at the following theorem:

Theorem 3 (Maximum floating-point error for unit vector dot products). *Calculating the dot product of two unit vectors with length n has a maximum error of $(n + 1) \times \epsilon$.*

Proof Sketch: To break down this theorem we decompose the dot product. A dot product of two vectors of length n consists of n multiplications and $n - 1$ additions. We will discuss the rounding error resulting from the multiplications first.

To do so consider the intervals of $[2^{-i}, 2^{-i+1})$ for all $i > 0$. These intervals correspond with the intervals in which the distance between two consecutive floats is always the same. Additionally, this distance decreases/increases by a factor of 2 when increasing/decreasing i by one. For example the distance between two consecutive floats in the interval $[0.5, 1.0)$ is twice as big as the distance between two consecutive floats from the interval $[0.25, 0.5)$. Conversely, the maximum number of float that sum to 1.0 out of each interval is inversely correlated to the distance between the floats in this interval. For the previous example: At most 2 floats from $[0.5, 1.0)$ can sum to 1.0 (exactly 0.5 two times) and equivalently at most 4 floats from the interval of $[0.25, 0.5)$ can sum to 1.0 (exactly four times 0.25). Furthermore, we know that the maximum rounding in any interval is equivalent to the maximum distance between two floats in that interval (modulo factor 2). So the maximum rounding error if only using floats of the interval $[0.5, 1.0)$ is $2 \times \epsilon$. We can now replace any value of this interval with at most 2 values of the next smaller interval however as we increase the number of elements by a factor of two the maximum rounding error decreases by the same factor. So the maximum rounding error overall stays identical. Using this argument recursively we can see that the maximum combined rounding error of all n multiplications is bound by $2 \times \epsilon$. This argument can be applied as long as the results of the multiplications are great enough to be representable as floats and are not rounded to 0.0.

The sum of all those products is unfortunately more prone to errors as the possibility of adding small values to big values multiple times is the opportunity for more errors. Thus we can only limit the error to $(n - 1) \times \epsilon$ as all additions add an error of e in the worst case (as they may all be carried out in the biggest interval from above). This leads to a maximum error of $(2 + n - 1) \times \epsilon = (n + 1) \times \epsilon$ for a dot-product of vectors of length n.

For simplicity, we argued with real-valued vectors here. An analogous argument can be made for complex-valued vectors which increases the maximum rounding error by a constant factor of 4 only.

3 Practical Application

In this section, we are going to show how the theoretical considerations we made in the previous section can be used in an existing tool to prove the absence of relevant rounding errors and thus prove soundness.

3.1 The Verification Tool QIn

In [9], we presented a tool that is able to prove the correctness of quantum circuits based on a translation of the circuits into a classical host language followed by the application of a verification tool. In the paper mentioned above, we used JJBMC [1] as a verification tool which is a bounded model checker for Java annotated with JML. The basic idea for the translation is that one can automatically translate a given quantum circuit into an equivalent Java program using the standard matrix representation of quantum gates. The main drawback of this approach is that the translation into Java introduces floats instead of reals as the main algebraic data type. As we discussed, this will introduce rounding errors, and as long as these are not bounded or somewhat quantified the resulting verification becomes unsound.

3.2 Implementing the Approach

As QIn introduces floats in its translation it is a perfect match to implement the theoretical considerations we made in Sect. 2. Given a quantum circuit, we can add appropriate assertions after each measurement thus showing that the occurring floating-point errors are not relevant regarding the most likely result. In particular, we use Theorem 2 and turn it into a Java assertion. This can be checked by the verification tool along with all other proof obligations to show the absence of relevant rounding errors. An example of a translation of a measurement including such an assertion is given in Listing 1.1. The two variables *measureProb1* and *measureProb2* capture the probability of each outcome of the measurement. This can then be used to decide which measurement outcome is more probable and thus will be applied. The state gets updated accordingly and the result is stored in *measureVar*. Eventually, we add an assertion to check whether or not the probabilities for each outcome are far enough apart such that rounding errors could not have influenced their order. We extended QIn to allow for the automatic addition of soundness assertions as described above. The translation remains fully automatic and the soundness check may be toggled on or off via a command line option. No additional user input is necessary as we can derive the number of necessary operations during the translation process.

Listing 1.1. Example of the translation of a measurement including the assertion guaranteeing irrelevance of floating-point errors (**maxError** varies depending on context)

```
boolean $$_measureVar;
$$_measureProb1 = q0[0] * q0[0] + q0[1] * q0[1] +... ;
$$_measureProb2 = 1.0f - $$_measureProb1;
if ($$_measureProb2 > $$_measureProb1) {
    q0 = new float[]{0.0F, 0.0F, 0.0F, ... };
    $$_measureVar = true;
    assert $$_measureProb2 > $$_measureProb1 + maxError;
} else {
    q0 = new float[]{q0[0], q0[1], q0[2], ... };
    $$_measureVar = false;
    assert $$_measureProb1 > $$_measureProb2 + maxError;
}
```

3.3 Evaluation

Using the implementation outlined in the previous subsection we were able to prove that for all existing case studies of QIn, the translation of the circuits into Java was not introducing relevant floating-point errors (based on the observations made in Sect. 2). Not only that but the additional proof obligations introduce only minor increases in run time of the verification tool for almost all case studies. We observed that the times for verification with and without the additional assertions are very similar. A table comparing run times with and without soundness assertions is given in Table 1.

Table 1. Overview of all Case Studies presented in the QIn paper with the number of gates and qubits as well as the time to verify with and without soundness assertions

Case Study	#gates	#qubits	time w/o soundness (s)	time w/ soundness (s)
BB84	3	1	2.0	1.8
DeutschJozsa	9	4	5.0	6.8
Grover	10	2	2.6	2.9
GroverBroken	10	2	2.1	2.4
Shor	15	7	19.3 (period) + 20.1 (rest)	31.3 (per) + 20.1 (rest)
SuperdenseCoding	6	2	1.9	2.4

4 Related Work

Considering the pitfalls of floating-point arithmetic is a topic that has been examined by many researchers under various different aspects. Several general examinations have been published that tackle floating-point arithmetic and its challenges as a whole (e.g. [6,10]). This differs from our approach in that we use a subset of floating-point numbers (e.g., only from a certain interval) as well as operations (e.g., only base operations) and try to exploit the special properties that come with those restrictions (including the fact the special values are not a concern for us).

Additionally, there is a plethora of tools and approaches that tackle the challenge of verifying floating-point programs on different languages and abstraction levels. Examples of such work include support for floating-point arithmetic provided by Why3 [5]. Also, floating-point arithmetic was formalized in several well-known interactive theorem provers which allow the verification of complex properties [2,8,12]. However, all these approaches require a relatively high amount of user interaction in order to conduct proofs. In contrast, our approach focuses on a very small set of properties that we are able to prove fully automatically without additional user-provided specifications or other input.

In the area of verifying or simulating quantum circuits, floating-point arithmetic apparently has not caught too much attention yet. Fatima and Markov [4] acknowledge the potential errors floating-point arithmetic may introduce and present methods to reduce the number of operations needed for simulating quantum circuits. Combining our approach with their ideas seems like a promising direction for further research.

5   Conclusion

In this work, we have demonstrated how properties of floating-point arithmetic can be exploited to formally prove that rounding errors do not exceed defined bounds. We use this knowledge to derive conditions under which the simulation of a given quantum circuit will always compute the most likely result correctly – regardless of any rounding errors. Furthermore, we show how this can be implemented in an existing verification tool for hybrid quantum programs to prove its soundness. We show that with this combined approach a number of well-known quantum algorithms including Shor, Grover, and Deutsch could be proven correct and any type of perturbance through rounding errors could be ruled out.

References

1. Beckert, B., Kirsten, M., Klamroth, J., Ulbrich, M.: Modular verification of JML contracts using bounded model checking. In: Margaria, T., Steffen, B. (eds.) ISoLA 2020. LNCS, vol. 12476, pp. 60–80. Springer, Cham (2020). https://doi.org/10.1007/978-3-030-61362-4_4
2. Boldo, S., Melquiond, G.: Flocq: a unified library for proving floating-point algorithms in Coq. In: 2011 IEEE 20th Symposium on Computer Arithmetic, pp. 243–252. IEEE (2011)
3. Deutsch, D., Jozsa, R.: Rapid solution of problems by quantum computation. Proc. Math. Phys. Sci. **439**(1907), 553–558 (1992)
4. Fatima, A., Markov, I.L.: Faster schrödinger-style simulation of quantum circuits. In: 2021 IEEE International Symposium on High-Performance Computer Architecture (HPCA), pp. 194–207. IEEE (2021)
5. Fumex, C., Marché, C., Moy, Y.: Automating the verification of floating-point programs. In: Paskevich, A., Wies, T. (eds.) VSTTE 2017. LNCS, vol. 10712, pp. 102–119. Springer, Cham (2017). https://doi.org/10.1007/978-3-319-72308-2_7
6. Goldberg, D.: What every computer scientist should know about floating-point arithmetic. ACM Comput. Surv. **23**(1), 5–48 (1991)
7. Grover, L.K.: A fast quantum mechanical algorithm for database search. In: Proceedings of the Twenty-Eighth Annual ACM Symposium on Theory of Computing - STOC 1996, pp. 212–219. ACM Press (1996)
8. Jacobsen, C., Solovyev, A., Gopalakrishnan, G.: A parameterized floating-point formalizaton in HOL light. Electron. Notes Theor. Comput. Sci. **317**, 101–107 (2015)
9. Klamroth, J., Beckert, B., Scheerer, M., Denninger, O.: QIn: enabling formal methods to deal with quantum circuits. In: 2023 IEEE International Conference on Quantum Software (QSW), pp. 175–185. IEEE (2023)
10. Muller, J.M., et al.: Handbook of Floating-Point Arithmetic. Springer, Heidelberg (2018). https://doi.org/10.1007/978-3-319-76526-6

11. Shor, P.W.: Polynomial-time algorithms for prime factorization and discrete logarithms on a quantum computer. SIAM Rev. **41**(2), 303–332 (1999)
12. Yu, L.: A formal model of IEEE floating point arithmetic. Arch. Formal Proofs 91–104 (2013)

Linear Structure of Training Samples in Quantum Neural Network Applications

Alexander Mandl[1]([✉]) [iD], Johanna Barzen[1] [iD], Marvin Bechtold[1] [iD],
Michael Keckeisen[2] [iD], Frank Leymann[1] [iD], and Patrick K. S. Vaudrevange[2] [iD]

[1] Institute of Architecture of Application Systems, University of Stuttgart,
Universitätsstraße 38, 70569 Stuttgart, Germany
{mandl,barzen,bechtold,leymann}@iaas.uni-stuttgart.de
[2] TWT GmbH Science & Innovation, Ernsthaldenstr. 17, 70565 Stuttgart, Germany
{michael.keckeisen,patrick.vaudrevange}@twt-gmbh.de

Abstract. Quantum Neural Networks (QNNs) use sets of training samples supplied as quantum states to approximate unitary operators. Recent results show that the average quality, measured as the error of the approximation, depends on the number of available training samples and the degree of entanglement of these samples. Furthermore, the linear structure of the training samples plays a vital role in determining the average quality of the trained QNNs. However, these results evaluate the quality of QNNs independently of the classical pre- and post-processing steps that are required in real-world applications. How the linear structure of the training samples affects the quality of QNNs when the classical steps are considered is not fully understood. Therefore, in this work, we experimentally evaluate QNNs that approximate an operator that predicts the outputs of a function from the automotive engineering area. We find that the linear structure of the training samples also influences the quality of QNNs in this real-world use case.

Keywords: Quantum Neural Networks · Entanglement · Risk function · No-Free-Lunch

1 Introduction

The field of Quantum Machine Learning (QML) aims to employ quantum computers for solving machine learning tasks [6,17]. One such task is the reproduction of quantum operators using Quantum Neural Networks (QNNs) [3,7,10]. Similar to classical machine learning, QNNs are trained by adapting a given model in a supervised fashion until it can reproduce the given operator faithfully. However, as opposed to classical machine learning methods, QNNs can

The authors would like to thank Thomas Wolf for providing the car-model data and for support with the use case and Rahul Banerjee for useful discussions. This work was partially funded by the BMWK projects *PlanQK* (01MK20005N), *EniQmA* (01MQ22007B), and *SeQuenC* (01MQ22009B).

make use of the properties inherent to quantum computers to improve this training process. For example, entangled quantum states can be used to improve the generalization error after training [18,22].

For classical training data, however, the data has to be transformed into quantum states first to perform the training process [4,11,25]. Similarly, the predictions of the QNN have to be extracted from the measurements on the quantum computer [5]. Thus, training and using QNNs is a hybrid quantum-classical task that requires classical pre- and post-processing in addition to the classical optimization of quantum circuit parameters [11,24]. How these steps are performed influences the quality of the resulting QNNs.

In particular, the encoding of training data as quantum states influences the linear structure of the resulting quantum training samples. The linear structure includes the degree of entanglement of the prepared quantum states [18], as well as their linear independence and orthogonality [12]. Previous work has shown that this linear structure plays a critical role in predicting the quality of QNNs after the training process: Theoretical estimates for the QNN quality indicate a reduction in the quality of a trained QNN if the used training samples are linearly dependent or orthogonal [12,18]. However, these results evaluate the expected performance of QNN algorithms with respect to all possible operators that are to be approximated. Thus, it is unclear whether or not these results readily apply to practical applications of QNNs, where only one specific operator is of interest.

Therefore, in this work, we apply QNNs to a specific problem from automotive engineering: predicting the movement of a car's suspension system depending on road conditions. We use a quantum implementation of this predictor as a black box operator to study the effect of different compositions of training inputs on approximations of this operator. This is done by experimentally comparing the average quality of trained QNNs with respect to the black box operator on a simulator. This investigation highlights the importance of the state preparation operator in training QNNs, showing that certain ways of preparing training samples on the device are detrimental to the quality of the trained QNN.

This paper proceeds by introducing the operator that is approximated in this evaluation and presenting the background and the motivation for this work in Sect. 2. Section 3 presents related work on QNNs and the training data structure. Section 4 describes the quality measures used in our experiments and the setup and input data used. The experiment results are presented and discussed in Sect. 5 and summarized in Sect. 6.

2   Background and Motivation

This section introduces the fundamentals for QNNs training in Sect. 2.1. To study the effect of different compositions of training samples for QNNs, we use an application from automotive engineering. This application is described in detail in Sect. 2.2, before showing existing results on how QNN training benefits from entanglement (Sect. 2.3). These existing results provide the motivation for this work, which is further elaborated in Sect. 2.4.

2.1 Quantum Neural Networks

QNNs are used to approximate unitary operators on quantum computers by approximating this operator's behavior on a set of training samples [3,8]. The operator $U : \mathcal{H}_X \to \mathcal{H}_X$ that is approximated is referred to as the *target operator* and the QNN that is learned using the training data is referred to as the *hypothesis operator*. The operator U acts on the d-dimensional Hilbert space $\mathcal{H}_X$. The training data is a set $S = \{(|\psi_j\rangle, |\phi_j\rangle) \mid 1 \le j \le t\}$ containing training input-output pairs, where each output is obtained by applying the target operator to the associated input: $|\phi_j\rangle = U|\psi_j\rangle$.

In this work, we use Parameterized Quantum Circuits (PQCs) [5,9,16,20] to implement the QNN. A PQC is a quantum circuit $V(\vec{\theta})$ that is parameterized by a collection of real numbers $\vec{\theta}$ that are adjusted during the training process. The goal is to obtain a set of optimal parameters $\vec{\theta}^*$, such that the deviation of the outputs $V(\vec{\theta}^*)|\psi_j\rangle$ from the expected outputs $|\phi_j\rangle$ is minimal for each pair $(|\psi_j\rangle, |\phi_j\rangle) \in S$ [3,18]. This deviation is minimized by maximizing the fidelity $|\langle\phi_j|V(\vec{\theta})|\psi_j\rangle|^2$ [13]. Thus, the training process minimizes the *loss function*

$$L(\vec{\theta}) := 1 - \frac{1}{t} \sum_{j=1}^{t} \left| \langle\phi_j|V(\vec{\theta})|\psi_j\rangle \right|^2 . \tag{1}$$

Herein, $t = \text{card}(S)$ is the size of the set of training samples. Since the loss function calculates the average deviation of the outputs with respect to S, minimal loss implies that the QNN can reproduce the training samples correctly. In the following, we refer to a QNN that is trained using S as V_S.

2.2 Predicting Suspension Movement

As the target operator for our work, we consider a use case from the automotive engineering process: a predictor for the chassis movement of a car driving on a bumpy road. We use a simulation model of a simplified car, which is made up of a rigid chassis body that sits on a suspension system comprised of springs and dampers. Using the simulation model, different dynamic behavior can be deduced in the systems transfer function, mapping road excitation at a given frequency $\nu \in [0 \text{ Hz}, 4 \text{ Hz}]$ to the unitless ratio $W_U(\nu)$ of vertical chassis displacement per road bump height. This ratio is referred to as the *displacement ratio*. Figure 1 shows the displacement ratios within the applicable frequency range.

Therefore, this problem is a function mapping real-valued frequencies ν to real-valued displacement ratios $W_U(\nu)$. It is comprised of the quantum operator U, which is used in a larger algorithm with two additional operators: the *state preparation* operator $SP(\nu)$ and the *readout operator* M. These operators encode the inputs and extract the outputs of the quantum circuit. The prediction of the displacement ratio is performed by the operator U, which serves as the black box target operator for the experiments. It was initially obtained by training a PQC using classical data to reproduce the function in Fig. 1. We use four

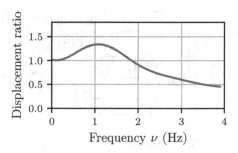

Fig. 1. The predictions of the simulation model using the unitary target operator U. It maps the real-valued frequency of road excitations to the real-valued displacement ratios according to the function in this plot.

qubits for this operator as this enabled us to reproduce the function accurately in the initial training step. The state preparation operator $SP(\nu)$ encodes the frequency ν as an input state $|\nu\rangle = SP(\nu)|0\rangle$ for U. It is implemented using RZ and RY rotations [2] that are parameterized by ν. After applying U, the readout operator extracts the displacement ratio from the state $U|\nu\rangle$. This is achieved by performing measurements to estimate the expectation value of $U|\nu\rangle$ with respect to an observable O. The readout operator uses the observable $O = (|0\rangle\langle 0| \otimes I^{\otimes 3})$ since its expectation value can be calculated by simple one-qubit measurements. Lastly, since the expectation value is in the interval $[0,1]$, it is rescaled with the maximal possible displacement ratio s that is predicted according to the function in Fig. 1. Thus the quantum circuit computes

$$W_U(\nu) = \langle \nu | U^\dagger O U | \nu \rangle \cdot s. \tag{2}$$

2.3   QNN Training with Entangled Training Samples

In this work, we use QNNs to reproduce the target operator U that is used in the chassis-movement prediction circuit $W_U(\nu)$. During the training of any QNN V_S, its accuracy is evaluated by the loss function (Eq. (1)). However, the loss function gives no indication of the quality of the hypothesis unitary on inputs that are unknown during training. To describe the quality of a QNN on unknown inputs, the *risk* $R(U, V_S)$ is used [12,15,18]. The risk is the average deviation between the expected output $U|x\rangle$ and the actual output $V_S|x\rangle$ with respect to all possible inputs $|x\rangle \in \mathcal{H}_X$ [12]. There are theoretical bounds on the expected risk in QNN training that can be used as estimates [15,18].

Particularly, the *Quantum No-Free-Lunch* (QNFL) theorem [15,18] gives a lower bound for the expected risk $\mathbb{E}_U [\mathbb{E}_S [R(U, V_S)]]$ with respect to all possible operators U and all possible sets of training samples S. It shows that the lower bound for the expected risk can be reduced by either increasing the number of training samples t or by using training samples of a high degree of entanglement [18]. This relationship is captured by the inequality

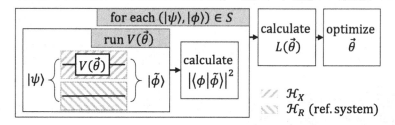

Fig. 2. One iteration of the optimization loop when training a PQC $V(\vec{\theta})$ with entangled states. Although the individual summands in the cost function are calculated with respect to the combined system $\mathcal{H}_X \otimes \mathcal{H}_R$, the PQC is applied to $\mathcal{H}_X$ only.

$$\mathbb{E}_U\left[\mathbb{E}_S\left[R(U, V_S)\right]\right] \geq 1 - \frac{(rt)^2 + d + 1}{d(d+1)}. \tag{3}$$

Herein, the degree of entanglement r is given by the Schmidt rank [13,18] with respect to the factorization $\mathcal{H}_X \otimes \mathcal{H}_R$ and $d = \dim(\mathcal{H}_X)$. Thus, the individual training sample inputs $|\psi\rangle$ and outputs $|\phi\rangle$ are elements of a combined space $\mathcal{H}_X \otimes \mathcal{H}_R$, where $\mathcal{H}_R$ is referred to as the *reference system*. Figure 2 shows one iteration of the adapted training process when a reference system is used for training a PQC with entangled quantum states. Since $V(\vec{\theta})$ is applied to $\mathcal{H}_X$ only, the output of the QNN for an input $|\psi\rangle$ is $|\tilde{\phi}\rangle = (V(\vec{\theta}) \otimes I)|\psi\rangle$. The loss function then averages the fidelity $|\langle\phi|\tilde{\phi}\rangle|^2$ with respect to S.

According to Eq. (3), the quality of the trained QNN is not governed solely by t but instead by the product $r \cdot t$. Therefore, sets of training samples comprised of t states of Schmidt rank r have the same lower bound for the risk in Eq. (3) as sets of training samples comprised of $r \cdot t$ states of Schmidt rank 1 [12]. However, this does not necessarily imply that this lower bound is saturated for a particular instance of minimal loss. Theoretical results show that two properties of the linear structure of the training samples influence the risk after training negatively. In particular, for pairwise orthogonal training samples or for linearly dependent training samples, the lower bound for the expected risk after training in Eq. (3) is not reached [12].

2.4   Motivation and Research Question

Although the theoretical restrictions on the structure of the training samples to minimize the risk in QNN training are known, so far these restrictions have only been experimentally evaluated for randomly generated target operators [12]. These experiments show that the risk increases depending on the linear structure of the training samples. However, they consider the average risk over all possible target operators, independently of possible pre- and post-processing of the algorithms [12]. Whether or not this increase in average risk also affects specific real-world use cases for QNNs is not fully understood. Therefore, in this work, we investigate the effect of the linear structure on the quality of a QNN in a real-world use case. As the use case, we consider the chassis movement predictor operator $W_U(\nu)$ presented in Sect. 2.2. Hence, the research question we investigate in this work is: *How does the structure of the input data influence the quality of a QNN for chassis movement prediction?* To answer this research question, we first discuss and select the applicable ways to measure the quality of the QNN prediction with respect to $W_U(\nu)$. We then experimentally evaluate QNNs that reproduce U on a simulator using training samples of varying linear structure using this quality measure.

3   Related Work

The theoretical results on QNFL theorems presented by Sharma et al. [18] and Poland et al. [15] build the fundamentals for the experiments in this work. These works give the bounds on the risk for arbitrary sets of training samples. For certain restricted sets of training samples, such as pairwise orthogonal and linearly dependent sets, these bounds are reevaluated and experimentally compared in [12]. These works evaluate the expected QNN quality with respect to all possible unitary target matrices and show that, in the worst case, an exponential-sized set S is required for the best approximations. However, Caro et al. [7] show that the required amount of training data is reduced when only efficiently implementable target operators are considered.

Our experiments require that the loss function for each training step is calculated by a quantum operator exactly. In practice, however, this loss function is estimated using a finite number of measurements. Wang et al. [23] show that the benefit of using entangled samples in QNN training is dependent on this number of measurements. Thus, their theoretical investigation serves as further guidelines on when training using entangled samples is beneficial.

4   Methods and Experiment Design

To answer the research question posed in Sect. 2.4, we experimentally evaluate the quality of QNNs that approximate the operator U. These QNNs are trained with training samples of varying linear structure on a simulator to compare the effect on the QNN quality. For this experimental evaluation, it is first required to specify how the quality of predictions for the displacement ratio (Eq. (2)) is measured. Thus, Sect. 4.1 describes the different error functions that are used in this work to evaluate the approximation quality. Afterward, Sect. 4.2 describes the properties of the different structures of training samples that are investigated, and Sect. 4.3 presents the experiment setup and implementation.

4.1   Quality Measurements

The first measure for the quality of the learned operators V_S is the risk. The risk is given as the average distance between the expected output $U|x\rangle$ and the actual output $V_S|x\rangle$ with respect to all possible inputs, i.e., all possible four-qubit states $|x\rangle \in \mathcal{H}^{\otimes 4}$ in our case. Since we train QNNs on a simulator, we can extract V_S as a matrix from the simulator. This allows to use an equivalent representation of the risk [15,18] to calculate it in our experiments as

$$R(U, V_S) = 1 - \frac{d + \left|\text{Tr}[U^\dagger V_S]\right|^2}{d(d+1)}, \tag{4}$$

for the $d = 2^4$ dimensional operator U from Sect. 2.2. Since $\left|\text{Tr}[U^\dagger V_S]\right|^2$ is maximal if and only if $V_S = U$ (see [12]), Eq. (4) further shows that the risk is minimal for exact reproductions of the target operator U.

Although the risk measures how well the QNN approximates the target operator U, it comes with two downsides. First, extracting the exact matrix that is learned by the QNN is not possible on a quantum computer. Thus, calculating Equation (4) as described above is not always possible. Second, the risk considers the quality of the QNN outputs with respect to all possible inputs. However, for our use case, only QNN outputs for inputs that are prepared by the state preparation operator SP (see Sect. 2.2) are relevant. Therefore, we consider a second measure for the quality of a QNN in the following.

Like the target operator U, the hypothesis operator V_S is used in a larger circuit $W_{V_S}(\nu)$. The displacement ratio $W_{V_S}(\nu)$ is the relevant quantity to measure the quality of V_S, when applied in the context of this application. Therefore, we use a function that quantifies the error with respect to the real-valued functions $W_U(\nu)$ and $W_{V_S}(\nu)$. A common choice for comparing functions is the *squared error* or L_2-loss $(W_U(\nu) - W_{V_S}(\nu))^2$ [17]. To approximate and compare the squared error over multiple hypothesis operators using a finite set of evaluations, we compute the *mean squared error* (MSE):

$$\hat{R}_{\text{MSE}}(U, V_S) = \frac{1}{N} \sum_{i=1}^{N} (W_U(\nu_i) - W_{V_S}(\nu_i))^2. \tag{5}$$

Herein, N is the number of function evaluations and ν_i is sampled uniformly at random in the applicable range $[0, 4]$.

4.2   Structure of Training Samples

Since we strive to reproduce the target operator U with maximal precision, we use training samples such that $r \cdot t = d$. This implies using Eq. (3) that the expected risk should be minimal after the training process. We evaluate if this is the case using the above quality measurements for training samples of maximal degree of entanglement and for training samples comprised of separable states. This section describes the *training sample compositions* that are summarized in Table 1, i.e. the different ways of composing sets of randomly generated training samples of varying linear structure that are studied in the experiments.

Table 1. The four different compositions of training samples for the experiments.

Training Sample Composition	Description
MAX_ENT	One maximally entangled training sample (Schmidt rank $r = d = 2^4$). Since there is only one training sample in this case, the studied sets of maximally entangled training samples are always linearly independent and pairwise non-orthogonal
LD_NONORTHO	Linearly dependent training samples of Schmidt rank 1 that are pairwise non-orthogonal
LI_NONORTHO	Linearly independent training samples of Schmidt rank 1 that are pairwise non-orthogonal
LI_ORTHO	Linearly independent training samples of Schmidt rank 1 that are pairwise orthogonal

Maximal Entanglement. We randomly create sets of training samples comprised of only one maximally entangled training sample, referred to as MAX_ENT in the following. The theoretical results in Sect. 2.3 show that the lower bound for the expected risk in this case is zero. Thus, the experiments investigate if this is also the case for concrete operators.

No Entanglement. As discussed in Sect. 2.3, there are two properties that influence the theoretical bounds on the risk for QNN training in the absence of entanglement. The first one is the linear dependence of the training samples. Thus, we compare training samples that are linearly independent (referred to as LI in the following) with training samples that are linearly dependent (referred to as LD). The second property is the orthogonality of the training samples. This property is evaluated by comparing sets of training samples that are pairwise orthogonal (referred to as ORTHO) with sets of training samples that are pairwise non-orthogonal (referred to as NONORTHO). Since it is not possible to create states that are linearly dependent and, at the same time, orthogonal, three combinations of these properties remain to be investigated for unentangled samples.

4.3   Implementation

The implementations and the results of the performed experiments are available online[1]. For the experiments, we simulate the training process of PQCs V_S using the four different compositions for training samples. The target operator for this training process is the operator U presented in Sect. 2.2. For the sets of training samples S, we use SciPy [21] to randomly sample training inputs $|\psi\rangle \in \mathcal{H}_X \otimes \mathcal{H}_R$ of the linear structure summarized in Table 1. For a detailed discussion on how these requirements are enforced for random training sample inputs, refer to the

---

[1] https://github.com/UST-QuAntiL/linear_struct_QNN.

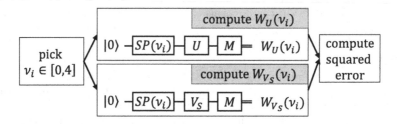

Fig. 3. We compare U and V_S by computing the predicted displacement ratios $W_U(\nu)$ and $W_{V_S}(\nu)$ respectively and compute $\hat{R}_{\mathrm{MSE}}(U, V_S)$ by averaging the squared difference of these outputs.

appendix of [12]. The expected output $|\phi\rangle$ for each training sample is computed by performing the multiplication $(U \otimes I)|\psi\rangle$ classically.

To obtain a sufficient number of evaluations to compute the average quality, we perform the training process described in Fig. 2 for 100 different randomly generated sets S for each composition. After the training process, we extract the prediction of the hypothesis operators as described in Fig. 3. Thus, for each trained V_S, we evaluate $W_U(\nu)$ and $W_{V_S}(\nu)$ for $N = 100$ frequency inputs ν_i selected uniformly at random and calculate $\hat{R}_{\mathrm{MSE}}(U, V_S)$ according to Eq. (5). Furthermore, we calculate the risk $R(U, V_S)$ for each operator according to Eq. (4) by extracting the complex-valued matrix V_S from the simulator.

As the PQCs for these experiments, we use an ansatz similar to the circuits given in [20] implemented in Pytorch [14]. The ansatz is comprised of 25 layers initiated by U3 gates, which entail generic single-qubit rotations with three Euler angles as parameters on each qubit [2]. These are subsequently followed by a circular application of CNOT gates on the qubits. The final layer of the ansatz ends with an additional layer of U3 gates. Lastly, the optimization routine uses the Pytorch implementation of the Adam optimizer [1] for 1000 iterations, where each iteration equates to one calculation of the cost function for the whole set of training samples S. We chose 1000 iterations since it allows us to reliably obtain QNNs with $L(\vec{\theta}) < 10^{-4}$.

5 Experiment Results and Discussion

In order to answer the research question of this work, the average quality of the QNNs for the different compositions of training samples is compared. The results are summarized in Fig. 4. The markers in this plot show $\hat{R}_{\mathrm{MSE}}(U, V_S)$ and $R(U, V_S)$ for each composition of training samples. The error bars show one standard deviation from the mean to indicate the spread of the obtained risks. Additionally, the dotted lines indicate the expected risk w.r.t. all possible quantum inputs for each composition of training samples. These expected risks are calculated according to the bounds in [12].

The results presented in Fig. 4 show a clear relationship between the expected risk and the experimentally evaluated average risk $R(U, V_S)$. The expected risk

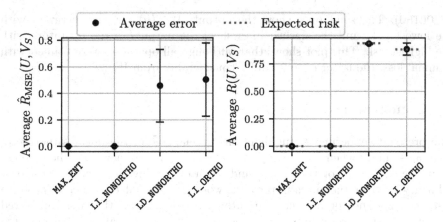

Fig. 4. Average of $\hat{R}_{\mathrm{MSE}}(U, V_S)$ and $R(U, V_S)$ for each of the compositions of the training samples given in Table 1. The error bars show one standard deviation from the average. The dotted lines indicate the lower bound for the expected risk.

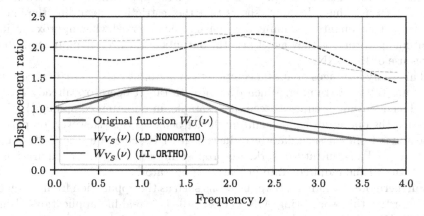

Fig. 5. The effect of the increased risk for LD_NONORTHO and LI_ORTHO training samples. This figure shows the learned unitary operators of the lowest error (solid lines) and the highest error (dashed lines) for these cases.

is within one standard deviation of the actual risk after training. Thus, they present additional evidence that, although the expected risk for QNNs is usually given as a lower bound with respect to all possible operators, it can also be used to estimate the performance of a learning algorithm in practice. Furthermore, an increase in the average error for LD_NONORTHO and LI_ORTHO is present for both $\hat{R}_{\mathrm{MSE}}(U, V_S)$ and $R(U, V_S)$, which shows that this increase in risk also negatively affects the classical predictions $W_{V_S}(\nu)$ of the application.

In Fig. 5, we specifically highlight the effect of this increased error. This plot shows the prediction of the displacement ratio $W_{V_S}(\nu)$ using two learned operators V_S each for the cases with non-zero average risk (LD_NONORTHO and

`LI_ORTHO`). The solid lines show the outputs $W_{V_S}(\nu)$ for the operators with the lowest risk, and the dashed lines show the outputs of the operators with the highest risk. This plot shows that, although all operators were trained with minimal loss, the latter outputs differ considerably from $W_U(\nu)$.

6   Conclusion

The presented experiments highlight the crucial role of the linear structure of training samples when training QNNs. The experiments show that the increase in approximation error that was found when evaluating the average error over arbitrary problem instances in previous work [12] also affects concrete problem instances. For the application from automotive engineering that was considered in this work, this error is apparent in the risk with respect to all possible quantum inputs for linearly dependent and for pairwise orthogonal inputs. Furthermore, even when the evaluation of the approximation error is restricted to only consider the error of the classical outputs of the predictor application, the increase in error is present. Thus, this work shows that the restrictions regarding the linear structure of the quantum training data have to be observed when approximating quantum operators, as they affect also the outputs of the overall application that makes use of the QNN.

This study leverages quantum computer simulators to easily create necessary quantum states for training. When dealing with target operators already represented as quantum circuits, as seen, for example, in quantum compiling [19,22], accessing the operator on the quantum device achieves this. However, preparing these states from classical data introduces further challenges in the QNN training process. Thus, in future work, we propose investigating the computational complexity of the required state preparation operator.

Furthermore, for industrial applications such as the application from automotive industry, this work brings QNNs closer to their real-life application. Using QNN training it is possible to derive simpler quantum circuits for the target operator, thus increasing its quality on noisy machines. We plan to continue our research into this direction by examining larger operators in the future.

References

1. Documentation on torch.optim.Adam. https://pytorch.org/docs/stable/generated/torch.optim.Adam.html. Accessed 31 Aug 2023
2. Qiskit: Summary of quantum operations: Standard rotations. https://qiskit.org/documentation/tutorials/circuits/3_summary_of_quantum_operations.html#Standard-Rotations. Accessed 30 Aug 2023
3. Beer, K., et al.: Training deep quantum neural networks. Nat. Commun. **11**(1), 808 (2020)
4. Benedetti, M., Garcia-Pintos, D., Perdomo, O., Leyton-Ortega, V., Nam, Y., Perdomo-Ortiz, A.: A generative modeling approach for benchmarking and training shallow quantum circuits. NPJ Quant. Inf. **5**(1), 45 (2019)

5. Benedetti, M., Lloyd, E., Sack, S., Fiorentini, M.: Parameterized quantum circuits as machine learning models. Quant. Sci. Technol. **4**(4), 043001 (2019)
6. Biamonte, J., Wittek, P., Pancotti, N., Rebentrost, P., Wiebe, N., Lloyd, S.: Quantum machine learning. Nature **549**(7671), 195–202 (2017)
7. Caro, M.C., et al.: Generalization in quantum machine learning from few training data. Nat. Commun. **13**(1), 4919 (2022)
8. Cerezo, M., et al.: Variational quantum algorithms. Nat. Rev. Phys. **3**(9), 625–644 (2021)
9. Du, Y., Hsieh, M.H., Liu, T., Tao, D.: Expressive power of parametrized quantum circuits. Phys. Rev. Res. **2**, 033125 (2020)
10. Du, Y., Hsieh, M.H., Liu, T., You, S., Tao, D.: Learnability of quantum neural networks. PRX Quant. **2**, 040337 (2021)
11. Leymann, F., Barzen, J.: The bitter truth about gate-based quantum algorithms in the NISQ era. Quant. Sci. Technol. **5**(4), 044007 (2020)
12. Mandl, A., Barzen, J., Leymann, F., Vietz, D.: On reducing the amount of samples required for training of QNNs: constraints on the linear structure of the training data. arXiv:2309.13711 [quant-ph] (2023)
13. Nielsen, M.A., Chuang, I.L.: Quantum Computation and Quantum Information. Cambridge University Press, Cambridge (2010)
14. Paszke, A., et al.: PyTorch: an imperative style, high-performance deep learning library. In: Advances in Neural Information Processing Systems, vol. 32 (2019)
15. Poland, K., Beer, K., Osborne, T.J.: No free lunch for quantum machine learning. arXiv:2003.14103 [quant-ph] (2020)
16. Schuld, M., Bocharov, A., Svore, K.M., Wiebe, N.: Circuit-centric quantum classifiers. Phys. Rev. A **101**(3) (2020)
17. Schuld, M., Petruccione, F.: Supervised Learning with Quantum Computers. Quantum Science and Technology. Springer, Heidelberg (2018). https://doi.org/10.1007/978-3-319-96424-9
18. Sharma, K., Cerezo, M., Holmes, Z., Cincio, L., Sornborger, A., Coles, P.J.: Reformulation of the no-free-lunch theorem for entangled datasets. Phys. Rev. Lett. **128**(7), 070501 (2022)
19. Sharma, K., Khatri, S., Cerezo, M., Coles, P.J.: Noise resilience of variational quantum compiling. New J. Phys. **22**(4), 043006 (2020)
20. Sim, S., Johnson, P.D., Aspuru-Guzik, A.: Expressibility and entangling capability of parameterized quantum circuits for hybrid quantum-classical algorithms. Adv. Quant. Technol. **2**(12), 1900070 (2019)
21. Virtanen, P., et al.: SciPy 1.0: fundamental algorithms for scientific computing in python. Nat. Methods **17**, 261–272 (2020)
22. Volkoff, T., Holmes, Z., Sornborger, A.: Universal compiling and (no-)free-lunch theorems for continuous-variable quantum learning. PRX Quant. **2**, 040327 (2021)
23. Wang, X., Du, Y., Tu, Z., Luo, Y., Yuan, X., Tao, D.: Transition role of entangled data in quantum machine learning. arXiv:2306.03481 [quant-ph] (2023)
24. Weder, B., Barzen, J., Leymann, F., Zimmermann, M.: Hybrid quantum applications need two orchestrations in superposition: a software architecture perspective. In: Proceedings of the 18th IEEE International Conference on Web Services (ICWS 2021), pp. 1–13. IEEE (2021)
25. Weigold, M., Barzen, J., Leymann, F., Salm, M.: Encoding patterns for quantum algorithms. IET Quant. Commun. **2**(4), 141–152 (2021)

Towards Higher Abstraction Levels in Quantum Computing

Hermann Fürntratt[1]([⊠]) [iD], Paul Schnabl[2] [iD], Florian Krebs[1] [iD],
Roland Unterberger[1] [iD], and Herwig Zeiner[1] [iD]

[1] JOANNEUM RESEARCH Forschungsgesellschaft mbH, Graz, Austria
{hermann.fuerntratt,florian.krebs,roland.unterberger,
herwig.zeiner}@joanneum.at
[2] University of Technology, Graz, Austria
paul.schnabl@student.tugraz.at

Abstract. This work is a survey and a position paper towards a higher abstraction in quantum computing (QC) programming frameworks and software development kits (SDKs). Since in 2003, Peter Shor complained about the limited increase in the number of QC algorithms [19], we see an urgent need to bridge the gap between well-established classical physics and quantum physics so that approaches become more intuitive, and - hopefully - more quantum algorithms can be discovered. In service-based hybrid QC frameworks, where algorithms need to be partitioned into quantum and classical tasks, we look at the methods available and the abstractions used.

For this paper we have investigated the various levels of abstraction in Silq, Qrisp, OpenQl, Qiskit, Cirq, IonQ, and Ocean, which are originated in the QC domain, as well as CUDA Quantum, rooted in the classical software domain. With the rise of Large Language Models (LLMs), we have also explored the capabilities of LLM-powered tools like GitHub Copilot, which currently represents the top level of abstraction.

Keywords: Abstraction · Quantum Computing · Software Engineering · Hybrid Systems

1 Introduction

Abstraction is a fundamental principle in software development that helps manage complexity, improve code readability, and enhance code reusability. It allows developers to focus on essential aspects of a problem while hiding unnecessary details [1,3]. In quantum computing, abstraction ensures hardware independence as well [4]. To make quantum devices work, an interdisciplinary approach is needed in two different domains:

- the physics domain, providing fundamental knowledge how to create devices that follow the rules of quantum mechanics.

Funded by the Federal Ministry of the Republic of Austria, responsible for Climate Action, Environment, Energy, Mobility, Innovation and Technology.

F. Monti et al. (Eds.): ICSOC 2023 Workshops, LNCS 14518, pp. 162–173, 2024.
https://doi.org/10.1007/978-981-97-0989-2_13

– the computer science domain, which controls QC hardware, but also tries to develop algorithms for solving a wide range of problems, preferably with quantum advantage.

A huge progress[1,2] has been made on quantum hardware in the last year, but challenges like a high error rate or limited scalability still have a significant impact on quantum software design [8]. Computation needs to be split between classical and quantum devices, and thus between the two domains. As their domain specific languages (DSLs) are remarkably different, adapting their levels of abstraction would facilitate heterogeneous computing.

This paper is organized in the following manner. In Sect. 2, we present a taxonomy of abstraction levels based on [15] and explore its impact from different points of view. In Sect. 3, we analyse the selected quantum computing frameworks and SDKs for their overall properties, and especially, which kind of abstraction they support. We evaluate, to what extend the revealed abstractions lead to a higher level of understanding. Finally, Sect. 4 draws a conclusion on what to improve in the near future and briefly discusses possible long-term developments.

2   Levels of Abstraction

In the computer science domain, we deal with different levels of abstraction. Our software engineering goal is to translate high-level requests (e.g. "solve the problem of climate change") into low-level commands for devices that compute possible solutions. Each level of abstraction represents a degree of complexity, i.e. the higher the level of abstraction, the lower the level of complexity.

So we define the level of *algorithms* above the level of *control flow* abstraction and *data* abstraction. As quantum computing is at a very early stage of development, the concepts for programming quantum devices are focused at a very low level (i.e. circuits and gates). Due to the nature of quantum physics, and - not yet perfect - hardware, we are currently only able to create small programs (circuits) that contain a very limited amount of global variables (qubits and ancillas) with no loops but a small amount of control flow branching (controlled gates). More abstractions such as *control flow loops* or *garbage collection* are on the way (with loop unrolling and uncomputation), as described in the next section.

From a classical software engineering point of view, with increased availability of well-known abstractions used in the QC domain (e.g. arithmetic operations, client-server, publisher-subscriber, . . .) and more qubits, we will get more classical algorithms on quantum devices. QC devices will evolve to contain additional

---

[1] Quantinuum Launches the Most Benchmarked Quantum Computer in the World; https://www.quantinuum.com/news/quantinuum-launches-the-most-benchmarked-quantum-computer-in-the-world-and-publishes-all-the-data; 2023.

[2] AQT erreicht Quantum Volume von 128; https://www.uibk.ac.at/de/newsroom/2023/aqt-erreicht-quantum-volume-von-128/; 2023.

functionality. Hence transferring classical abstractions to the quantum domain is one way to go. The other, much harder way for pure quantum computing is to recognise, that we don't have any solid mental model yet, on which to build new quantum algorithms like those of Shor, Grover or HHL. One possible reason might be human convenience, because it would require us to think radically differently than we are used to. And after Mermin's famous quote to better "Shut up and calculate!" than to think of new ways in the quantum domain, it seems difficult to motivate people to leave the established paths and to explore new territories (which is considered as embarrassing by physicists such as Sean Carroll).

Table 1 shows a selection of abstractions used for evaluation in the following section. The items are ordered by increasing complexity.

Table 1. Taxonomy of selected abstractions.

Abstraction type	Example
Textual description	"Write a grover algorithm in qiskit"
Algorithms in hybrid systems	QAOA()
Control flow between systems	Compiler pragma "__qpu__", "__cpu__", "__gpu__"
Algorithms within QC system	HHL()
Control flow within QC system	for_loop()
Circuit abstractions	DAGCircuit
Data abstractions	$\mathbb{B}$, QuantumFloat

3   Analysed SDKs

3.1   Silq - ETH Zurich

Created 2020. An imperative programming language [2] which claims to provide a higher level of abstraction and to be more intuitive than traditional quantum computing languages (e.g. Quipper [6]).

Benefits. Usage of subroutines with generic parameters. Increased readability of code. Silq introduces a type system for classical and quantum data types. It allows (explicit) data type conversion. Silq supports safe automatic uncomputing (disentangling ancillas via `qfree` annotation). It provides control flow pattern like `for/while` loops and conditionals that transform to proper gate representation.

```
def solve[n:!ℕ](x:𝔹^n)lifted{
    y:=0:𝔹;
```

Fig. 1. Silq: function definition with parameter x, which is a variable array of n boolean quantum states.

Drawbacks. Silq's domain specific language is designed to be easily processed by the Silq parser, but does not necessarily lead to better readability in the context of classical programming languages. Silq provides no backend interface.

Abstractions

- Data types $\mathbb{1}, \mathbb{B}, \mathbb{N}, \mathbb{Z}, \mathbb{Q}, \mathbb{R}$ (only $\mathbb{B}$, which is boolean, is quantum-allowed)
- Control flow loops and conditionals
- Uncomputation[3]

Conclusion. Silq is a pionieer among quantum programming languages, as it initiates the evolution from plain quantum circuits programming to imperative programming with mixed data types. The claim to be "more intuitive" is clearly within the domain of physics. In the domain of computer science many abstractions are partly counter intuitive - i.e. they evoke different meanings (e.g. $\tau\hat{}\text{n}$ for a vector definition τ of length n, vs. τ to the n exponentiation) (See footnote 3). See Fig. 1.

3.2   Qrisp - Fraunhofer FOKUS

Created 2023. A programming language[4], strongly inspired by Silq, and intentionally similar to Qiskit. Qrisp is a modern Python framework for higher level quantum computer programming. It offers a classically inspired type system, with integrated floating point arithmetic and a RESTful backend interface.

Benefits. Qrisp is a lightweight framework using the Python idiom [20] aiming towards user-friendly programming[5]. Qrisp defines base data types like `Qubit` and `Clbit` (classical). It has a sophisticated qubit management (`QuantumVariable`), and a sophisticated circuit management (parameterised circuits) as well. Qrisp offers a fine grained abstraction for `Operation` and `Instruction`. It provides additional quantum data types (e.g. `QuantumArray` or `QuantumDictionary`) Qrisp supports safe (automatic) uncomputing (disentangle ancillas via `@auto_uncompute` decorator or manual `uncompute()` call). It provides optimised control flow pattern like `for/while` loops (`IterationEnvironment`) and conditionals (`ConditionalEnvironment`). Qrisp contains a submodule with 9 well-known quantum algorithms (e.g. QFT, QPE, HHL, . . .). A small client-server simulation of several quantum computers within a network is available.

Drawbacks. Floating point encoding is restricted by phase angle resolution. 32-bit arithmetic may require a large (40k+) amount of RZ and CX gates.

Abstractions

- Data abstraction with types: `QuantumFloat, Bool, Char, String, Array, Dictionary`

---

[3] Documentation Silq - High-level Quantum Programming; https://silq.ethz.ch; ETH Zurich.

[4] Qrisp 0.2 - documentation; https://www.qrisp.eu/general/changelog/0.2.html#v0-2; Fraunhofer FOKUS.

[5] Python is ranked within the top 3 of currently most popular programming languages according to rating sites.

- Control abstraction with array processing
- Control flow loops and conditionals
- Supports symbolic development
- Abstract parameters for parameterised circuits (e.g. `Symbol('phi')`)
- Algorithm abstraction (e.g. for QFT, QPE, HHL)
- Automatic uncomputation [18]
- Sevice abstraction with `VirtualBackend`
- Distributed client-server communication model

Conclusion. Qrisp is a lightweight quantum programming framework that continues the evolution from pure gate-based quantum programming - which is considered to be low level - towards programming paradigms used in modern classical programming languages. With the abstraction of classical data types like float and its corresponding arithmetic implementation based on semi-boolean polynomials [17], it tries to open the door to classical algorithms. Apart from the abstraction, Qrisp also provides specialised components (e.g. global Mølmer-Sørensen gates) to optimize low-level circuits for specific quantum hardware (i.e. ion traps).

3.3   OpenQl - QuTech

Created 2017. Hardware-agnostic programming is an important step towards an algorithm-centred development. The OpenQl quantum computing framework offers that possibility. It has been developed at the university of Delft, with a layered programming interface in Python and C++ and its own compiler - cQasm [10] that decomposes gates, and compiles the circuit sources to platform independent assembler code, which is then transpiled and optimised for various simulation and hardware backends (e.g. the spin-2 or starmon-5 instance, which can be accessed via the Quantum Inspire platform [21]). For a Python based example[6] see Fig. 2. OpenQl's clear preference is on circuit based algorithm development with cQasm.

Benefits. OpenQl uses the Python and C++ idiom. It supports a common quantum gate set [9] that allows access to an electron spin based quantum dot system.

```
import openql as ql

ql.initialize()

ql.set_option('output_dir', 'output')
ql.set_option('log_level', 'LOG_INFO')

platform = ql.Platform('my_platform', 'none')

nqubits = 3
program = ql.Program('my_program', platform, nqubits)
kernel = ql.Kernel('my_kernel', platform, nqubits)

for i in range(nqubits):
    kernel.prepz(i)

kernel.x(0)
kernel.hadamard(1)
kernel.cz(2, 0)
kernel.measure(0)
kernel.measure(1)

program.add_kernel(kernel)

program.compile()
```

Fig. 2. OpenQl example algorithm in Python.

---

[6] OpenQl read the docs; QuTech TU Delft; https://openql.readthedocs.io/en/latest/,.

Drawbacks. The Qubit topology must be given manually before compiling. Currently, no error occurs if the hardware topology does not match with the compiled program.

Abstractions

- Uses layered approach from `Platform` to `Program`, incorporating one or more SPSVERBc24s to describe an algorithm.
- Abstraction also aims at compiler level.

Conclusion. QuTech is mainly focusing in their high level program language OpenQl, which provides a library of common quantum expression. The input file is a Pyhton script that imports modules, and gives a representation of an algorithm that OpenQl understands. An OpenQl algorithm is usually a complete program and consists of different kernels. Each of these kernels represents gates of different kinds in the low level cQasm language or other quantum backends.

3.4   Qiskit - IBM

Created 2017. Qiskit is by far the most prominent collection of quantum software for gate-based programming. It offers hardware access to various backends - not only IBM ones, and several simulation environments. Due to a large amount of education resources (examples, tutorials, classes, . . .), which are available online (e.g.[7]), and a concise development roadmap[8], Qiskit continues to drive innovation towards distributed heterogeneous computing for quantum advantage.

Benefits. Qiskit is a comprehensive development platform with multiple SDKs (3–5, depending on Qiskit version). It uses the Python idiom and offers a sophisticated circuit management (parameterised circuits and sub-circuits). Furthermore, algorithms for variational *threaded primitives* for improved modularity (`PrimitiveJob`). Qiskit has a *quantum serverless* cloud-based programming model for distributing tasks easily between CPU, GPU and quantum processors (QPUs) (announced for 2023). The comprehensive implementation of (68) gates is partly templated. Backends (`BackendV2`) have a more intuitive semantic than in the previous version.

Drawbacks. Due to the fast pace in the Qiskit software development life cycle (in 2022: 15 version updates, 2023: 12 updates until Sept.) [16], deprecated methods/classes are keeping the learning curve steep.[9] IBM's convention of *little endian* qubit order causes interoperability issues.

Abstractions

- Abstraction of opaque gates, i.e. gates that are not unrolled.

---

[7] IBM Quantum Documentation; https://docs.quantum-computing.ibm.com/; IBM Corporation.

[8] IBM Quantum Computing Roadmap; https://www.ibm.com/quantum/www.ibm.com-/quantum/roadmap; IBM Corporation.

[9] Steep in the sense of *requiring effort to stay up-to-date.*

- Abstraction of composite gate, which represents a sub-circuit
- Representation of `DAGCircuit`, as directed acyclic graph (for scheduling optimisation)
- Control flow with conditionals and `for_loop()`, but only for classical registers
- Some high level algorithm abstraction (e.g. Grover), but in general more explicit versions (e.g. `SciPyRealEvolver`)
- Abstraction of devices/simulators (i.e. `QiskitRuntimeService`) with job based communication

Conclusion. Qiskit offers plenty of functionality, especially in the circuit and backend area. Algorithms are also provided, but due to a software paradigm switch recently, many algorithms are marked deprecated. Abstraction is currently focused on job distribution in a cloud environment, which is important for heterogeneous computing.

3.5 Cirq - Google AI Group

Created 2018. Cirq is a lightweight quantum SDK from the Google AI Group. Cirq aims to build quantum algorithms with gates. The algorithms can run on a simulator or one of several hardware backends (Google's own hardware devices are accessible only in limited special cases). Realistic conditions can be simulated using noise models. For control flow, conditionals are available, but only for classical registers. Qubit topologies may be linear or in 2D grid order. To simulate error correction, stabilizer classes are available.

Benefits. Cirq is focused on algorithm development. It uses the Python idiom. Tutorials[10] cover a large area of research topics. The framework allows to create custom gates with higher logic levels (Qutrits, ...).

Drawbacks. The fact that the qubit topology has to be specified by the user (e.g. `GridQubit()`) might be a requirement for certain algorithms like quantum walk(See footnote 10), but is in general not considered to be of advantage for algorithm development. It is better to hide the topology, as transpilers take care of optimising the circuit for a target device.

Abstractions.

- Control workflow abstraction covers conditional branching for classical registers.
- Properties of single qubits (or qubit pairs) may be visualised as heatmap.

Conclusion. Cirq's aims towards the circuitry. It allows to create and run quantum circuits with different topologies (linear or 2d-grid) in simulators or on quantum hardware. Noise models can be applied and custom n-level logic (Qutrits or n-Qudits) can be developed and tested.

---

[10] Experiments using quantum circuits; https://quantumai.google/cirq/experiments; Google AI.

3.6   IonQ

IonQ has built several generations of high performance quantum hardware which are available via Google Cloud Marketplace or Amazon and Microsoft web services. The provided API uses a RESTful architecture, where quantum programs can be send to the cloud service which return an HTTP-based response. Additionally an *OpenAPI* service is provided to use any code of any programming language.

Benefits. IonQ offers a cloud service based approach. It can run Qiskit programs with IonQ backends. IonQ understands Q# programs and most of the common programming language of the user choice.

Drawbacks. Only a few tutorials are available.

Abstractions

– Cloud service based approach, with companies such as Microsoft, Amazon and Google as cloud provider. User which are familiar with those services can easily execute quantum based algorithms.

Conclusion. IonQ focuses on delivering the quantum computers into big cloud service providers, which provide a common user interface that has already been established with classical services.

3.7   Ocean - D-Wave

D-Wave has been one of the first companies to offer commercial quantum annealing technology. Ocean software is a suite of open source Python tools for solving problems with D-Wave quantum annealing hardware. The first release dates back to 2018. It offers hardware access to D-Wave QPUs and simulation environments on the local CPU.

Benefits. Ocean is an open-source SDK with a Python idiom. It offers hybrid solvers that combine quantum and classical computing resources. Furthermore, high level abstractions for optimization problems are available, but also plugins to interface Qiskit via D-Wave.

Drawbacks. Since annealing systems are not considered to be universal QC devices, the problem domain for annealer is mainly limited to optimization. The graph of a formulated Ising (QUBO) model has to match the topology of the hardware, otherwise qubits are unused and constrain the problem size [22]

Abstractions

– Abstraction of various optimisers are available
– Abstractions for (hybrid) workflows are available as well.

Conclusion. The Ocean SDK is focused on solving optimization problems and offers many tutorials and an ease-to-use interface to quantum annealers.

3.8 CUDA Quantum

Created 2022. The CUDA Quantum framework is Nvidia's approach to close the gap between the QC domain an the classical domain with a scalable and performant heterogeneous system [13]. The platform offers a unified programming model to run distributed computing tasks on QPUs along with GPUs and CPUs. Programming language is a templated version of C++. The compiler and simulator are part of the Nvidia ecosystem.

Benefits. The framework uses the C++ idiom with meta templates. Communication channels are abstracted away by the compiler using pragmas. Simulations can take advantage of GPU acceleration. It allows great flexibility in the interplay

```
// A qubit is a qudit with 2 levels.
using qubit = qudit<2>;
```

Fig. 3. Cuda Quantum: templated type definition of quantum data types with focus on future developments.

between simulator and hardware backend. Just by switching the startup parameter --qpu, the application may target different devices. Due to containerisation, the platform may easily migrate from on-premises into the cloud.

Drawbacks. Levels of abstraction beyond a distributed hybrid computing are not currently expected.

Abstractions

- Nvidia offers data abstraction towards an intermediate type representation with respect to handle data uniformly for different hardware platforms [14]
- In the QC domain, a basic data type is a (C++) templated qudit, which anticipates higher order quantum systems (see [7]). The plain qubit definition starts as qudit with 2 levels (see Fig. 3).

Conclusion. Nvidia is one of the first vendors that start the integration process for QPUs from the 'classical' side. Since the company offers experience integrating different classical hardware systems, the step towards a hybrid environment with QC systems seems promising.

3.9 GitHub Copilot

Created 2021. GitHub Copilot is a cloud-based LLM-powered development assistant that can respond to text input. It is considered to be at the highest level of abstraction and involves LLM-generated recommendations, optimization, and auto-completion functionality that assists programmers in writing quantum code more efficiently. LLMs can analyse patterns in quantum programs, suggest improvements and generate optimised snippets of code based on desired behaviour or performance requirements. Trained on a large language model, the assistant can only use pre-trained knowledge that is neither complete nor perfectly correct. This means that a developer can never rely on generated code, but must always use their own knowledge to check and correct the code. See Fig. 4 for a generated Grover algorithm.

Benefits. Copilot may be a start for programming beginners. It may increase the productivity. Over time, the assistant may learn the developer's coding style to produce similar code.

Drawbacks. Although the percentage of accepted code rises constantly (currently 26%[11] every line of code has to be examined and double-checked by the developer. Because developer fatigue may occur after a while of using such tools, all sorts of bugs and security issues may be introduced. With pre-trained knowledge, only existing code can be generated. There is no incentive to find new solutions. Such effort would require a different ansatz, e.g. Reinforcement Learning.

Abstractions

– With a text input like "write grover's algorithm in qiskit" you abstract away all implementation details

Conclusion. LLM-driven assistance services have the potential to increase the knowledge about QC programming quickly. This means more people can get involved and try out new ideas in quantum computing, which seems to be a good precondition for further discoveries and inventions.

```
# Generated by LLM
from qiskit import QuantumCircuit, Aer,\
execute
from qiskit.visualization import \
plot histogram
```

```
# Define the number of qubits and target
n = 3
target = '010'
# Create the circuit
qc = QuantumCircuit(n, n)
# Apply Hadamard gates to all qubits
for i in range(n):
    qc.h(i)
# Apply the oracle
qc.barrier()
for i in range(n):
    if target[n-i-1] == '1':
        qc.x(i)
qc.barrier()
qc.h(n-1)
qc.mct(list(range(n-1)), n-1)
qc.h(n-1)
qc.barrier()
# Apply the diffusion operator
for i in range(n):
    qc.h(i)
    qc.x(i)
qc.h(n-1)
qc.mct(list(range(n-1)), n-1)
qc.h(n-1)
for i in range(n):
    qc.x(i)
    qc.h(i)
# Measure the qubits
qc.measure(range(n), range(n))
# Run the circuit on a simulator
backend=Aer.get_backend('qasm_simulator')
job = execute(qc, backend, shots=1024)
result = job.result()
# Print the results
counts = result.get_counts()
result = plot histogram(counts,
title="Github Copilot Test")
# Manually added
print(qc)
result.show()
```

```
# Corrected code example
from qiskit import QuantumCircuit, Aer, \
execute
from qiskit.visualization import \
plot histogram
from qiskit.circuit.library import MCMT, \
ZGate

def grover_oracle(marked_states, qc):
    if not isinstance(marked_states, list):
        marked_states = [marked_states]
    num qubits = len(marked_states[0])
    for target in marked_states:
        # Flip target bit-string
        # to match Qiskit bit-ordering
        rev_target = target[::-1]
        zero_inds = [ind for ind in \
        range(num_qubits) \
        if rev_target.startswith("0",ind)]
        qc.x(zero_inds)
        qc.compose(MCMT(ZGate(), \
        num_qubits - 1, 1), inplace=True)
        qc.x(zero_inds)
    return qc
```

```
n = 3
target = '010'
# Create the circuit
qc = QuantumCircuit(n, n)
# Apply Hadamard gates to all qubits
for i in range(n):
    qc.h(i)
# Apply the oracle (flip the sign of the
# target object, which we are searching)
qc.barrier()
cq = grover_oracle(target, qc)
qc.barrier()

# Apply the diffusion operator
for i in range(n):
    qc.h(i)
    qc.x(i)
qc.h(n-1)
qc.mct(list(range(n-1)), n-1)
qc.h(n-1)
for i in range(n):
    qc.x(i)
    qc.h(i)
# Measure the qubits
qc.measure(range(n), range(n))
# Run the circuit on a simulator
backend=Aer.get_backend('qasm_simulator')
job = execute(qc, backend, shots=1024)
result = job.result()
# Print the results
counts = result.get_counts()
result = plot histogram(counts, title=\
"User Corrected Github Copilot Test")

print(qc)
result.show()
```

Fig. 4. Left: incorrect LLM-generated code. Right: manually user corrected code.

---

[11] GitHub Copilot YourAI pair programmer; https://github.com/features/copilot.

4   Conclusion and Discussion

Without claiming to be exhaustive, as more QC frameworks are becoming available [5,11], we have analysed 9 current quantum software frameworks and SDKs. Starting from a low level of abstraction in SDKs that allow direct access to the underlying hardware, new approaches have developed that incorporate concepts from classical computer science - like in Qrisp. This facilitates the migration of classical algorithms into the QC domain in a hybrid way. In addition, new approaches are also emerging on how classical and QC systems can communicate with each other in a more user-friendly way. These developments are paving the way for more intense hybrid computing.

On the other hand, no major expansion can currently be observed in the area of pure QC algorithm development. Efforts are underway to change the mental model (e.g. via pattern building blocks [12]) but for the long term, the question still remains: How can we provide new stimuli for future QC algorithms?

References

1. Aho, A.V., Ullman, J.D.: Foundations of Computer Science. Computer Science Press, April 1994. google-Books-ID: ZXHAHAAACAAJ
2. Bichsel, B., Baader, M., Gehr, T., Vechev, M.: Silq: a high-level quantum language with safe uncomputation and intuitive semantics. In: Proceedings of the 41st ACM SIGPLAN Conference on Programming Language Design and Implementation, pp. 286–300. PLDI 2020, Association for Computing Machinery, New York, NY, USA, June 2020. https://doi.org/10.1145/3385412.3386007
3. Colburn, T., Shute, G.: Abstraction in computer science. Minds Mach. **17**, 169–184 (2007). https://doi.org/10.1007/s11023-007-9061-7
4. Dominguez, F., Unger, J., Traube, M., Mant, B., Ertler, C., Lechner, W.: Encoding-independent optimization problem formulation for quantum computing. Front. Quantum Sci. Technol. **2**, 1229471 (2023). https://doi.org/10.3389/frqst.2023.1229471, arXiv:2302.03711 [quant-ph]
5. Efthymiou, S., et al.: Quantum-TII/qibo: Qibo, August 2020. https://doi.org/10.5281/ZENODO.3997195, https://zenodo.org/record/3997195
6. Green, A., LeFanu Lumsdaine, P., Ross, N., Selinger, P., Valiron, B.: The Quipper System. https://www.mathstat.dal.ca/~selinger/quipper/doc/
7. Hrmo, P., et al.: Native qudit entanglement in a trapped ion quantum processor. Nat. Commun. **14**(1), 2242 (2023). https://doi.org/10.1038/s41467-023-37375-2, https://www.nature.com/articles/s41467-023-37375-2, number: 1 Publisher: Nature Publishing Group
8. Ichikawa, T., et al.: A comprehensive survey on quantum computer usage: how many qubits are employed for what purposes?, July 2023. https://doi.org/10.48550/arXiv.2307.16130, arXiv:2307.16130 [quant-ph]
9. Khammassi, N., et al.: OpenQL: a portable quantum programming framework for quantum accelerators (2020)
10. Khammassi, N., Guerreschi, G.G., Ashraf, I., Hogaboam, J.W., Almudever, C.G., Bertels, K.: cQASM v1.0: towards a common quantum assembly language, May 2018. https://doi.org/10.48550/arXiv.1805.09607, arXiv:1805.09607 [quant-ph]

11. LaRose, R.: Overview and comparison of gate level quantum software platforms. Quantum **3**(130), 10 (2019). 22331/q-2019-03-25-130, https://quantum-journal.org/papers/q-2019-03-25-130/

12. Leymann, F.: Towards a pattern language for quantum algorithms. In: Feld, S., Linnhoff-Popien, C. (eds.) Quantum Technology and Optimization Problems. QTOP 2019. LNCS, vol. 11413, pp. 218–230. Springer, Cham (2019). https://doi.org/10.1007/978-3-030-14082-3_19

13. Nvidia: CUDA Quantum, July 2022. https://developer.nvidia.com/cuda-quantum. Accessed 23 June 2023

14. Nvidia: Create your Own MLIR Pass – NVIDIA CUDA Quantum documentation, June 2023. https://nvidia.github.io/cuda-quantum/latest/using/advanced/mlir_pass.html. Accessed 23 June 2023

15. Reed, S.K.: A taxonomic analysis of abstraction. Perspect. Psychol. Sci. J. Assoc. Psychol. Sci. **11**(6), 817–837 (2016). https://doi.org/10.1177/1745691616646304

16. Research, I.: Qiskit Release Notes, September 2023. https://qiskit.org/documentation/release_notes.html

17. Seidel, R., Tcholtchev, N., Bock, S., Becker, C.K.U., Hauswirth, M.: Efficient Floating Point Arithmetic for Quantum Computers, December 2021. https://arxiv.org/abs/2112.10537v1

18. Seidel, R., Tcholtchev, N., Bock, S., Hauswirth, M.: Uncomputation in the qrisp high-level quantum programming framework. In: Kutrib, M., Meyer, U. (eds.) Reversible Computation. RC 2023. LNCS, vol. 13960, pp. 150–165. Springer, Cham (2023). https://doi.org/10.1007/978-3-031-38100-3_11, arXiv:2307.11417 [quant-ph]

19. Shor, P.W.: Why haven't more quantum algorithms been found? J. ACM **50**(1), 87–90 (2003). https://doi.org/10.1145/602382.602408

20. Stackscale: Most popular programming languages in 2023 [Ranking], September 2023. https://www.stackscale.com/blog/most-popular-programming-languages/, section: General

21. Staff, A.J.B.C.: First European Quantum Computing Facility Goes Online. https://cacm.acm.org/news/248166-first-european-quantum-computing-facility-goes-online/fulltext?mobile=false

22. Villar-Rodriguez, E., Osaba, E., Oregi, I.: Analyzing the behaviour of D'WAVE quantum annealer: fine-tuning parameterization and tests with restrictive Hamiltonian formulations. In: 2022 IEEE Symposium Series on Computational Intelligence (SSCI), pp. 938–946. IEEE, Singapore, Singapore, December 2022. https://doi.org/10.1109/SSCI51031.2022.10022300, https://ieeexplore.ieee.org/document/10022300/

Hybrid Data Management Architecture for Present Quantum Computing

Markus Zajac[(⊠)] and Uta Störl

Databases and Information Systems, FernUniversität in Hagen, Hagen, Germany
{markus.zajac,uta.stoerl}@fernuni-hagen.de

Abstract. Quantum computers promise polynomial or exponential speed-up in solving certain problems compared to classical computers. However, in practical use, there are currently a number of fundamental technical challenges. One of them concerns the loading of data into quantum computers, since they cannot access common databases. In this vision paper, we develop a hybrid data management architecture in which databases can serve as data sources for quantum algorithms. To test the architecture, we perform experiments in which we assign data points stored in a database to clusters. For cluster assignment, a quantum algorithm processes this data by determining the distances between data points and cluster centroids.

Keywords: Data management for quantum computing · hybrid quantum computing · data loading · data encoding

1 Introduction from the Database Perspective

Quantum computers have the potential to perform certain calculations much faster than classical computers. They can be used in various application areas, such as optimization, machine learning or search algorithms, to name just a few examples [1,6,8]. Depending on the problem, a polynomial or exponential acceleration can be assumed compared to a classical computer [20]. It is foremost a mathematical superiority. However, for practical use, certain hurdles must be addressed.

First of all, the current generation of quantum computers (NISQ) can be termed as noisy and limited in scalability [12,26]. This means that the number of qubits is limited, and the qubits themselves are error-prone. Next difficulty concerns loading data into the quantum computer. From the perspective of a database, data is managed in various database models that need to be processed to solve a particular problem or query. In principle, it may be interesting to perform this processing on a quantum computer for certain problems or queries. We

This work has been funded by Deutsche Forschungsgemeinschaft (DFG, German Research Foundation) grant #385808805. We would like to thank Stefanie Scherzinger from University of Passau for many prolific discussions as well as helpful suggestions.

F. Monti et al. (Eds.): ICSOC 2023 Workshops, LNCS 14518, pp. 174–184, 2024.
https://doi.org/10.1007/978-981-97-0989-2_14

introduce some computationally intensive queries later on. Quantum computers, however, cannot access databases directly [23]. Moreover, today's quantum algorithms assume its input data is already in the desired form [10]. The data to be processed has therefore first to be encoded in a suitable way in order to be used on a quantum computer at all. The encoding must reflect the structure of the data, for example, when data is organized hierarchically (in trees) or semi-structured (in documents). Efficient encoding of data is a challenge [7,10] as well as a future research direction [8]. Last but not least, workflows and interfaces for data exchange between classical systems (such as applications but also databases) and quantum computers are an issue. An important design goal of such hybrid systems should be the reduction and manageability of complexity. Our contributions are therefore the following:

1. In this vision paper, we describe a hybrid system that enables the exchange of data between applications and databases and quantum computers and call it Hybrid Data Management Architecture (HDMA). The architecture acts as a framework for researching and piloting appropriate encoding methods for data in different data structures and models. It is also a framework for designing future data-centric applications for quantum computing.
2. We validate an early prototype of this architecture on an example.

The remainder of the paper is structured as follows: In Sect. 2 we discuss related work. In the following, we describe the HDMA (Sect. 3) and in Sect. 4 its proof of concept. In doing so, we use a quantum distance estimation algorithm. Section 5 provides a summary and outlines next steps.

2   Related Work

We review work on computationally intensive database queries, quantum technologies in the database environment, data encoding, and data exchange.

Computationally Intensive Queries. We first addressed the question of whether data models and corresponding queries exist that are of interest for quantum computing. We first look at queries that are computationally intensive and therefore represent interesting objects of investigation to determine whether quantum computers can generally enable their acceleration. As an example, data organization in labeled trees (like XML trees) can be given here. David [2] describes an NP-Complete problem involving data tree patterns as a query language for such trees. Gottlob et al. [5] discuss the complexity of *XPath* queries (used for node selection) on such trees. These queries exhibit a polynomial runtime, and for some the polynomial degree can be 4 or 5. Another NP-hard problem is the keyword search in (graph) databases, which is related to the so-called *Group Steiner Tree* problem [14]. This non-exhaustive list of examples shows that interesting query candidates exist for quantum computing.

Quantum Technologies in the Database Environment. In [1] quantum algorithms (such as *Grover*) and heuristics (such as *Variational Quantum Algorithms* or *Quantum Annealing*) for optimizing queries and transaction plans are presented. The development of hybrid algorithms for database problems is mentioned as a future research direction. Yuan et al. [27] also conduct a literature review on quantum computing for database problems (such as database search, database manipulation, or query optimization). In addition, the paper outlines a vision of a quantum-based multi-modal database. Jóczik and Kiss [9] describe some possible applications for database systems based on *Grover's* algorithm. In [13], the idea of a so-called data center with *Quantum Random Access Memory* (QRAM) is presented. Classical or quantum information should be able to be uploaded and downloaded to the center. This uploaded information can be processed, e.g. by suitable quantum algorithms. However, the authors assume that QRAM has been constructed in a fault tolerant manner and has been error corrected. Today, however, noise resilience and scalability represent major unsolved hurdles [17]. An implementation of a sufficiently large memory therefore seems to be impossible today [15].

In summary, the papers present visionary ideas, future research directions, and reviews of the literature. Our contribution is to develop not only concepts for the use of quantum technologies in the database environment, but also a hybrid architecture that can be implemented today to successively realize these concepts. The architecture is a framework for exploring and testing appropriate encoding methods for data in various data structures and models, and implementing certain queries using quantum computing. To the best of our knowledge, there is no other work that addresses a framework for realizing the above database queries using database systems or classical technologies and quantum technologies.

Data Encoding. Encoding represents the transformed classical data by means of qubits [10]. Only then can the data be processed on a quantum computer. In [23–25], various encoding procedures are explained, which are understood as patterns. These patterns are reusable self-contained building blocks that can be reused in the construction of quantum algorithms.

As mentioned earlier, data can be organized in different data models and structural information must be preserved when encoding. A first idea of how to encode data organized in labeled trees was presented in [28]. We are not aware of any other work on encoding specific database data models. In general, the encryption methods we are developing are also intended to serve as a blueprint for future improved quantum hardware. For these, roadmaps are given, accompanied by appropriate research [19].

Data Exchange. Another aspect concerns the exchange of data between classical components and quantum computers. Data wrangling, pre-processing, job management, post-processing, and feeding back the results to applications or a databases are individual processes here. The work of Weder et al. [22] deals with orchestration using *BPMN* workflows. The described approach with many steps and modeling aspects seems complex to us. It can be generally stated that more complex systems (such as so-called *data mesh architectures*) tend towards complexity and cause considerable additional expenses for their operation [11].

To reduce complexity, we propose a decentralized approach with a lightweight, asynchronous communication mechanism by adopting the microservice paradigm. Microservices are typically used to manage the increase in complexity of systems [4].

3   Architectural Description

This Section introduces the Hybrid Data Management Architecture (HDMA). We derive these from the introductory Sect. 1 and the considered work of Sect. 2. Figure 1 shows the schematic structure of the architecture. The classic components include a series of loosely coupled services that follow the microservice paradigm. These are the following services: *Decision Service*, *Circuit Service*, *Data Service*, *Backend Service* and *Result Manager*. Some services communicate with a *Gate-based Quantum Computer* that processes data to solve a task. A *Gate-based Quantum Computer* is characterised by its ability to be used for a wide range of problems. This type of quantum computer is based on quantum gates for encoding and processing data, which form a *Quantum Circuit*. Today, quantum computers are usually provided as cloud services. Instead of quantum computer, a simulator can also be used.

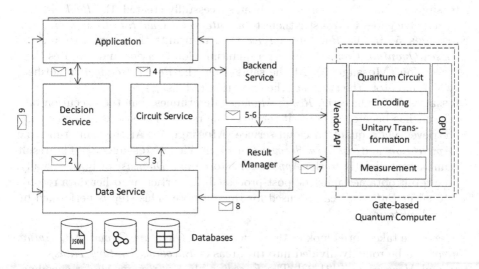

Fig. 1. Hybrid Data Management Architecture [Source: Own representation]

We will first provide a brief overview of the services before focusing on communication. As motivation, we imagine an *Application* that would initiate a computationally intensive query or intends to solve another computationally intensive problem. The decision as to whether a problem is calculated using a *Gate-based Quantum Computer* or completely classically is made by the *Decision Service*. The data required to solve a problem, as well as the results of the calculations, are stored in *Databases* and managed by the *Data Service*. The *Circuit Service* generates *Quantum Circuits* for the *Gate-based Quantum Computer* that contain the data and processing instructions. The transmission of *Quantum Circuits* to *Gate-based Quantum Computer* is the responsibility of the *Backend Service*. The *Result Manager* determines whether previously transmitted *Quantum Circuits* have been executed and notifies the *Application* and/or *Data Service* if a result is available. Based on the services and the *Gate-based Quantum Computer*, we define the following reference procedure in which messages are exchanged asynchronously between the services.

Message 1. An *Application* notifies the *Decision Service* of the problem to be solved. This first verifies whether a problem should be calculated using a *Gate-based Quantum Computer* or not and notifies the *Application* of the decision. We assume in the following that a *Gate-based Quantum Computer* is to be used. Otherwise, the problem is solved classically and the *Application* communicates directly with the *Data Service* for the purpose of data exchange (**Message 9**).

Message 2. The *Data Service* is notified in order to extract the data required to solve the problem.

Message 3. After all data is available, the *Circuit Service* is notified to generate a corresponding *Quantum Circuit*. If appropriate, several circuits are created.

Message 4. Once the circuits have been successfully created, the *Backend Service* is triggered to transfer them to a *Gate-based Quantum Computer*.

Messages 5–6. The *Backend Service* then transmits the circuits to a *Gate-based Quantum Computer* using a quantum cloud service and initiates their execution (**Message 5**). At the same time, the *Result Manager* is notified, which monitors the status of the execution (**Message 6**).

Messages 7–8. Once the *Result Manager* determines that the execution of a circuit has been completed, it retrieves the result. The status and result are retrieved via a quantum cloud service (**Message 7**). At the same time, the *Application* and/or *Data Service* can be notified (**Message 8**). The result can be sent directly to the *Application*, stored in a *Database* or both. Usually, the result obtained must be post-processed. In particular, other data records stored in *Databases* can be used for this purpose. This step is performed by the *Application*.

Next, we take a brief look at the structure of a *Quantum Circuit*. A *Quantum Circuit* can be roughly divided into the areas of *Encoding*, *Unitary Transformation* and *Measurement* [21,23]. The *Encoding* block is responsible for encoding, which means that data and, if necessary, parameters are loaded and encoded in a quantum state. This quantum state forms the starting point for the actual quantum algorithm in the *Unitary Transformation* block, which can manipulate the initial state. The execution of an algorithm ends with the *Measurement* of the final quantum state, which represents the result.

Finally, we address two aspects that are to be supported by the HDMA.

Circuit Generation. In some cases, the circuits are generated on demand, in others automatically, e.g. when data changes. The first method can be useful if, for example, different small portions of historical data or predefined problem instances are to be processed. In the second case, data changes (e.g. new or updated data records) must be detected automatically and the circuit generation must then be triggered automatically at certain times. In this scenario, a quantum algorithm works with data set at a given time or the most recent time.

Data Restrictions/Data Economy. Considering data restrictions in the architecture is central to quantum computing. More data requires more qubits and longer runtimes of state preparation routines. We propose to store data constraints in profiles to define only a reasonable minimum amount of data to be processed on a quantum computer. For a given use case, different profiles can be used, e.g. to manage different data value ranges or different graph partitions. In the latter case, different circuits could be generated for the different node sets (each partition forms the input for a calculation task). Some use cases (which especially process historical data) allow different circuits to be executed independently of each other. In the NISQ era, this is of particular interest. Due to the hardware limitations, the width and depth of quantum circuits should be reduced as much as possible [3]. In general, validation of use cases respectively the aforementioned computationally intensive queries is only possible with small problem instances in the NISQ era.

4   Experimentation

In this Section, we describe the experiment to test the hybrid architecture. For the development of the first prototype, we use *Python, FastAPI, Docker* and *ch1Qiskit* [18] as implementation technologies. The objective is to verify the functioning of the reference procedure described in Sect. 3. To validate the procedure, we resort to well-known quantum routines. We first consider the following Table 1.

Table 1. Test Data

	ID	Feature1	Feature2	Cluster
Centroid A	0	−0.5	0.5	blue
Centroid B	1	0.2	−0.2	green
Data Point	2	0.15	−0.15	?
Data Point	3	−0.45	0.45	?

This represents some relational data. Each row (tuple) represents a data point that has two properties (called features) *Feature1* and *Feature2*. Each tuple also has a unique ID. The first two tuples are data points, each representing a cluster centroid. The remaining data points are now to be assigned to a cluster. We aim to achieve this with the support of a routine or algorithm for distance estimation as used in the Quantum K-Means algorithm [3,16].

According to the reference procedure in Sect. 3, we implement the following services and functionalities in the prototype:

1. The *Decision Service* receives a request from the *Application* for the assignment of data points to clusters and decides to solve this problem using a *Gate-based Quantum Computer*. The *Application* is informed of this.
2. Next, a defined amount of data records is extracted via the *Data Service*.
3. The *Circuit Service* creates several circuits. We create a circuit for each pair of data point and centroid. In this first experiment, we have opted for this simple approach. First, the data provided is encoded. In our case, these are the features and the ID of the data points. We need the latter for post-processing (cf. step 5). For the encoding of the features we use the so-called *angle embedding* [3,16]. For this we calculate per tuple the two angles $\theta = (Feature1 + 1)\frac{\pi}{2}$ and $\varphi = (Feature2 + 1)\frac{\pi}{2}$, whereby angle values between 0 and π are allowed. For the encoding of the IDs we use the basis encoding in this example [25]. Next the distance estimation algorithm follows, which works on the encoded information (cf. Subsect. 4.1). Note: For the encoding of the IDs, we have chosen basis encoding in this first example. Other implicit encoding types (as in [15]) are also of interest. In addition, the identification of records in a distributed database system requires more comprehensive identifiers than just an ID as in this example. This was reported in [29].
4. The generated circuits are transmitted to a *Gate-based Quantum Computer* via the *Backend Service* and their execution is triggered. In our case, it is the quantum cloud service from IBM Quantum[1], which we used for our tests.
5. In the final step, the *Result Manager* checks the execution status and retrieves the result after a circuit has been executed. The result is then forwarded to the *Application*. The corresponding cluster of each data point can be derived from the overall result (comparison of all points with both centroids, cf. Subsect. 4.2). The IDs of these data points are included in the individual results. The *Application* is responsible for post-processing the overall result. Based on the IDs, the Table 1 can be supplemented with the information of the correct cluster. In a relational database, we can imagine that this table is indexed by ID, so that records can be efficiently identified by ID for an update.

4.1 Circuit

The circuit created in Step 3) can be roughly divided into two sections *Encoding* and *Algorithm*. Figure 2 shows the circuit as an example for a data point centroid pair. The encoding is marked. To encode the features, so called $U_3(\theta, \varphi, 0)$ gates can be used. The parameters of the gates are the previously calculated angles. *Pauli X* gates can be used for encoding the IDs. In this case, an ID is represented by a corresponding bit string.

The core of the actual algorithm is the estimation of the distance between a data point and a centroid. The basis of the algorithm is described in [16].

---

[1] IBM Quantum. https://quantum.ibm.com/, 2023.

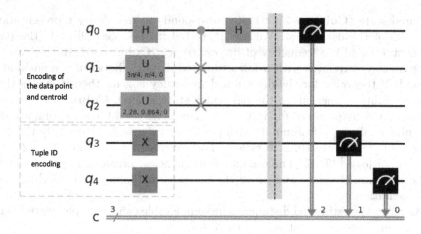

Fig. 2. Distance Estimation Algorithm following [16] with additional encoding of the Tuple IDs to utilize them in post-processing. Parameterized with Data Point ID = 3 and Centroid A. Drawn by *Qiskit*.

We supplement it with the encoding of the IDs. The distance is reflected in the measurement result and how often a particular measurement result occurs. We will deal with this in Subsect. 4.2.

4.2   Results

In this Subsection we review the results, which are shown in the Table 2.

Table 2. Experiment Results

	Data Point ID	Bit sequence for $c[2] = 1$	Determined Frequency	Calculated Frequency
Centroid A	2	110	43	≈47
Centroid B	2	–	0	≈0.513
Centroid A	3	–	0	≈0.061
Centroid B	3	111	43	≈46

Each data point (**Column 1**) is compared to the two centroids to determine the proximity in each case. In quantum-based distance estimation, the estimated distance between points can be derived from the frequency of a particular state that we obtain from the measurements. For this purpose, we use the *ibmq_ qasm_ simulator* with 1000 shots (number of repetitions) per centroid/data point comparison. According to the Fig. 2, we measure $q_0 \rightarrow c[2]$, $q_3 \rightarrow c[1]$, and $q_4 \rightarrow c[0]$ and obtain in this way a bit sequence representing the measured state (**Column 2**). $c[1]c[0]$ corresponds to the binary representation of the ID of the data point. We are interested in the case $c[2] = 1$ (the particular state) and the frequency of its occurrence (**Column 3**). In this case, a low frequency correlates with a low estimated distance between a point and a centroid (if the value for the determined frequency is zero, then it means that the probability of measuring the particular state is low). **Column 4** contains the calculated frequencies (for 1000 repetitions). We need these to compare the determined values (in Column 3) with predicted values and thus verify the correctness of the architectural workflow. The calculated probability for $c[2] = 1$ is: $\frac{1}{2} - \frac{1}{2}|\langle q_1|q_2 \rangle|^2$ [3,16]. The calculated frequencies correspond approximately to the determined values and prove the correct functioning of the architecture implementation.

Based on the estimated distances, the source table can be supplemented. The supplemented entries are shown in Table 3.

Table 3. Updated Test Data

	ID	Feature1	Feature2	Cluster
...	...	...	...	...
Data Point	2	0.15	−0.15	**green**
Data Point	3	−0.45	0.45	**blue**

The architecture thus allows data from a database to be processed by a quantum algorithm to assign data points to the correct clusters. The correct generation of the corresponding circuits was ensured by the previously mentioned comparison of determined and calculated frequencies.

5   Summary and Future Work

In this paper, we have presented a Hybrid Data Management Architecture to enable data exchange between databases and quantum computers. We have experimentally proven a correct functioning of the architecture. In the experiments, quantum circuits were created and executed based on relational data. The circuits implement an algorithm for the distance estimation between data point and centroid and includes the encoding of the classical data. However, the architecture is not limited to this use case.

Next, we would like to leverage the architecture to implement more data-centric applications. In doing so, we would like to encode data organized in hierarchical structures (for example, labelled trees for which we have outlined an initial idea [28], or graphs) in order to execute selected queries on the encoded data using appropriate quantum algorithms. The implemented routines are also accompanied by time and space complexity analysis to deduce any advantages over purely classical solutions.

References

1. Çalikyilmaz, U., et al.: Opportunities for quantum acceleration of databases: optimization of queries and transaction schedules. Proc. VLDB Endow. **16**(9), 2344–2353 (2023)
2. David, C.: Complexity of data tree patterns over XML documents. In: Ochmański, E., Tyszkiewicz, J. (eds.) MFCS 2008. LNCS, vol. 5162, pp. 278–289. Springer, Heidelberg (2008). https://doi.org/10.1007/978-3-540-85238-4_22
3. DiAdamo, S., O'Meara, C., Cortiana, G., Bernabé-Moreno, J.: Practical quantum K-means clustering: performance analysis and applications in energy grid classification. IEEE Trans. Quant. Eng. **3**, 1–16 (2022)
4. Dragoni, N., et al.: Microservices: yesterday, today, and tomorrow. In: Mazzara, M., Meyer, B. (eds.) Present and Ulterior Software Engineering, pp. 195–216. Springer, Cham (2017). https://doi.org/10.1007/978-3-319-67425-4_12
5. Gottlob, G., Koch, C., Pichler, R.: The complexity of XPath query evaluation. In: Proceedings of the PODS 2003, pp. 179–190. ACM (2003)
6. Hassija, V., Chamola, V., Goyal, A., Kanhere, S.S., Guizani, N.: Forthcoming applications of quantum computing: peeking into the future. IET Quant. Commun. **1**(2), 35–41 (2020)
7. Herbert, S.: Quantum computing for data-centric engineering and science. Data-Cent. Eng. **3**, e36 (2022)
8. Houssein, E.H., Abohashima, Z., Elhoseny, M., Mohamed, W.M.: Machine learning in the quantum realm: the state-of-the-art, challenges, and future vision. Expert Syst. Appl. **194**, 116512 (2022)
9. Jóczik, S., Kiss, A.: Quantum computation and its effects in database systems. In: Darmont, J., Novikov, B., Wrembel, R. (eds.) ADBIS 2020. CCIS, vol. 1259, pp. 13–23. Springer, Cham (2020). https://doi.org/10.1007/978-3-030-54623-6_2
10. Kieferová, M., Sanders, Y.: Assume a quantum data set. Harv. Data Sci. Rev. **4**(1) (2022)
11. Kraska, T., et al.: Check out the big brain on BRAD: simplifying cloud data processing with learned automated data meshes. Proc. VLDB Endow. **16**(11), 3293–3301 (2023)
12. Leymann, F., Barzen, J.: The bitter truth about gate-based quantum algorithms in the NISQ era. Quant. Sci. Technol. **5**(4), 044007 (2020)
13. Liu, J., Hann, C.T., Jiang, L.: Data centers with quantum random access memory and quantum networks. Phys. Rev. A **108**, 032610 (2023)
14. Manolescu, I., Mohanty, M.: Full-power graph querying: state of the art and challenges. Proc. VLDB Endow. **16**(12), 3886–3889 (2023)
15. Matteo, O.D., Gheorghiu, V., Mosca, M.: Fault-tolerant resource estimation of quantum random-access memories. IEEE Trans. Quant. Eng. **1**, 1–13 (2020)
16. Ouedrhiri, O., Banouar, O., Raghay, S., el Hadaj, S.: Comparative study of data preparation methods in quantum clustering algorithms. In: NISS (ACM), pp. 28:1–28:5. ACM (2021)
17. Phalak, K., Chatterjee, A., Ghosh, S.: Quantum random access memory for dummies. CoRR abs/2305.01178 (2023)
18. Qiskit contributors: Qiskit: An Open-source Framework for Quantum Computing (2023). https://doi.org/10.5281/zenodo.2573505
19. Riel, H.: Quantum computing technology. In: 2021 IEEE International Electron Devices Meeting (IEDM) (2021)

20. Schuld, M., Petruccione, F.: Quantum computing. In: Schuld, M., Petruccione, F. (eds.) Machine Learning with Quantum Computers. Quantum Science and Technology, pp. 79–146. Springer, Cham (2021). https://doi.org/10.1007/978-3-030-83098-4_3

21. Schuld, M., Petruccione, F.: Representing data on a quantum computer. In: Schuld, M., Petruccione, F. (eds.) Machine Learning with Quantum Computers. QST, pp. 147–176. Springer, Cham (2021). https://doi.org/10.1007/978-3-030-83098-4_4

22. Weder, B., Barzen, J., Leymann, F., Zimmermann, M.: Hybrid quantum applications need two orchestrations in superposition: a software architecture perspective. In: 2021 IEEE International Conference on Web Services (ICWS), pp. 1–13 (2021)

23. Weigold, M., Barzen, J., Leymann, F., Salm, M.: Encoding patterns for quantum algorithms. IET Quant. Commun. **2**(4), 141–152 (2021)

24. Weigold, M., Barzen, J., Leymann, F., Salm, M.: Expanding data encoding patterns for quantum algorithms. In: 2021 IEEE 18th International Conference on Software Architecture Companion (ICSA-C), pp. 95–101. IEEE (2021–03)

25. Weigold, M., Barzen, J., Leymann, F., Salm, M.: Data encoding patterns for quantum computing. In: Proceedings of the 27th Conference on Pattern Languages of Programs, PLoP 2020. The Hillside Group (2022)

26. Weigold, M., Barzen, J., Leymann, F., Vietz, D.: Patterns for hybrid quantum algorithms. In: Barzen, J. (ed.) SummerSOC 2021. CCIS, vol. 1429, pp. 34–51. Springer, Cham (2021). https://doi.org/10.1007/978-3-030-87568-8_2

27. Yuan, G., et al.: Quantum computing for databases: a short survey and vision. In: VLDB Workshops. CEUR Workshop Proceedings, vol. 3462. CEUR-WS.org (2023)

28. Zajac, M.: Encoding and provisioning data in different data models for quantum computing. In: PhD@VLDB. CEUR Workshop Proceedings, vol. 3452, pp. 45–48. CEUR-WS.org (2023)

29. Zajac, M., Störl, U.: Towards quantum-based search for industrial data-driven services. In: Proceedings of the 2022 IEEE International Conference on Quantum Software (QSW). IEEE (2022)

Quantum Block-Matching Algorithm Using Dissimilarity Measure

M. Martínez-Felipe[1]([✉]) [iD], J. Montiel-Pérez[1] [iD], Victor Onofre[2] [iD],
A. Maldonado-Romo[1,2,3] [iD], and Ricky Young[2,3]

[1] Centro de Investigación en Computación, Instituto Politécnico Nacional,
07738 Ciudad de México, Mexico
{mmartinezf2020,jyalja,amaldonador2021}@cic.ipn.mx
[2] Quantum Open Source Foundation, Santander, Spain
[3] qBraid, Chicago 60615, USA
rickyyoung@qbraid.com
https://www.qosf.org/

Abstract. Finding groups of similar image blocks within an ample search area is often necessary in different applications, such as video compression, image clustering, vector quantization, and nonlocal noise reduction. A block-matching algorithm that uses a dissimilarity measure can be applied in such scenarios. In this work, a measure that utilizes the quantum Fourier transform through the draper adder or the Swap test based on the Euclidean distance is proposed. Experiments on small representative cases with ideal and depolarizing noise simulations are implemented. In the case of the Swap test, the IBM, OQC and IonQ quantum devices have been used through the qBraid services, demonstrating potential for future near-term applications.

Keywords: Quantum Block-Matching · Quantum Image Processing · Quantum Noise Models · Quantum Euclidean Distance

1 Introduction

Block-matching (BM) is a way to locate patch blocks in a sequence of digital images. These BM algorithms use a similarity or dissimilarity measure to compare images or some regions of an image [3]. There are various applications for BM, mainly in video compression, image clustering, nonlocal noise reduction, and vector quantization [5].

Quantum image processing (QIP) opens the possibility to design, store, develop, and implement new methods applied to image processing algorithms. For example, there are some quantum image representations such as flexible representation (FRQI) [11], multi-channel (MCQI) [17], and novel enhanced (NEQR) [19], which is one of the earlier forms of quantum image representation. It uses a normalized superposition to store pixels in an image. NEQR

CONAHCYT, IPN and qbraid.

was created to leverage the basis state of a qubit sequence to store the image's grayscale value.

Developing new methods and algorithms using the quantum computing framework offers a possible advantage over classical computing. Nevertheless, these quantum computers contain hundreds of noisy qubits and perform imperfect operations in a limited coherence time. We are in the Noisy intermediate-scale quantum (NISQ) era [13], it is necessary to mitigate the error rates. Recent theoretical works have shown improvements in implementing error mitigation techniques with these NISQ devices [2,7,10], opening opportunities for near-term applications.

In this work, we develop quantum circuits in order to map the BM problem in a noisy environment using dissimilarity measurement based on Euclidean distance. Since low-complexity block-matching algorithms based on patch recognition in image processing are required for comparing images, exploring some regions of one image plays a crucial role in standard video codec due mainly to the motion estimation process but also in applications previously mentioned. Nevertheless, using the properties of quantum computing as superposition or the amplitude encoding of a qubit, the quantum block-matching algorithm could help to reduce the complexity in many operations since $n = log_2(M) + 1$ we could use only n qubits to encode M classical data.

This paper is structured as follows: Sect. 2 explores the block-matching algorithms, and Sect. 3 explains the methodology used. Section 4 is dedicated to explaining the result for different quantum noise models. Finally, Sect. 5 summarizes this proposal work and experimental results.

2   Block-Matching Algorithms

In previous works [9], there has been an implementation of the generalized quantum image representation (GQIR), where the size of an image is $2^m \times 2^m$ and $I(x, y) \in \{0, 1, \cdots, 2^n - 1\}$, where m is an integer related to the size of images and n the number of qubits. The idea is to find a small image in a big image using Grover's algorithm. Nevertheless, noisy environments to find a particular patch in an image are not applied. Although this algorithm improved in [4] to solve the error of matching at the upper left corner of one pixel, maintaining an advantage with less complexity than classical algorithms. On the other hand, there are methods based on the quantum-classical approach. In [16], a method for image matching with a scale-invariant feature transform (SIFT) algorithm is presented. In this last work, feature extraction from images is done to assign an orientation to each key point location. Although these related works present novel solutions, none of the previous works study how quantum noise affects the results in a Quantum Processing Unit (QPU). These works are compared in the Table 1.

Table 1. Comparison between block-matching related works.

Related works	Algorithms	Noisy models
Analysis and improvement of the quantum image matching [4]	NEQR + Grover's algorithm + improvement	No
Quantum image matching [9]	NEQR + Grover's algorithm	No
A Hybrid Quantum Image-Matching Algorithm [16]	SIFT + amplitude encoding + similarity measure	No
Proposal methodology	Hierarchical search + encode + Quantum Swap Test or Quantum Fourier Transform	Yes

2.1 QFT Approach

The standard dissimilarity measure is obtained between two vectors using the Draper adder [6], arguably one of the most elegant quantum adders, as it directly invokes quantum properties to perform addition. The insight behind the algorithm is that the Fourier transform can be used to translate phase shifts into a bit shift. It follows the implementation with an adder by applying a Fourier transform, applying appropriate phase shifts, and then the Fourier transform inverse is done. Unlike many other adders that have been proposed, the Draper adder does not have a natural classical counterpart.

2.2 Swap Test

A dissimilarity measure based on a swap test [18] to compare two states, $|\phi\rangle$ and $|\psi\rangle$ to compute the Euclidean distance [12,20] is implemented. First, the classical data, represented by the vectors A and B is encoded in quantum states:

$$A \longrightarrow |A\rangle = \frac{1}{|A|} \sum_i A_i |q_i\rangle$$

$$B \longrightarrow |B\rangle = \frac{1}{|B|} \sum_i B_i |q_i\rangle \qquad (1)$$

then, the quantum states $|\psi\rangle$ and $|\phi\rangle$ are defined:

$$|\psi\rangle = \frac{|0\rangle \otimes |A\rangle + |1\rangle \otimes |B\rangle}{\sqrt{2}}$$

$$|\phi\rangle = \frac{|A||0\rangle - |B||1\rangle}{\sqrt{Z}} \qquad (2)$$

where, $Z = |A|^2 + |B|^2$. The advantage of this methodology is to perform a few qubits, specifically $n = \log_2(M) + 1$ where n is the number of qubits and M the classical data coded with amplitude embedding [15]. The quantum circuit is shown in the Fig. 1. Now, to obtain the quantum Euclidean distance, the following equation is solved:

$$D^2 = 2Z|\langle \phi | \psi \rangle|^2 \tag{3}$$

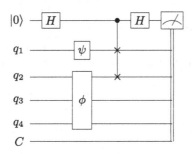

Fig. 1. Quantum circuit swap test to compute the quantum Euclidean distance.

3   Methodology

The proposal work is introduced, and the general diagram of the present methodology is shown in Fig. 2.

3.1   Classical Approach

In this first part, it is essential to resize the tested images in order to obtain experimental results implementing quantum circuits. So, the original images are contaminated with Gaussian noise $I_r = I_o + G$, where I_r is the image with noise, I_o is the original image and G is a normally distributed random variable of mean μ and variance σ^2. In the present work $\mu = 0$ and $\sigma^2 = 20$ [1]. After this, since the original images are 512×512 pixels, size reduction is applied to obtain an image with 64×64 pixels. For the last stage in image processing, a grayscale palette reduction is applied from 8-bit grayscale to 4-bit grayscale Fig. 3.

The resulting image from Fig. 3 can be smoothed in a spatial domain transform or a low pass filter. Such transformation can introduce some robustness in a noisy environment. In order to reduce the complexity of some operations, a hierarchical search algorithm is implemented in comparison to the full search algorithm [3]. With this proposal, the complexity can be reduced from $O(n^2 K)$ to $O((\frac{n}{2})^2 K)$, where K is the search area and n is the size of the window for each patch image. Once the search algorithms are introduced, the next step is to define the experiment parameters. In the present work, $k = 10$ and $n = 8$ are chosen; considering the hierarchical search, the size of the vectors is reduced from $n = 8$ to $n = 4$.

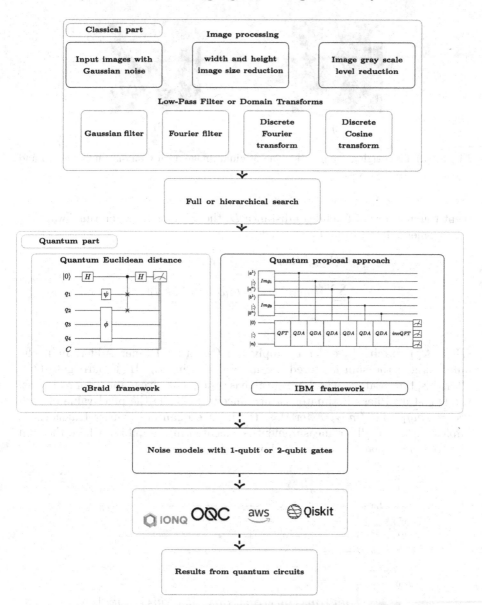

Fig. 2. Diagram of the proposal methodology for a quantum block-matching algorithm using dissimilarity measure.

3.2 Quantum Approach

The standard dissimilarity measure is obtained between two image blocks. Firstly, the image blocks are flattened in vectors of size r_x. Secondly, to imple-

(a)   (b)

Fig. 3. (a) The original image. (b) The original image with Gaussian noise $\mu = 0$ and $\sigma = 20$ and 4-bit grayscale.

ment the measure of Euclidean distance D, the QFT or the Quantum swap test is implemented; it can be formulated as [14]:

$$D\left(Img_1, Img_2\right) =$$
$$\sum_{i=0}^{r_x-1} \left[Img_1\left(x+i\right) - Img_2\left(x+o_x+i\right)\right]^2, \tag{4}$$

QFT Approach. In order to apply the Quantum Draper Adder, first, the qubits where the sum is stored are initialized using the Hadamard gate (H); after this, the rotation of each pixel value is coded. For save numbers of rotations, the Quantum Phase Estimator is introduced to encode the pixel value of each vector $\vec{Img_1}$ and $\vec{Img_2}$. After this, the inverse quantum Fourier transform is implemented. Finally, a measurement is executed in the qubits, where the sum is stored. The quantum circuit is shown in Fig. 4.

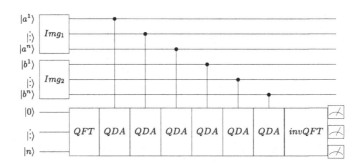

Fig. 4. Quantum Circuit for the QFT approach.

Quantum Swap Test Approach. The advantage of this approach is the number of qubits. In performing the quantum circuit Swap Test, $n = log_2(M) + 1$

qubits are implemented. From the Eq. 2 and Eq. 3, the dissimilarity measure can be executed. So $|\psi\rangle$ and $|\phi\rangle$ are obtained since $A = \vec{Img_1}$ and $B = \vec{Img_2}$. The quantum circuit is shown in the next Fig. 5.

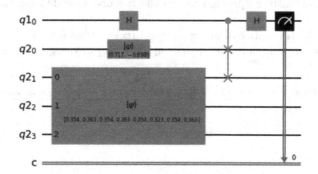

Fig. 5. Quantum Euclidean Distance using Swap Test approach with the vectors $\vec{Img_1} = [9,9,9,9]$ and $\vec{Img_2} = [9,9,8,9]$.

3.3   Quantum Noise Models

A method to analyze the behavior of quantum circuits before running it on a QPU is to create a noise model that considers the noise in the real QPU. The main errors in a QPU are decoherence and gate errors. We focused on a noise model with different gate errors - fidelities of the two qubits gates. Decreasing the fidelity will affect the results considerably. Finding a reasonable fidelity in the simulations will give us an estimate of the resources we will need for a perfect outcome of the circuits in real QPU.

4   Results

The experiments were implemented with Qiskit [14] using the qBraid environment [8] and with AWS braket in the case of Hardware jobs with IonQ and Oxford Quantum Circuits (OQC).

4.1   Results for QFT Approach

The results using the QFT approach are ideal in the perfect simulation. Nevertheless, many qubits are needed since the quantum circuits have a considerable depth. Therefore, this approach is unreasonable for the current NISQ devices. To showcase the disadvantage of this approach, a simple subtraction operation of two integers, as shown in the Fig. 6 is simulated. In the worst case, at least 12 qubits with more than 200 CNOT gates will be used. In implementing the

BM problem, each vector represents sections of an image with multiple subtractions needed to compute the Euclidean distance. Despite this approach having many quantum resources, the result will always be accurate in a fault-tolerant device. The error increases rapidly once a slight noise into the CNOT gates is introduced. Currently, improvements to the resources needed for this approach are being made.

Given the high number of quantum resources needed for the QFT approach, the Swap Test, a more suitable algorithm for NISQ devices, is explored.

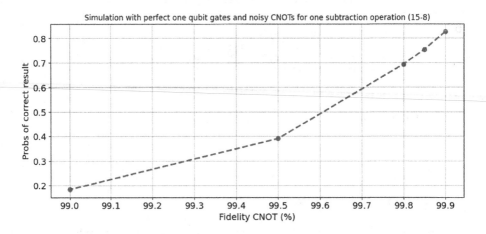

Fig. 6. Noisy simulation with different CNOT gate fidelities using the QFT approach for the subtraction operation

4.2   Results for Swap Tets Approach

The results with the Swap Test approach were done with 17 pairs of vectors of 4 dimensions. Based on the classical part similar to those representing the different sections of images for the BM problem.

The Fig. 7 shows results with noiseless simulations of 20 runs with 4000 shots each for the different vectors. In Fig. 8, a noise simulation results with depolarising errors in the CNOTs (with 99% gate fidelity), and one qubit gate (with 99.99% gate fidelity) is shown. For both cases, the results are accurate when the distance is more significant, starting on the order of 5 units in the case of perfect simulation and 10 in the noisy model.

The error in the small distance area is attributed to the encoding in the angle of rotations; when the two vectors are close to each other, the angle will become small enough to create errors. As seen in the transpiler circuit shown in Fig. 9, the swap test involves fewer CNOT gates than the QFT approach.

Given the applicability of the Swap test in current NISQ devices, the experiments for different pairs of vectors in several QPUs using the qBraid environment

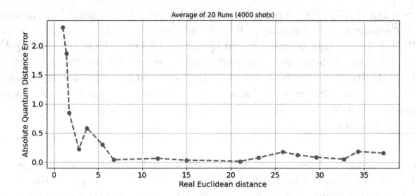

Fig. 7. Noiseless simulation of the computation of the Euclidean distance using the Swap Test for 17 pairs of vectors. With an average of 20 runs and 4000 shots each.

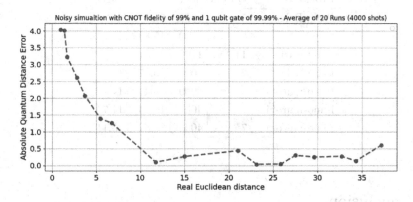

Fig. 8. Noisy simulation with a CNOT fidelity of 99% and one qubit gate of 99.99% of the Swap Test for 17 pairs of vectors. With an average of 20 runs and 4000 shots each.

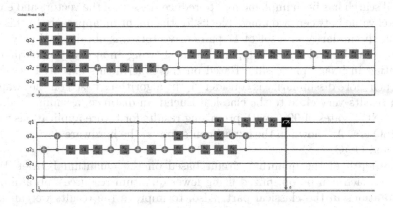

Fig. 9. Transpiled circuit for the Swap Test with the gate basis $[cx, id, rz, sx]$

are executed. The proposal quantum-classical hybrid block-matching algorithm with the image vectors $\vec{Img_1} = [9,9,9,9]$ and $\vec{Img_2} = [9,9,8,9]$ in the following QPU's: IonQ Harmony device, Oxford Quantum Circuits (OQC) and IonQ Aria device and Ibmq-Belem were executed. The experimental results are shown in the Table 2 with the number of qubits and shots used in each case. As expected with the noise models Fig. 8, we found that when less dissimilarity is considered, the error is more significant than in the cases of bigger distances from the vectors previously presented.

Table 2. Comparison between the Quantum Euclidean Distance (QED) and the Classical Euclidean Distance (CED) using vectors $\vec{Img_1}$ and $\vec{Img_2}$. The proposal quantum-classical hybrid block-matching algorithm was executed in IonQ Harmony, OQC, IonQ Aria, and Ibmq-Belem.

Provider	Qubits	Shots	QED	CED
Ibmq-Belem	5	1000	6.55	1
OQC	8	1000	15.887	1
IonQ Harmony	11	1000	7.452	1
IonQ Aria	25	1000	10.173	1
Ibmq-nairobi	7	4000	5.54	1
Ibmq-nairobi	7	4000	16.74	11.747
Ibmq-nairobi	7	4000	26.82	23.11

5   Conclusions

This work presented a proof of concept of the standard dissimilarity measure using the Euclidean distance in a quantum computing approach. Also, the hierarchical search has been implemented to reduce the size of the vectors and encode the pixel value between two image blocks for the quantum approach. In this case, only the dissimilarity of a set of 17 pairs of vectors was obtained. However, the approach can be scaled to a complete image showing an application of quantum computing in image processing. Based on the experiments executed, we found that when more dissimilarity is considered, the algorithms based on the swap test obtain results very close to the classical Euclidean distance, assuming a fidelity in the CNOT gates of 99%, with promising results for future applications within the NISQ era. As shown in the experiments run on the hardware devices of IBM, IonQ, and OQC.

The depth of the quantum circuit based on the Quantum Fourier Transform approach can be optimized using fewer quantum resources, obtaining the final rotations in the classical part. Also, to improve the results we can apply error mitigation techniques as Zero-Noise Extrapolation to both approaches. In addition, we plan to use this work in a sequence of digital videos.

Acknowledgments. This work is supported by the Consejo Nacional de Humanidades, Ciencias y Tecnologías (CONAHCYT), Instituto Politécnico Nacional (IPN) and Quantum Open Source Foundation (QOSF). Also this work was sponsored by qBraid, a cloud-based platform for quantum computing.

References

1. Al-Ghaib, H., Adhami, R.: On the digital image additive white gaussian noise estimation. In: 2014 International Conference on Industrial Automation, Information and Communications Technology, pp. 90–96 (2014). https://doi.org/10.1109/IAICT.2014.6922089
2. Bharti, K., et al.: Noisy intermediate-scale quantum algorithms. Rev. Mod. Phys. **94**, 015004 (2022). https://doi.org/10.1103/RevModPhys.94.015004
3. Brunelli, R.: Template Matching Techniques in Computer Vision (2009). https://doi.org/10.1002/9780470744055
4. Dang, Y., Jiang, N., Hu, H., Zhang, W.: Analysis and improvement of the quantum image matching. Quantum Inf. Process. **16** (2017). https://doi.org/10.1007/s11128-017-1723-7
5. De Jesús Martínez Felipe, M., Felipe Riverón, E.M., Martínez Castro, J.A., Pogrebnyak, O.: Noisy image block matching based on dissimilarity measure in discrete cosine transform domain. J. Intell. Fuzzy Syst. **36**(4), 3169–3176 (2019). https://doi.org/10.3233/JIFS-18533. Cited by: 1
6. Draper, T.G.: Addition on a quantum computer. arXiv preprint quant-ph/0008033 (2000)
7. Georgopoulos, K., Emary, C., Zuliani, P.: Modeling and simulating the noisy behavior of near-term quantum computers. Phys. Rev. A **104**, 062432 (2021). https://doi.org/10.1103/PhysRevA.104.062432
8. Hill, R.J., et al.: qBraid-SDK: Python toolkit for cross-framework abstraction of quantum programs (2023). https://github.com/qBraid/qBraid
9. Jiang, N., Dang, Y., Wang, J.: Quantum image matching. Quantum Inf. Process. **15**(9), 3543–3572 (2016). https://doi.org/10.1007/s11128-016-1364-2
10. Kandala, A., Temme, K., Córcoles, A.D.: Error mitigation extends the computational reach of a noisy quantum processor. Nature **567** (2019). https://doi.org/10.1038/s41586-019-1040-7
11. Le, P.Q., Dong, F., Hirota, K.: A flexible representation of quantum images for polynomial preparation, image compression, and processing operations. Quantum Inf. Process. **10**, 63–84 (2011)
12. Li, P., Wang, B.: Quantum neural networks model based on swap test and phase estimation. Neural Netw. **130**, 152–164 (2020). https://doi.org/10.1016/j.neunet.2020.07.003. https://www.sciencedirect.com/science/article/pii/S0893608020302446
13. Preskill, J.: Quantum computing in the NISQ era and beyond. Quantum **2**, 79 (2018)
14. Qiskit contributors: Qiskit: an open-source framework for quantum computing (2023). https://doi.org/10.5281/zenodo.2573505
15. Schuld, M., Petruccione, F.: Quantum models as kernel methods. In: Machine Learning with Quantum Computers. QST, pp. 217–245. Springer, Cham (2021). https://doi.org/10.1007/978-3-030-83098-4_6
16. Shu, G., Shan, Z., Di, S., Ding, X., Feng, C.: A hybrid quantum image-matching algorithm. Entropy **24**, 1816 (2022). https://doi.org/10.3390/e24121816

17. Sun, B., Iliyasu, A., Yan, F., Dong, F., Hirota, K.: An RGB multi-channel representation for images on quantum computers. J. Adv. Comput. Intell. Intell. Inform. **17**(3) (2013)

18. Urgelles, H., Picazo-Martínez, P., Monserrat, J.F.: Application of quantum computing to accurate positioning in 6g indoor scenarios. In: IEEE International Conference on Communications, ICC 2022, pp. 643–647 (2022). https://doi.org/10.1109/ICC45855.2022.9838523

19. Zhang, Y., Lu, K., Gao, Y., Wang, M.: NEQR: a novel enhanced quantum representation of digital images. Quantum Inf. Process. **12**, 2833–2860 (2013)

20. Zhao, J., Zhang, Y.H., Shao, C.P., Wu, Y.C., Guo, G.C., Guo, G.P.: Building quantum neural networks based on a swap test. Phys. Rev. A **100**, 012334 (2019). https://doi.org/10.1103/PhysRevA.100.012334

Some Initial Guidelines for Building Reusable Quantum Oracles

Javier Sanchez-Rivero[3] , Daniel Talaván[1] , Jose Garcia-Alonso[2(✉)] ,
Antonio Ruiz-Cortés[3] , and Juan Manuel Murillo[2]

[1] COMPUTAEX, Cáceres, Spain
[2] University of Extremadura, Badajoz, Spain
jgaralo@unex.es
[3] Universidad de Sevilla, Seville, Spain

Abstract. The evolution of quantum hardware is highlighting the need for advances in quantum software engineering that help developers create quantum software with good quality attributes. Specifically, reusability has been traditionally considered an important quality attribute. Increasing the reusability of quantum software will help developers create more complex solutions. This work focuses on the reusability of oracles, a well-known pattern of quantum algorithms that can be used to perform functions used as input by other algorithms. In this work, we present several guidelines for making reusable quantum oracles. These guidelines include three different levels for oracle reuse: the reasoning behind the oracle algorithm, the function which creates the oracle, and the oracle itself. To demonstrate these guidelines, two different implementations of a range of integers oracle have been built by reusing simpler oracles. The quality of these implementations is evaluated in terms of functionality and quantum circuit depth. Then, we provide an example of documentation following the proposed guidelines for both implementations to foster reuse of the provided oracles. This work aims to be a first point of discussion towards quantum software reusability.

Keywords: quantum computing · quantum software reuse · oracle · reuse guidelines · quantum algorithms

1 Introduction

Quantum software is beginning to become a reality and with it, the first forums have begun to appear that address the discipline of Quantum Software Engineering (IEEE QSW, ICSE Q-SE, Q-SET, etc). One of the problems to be addressed by this discipline is that of achieving good quality attributes in quantum programs [24].

The standard ISO/IEC 25010:2011 - Systems and software Quality Requirements and Evaluation (SQuaRE) [9] identifies *Reusability* as one of the sub-characteristics of the quality attribute *Maintainability*. It is defined as the *degree*

F. Monti et al. (Eds.): ICSOC 2023 Workshops, LNCS 14518, pp. 197–208, 2024.
https://doi.org/10.1007/978-981-97-0989-2_16

to which an asset can be used in more than one system, or in building other assets. Thus, in terms of efficiency of cost and effort, software is of better quality the more reusable it is. Modularity can contribute to reusability in that the asset to be reused needs not be a complete program but a smaller module of whatever it may be (procedure, function, component, service, etc.).

If one tries to port these concepts to the realm of quantum programming, oracles would be a good asset to promote modularity, reusability and maintainability. The oracle has been identified as a pattern for quantum algorithms [13]. An oracle can be thought as a black box performing a function that is used by another algorithm [14]. Following the principles of Separation of Concerns [3], they can be designed in isolation and then applied in solving different problems.

The above features make oracles a good candidate asset for quantum software reuse. However, oracles are not reusable by themselves. As in classical systems programming [15], quantum programmers must apply techniques that make the code they build reusable by design. In addition, proper documentation is a necessity for the systematic reuse of software [19].

This work focuses on how to properly document quantum software and more specifically quantum oracles. In this scope, some guidelines for documenting oracles are proposed. With this, the authors of this work seek to contribute to enable programmers to build complex quantum software by reusing and composing simpler pieces. To demonstrate the use of the guidelines two different implementations of the *range of integers* are provided. One of them corresponds to the reuse and composition of two oracles: *less than* and *addition*. While the other one corresponds to the reuse and composition of two *less than* oracles.

The remainder of this paper is structured as follows. Section 2 introduces some background and related works about oracles and their usage. Then, Sect. 3 introduces two different implementations for the *range of integers* oracle. One of them is based on the composition of two oracles *less than* and *greater than*. The second one corresponds to a direct implementation optimizing the depth of the produced quantum circuit. Section 4 analyses the documentation needs for oracles to be reused. We analyse three different levels of re-usability said reuse of the ideas inspiring the oracle, reuse of the oracle and reuse of the classical function that builds the implementation of the oracle. Finally, Sect. 5 gives some conclusions and explores future works.

2   Background and Related Work

A well-known example of a quantum algorithm that uses an oracle is Grover's algorithm [6]. This quantum algorithm can search a value in an unordered data sequence faster than any classical algorithm. To do that, it needs an oracle that encodes the desired value. There are many other quantum algorithms that use oracles such as Deutsch-Jozsa [2], Simon [23] or Bernstein-Vazirani [1]. This can be seen as one of the first cases of quantum software reuse.

It is desired that reusable software has the best possible quality attributes. This is especially relevant in quantum software as actual quantum computers are prone to decoherence. One of the crucial factors regarding reliability of results is the depth of circuits. As depth is a measure of the execution time of a given circuit, the deeper the circuit, the greater the exposition to noise and lower its reliability [18]. Consequently, disregarding the depth of the circuit may arise results indistinguishable from noise [16]. Many of the works being developed nowadays in the area of quantum computing is focused on improving existent oracles to reduce depth [10], reduce the number of required qubits [7] or simplifying the gates they use [11]. However, those works are very difficult to reuse. Usually they provide a description of the oracle being very unusual to find, for example, an algorithm to implement the oracle parameterizing magnitudes like the number qubits or the state to which they must be applied. So, reusing those oracles requires a deep understanding and a big effort of programming. To help with this situation some standard to describe oracles would be very helpful.

In this paper we present an example of quantum software reutilization by combining existing quantum software to build a range of integers phase-marking oracle. We present two different implementations of the same oracle to showcase the need for a good description to have easily reusable oracles. Based on this example, we provide some guidelines for making reusable oracles.

3   Oracle for Range of Integers

In this section we present two different implementations of what is, in principle, the same oracle. These two different implementations exemplify how already existing oracles can be reused to achieve a different purpose.

The aim is to design a phase-marking oracle which, assuming quantum states encode natural numbers (including 0), gives a π-phase to those numbers within a given range, $[n_1, n_2]$. This oracle ideally would encode the following function:

$$f(x) = \begin{cases} -1 & \text{if } x \in [n_1, n_2] \\ 1 & \text{otherwise} \end{cases} \tag{1}$$

These two implementations of a phase-marking oracle for a range of integers have been developed by reusing existing quantum software. We have used, in all cases, the linear-depth multi-controlled Z-gate as provided in [22]. The less-than oracle presented in [21] is also used in both implementations (another, similar, oracle was also created from this line of work for marking multiples of an integer, additional information can be found in [20]). The quantum addition presented in [4] is used in implementation B. As all these quantum software pieces have a depth with polynomial growth with the number of qubits, the resulting compositions of these oracles have polynomial depth. The code for both implementations as well as the data of experiments conducted in this work can be found here[1].

---

[1] https://github.com/JSRivero/range-integers-oracle

3.1   Implementation A: Two Less-Than Oracles

The first way of implementing a range of integers oracle is by combining two less-than oracles. If the aimed range is $[n_1, n_2]$, notice the close interval, the oracle which marks these states can be obtained by applying oracles less-than $n_2 + 1$ and less-than n_1. It is noticeable that this oracle marks the desired states regardless of the order. This happens because the states smaller than n_1 are marked twice, so the second phase-marking applied to already marked states return them to 0-phase. This implementation does perform the function 1 for any input state.

An example of this oracle is shown in Fig. 1. The upper part of the figure corresponds to the quantum states after applying the circuits displayed in the bottom part. In blue, the states with a 0-phase, in red, the states with a π-phase. Figure 1a represents the states after the initialization to full superposition. Figure 1b shows in red the quantum states marked after applying a less-than 4 oracle to the circuit. Figure 1c shows the states within the desired range successfully marked after a less-than 8 oracle is applied to the circuit.

3.2   Implementation B: Less-Than Oracle and Displacement

The second way of implementing this oracle is by applying a less-than oracle followed by a displacement of the marked states by using quantum addition. If the aimed range is $[n_1, n_2]$, the oracle can be obtained by applying the oracle less-than $n_2 - n_1 + 1$ followed by quantum addition of n_1. Contrary to the first implementation, the order of the oracles in this implementation must always be as explained.

However, this implementation possesses some drawbacks. A hard condition on the input state is needed as the oracle only performs function (1) given a full superposed input state without relative phases, formally:

$$\frac{1}{\sqrt{N}} \sum_{i=0}^{N-1} |i\rangle \tag{2}$$

where $N = 2^n$ being n the number of qubits.

An example of this oracle is shown in Fig. 2. The upper part of the figure corresponds to the quantum states after applying the circuits displayed in the bottom part. In blue, the states with a 0-phase, in red, the states with a π-phase. Figure 2a represents the states after the initialization to full superposition. Figure 2b shows in red the quantum states marked after applying a less-than 4 oracle to the circuit. Figure 2c shows the states within the desired range successfully marked after an addition of 4 is applied to the circuit. This addition may be seen as a displacement of the already marked states.

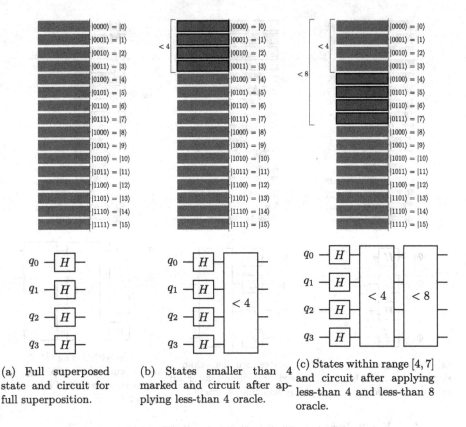

(a) Full superposed state and circuit for full superposition.

(b) States smaller than 4 marked and circuit after applying less-than 4 oracle.

(c) States within range [4, 7] and circuit after applying less-than 4 and less-than 8 oracle.

Fig. 1. Implementation A of range of integers oracle for [4, 7].

3.3   Depth Comparison of both Implementations

To properly compare the depth of these two methods, we have transpiled both circuits to the gate set used in one of the IBM quantum computers (*ibm_washington*), using the fake provider[2].

In order to do the comparison we generate a range of integers circuit for each possible interval $[n_1, n_2]$ where $0 < n_1 < n_2 < N - 1$, where N is the total number of states. We have conducted this analysis from 3 to 12 qubits, both included. Figure 3 shows the comparison of the two implementations of the range of integers oracle. While both implementations have polynomial depth on the number of qubits, it can be noted that Implementation B has a lower depth than Implementation A. It is more suitable to be used in NISQ devices given a full superposed initial state without relative phases. However, Implementation A, as stated, does not have this constraint and would work on any input state.

---

[2] Fake providers are built to mimic IBM quantum systems, they have the same properties (gate set, coupling map, etc.) as the real devices.

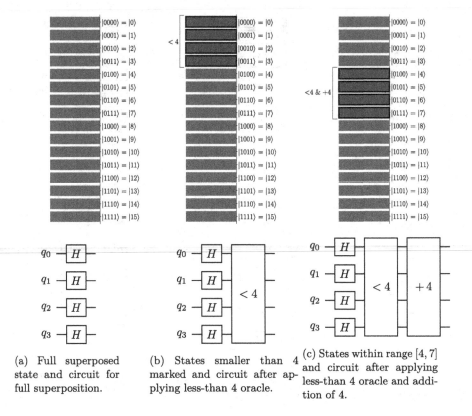

(a) Full superposed state and circuit for full superposition.

(b) States smaller than 4 marked and circuit after applying less-than 4 oracle.

(c) States within range [4, 7] and circuit after applying less-than 4 oracle and addition of 4.

Fig. 2. Implementation B of range of integers oracle for $[4, 7]$.

4   Guidelines for Making Reusable Oracles

From the above examples, it is clear that is not enough to document the function that an oracle is performing in order for them to be reused later. Both oracles perform the same function in the adequate input, however choosing one of them over the other can have a significant impact in the final quantum software. From the current version of the oracles, it seems clear that implementation B of the oracle is the preferred one due to the lesser depth of the circuit. However, this could change if a more efficient implementation of the less than oracle that is used twice to create implementation A is discovered. For developers to be able to effectively reuse quantum oracles, they should be aware of all the aspects of the oracle that could have an impact in their software.

In order to facilitate the creation of such reusable oracles, and based on the experience of the creation of the two implementations of the range of integers oracle, in this section we present some initial guidelines for making reusable oracles. We present these guidelines organized in three subsections that represent three different levels of oracle reuse in quantum software.

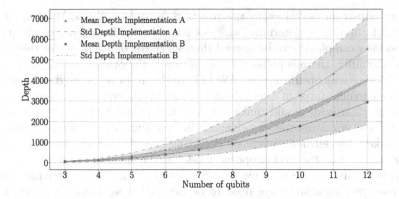

Fig. 3. Depth comparison of implementations A and B.

First, we propose some guidelines for making the fundamental reasoning behind the oracle algorithm easier to reuse. Given the current state of quantum software development, oracles are usually based on algorithms with low abstraction levels. As has been demonstrated in classical software reuse, this kind of low abstraction level patterns or algorithmic paradigms, if well understood, can help developers in the development process.

Then, we consider two different levels of specification for the reuse of the oracles. On one side, we consider the classical algorithm that is used to create the oracle circuit. This algorithm is needed for generating the actual quantum circuit that would be used as part of the quantum program, adapted to the required size of the input. And on the other side, we considered the oracle itself. This will be the final piece of software that could be reused to create more complex functions by composing them with others and, therefore, developers should be made aware of how to reuse it, how it can be composed, its effects on the quantum state, the impact in the resulting circuit and many other elements needed for effective reuse.

4.1   Reuse of the Reasoning Behind the Oracle Algorithm

As is well known from classical software, all approaches to software reuse refers to some form of abstraction [12]. One of the higher level abstractions in classical software are algorithmic paradigms, a generic model or framework that underlies the design of a class of algorithms. Oracle, as patterns for quantum algorithms, can be considered as an algorithmic paradigm and, therefore, a prime candidate for reuse.

Nevertheless, a high abstraction level is not enough. Any approach to reusability should help software developers locate, compare, and select reusable software artifacts [12]. By treating oracles as black box functions, we might provide enough information for quantum software developers to understand how an oracle can be used. However, as demonstrated by the presented examples, is not enough if they need to compare them and select the best suited one.

If we constrain ourselves to the function of oracles A and B, there is not enough information to determine which oracle is better for a given situation. For this specific example, it can be argued that, since the depth of one of the oracles is always smaller, there is no need to select one of the oracles, as the answer will always be the most optimized one. We believe this to be a shortsighted approach given the current status of quantum devices and software. The current diversity in quantum hardware could make a more efficient oracle to perform worse in a given quantum computer or advances in quantum algorithms or transpilers could make a less efficient oracle suddenly improve its performance over others.

For this reason, the first proposed guideline for oracle reuse is that it is not enough to document the function that oracles perform. The underlying components used to create an oracle need to be detailed if we want the oracle to be reused effectively. In the Documentation of implementation A and Documentation of implementation B (included in the above mentioned repository[3]) the Oracle as a Black Box and Oracle as its components show the difference between the two types of oracle documentation.

Additionally, by providing a more detailed description of the oracle we not only make them more reusable by themselves, we allow developers to reuse the reasoning behind the oracle algorithm for the creation of other oracles. An example of this can be found in implementation A. As mentioned above, one of the key ideas of this implementation is that if a given state is marked two times (in this case by both less-than oracles) it returns to 0-phase. This is not an obvious behavior of the less-than oracle, and by making developers aware of it they could be inspired for the creation of new software that can take advantage of this property.

Taking this into account we can propose another guideline for creating reusable oracles. To foster reuse, a developer must be able to navigate through, and reason about, the source code and its dependencies in order to identify program elements that are relevant [8]. In the specific case of quantum oracles this means that the reasoning behind the oracle algorithm should be thoroughly documented alongside the oracle for the developer to be able to reason about them and get inspired for the creation of new oracles based on such ideas.

Another example of this kind of reuse can be found in implementation B of the proposed oracle. In that oracle, we make use of the quantum addition to shift the states the marked states to the desired one.

4.2   Reuse of the Algorithm that Creates the Oracle

Once the reasoning behind the oracle algorithm is clearly documented, another relevant level of reuse to consider is the reuse of the function that creates the oracle circuit. For most oracles, a classical algorithm is used in order to generate a specific quantum circuit that implements the oracle for a given size of the input. As such, to foster reuse its documentation should focus on some of the metrics

---

[3] https://github.com/JSRivero/range-integers-oracle

that traditionally help software reuse like the ratio of input/output parameters or the ratio of comments [5].

Additionally, some aspects have to be considered that are specific of quantum software in general and oracles in particular. Specifically, a relevant guideline when documenting for reuse an algorithm that creates oracles is to differentiate between input parameters that are only used by the algorithm that those that are used by the oracle itself.

One example of such parameters in the case of the range of integers oracle are the two specific integers that define the limits of the range. These values are used by the function to create the quantum circuit. However, once the circuit is generated those are not input parameters of the oracle. The circuit that implements the oracle for the range $[4, 7]$ will only work for those values and a completely different circuit should be created for the range $[3, 8]$ or any other range.

How this kind of parameters of the function but not of the oracle work may not be obvious for developers wanted to reuse an oracle, especially for those coming from classical software engineering, and therefore should be clearly documented as such. To make these functions more reusable, the user must clearly understand their interface (i.e., those properties of the function that interact with other artifacts) [12].

To improve reuse these parameters should be clearly distinguished from other types of input parameters like those that are only used by the oracle and not by the function that creates it or those parameters used by both. An example of the first type is the specific qubits to which the oracle is going to be applied. This information is relevant for the oracle itself, and therefore it would be discussed in the next section, but is irrelevant for the function that creates the oracle. The quantum circuit for the range $[4, 7]$ would be the same regardless of whether it is applied to qubits from q_0 to q_4 or from q_5 to q_8.

4.3   Reuse of the Oracle

Finally, the last level of reuse to consider when creating oracles is the reuse of the oracle itself. Similar to classical software, using a formalized process to foster reuse, as the one proposed by these guidelines, increases the chance that the software can be reused successfully [17]. In the specific case of quantum oracles, some additional aspects should be considered that are not included in the reuse of classical software.

As part of classical software documentation, pre and postconditions are fundamentals aspects of software reuse. For oracles, one of the most relevant preconditions is the quantum state that the oracle is expecting as input. This is a key difference between implementations A and B. Whereas implementation A marks the states regardless of their amplitude, implementation B requires a superposition of all possible states with no relative phase. If the input does not meet this precondition, the oracle B will not behave as expected. In other oracles, the expected state could be different.

As important as the input quantum state are the postconditions that can be guaranteed after the oracle has been applied to the quantum state. Specifically, the quantum state in which the qubits are left once the oracle has been applied. This can be extrapolated from the oracle's unitary matrix (as shown in Sect. 3 for the range of integers example), however a textual description of the state would improve readability and foster reuse. For both implementations of the range of integer oracles, the postcondition of the quantum state is that states that represent integers in the selected range would have π-phase without any other change to the input quantum state (as long as input state fulfills the preconditions). Another example would be the addition oracle. The postcondition of this oracle is just a displacement on any given input state, i.e., for an input state $|4\rangle = |100\rangle$ an addition of 3 results in the state $|7\rangle = |111\rangle$. It also maintains the phases of the displaced states.

Therefore, an important guideline for creating reusable quantum oracles is to clearly document the pre and postconditions of the quantum state manipulated by the oracle. Providing this information will make oracles easier to reuse, since developers understand the expected state and how to keep working with the output state once the oracle has been applied.

Finally, the last proposed guideline is to document the properties of the oracles' quantum circuits that are relevant for future users.

One of the most relevant properties of the circuit to be documented is the depth of the oracle's circuit. This property is crucial to determine if a given oracle can be used in a NISQ era quantum computer and, therefore, it should be known by developers willing to reuse the oracle. The depth of the circuits should be measured by transpiling them to a specific device, as the architecture of quantum chips is not yet standardized and can affect the resulting depth.

Nevertheless, other aspects of the circuit should also be considered. For example, the quantum gates used in the circuit are also a relevant aspect to consider if it is going to be run a real device. Although not available quantum gates can be replaced by alternative circuits, this could heavily impact the circuit's depth or other properties, so it should be documented for reuse. Something similar happens with the assumption of connections between given qubits for entanglement. Although this is usually handled by the transpiler it can affect the circuit properties. In general, any aspect of the circuit that could affect to its performance should be thoroughly documented.

For the range of integer oracles, both implementations need the universal set of quantum gates. Moreover, all qubits require connections between them, because the less-than oracle and the Quantum Fourier Transform.

5   Conclusions and Future Work

We have presented two implementations of a range of integers oracle built by reusing two different oracles. This is done to exemplify the reusability of oracles. The functionality of both implementations has been shown with the same example. A study on the depth of both implementations has been made. An improvement in depth is clearly shown with one of the implementations. Moreover, we have presented several guidelines for making reusable oracles, including the reasoning behind the oracle algorithm, the function which creates the oracle and the oracle itself. We have provided an example of a documentation that follows those guidelines for both implementations presented.

This work aims to be a first point of discussion towards quantum software reusability. There is still work to do in establishing proper criteria for quantum software reusability. Further guidelines may be presented not only on oracles, but also on any type of quantum software, such as full algorithm implementations.

Acknowledgments. This work has been financially supported by the Ministry of Economic Affairs and Digital Transformation of the Spanish Government through the QUANTUM ENIA project call - Quantum Spain project, by the Spanish Ministry of Science and Innovation under project PID2021-124054OB-C31, by the Regional Ministry of Economy, Science and Digital Agenda, and the Department of Economy and Infrastructure of the Government of Extremadura under project GR21133, and by the European Union through the Recovery, Transformation and Resilience Plan - NextGenerationEU within the framework of the Digital Spain 2026 Agenda. We are grateful to COMPUTAEX Foundation for allowing us to use the supercomputing facilities (LUSITANIA II) for calculations.

References

1. Bernstein, E., Vazirani, U.: Quantum complexity theory. SIAM J. Comput. **26**(5), 1411–1473 (1997). https://doi.org/10.1137/S0097539796300921
2. Deutsch, D., Jozsa, R.: Rapid solution of problems by quantum computation. Proc. R. Soc. Lond. Series A: Math. Phys. Sci. **439**, 553–558 (1992). https://doi.org/10.1098/rspa.1992.0167
3. Dijkstra, E.W.: On the role of scientific thought (EWD447). In: Dijkstra, E.W. (ed.) Selected Writings on Computing: A Personal Perspective, pp. 60–66. Springer, Cham (1982). https://doi.org/10.1007/978-1-4612-5695-3_12
4. Draper, T.G.: Addition on a quantum computer. arXiv preprint quant-ph/0008033 (2000)
5. Frakes, W., Terry, C.: Software reuse: metrics and models. ACM Comput. Surv. (CSUR) **28**(2), 415–435 (1996)
6. Grover, L.K.: A fast quantum mechanical algorithm for database search (1996). https://doi.org/10.48550/ARXIV.QUANT-PH/9605043. https://arxiv.org/abs/quant-ph/9605043
7. Henderson, J.M., Henderson, E.R., Sinha, A., Thornton, M.A., Miller, D.M.: Automated quantum oracle synthesis with a minimal number of qubits. In: Quantum Information Science, Sensing, and Computation XV, vol. 12517, pp. 50–67. SPIE (2023)
8. Holmes, R., Walker, R.J.: Systematizing pragmatic software reuse. ACM Trans. Softw. Eng. Methodol. (TOSEM) **21**(4), 1–44 (2013)
9. ISO/IEC: Systems and software engineering - systems and software quality requirements and evaluation (square) - system and software quality models (2011). https://www.iso.org/standard/35733.html

10. Jaques, S., Naehrig, M., Roetteler, M., Virdia, F.: Implementing Grover oracles for quantum key search on AES and LowMC. In: Canteaut, A., Ishai, Y. (eds.) EUROCRYPT 2020. LNCS, vol. 12106, pp. 280–310. Springer, Cham (2020). https://doi.org/10.1007/978-3-030-45724-2_10

11. Kissinger, A., van de Wetering, J.: Reducing the number of non-clifford gates in quantum circuits. Phys. Rev. A **102**(2), 022406 (2020)

12. Krueger, C.W.: Software reuse. ACM Comput. Surv. (CSUR) **24**(2), 131–183 (1992)

13. Leymann, F.: Towards a pattern language for quantum algorithms. In: Feld, S., Linnhoff-Popien, C. (eds.) QTOP 2019. LNCS, vol. 11413, pp. 218–230. Springer, Cham (2019). https://doi.org/10.1007/978-3-030-14082-3_19

14. Liu, J., Zhou, H.: Hardware efficient quantum search algorithm (2021). https://doi.org/10.48550/ARXIV.2103.14196. https://arxiv.org/abs/2103.14196

15. Mili, H., Mili, F., Mili, A.: Reusing software: issues and research directions. IEEE Trans. Softw. Eng. **21**(6), 528–562 (1995). https://doi.org/10.1109/32.391379

16. Preskill, J.: Quantum Computing in the NISQ era and beyond. Quantum **2**(79), 10 (2018). https://doi.org/10.22331/q-2018-08-06-79

17. Rothenberger, M.A., Dooley, K.J., Kulkarni, U.R., Nada, N.: Strategies for software reuse: a principal component analysis of reuse practices. IEEE Trans. Softw. Eng. **29**(9), 825–837 (2003)

18. Saki, A.A., Alam, M., Ghosh, S.: Study of decoherence in quantum computers: a circuit-design perspective (2019). https://doi.org/10.48550/ARXIV.1904.04323. https://arxiv.org/abs/1904.04323

19. Sametinger, J.: Software Engineering with Reusable Components. Springer, Cham (1997)

20. Sanchez-Rivero, J., Talaván, D., Garcia-Alonso, J., Ruiz-Cortés, A., Murillo, J.M.: Operating with quantum integers: an efficient 'multiples of' oracle. In: Aiello, M., Barzen, J., Dustdar, S., Leymann, F. (eds.) Service-Oriented Computing, pp. 105–124. Springer, Cham (2023). https://doi.org/10.1007/978-3-031-45728-9_7

21. Sanchez-Rivero, J., Talaván, D., Garcia-Alonso, J., Ruiz-Cortés, A., Murillo, J.M.: Automatic generation of an efficient less-than oracle for quantum amplitude amplification (2023). https://doi.org/10.1109/Q-SE59154.2023.00011

22. da Silva, A.J., Park, D.K.: Linear-depth quantum circuits for multiqubit controlled gates. Phys. Rev. A **106**, 042602 (2022). https://doi.org/10.1103/PhysRevA.106.042602

23. Simon, D.R.: On the power of quantum computation. SIAM J. Comput. **26**(5), 1474–1483 (1997). https://doi.org/10.1137/S0097539796298637

24. Sodhi, B., Kapur, R.: Quantum computing platforms: Assessing the impact on quality attributes and SDLC activities. In: 2021 IEEE 18th International Conference on Software Architecture (ICSA), pp. 80–91 (2021). https://doi.org/10.1109/ICSA51549.2021.00016

SSCOPE: Sustainable Service-Oriented Computing: Addressing Environmental, Social, and Economic Dimensions
Introduction

Introduction to the 1st International Workshop on Sustainable Service-Oriented Computing: Addressing Environmental, Social, and Economic Dimensions (SSCOPE 2023)

Roberta Capuano⬤, Daniele Di Pompeo⬤, and Michele Tucci⬤

University of L'Aquila, Italy
{roberta.capuano,daniele.dipompeo,michele.tucci}@univaq.it

The Sustainable Service-Oriented Computing Workshop (SSCOPE 2023) was held as an integral part of the 21st International Conference on Service-Oriented Computing (ICSOC 2023). SSCOPE 2023 was dedicated to exploring the critical intersection of sustainability and service-oriented computing, providing a forum for professionals and researchers interested in embedding environmental, social, and economic sustainability into service-oriented architectures and processes.

From the pool of submissions to SSCOPE 2023, 3 were desk rejected and 1 was accepted. The single blind reviewing process was thorough and involved a senior Program Committee member and at least two regular Program Committee members. This rigorous review ensured the high quality and relevance of the accepted paper, fostering a robust and insightful discussion at the workshop.

November 2023   SSCOPE 2023 Workshop Organizers

Organization

Workshop Organizers

Roberta Capuano   University of L'Aquila, Italy
Daniele Di Pompeo   University of L'Aquila, Italy
Michele Tucci   University of L'Aquila, Italy

Program Committee

Marco Autili   University of L'Aquila, Italy
Ivona Brandic   Vienna University of Technology, Austria
Matteo Camilli   Politecnico di Milano, Italy
Ilias Gerostathopoulos   Vrije Universiteit Amsterdam,
    The Netherlands
Gabriele Russo Russo   University of Rome Tor Vergata, Italy
Davide Taibi   University of Oulu, Finland
Roberto Verdecchia   University of Florence, Italy

Carbon-Awareness in CI/CD

Henrik Claßen, Jonas Thierfeldt, Julian Tochman-Szewc(iD),
Philipp Wiesner$^{(\boxtimes)}$ (iD), and Odej Kao(iD)

Technical University Berlin, Berlin, Germany
{h.classen,thierfeldt,tochman-szewc}@campus.tu-berlin.de,
{wiesner,odej.kao}@tu-berlin.de

Abstract. While the environmental impact of cloud computing is increasingly evident, the climate crisis has become a major issue for society. For instance, data centers alone account for 2.7% of Europe's energy consumption today. A considerable part of this load is accounted for by cloud-based services for automated software development, such as continuous integration and delivery (CI/CD) workflows.

In this paper, we discuss opportunities and challenges for greening CI/CD services by better aligning their execution with the availability of low-carbon energy. We propose a system architecture for carbon-aware CI/CD services, which uses historical runtime information and, optionally, user-provided information. Our evaluation examines the potential effectiveness of different scheduling strategies using real carbon intensity data and 7,392 workflow executions of Github Actions, a popular CI/CD service. Results show, that user-provided information on workflow deadlines can effectively improve carbon-aware scheduling.

Keywords: continuous integration · carbon-aware scheduling · carbon intensity · sustainability

1 Introduction

It is widely accepted that the main cause of anthropogenic climate is the release of greenhouse gases, such as carbon dioxide (CO_2), into the atmosphere. The burning of fossil fuels such as coal and gas for energy production is a major contributor to the release of greenhouse gases. Globally, data centers, which are an important part of modern digital infrastructure, consumed about 205 TWh of electricity in 2018, representing about 1% of global energy consumption [1], while in the EU they accounted for 2.7% of energy consumption [2]. Many cloud providers are taking steps to reduce the environmental impact of their data centers by utilizing more renewable energy. However, the production of renewable energy sources such as solar and wind varies greatly over time and different locations, making it difficult to ensure a constant supply of energy. A common metric to quantify the operational carbon emissions of energy consumption is called *carbon intensity*, which describes the grams of CO_2-equivalent greenhouse gases emitted per killowatt-hour of consumed energy (gCO_2/kWh).

© The Author(s), under exclusive license to Springer Nature Singapore Pte Ltd. 2024
F. Monti et al. (Eds.): ICSOC 2023 Workshops, LNCS 14518, pp. 213–224, 2024.
https://doi.org/10.1007/978-981-97-0989-2_17

A significant portion of the work performed in cloud data centers pertains to services that enable the automated testing, building, and delivery of software, often referred to as continuous integration and delivery (CI/CD) [3]. According to a survey conducted by the CD Foundation [4], the use of CI/CD in the context of development and operation has become a standard practice today and has steadily increased. Out of 70,000 developers, about 47% reported to use CI or CD in their software engineering process, as they increase productivity, software quality, and enable faster release cycles.

The operation of CI/CD services is a promising target for carbon-aware computing – the alignment of a computing system's power usage with the availability of energy with low carbon intensity – as they often include recurring or non-time-critical jobs. Moreover, the execution of CI/CD workflows can be resource-intensive and thus energy-intensive, since separate virtual machines or containers are usually used for each individual job. On the other hand, many CI/CD workflows are expected to execute as fast as possible and therefore have no temporal flexibility that can be leveraged. In this paper

- we discuss challenges and opportunities for carbon-aware CI/CD and propose a system architecture for more sustainable CI/CD services.
- we quantify potential improvements of carbon-aware scheduling using real-world carbon intensity and CI/CD workflow execution data.

The remainder of this paper is structured as follows. Section 2 reviews related work. Section 3 discusses the main opportunities and challenges of carbon-awareness in CI/CD followed by a carbon-aware system architecture in Sect. 4. Section 5 evaluates different scheduling scenarios. Section 6 concludes the paper.

2 Related Work

In this section we survey related works on CI/CD job management as well as general carbon-aware scheduling approaches.

2.1 CI/CD Workflow Scheduling

Major cloud and CI/CD service providers typically do not publicly disclose the specifics of their workflow scheduling heuristics. Jenkins, an open-source CI/CD automation server, employs a controller-agent architecture where a controller server schedules jobs to available agent nodes based on user-defined criteria, such as labels and priorities. While cloud providers keep their scheduling algorithms under wraps, the research community has been advancing cloud computing scheduling algorithms. For example, in the work of Ibrahim et al. [5] different state of the art scheduling heuristics that aim to optimize resource allocation and load balancing in cloud environments were compared and evaluated. However, to the best of our knowledge, no service provider inherently includes features for carbon-aware job scheduling at this point.

2.2 Carbon-Aware Computing

Due to an increasingly critical public perception of unsustainable business practices and the fact that carbon pricing mechanisms, such as emission trading systems or carbon taxes, are being implemented on a global scale [6], the IT industry is actively striving to increase the utilization of low-carbon energy within datacenters. Carbon-aware computing aims to reduce the emissions linked to computing by adjusting flexible workloads in terms of both timing [7–9] and geographic locations [10–12] to align with clean energy sources.

Like the concept proposed in this paper, the majority of carbon-aware approaches aims at consuming cleaner energy from the public grid [7,8,11,13,14]. For example, Google defers delay-tolerant workloads during periods when power generation is associated with high carbon intensity [8], which describes the amount of greenhouse gas emissions per unit of consumed energy (gCO_2/kWh). Although CI/CD workflows are sometimes used as exemplary use cases in evaluation scenarios [7], none of these works explicity addresses the opportunities and challenges arising when implementing carbon-awareness in CI/CD services.

Besides optimizing for grid carbon intensity, recent works also try to better exploit renewable energy fluctuations directly. For example, GreenSlot [15] is a scheduler that predicts the near-future availability of solar energy and schedules workload to maximize green energy consumption while also meeting job submission deadlines. Similarly, Cucumber [16] is an admission control policy which accepts low-priority workloads on underutilized infrastructure, only if they can be computed using excess energy. Zheng et al. [10] explore workload migration on underutilized data centers as a measure to reduce curtailment.

3 Opportunities and Challenges

In this section, we discuss ways in which existing CI/CD services can be made more carbon-aware and debate what challenges arise in doing so. After that, we look into the possibilities of utilizing additional user-supplied information to further improve carbon-aware scheduling.

3.1 Leveraging Temporal Flexibility vs. *Fail Fast*

The *fail fast* concept is a fundamental concept of CI/CD. It involves providing fast feedback to developers on whether their code changes meet the requirements or not. This helps to identify issues early in the development process, which can save time and resources in the long run.

Many carbon-aware scheduling strategies involve shifting workloads to times when there is a greener energy mix or when there is renewable excess energy available. However, as the *fail fast* concept demands workflows to be executed as soon and as fast as possible, it strongly conflicts with one of the most important properties of jobs suitable for carbon-aware computing: Temporal flexibility. This conflict highlights the need for a careful analysis of which jobs are eligible and to what extent carbon-aware scheduling can be implemented without compromising the speed and efficiency of the development process. Thus, a balance must be struck between these two concepts to achieve both fast feedback for developers and reduced carbon emissions.

3.2 Promising CI/CD Workflows for Carbon-Aware Scheduling

As stated above, not every CI/CD job is viable for full emission reducing scheduling, i.e. scheduling in time and location. Identifying this subset of jobs is the important first step in making CI/CD more carbon friendly.

- The first and most important category is made up of periodically running jobs. These are triggered by a date and time and not by a code change, such as nightly builds, integration test pipelines, or database backups. They are often not subject to the fail fast constraint: For example, the very requirement to perform a workflow *nightly* is often to perform it *outside of business hours*, which is usually more than half a day. The size of flexibility windows significantly impacts the potential for carbon footprint reduction [7].
- Second, CI/CD workflow often comprise of a multitude of interdependent jobs that are sometimes executed in parallel. Some of these steps may take multiple hours to complete, while other finish in a few minutes. Through the use of historical runtime data, carbon-aware schedulers can estimate flexibility windows for shorter tasks and leverage this information for carbon-aware scheduling.
- The third and last category is made up of jobs which are unnecessarily executed. Some code changes to a repository, e.g. changes to documentation, do not warrant the execution of, for example, unit tests. Some research has already been done in this direction [17]. Detecting these cases and aborting the workflow yields the greatest benefit because their carbon emissions can be reduced by 100%. However, identifying unnecessary CI/CD workflow executions is not the focus of this paper.

If there are multiple datacenters available to the CI/CD service to schedule workflows on, even workflows that cannot be shifted in time have a large potential in carbon reduction through the use of carbon-aware scheduling. This potential, however, highly depends on data locality and data protection regulations of the specific workflow.

3.3 Leveraging Historical Runtime Data

Integrating carbon awareness into existing CI/CD solutions is the most sensible way to achieve a high level of adoption. Therefore, we will now examine which information could be extracted from existing services without external input for carbon-aware scheduling.

The first bit of information needed is to identify a job's category (as defined above). Since a key concept of CI/CD services is automation, workflow definitions are seldom created on the fly but instead are defined in some machine readable format. These are then passed to the CI/CD framework used to execute. These configuration files, typically in YAML format, can also be fed into the scheduler to extract information about the parallelism, dependencies as well as periodicity of the jobs. This information can then be used to try to determine the category and make decisions on the scheduling. Additionally, configuration files may contain further execution requirements such as build system, mockup, or test data. As data transmission can also generate carbon emissions [18], it is furthermore important to inform the scheduler about where data is stored.

Data points produced by one or more actual executions of a job can also be used to influence scheduling decisions. For example, knowing the average and maximum runtime allows to better choose a time frame for execution. Moreover, start and finish times of jobs can be used to guess dependencies between jobs which might have not been included in their definitions. The time frame between the end of one job and the start of the next earliest depending job offers flexibility for scheduling. Even if a job is not dependent on another job, the start and end times can give an indication of a possible deadline: Consider a job that is not triggered by some user activity, starting after office hours or in the night and finishing before the start of the next days office hours. In this case, it can be assumed that this job is some kind of over night build or test and the time frame deducted from this can then be used for scheduling. This is especially useful for jobs which run periodically.

The last source of information is the current state of the CI/CD system. As service providers try to optimize their computing resources they cache container/VM images as well as required data at certain locations. Furthermore, providers have to keep spare computing resources available at different sites to guarantee fast response times (fail fast) under high system load. A scheduler can make use of this information and the learned workflow execution requirements to influence where (machine, data center, or region) a job will be executed. For example, starting a new server creates higher associated carbon costs than consolidating work on running machines. As outlined before, moving data to a desired location also consumes energy and therefore produces carbon emissions. Following, if some or all data requirements for a job execution are present at a certain data center it can be more efficient to run the job there even if the carbon footprint of the electricity is higher than elsewhere.

3.4 Improving Scheduling with User-Supplied Information

To further increase the effect of carbon-aware scheduling, we now investigate the potential effect of user-supplied information on the scheduling. To implement this, a user interface must be provided by the CI/CD service provider. An example is provided in Listing 1.1. Furthermore, users should be incentivized to provide additional information on their workflow runs and to accept potential delays in workflow executions.

One example of useful information that users can provide to the scheduler is runtime estimates. Especially for new workflows where historical information is not available, the cold-start problem significantly hinders the scheduler's ability

Listing 1.1. Exemplary interface which allows users to provide additional information on a workflow's duration, deadline, and allowed regions for execution.

```
---
name: CI/CD jobs
on: [push]
jobs:
  job-a:
    runs-on: ubuntu-latest
    carbon-aware: yes
    steps:
      - name: My first step
        uses: actions/hello_world@main
        with:
          duration: 1h
          deadline: 3h
          allowed-regions: [eu-central-1]
---
```

to perform sensible carbon-aware decisions. If users are able to provide estimates of the duration of the job we can incorporating this information into the planning process to enable adjustments to the schedule, as needed. However, it is important to consider the validity and accuracy of user information. This especially applies to the estimated runtime. It is known from high-performance computing that users more often than not tend to overestimate the runtime [19–22]. We expect the same to be true for CI/CD jobs. One possibility to counteract that is to gradually move to using historical data as it becomes available. The user should be informed of this change.

Another highly valuable input for carbon-aware schedulers are deadlines. As described above, if this information is not provided we can only try to guess a job's deadline based on interdependecies with other workflows. Since estimates must be conservative to avoid introducing delays or even errors, the potential carbon reductions can not be fully exploited. With a user-specified deadline, this ambiguity is removed, jobs are still guaranteed to finish on time, and the full potential can be realized. As described above, periodic jobs benefit the most from this.

Lastly, users should also be able to specify allowed regions for scheduling, for example, to avoid the scheduling in regions that require the migration of large volumes of data or that contradict with data protection regulations. This information can is used to influence the selection of the assigned region, as shorter transfer times are taken into account.

4   A Carbon-Aware CI/CD Service Architecture

In the following, we present a high-level systems architecture for carbon-aware CI/CD services in a distributed computing environment. We intentionally describe the concept in a general manner and do not specify whether it is an internal part of a CI/CD framework or provided by a third party to ease the integration into existing solutions such as GitHub Actions, Jenkins, or proprietary services. We assume that the scheduler is fed on a job-by-job basis and that it can query the information outlined in Sect. 3 in an effective manner.

To reduce the carbon footprint of CI/CD services, we first filter out promising jobs for carbon-aware scheduling and then plan their execution using information about previous runs, the state of the CI/CD system, and carbon intensity forecasts at different locations. The overall concept is depicted in Fig. 1. When a CI/CD workflow starts, a request is made to the scheduler. The result then contains when the job should be run, the region where to run and optionally the estimated duration that was used in the scheduling process. If the job should run at a later point in time we need to store meta information about the job.

A preprocessor filters all incoming requests, to sort out jobs which cannot or should not be processed further. Jobs cannot be processed further if it is not possible to apply carbon-aware scheduling (see Sect. 3) and should not be processed further if the expected carbon savings are smaller than the costs of the scheduling. Calculating this difference depends on many factors such as resource consumption of the scheduling process or length of the job. Therefore, we can not give a general answer when to apply the scheduling to a job and when not. If a user provides an estimate for the runtime of a job, the duration used in the scheduling process is a combination of this estimate and historical data. The weight of the user input decreases with increasing historical data. Additionally,

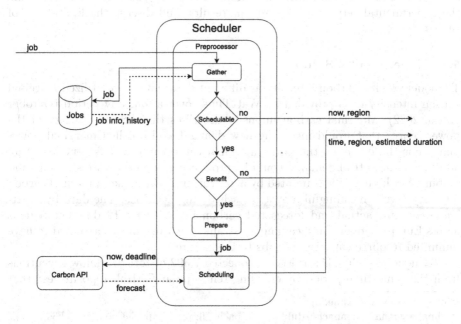

Fig. 1. High-level systems architecture

a time buffer is added to account for unforeseen increases in the duration, e.g. a sudden increase in the code base or tests. With an increasing number of previous runs the buffer is reduced.

The second step is the actual scheduling, which is the most important step, since the carbon reduction happens here. To estimate the carbon footprint, forecast data predicting the future carbon intensity per time and region is used. This data is fetched from an API for the time frame spanning the arrival time of the request to the (estimated) deadline of a job. An algorithm then uses this and available data of the CI/CD framework to estimate the total carbon footprint for each possible start time and region and selects the best result in terms of carbon intensity. For jobs that were previously filtered out, the currently best region in terms of carbon intensity is selected. To compare the prediction with the actual carbon emissions and provide feedback to the user, the runtime and energy consumption of a finished job is used to estimate the actual carbon intensity.

The interface for the human user to input information about a job (e.g. estimated runtime) can be implemented by a extending existing specification formats, see Listing 1.1. This also applies to reporting results back to the user, by adding this data to CI/CD framework's reporting mechanisms.

5   Evaluation of Carbon-Aware Scheduling Strategies

We implemented a first prototype of our proposed architecture using Node.js and evaluate different carbon-aware scheduling strategies against it. After describing the experimental setup, we present our results, and discuss the limitations of this analysis.

5.1   Experimental Setup

To model varying carbon intensity at different datacenters, we utilized marginal carbon intensity data provided by WattTime[1] over a four day period (October 12–16, 2022). Marginal carbon intensity describes the carbon intensity of the power source that would meet any new demand – also called marginal power plant. For the example, the grid's marginal carbon intensity is very low if an additional kilowatt of demand would be produced by an otherwise shut-off wind turbine, but high, if it is generated by a gas turbine. This makes marginal carbon intensity a very meaningful metric for scheduling decisions. The data by WattTime contains actual and forecasted carbon intensity for 12 different regions across Europe, North America, and Australia. Each region was assumed to have unlimited resource capacity for jobs to be executed.

To model the CI/CD service, we collected 7,392 historic workflow executions from the same time period by crawling ten popular GitHub repositories[2] that

---

[1] https://www.watttime.org.
[2] alibaba/arthas,   apache/dubbo,   apache/flink,   apache/spark,   k3s-io/k3s, kubernetes/minikube, microsoft/typescript, microsoft/vscode, netdata/netdata, Tencent/ncnn.

perform their CI/CD using Github Actions. The resulting dataset included the workflow name, start date, and runtime for each workflow execution.

We analyzed five experiments using different scheduling strategies. For each experiment, we iterate over all jobs in the dataset in temporal order. The five scheduling strategies are

- **Round-robin.** This naive strategy uses round-robin scheduling establishing a baseline to assess the improvements introduced by carbon-awareness.
- **Location Shifting.** This strategy demonstrates the effectiveness of scheduling CI/CD jobs at locations of low carbon intensity. Yet unknown jobs - those for which we lack historical data to estimate the runtime - are scheduled using the round-robin method.
- **Location + Time Shifting ({1, 3, 6} h).** The remaining strategies show the full potential of carbon-aware scheduling by additionally enabling the scheduler to exploit temporal flexibility of jobs. This approach is tested across three cases with varying deadline buffers (1 h, 3 h, 6 h) – information which, in practice, could be provided by users. The job's deadline was set to the sum of the duration and the buffer, ensuring each job had the same flexibility window for rescheduling. We will abbreviate this strategy in the following section as LTS-{1, 3, 6}.

5.2   Results

For each scenario, we report the distribution of jobs and accumulated carbon emissions over time relative to the round-robin baseline. We opted for relative results, as our dataset did not contain any energy consumption values and therefore we could not calculate carbon emissions in grams of CO_2eq or similar. This means that our findings provide an indication of the relative carbon intensity of different scheduling strategies, but not an absolute measure of carbon emissions.

In Fig. 2, it can be observed that in the round-robin baseline, the number of jobs is relatively evenly distributed, except for October 15th (Saturday), when the number of jobs is reduced over the weekend. Carbon emissions show some spikes on the afternoon of October 13th, as well as the early morning of October 12th and 14th. However, there are only a few periods where there are no or very low carbon emissions.

Since the *Location Shifting* strategy involves no temporal scheduling, the distribution of jobs over time remained the same, but the carbon emissions in Fig. 2 are noticeable lower overall. As a result, the overall carbon emissions could already be reduced by 25.31%.

In the *Location + Time Shifting* strategy, the effect of additionally leveraging temporal flexibility becomes apparent. For LTS-1, there was a noticeable reduction in carbon emissions, with some of the spikes shifting in time, which led to an improvement of 28.59% compared to the baseline. In the cases of LTS-3 and LTS-6, the impact was even more pronounced: jobs were significantly shifted to periods with lower carbon intensity. This redistribution resulted in more concentrated job clusters, along with intermittent gaps that featured fewer or no jobs. The overall carbon emissions were reduced by 31.20%.

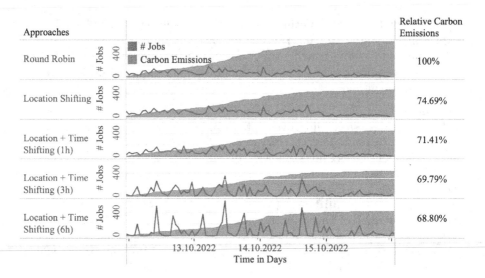

Fig. 2. Amount of currently running jobs and accumulated carbon emissions for all five strategies.

5.3 Limitations

Although our data set used real-world data, we do not have the necessary information about data locality, the carbon cost of moving data, or resource utility. Furthermore, power consumption was assumed to be steady, constant, and equal for each job – meaning it only scales with its duration. This assumption simplifies the evaluation but may not reflect real-world scenarios accurately. Lastly, the data set also lacks information about sequential jobs and dependencies. Since our scheduler does not account for these cases, it would have been useful to evaluate dependency violations as well. This would provide insights into how our scheduler handles complex job dependencies and potential improvements needed in this area. Therefore, our results are to be considered rather indicative, and results in real environments may be different.

6 Conclusion and Future Work

In this paper, we presented the idea of integrating approaches from carbon-aware computing into CI/CD services. We discussed the opportunities and challenges when doing so and evaluated different carbon-aware scheduling strategies to demonstrate their possible effectiveness in carbon footprint reduction.

Solely relying on historical runtime data for estimating the job duration and immediately allocating jobs to the region with the best window already resulted in a 25.31% reduction in overall carbon emissions. A key observation was that the effective distribution of jobs across multiple regions with varying carbon intensities was a significant factor in reducing emissions. Building on this, our complete scheduling approach introduces user input for estimated durations and deadlines, giving jobs the flexibility to be rescheduled in more carbon-efficient time windows. When we employed this strategy, the improvement further increased by an additional 3.28–5.89%, bringing the total improvement to approximately 31.2%. It is important to clarify that our test data did not accurately represent real-world user input; the estimated durations were closely aligned with actual runtimes. Thus, we anticipate even greater improvements when accounting for the inaccuracies commonly found in real user input.

As a next step, we will investigate the practical implications of different carbon-aware CI/CD scheduling by testing them on the internal CI/CD service of a large industrial company. We anticipate that real-life deployments with global knowledge about the number and types of jobs offer additional opportunities as, for example, workflow duration and deadline estimates can be performed in a more sophisticated manner. On the other hand, we expect new challenges in terms of data locality, resource constraints, and interdependencies between workflows which limit scheduling flexibility. Lastly, we plan to simulate different seasons and datacenter locations through the use of a carbon-aware computing testbed [23] to give us a better picture of when and where there is substantial potential for savings.

Acknowledgments. We sincerely thank WattTime for providing us with access to their marginal carbon intensity data. This research was supported by the German Ministry for Education and Research (BMBF) as Software Campus (grant 01IS17050).

References

1. Masanet, E., Shehabi, A., Lei, N., Smith, S., Koomey, J.: Recalibrating global data center energy-use estimates. Science **367**(6481), 984–986 (2020)
2. Montevecchi, F., Stickler, T., Hintemann, R., Hinterholzer, S.: Energy-efficient Cloud Computing Technologies and Policies for an Eco-friendly Cloud Market. Final Study Report. Publications Office of the European Union, LU (2020)
3. Meyer, M.: Continuous integration and its tools. IEEE Softw. **31**(3), 14–16 (2014)
4. CD Foundation. State of Continuous Delivery Report: The Evolution of Software Delivery Performance (2022)
5. Ibrahim, M., et al.: An in-depth empirical investigation of state-of-the-art scheduling approaches for cloud computing. IEEE Access **8**, 128282–128294 (2020)
6. World Bank. State and trends of carbon pricing 2022. Technical report. World Bank, Washington, DC (2022)
7. Wiesner, P., Behnke, I., Scheinert, D., Gontarska, K., Thamsen, L.: Let's wait awhile: how temporal workload shifting can reduce carbon emissions in the cloud. ACM Middleware (2021)
8. Radovanovic, A., et al.: Carbon-aware computing for datacenters. IEEE Trans. Power Syst. (2022)
9. Fridgen, G., Körner, M.-F., Walters, S., Weibelzahl, M.: Not all doom and gloom: how energy-intensive and temporally flexible data center applications may actually promote renewable energy sources. Bus. Inf. Syst. Eng. **63**(3) (2021)
10. Zheng, J., Chien, A.A., Suh, S.: Mitigating curtailment and carbon emissions through load migration between data centers. Joule **4**(10) (2020)

11. Zhou, Z., et al.: Carbon-aware load balancing for geo-distributed cloud services. In: International Symposium on Modelling, Analysis and Simulation of Computer and Telecommunication Systems (MASCOTS) (2013)
12. Moghaddam, F., Farrahi Moghaddam, R., Cheriet, M.: Carbon-aware distributed cloud: multi-level grouping genetic algorithm. Cluster Comput. **18**, 477–491 (2015)
13. Hanafy, W.A., Liang, Q., Bashir, N., Irwin, D., Shenoy, P.: CarbonScaler: leveraging cloud workload elasticity for optimizing carbon-efficiency. In: ACM SIGMETRICS/IFIP Performance (2024)
14. Lin, L., Zavala, V.M., Chien, A.: Evaluating coupling models for cloud datacenters and power grids. ACM e-Energy (2021)
15. Goiri, I., et al.: Matching renewable energy supply and demand in green datacenters. Ad Hoc Netw. **25**, 520–534 (2015)
16. Wiesner, P., Scheinert, D., Wittkopp, T., Thamsen, L., Kao, O.: Cucumber: renewable-aware admission control for delay-tolerant cloud and edge workloads. In: Cano, J., Trinder, P. (eds.) Euro-Par 2022. LNCS, vol. 13440, pp. 218–232. Springer, Cham (2022). https://doi.org/10.1007/978-3-031-12597-3_14
17. Abdalkareem, R., Mujahid, S., Shihab, E., Rilling, J.: Which commits can be CI skipped? IEEE Trans. Softw. Eng. **47**(3), 448–463 (2021)
18. Ficher, M., Berthoud, F., Ligozat, A.-L., Sigonneau, P., Wisslé, M., Tebbani, B.: Assessing the carbon footprint of the data transmission on a backbone network. In: Conference on Innovation in Clouds, Internet and Networks (ICIN) (2021)
19. Cirne, W., Berman, F.: A comprehensive model of the supercomputer workload. In: 4th IEEE International Workshop on Workload Characterization (2001)
20. Tsafrir, D., Etsion, Y., Feitelson, D.G.: Backfilling using system-generated predictions rather than user runtime estimates. IEEE Trans. Parallel Distrib. Syst. **18**(6), 789–803 (2007)
21. Tang, W., Lan, Z., Desai, N., Buettner, D.: Fault-aware, utility-based job scheduling on Blue, Gene/P systems. In: IEEE CLUSTER (2009)
22. Ward, W.A., Mahood, C.L., West, J.E.: Scheduling jobs on parallel systems using a relaxed backfill strategy. In: Feitelson, D.G., Rudolph, L., Schwiegelshohn, U. (eds.) JSSPP 2002. LNCS, vol. 2537, pp. 88–102. Springer, Heidelberg (2002). https://doi.org/10.1007/3-540-36180-4_6
23. Wiesner, P., Behnke, I., Kao, O.: A testbed for carbon-aware applications and systems. arXiv:2306.09774 [cs.DC] (2023)

WESOACS: Workshop on Engineering Service-Oriented Applications and Cloud Services Introduction

Introduction to the 19th International Workshop on Engineering Service-Oriented Applications and Cloud Services (WESOACS 2023)

Andreas S. Andreou[1] , George Feuerlicht[2] , Willem-Jan van den Heuvel[3] ,
Winfried Lamersdorf[4] , Guadalupe Ortiz[5] , and Christian Zirpins[6]

[1]Cyprus University of Technology, Cyprus
andreas.andreou@cut.ac.cy
[2]Unicorn University, Czechia
george.feuerlicht@unicornuniversity.net
[3]Tilburg University, The Netherlands
wjheuvel@uvt.nl
[4]University of Hamburg, Germany
winfried.lamersdorf@uni-hamburg.de
[5]University of Cádiz, Spain
guadalupe.ortiz@uca.es
[6]Karlsruhe University of Applied Sciences, Germany
christian.zirpins@h-ka.de

The International Workshop on Engineering Services-Oriented Applications and Cloud Services (WESOACS), formerly known as WESOA, was established in 2005 in Amsterdam with the aim of promoting innovative ideas in research and practice of engineering of service-oriented applications. WESOACS 2023 took place on November 28th, 2023, in conjunction with the 21st International Conference on Service-Oriented Computing (ICSOC 2023) in Rome, Italy.

Service-oriented applications and cloud computing play an increasingly important role in enterprise computing today. While there is a good agreement about the main principles for designing and developing application systems based on the principles of distributed software services, there is still intense interest in this research area. In particular, areas of ongoing research include software service life cycle methodologies, service-oriented enterprise architectures and, more recently, engineering methods for cloud computing environments. The recent shift towards DevOps and microservices and the extensive use of container-based technologies and architectures necessitates revision of current approaches for developing service-oriented applications.

The WESOACS 2023 program included a keynote presentation by Marco Aiello titled Service Composition in the ChatGPT Era and four high-quality research papers that were carefully selected based on at least three expert reviews:

- *"Smart public transport with Be-in/Be-out system and iBeacon devices"* by Aneta Poniszewska-Maranda and Mateusz Kubiak,
- *"Towards a Systematic Comparison Framework for Cloud Services Customer Agreements"* by Elena Molino-Peña and José María García,

- *"Privacy Engineering in the Data Mesh: Towards a Decentralized Data Privacy Governance Framework"* by Nemania Borovits, Indika Kumara, Damian Tamburri and Willem-Jan van den Heuvel,
- *"Formalizing Microservices Patterns with Event-B: the case of Service Registry"* by Sebastián Vergara, Laura González and Raúl Ruggia.

We regard the 19th edition of the workshop as highly successful and wish to thank all authors for their contributions as well as the program committee members whose expert input made this workshop possible. Special thanks go to the ICSOC 2023 workshop chairs Pierluigi Plebani and Naouel Moha.

November 2023   WESOACS 2023 Workshop Organizers

Organization

Workshop Organizers

Andreas S. Andreou	Cyprus University of Technology, Cyprus
George Feuerlicht	Unicorn University, Czech Republic
Willem-Jan van den Heuvel	Tilburg University, The Netherlands
Winfried Lamersdorf	University of Hamburg, Germany
Guadalupe Ortiz	University of Cadiz, Spain
Christian Zirpins	Karlsruhe University of Applied Sciences, Germany

Program Committee

Marco Aiello	University of Stuttgart, Germany
Javier Berrocal	University of Extremadura, Spain
Juan Boubeta-Puig	University of Cadiz, Spain
Alena Buchalcevova	Prague University of Economics, Czech Republic
Javier Criado	University of Almería, Spain
Schahram Dustdar	Technical University of Vienna, Austria
Laura Gonzalez	Universidad de la República, Uruguay
Herodotos Herodotou	Cyprus University of Technology, Cyprus
Dimka Karastoyanova	University of Groningen, The Netherlands
Mark Little	Red Hat, USA
Andres Muñoz	University of Cádiz, Spain
Philippe Roose	Université de Paud es des Pays de l'Adour, France
Rebecca Parsons	ThoughtWorks, USA
Cesare Pautasso	University of Lugano, Switzerland
Olaf Zimmermann	Eastern Switzerland University of Applied Sciences, Switzerland

Smart Public Transport with Be-in/Be-out System Supported by iBeacon Devices

Aneta Poniszewska-Marańda[✉] [ID], Mateusz Kubiak, and Lukasz Chomątek [ID]

Institute of Information Technology, Lodz University of Technology, Lodz, Poland
{aneta.poniszewska-maranda,lukasz.chomatek}@p.lodz.pl,
mateuszkubiak@protonmail.com

Abstract. The paper likely introduces the concept of "Be-in/Be-out" system, discussing the need for more efficient and user-friendly transportation systems in urban areas. This system often relies on technology like RFID or Bluetooth to automatically detect when passengers board and exit public transport. This can provide a seamless and convenient experience for travellers. iBeacon technology is commonly used for location-based services and could be applied to enhance the passenger experience or optimize operations. The paper also explains how iBeacon devices are used in the context of smart public transport and discusses the advantages of implementing such systems, including improved passenger convenience and better data collection.

Keywords: Smart cities · mobile ticketing · Be-in/Be-out system · iBeacon devices

1 Introduction

Significant technological development in recent years has affected every sphere of human life, including a change in the approach to the infrastructure of urban areas. In response to these greatest inconveniences, the concept of smart cities was born. This idea is aimed at solving problems with the deteriorating living comfort of residents. This idea is related to the parallel development of intelligent public transport. It assumes the development of IT systems that will be able to eliminate problems in the provision of communication services. This issue aims to revolutionize the approach of residents to transport by changing the manual interaction with vehicles.

The constant boom of technologies based on the paradigm of the Internet of Things has opened up the possibility of introducing changes in the calculation of tolls. One solution involves the introduction of the Be-in/Be-out (BIBO) model. This is the most advantageous solution, as it allows passengers to travel by public transport, excluding manual interactions. This model enables the implementation of a non-contact form of payment, thus replacing the outdated method of ticket validation. When creating an effective solution based on the Be-in/Be-out model, you can use the technology of energy-saving Bluetooth devices. One of

F. Monti et al. (Eds.): ICSOC 2023 Workshops, LNCS 14518, pp. 229–240, 2024.
https://doi.org/10.1007/978-981-97-0989-2_18

the types of devices that use this idea are devices of the iBeacon type. These small-sized technological innovations are able to initiate interactions with passengers' phones. The main problem of this model is the correct registration of the presence of a passenger in the vehicle. When this problem is solved, it will be possible to create a fully functioning system based on the Be-in/Be-out model that meets the assumptions of the smart city concept.

The paper likely introduces the concept of "Be-in/Be-out" system, discussing the need for more efficient and user-friendly transportation systems in urban areas. This system often relies on technology like RFID or Bluetooth to automatically detect when passengers board and exit public transport. From other point of view, iBeacon technology is commonly used for location-based services and could be applied to enhance the passenger experience or optimize operations. The paper is likely to explain how iBeacon devices are used in the context of smart public transport. Finally, the paper discusses the advantages of implementing such systems, including improved passenger convenience, better data collection for transit planning, and cost-efficiency.

2   Be-in/Be-out Systems in Public Transport

The Be-in/Be-out system is an innovative concept, characterized by an unconventional approach to collecting payments for the journey made by public transport. This variant is characterized by full automation of the operation of starting and ending the calculation of tolls. In addition, the passenger automatically purchases a ticket while on the move. Such system focuses on introducing new interactions with the public transport system, thus simplifying the process of purchasing the tickets. This system is attractive to all social groups. This solution eliminates the queues that occurred when using the classic system. It is worth noting that this system is an extension of the Check-in/Be-out system, which introduced a partial automation process and showed technological possibilities [1,3,7,8].

Focusing on the method of purchasing virtual tickets, two methods that can be used by passengers should be mentioned. The first form of interaction with this system is the use of a card that does not differ in appearance from a bank card. The card stores basic information about the person who is its owner and an electronic identification number. The number stored on the card is read by sensors located at the vehicle doors using RFID technology [2,9–11].

Fig. 1. General operation of the Be-in/Be-out system.

The second way to interact with the Be-in/Be-out system is by using a mobile phone, which replaces the card with RFID technology. To use the services, a passenger needs a dedicated application provided by the carrier [2, 3, 13, 14]. The requirement for the proper functioning of the software on a mobile device is the availability of network services and Bluetooth technology. For the application to work properly, the passenger must provide information about his bank card, from which the carrier will be able to collect the accrued fares. A passenger who wants to use this method of payment must run the application and must have Bluetooth technology turned on. The application on the passenger's phone will automatically recognize the means of transport, because information about the vehicle is propagated using iBeacon devices located in the vehicles. The communication system with Internet of Things devices is based on the Check-in/Be-out system (Fig. 1).

3   Related Works on Be-in/Be-out Systems

It is possible to use Internet of Things devices supporting wireless communication to identify the passengers in public transportation, e.g. by using Bluetooth technology in Be-in/Be-out system. The analysis of state-of-the-art on wireless communication for systems using transmitters keeped by passengers, systems using Bluetooth technology supported by GPS services and systems supported by sensors built-in in passengers' mobile devices focused on finding out the answers to the following questions:

- How could an architecture using Bluetooth communication work?
- How to effectively check whether a passenger is actually in the vehicle?
- Does the use of wireless communication methods give promising results?
- How far does Bluetooth technology work?
- Are wireless technologies immune to external factors such as interference?
- Does the location of transmitters in the vehicle matter?
- Is it possible to obtain a more efficient version of the system by extending the Be-in/Be-out system with another technology?

In [4], the authors conducted research on the possibility of using Bluetooth technology in the Be-in/Be-out system. The aim of researchers was to propose an effective Be-in/Be-out system that would replace the outdated payment methods included in the classic system. The authors based on the architecture in which it is possible to simultaneously use mobile devices supporting Bluetooth technology and IBeacon devices that "spread" a unique passenger number. In this concept, the passenger would communicate wirelessly with a minicomputer placed in the vehicle. The minicomputer would be an intermediary device in contact with the carrier's IT systems.

The authors of [5] are of the opinion that the combination of two technologies, such as Bluetooth and GPS, gives a lot of benefits in terms of facilitating user detection. The aim of the authors was to create a prototype of Be-in/Be-out system using Bluetooth technology and geolocation services. The authors have created a prototype of the system, which is based on the approach that the passenger carries an iBeacon device that is able to broadcast a unique MAC address. This address is assigned by the manufacturer and is then associated with a specific passenger in the carrier's system.

In the paper [6], the authors created a prototype of a Be-in/Be-out system using sensors such as Bluetooth, GPS and an accelerometer. Their main goal was to design a Be-in/Be-out system that would enable manual ticket purchase. At the very beginning of their work, the researchers created a prototype of Check-in/Check-out system, and then added automatic ticket validation to it. The proposed system uses iBeacon devices installed in vehicles and stops. The prototype designed for passengers can interact with these devices in two ways: by monitoring the zone change area and by creating a ranking of iBeacon devices. Analysis of collected material shows that the use of additional sensors installed in the device can help to determine whether the user is actually in vehicle.

The main problems of the created and analysed solutions are: checking by applications whether the user is in the vehicle; checking whether the user is not mistakenly scanned by the system because he is standing at a stop where a given means of transport has just stopped; detecting whether the passenger has left the vehicle he/she was travelling in; constructing an efficient user detection algorithm; implementation of a secure solution, without the participation of an intermediary computer. The software architecture plays an important role in the Be-in/Be-out system. The system may incorrectly charge travel costs when the system is heavily loaded. Moreover, the analysed prototypes of systems had a problem with maintaining an appropriate level of security of the processed data.

4   Be-in/Be-out System Concept Using iBeacon Devices

This section presents the concept of effective Be-in/Be-out system prototype, using wireless communication based on iBeacon devices and supported by the geolocation service. Summing up the analyses carried out in the subject of Be-in/Be-out systems, it can be said that most of the prototypes performed calculations regarding the presence of a passenger in the vehicle using mobile devices, without taking into account the aspects of sensitive data protection. Additionally, portable devices have insignificant amounts of computing resources that can significantly impact the performance and accuracy of a Be-in/Be-out system. The analysed materials do not take into account anomalies that may occur on mobile devices in the context of operation of the devices themselves and the signals they receive. Taking into account the concept of Smart Cities, an important aspect is to be able to conduct further analyses related to the study of human behaviour patterns. By implementing data processing on mobile devices, we significantly complicate the processes of transferring information to IT systems.

The main task of the proposed approach is to simplify the computational complexity involved in charging users for the stations travelled. In addition, this concept shows a new approach to detecting the user of the system in the vehicle. This idea is based on iBeacon devices with unique identifiers that are assigned to vehicles. With the use of mobile devices with the Bluetooth function turned on, it is possible to detect the vehicle in which the system user is moving. The main use of mobile devices is to provide information about the current position of the user and RSSI (Received Signal Strength Indication) measurement of detected iBeacon devices. The server software, having an archival record of RSSI measurements, coordinates of the user's position and vehicle routes, is able to calculate the number of routes travelled by the system user. It is worth noting that the calculation of fees is based on historical data. The model of the Be-in/Be-out system designed in this way, performing calculations on the server software, is resistant to the factors:

- anomalies resulting from the lack of continuity of operation of user's device,
- irregularities resulting from the performance of the device,
- battery charge level in the user's device,
- interference with the operation of the user's device,
- irregularities resulting from the inattention of system user.

The main function of the Be-in/Be-out system is represented by an algorithm that counts the number of stops travelled by individual users of the system. This function uses the following data: record of the received RSSI signal from Bluetooth devices, user's coordinates, time interval, coordinates of stops registered in the system, identifiers of iBeacons detected during the journey. It is worth emphasizing the role of recording the received RSSI signal. This indicator measures the amount of power present in the radio signal emitted by the iBeacon.

In the proposed algorithm, the calculation of distance between the coordinates of user's device and the stops saved on the route have the greatest impact on the final result. The algorithm takes into account only the coordinates of stops assigned to the route. It is worth noting that routes are searched on the basis of devices assigned to vehicles registered in the system. The distance between two points is calculated using the Haversine formula. It defines the shortest path between two points on the globe. This formula takes into account the longitude and latitude of these points – Algorithm 1 [12]:

1. Set variables *lat1*, *lon1*, which are latitude and longitude of first point.
2. Set variables *lat2*, *lon2*, which are latitude and longitude of second point.
3. $R = 6371e3;$ // Approximate radius of Earth in meters.
4. $\phi 1 = lat1 * Math.PI/180;$
5. $\phi 2 = lat2 * Math.PI/180;$
6. $\Delta\phi = (lat2 - lat1) * Math.PI/180;$
7. $\Delta\lambda = (lon2 - lon1) * Math.PI/180;$
8. $a = Math.sin(\Delta\phi/2) * Math.sin(\Delta\phi/2) + Math.cos(\phi 1) * Math.cos(\phi 2) * Math.sin(\Delta\lambda/2) * Math.sin(\Delta\lambda/2);$
9. $c = 2 * Math.atan2(Math.sqrt(a), Math.sqrt(1 - a));$
10. Return $R * c;$

Based on the above information, the algorithm can be defined to count the number of stops travelled by individual users travelling with different vehicles saved in the system – Algorithm 2 [12]:

1. Set *userId* variable (specifies system user ID).
2. Set *fromDate* variable (defines from when user's trip data should be fetched).
3. Set *toDate* variable (defines when user's trip data should be fetched by).
4. Retrieve list of user's travel waypoints based on RSSI that was less than -90 dBm and assign them to the *userTracks* array.
5. If *userTracks* array contains no elements, exit the program.
6. Get list of devices from *userTracks* array and assign them to *devices* array.
7. If *devices* array contains no elements, exit the program.
8. Retrieve list of vehicles from *devices* array and assign them to *vehicles* array.
9. If *vehicles* array contains no elements, exit the program.
10. Retrieve list of assigned routes from *vehicles* array and assign them to *route* array.
11. variable *results* = *[]*
12. For each *vehicle* from *vehicles* array:
    (a) *matchedStops* = *[]*
    (b) Find list of routes assigned to *vehicle* variable and assign them to *routesAssignedToVehicle* array.
    (c) For each *userTrack* element in *userTracks* array:
        i. For each *stop* element from *routesAssignedToVehicle.stops* array:
            A. Calculate distance between *userTrack* - *stop* and result in meters assign to *distanceBetweenUserTrackAndStop* variable
            B. If *distanceBetweenUserTrackAndStop* <= 0.3 and *userTrack.rssi* < -70:
                – Add *stop* element to *matchedStops* array
    (d) Add structured element to *results* array
        i. *matchedStops*, //stops travelled
        ii. *matchedStops.length* * 0.35, // travel cost where 0.35 is the base rate per stop
13. Return *results*

The Algorithm 2 counts the number of stops travelled for one user in the Be-in/Be-out system. This implementation uses the entered identifier that is assigned to the user in the system. A unique identification number is generated when basic user information is entered into the system. An additional parameter passed to the function is information on the period of data processing. This parameter defines from when and to when historical data on the received radio signal strength indicator and GPS coordinates should be downloaded. This information is transferred to the system when the user is within the range of iBeacon devices propagating a unique identification number. It is worth noting that the algorithm downloads historical data that contains non-empty information about the signal strength, which cannot be lower than −90 dBm. This condition introduces the minimum value of the signal that allows the correct transmission of the iBeacon device identification number. This condition also screens out mobile devices, which are likely to be within 15 m of the transmitting device. The algorithm, taking into account historical information about detected iBeacon devices, retrieves information about the vehicles assigned to them and their routes.

The main part of this algorithm calculates the number of stops travelled for individual vehicles with which the system user had radio contact. It takes into account the calculated distance between the coordinates of the user's position and the stops assigned to the detected route. The distance is calculated using the formula described in Algorithm 1. If the calculated distance between the stop and the user is less than or equal to 3 m and the power of received radio signal is greater than −70 dBm, the algorithm recognizes the stop as passed. As the final result of the algorithm, the function returns information on the qualified stops and the total cost of trip, which depends on the base rate for the travelled stop.

5 Implementation of Be-in/Be-out System Using iBeacons

The implementation of Be-in/Be-out system includes server application, mobile application that is available directly to the passengers and set of IoT devices that act as iBeacon devices. The devices used diffuse unique UUID (Universally unique identifier) version 4 through Bluetooth Low Energy technology.

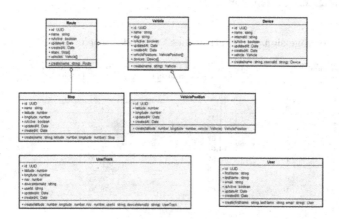

Fig. 2. Entity class diagram for implemented Be-in/Be-out server software.

The server application is characterized by following functional and non-functional requirements (Fig. 2): (1) software calculates the cost of the trip based on number of stops travelled by the user, (2) cost of the trip is calculated based on the base price per stop, (3) system user has the options to introduce the route representations, representation of stops, vehicle representation, (4) system has unique representations of iBeacon devices and makes it possible to assign IBeacon devices to vehicles, (5) system has the ability to enter basic information about the user, (6) user has the option to add the information about geographical location to the stop and communicates using an endpoint management tool, (7) system has the ability to prescribe many unique devices to the vehicle, (8) server application processes iBeacon devices that have a verified device ID and queues the entry of vehicle positions, (9) server application stores historical data and algorithm for calculating the route travelled by users must work on this historical data, (10) unique identifiers of objects in the database are based on UUID version 4, (11) server software calculates the distance based on geographical coordinates using Haversine pattern and it should automatically call the method.

6 Evaluation of Implemented Be-in/Be-out System

The evaluation tests of implemented system concerned the analysis of signals propagated by used iBeacon devices and the detection of user in and outside the vehicle. The aim of tests was to determine the arithmetic average value of the signal strength for used individual iBeacon devices. This test shows the general characteristics of the signals transmitted by both types of devices and checks for possible differences in signal strength. The measurement set for determining the average signal strength included the following elements: mobile device with Bluetooth version 5.0, iNode Beacon device, ESP32 device.

At the very beginning of the experiment, iNode Beacon and ESP32 devices were placed on a flat surface at a distance of 20 cm from each other. Then, every meter, the values of the emitted signals of both devices were measured three times. The measurement was carried out by the created mobile application. Measurements were carried out in a closed room (Table 1).

Table 1. Average signal strength values for iNode Beacon and ESP32 devices.

Test number	Distance [m]	Average signal strength for iNode Beacon [dBm]	Average signal strength for ESP32 [dBm]
1	0	−39,33	−39,67
2	1	−66,33	−67,67
3	2	−71,33	−71,67
4	3	−72,33	−72,67
5	4	−72,67	−73,67
6	5	−73,67	−75,67
7	6	−74,67	−75,33
8	7	−73,67	−75,00
9	8	−75,33	−75,67
10	9	−74,33	−78,33
11	10	−75,67	−78,00

The average value of the signal strength decreases with increasing distance between the devices transmitting the Bluetooth signal and the receiver. The greatest difference in the average signal strength can be seen at a distance of 2 m from the transmitting device. This value decreases by about 30 dBm at the border of 1 m from the transmitting device. Based on the obtained results of the average signal strength propagated by iBeacon devices, it can be concluded that the mobile device receives similar signal strength for both devices. The biggest difference in the strength of signals can be seen in the distance of 2 m from the device propagating the signal. At a distance greater than 2 m, the signal shows a downward trend and tends towards noise.

The aim of next experiment was to check the function of detecting the presence of human moving in a vehicle registered in the prototype of Be-in/Be-out system. This study also checked the correctness of calculations of the algorithm counting the number of travelled stops. This experiment simulated realistic conditions of using the prototype. When creating a research platform, a 2.8 km long route was introduced to Be-in/Be-out system software, which corresponds to a realistic public transport route. There are 11 stops along the route assigned to the ride route. Then, the route was assigned to the vehicle entity. Two iBeacon devices were assigned to the vehicle with which the user could communicate. Simulated data were introduced into the prototype, which concerned the read RSSI signals and GPS coordinates. The number of such samples was 122.

Figure 3 shows the simulated route of a public transport vehicle marked with a blue line. Table 2 shows sample samples of user readings entered into the prototype Be-in/Be-out system (simulated RSSI values were randomly generated in the range <−30, −85>).

Analysing the data in Table 2, it can be concluded that the system correctly classifies samples 1, 2, 3, because the average value of the signal strength is not lower than

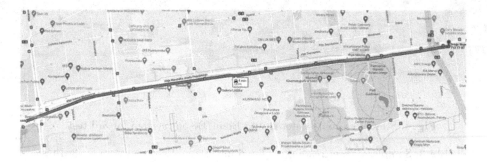

Fig. 3. Simulated route entered into Be-in/Be-out system for 2nd test.

Table 2. Samples of user readings entered into Be-in/Be-out system for 2nd test.

Sample number	iBeacon device ID	RSSI [dBm]	Coordinates (latitude, longitude)
1	dc02f682-82ad-439e-973a-566970c899c3	−31	51.7614565267312, 19.483516348218163
2	dc02f682-82ad-439e-973a-566970c899c3	−45	51.7614241292915, 19.483157420201234
3	24578b5f-3c4c-4c78-9435-b303542d9317	−61	51.76137553308835, 19.48271997669032
4	dc02f682-82ad-439e-973a-566970c899c3	−78	51.76134544969958, 19.482103069173554
5	24578b5f-3c4c-4c78-9435-b303542d9317	−98	51.76130770453379, 19.481522369549086

−70 dBm and the distance between the user and any stop is not greater than 0.3 m. However, the system does not take into account samples 4, 5 when calculating the number of stops driven by the user, due to the fact that these conditions are not met.

By calling the endpoint responsible for counting the number of stops travelled for the test user, it can be concluded that the algorithm is working correctly, because the system has detected all stops travelled by the user. The prototype of the system qualified 10 completed stops, did not correctly qualify 1 stop not travelled by the user. In addition, the software did not generate any errors during the calculations.

The purpose of the next study was to check the function of detecting the presence of a person moving parallel to the vehicle in which the prototype of Be-in/Be-out system operates. This study checks correctness of the algorithm counting the number of stops travelled by system users who have the application turned on, but do not use a means of transport.

When creating the simulation, a 400 m long route was entered into the system software, which corresponds to a realistic public transport route. There are 2 stops assigned to the route, which are located along the route. The route was then assigned to the vehicle. Two iBeacon devices were assigned to the means of transport, whose signal could be received by the user walking parallel to the vehicle and having the mobile application of Be-in/Be-out system turned on. Simulated data were introduced into the prototype, which concerned the read RSSI signals and GPS coordinates. The number of such samples was 21.

Figure 4 shows the simulated route of a public transport vehicle for the 3rd test, marked with a blue line. The values in RSSI column of Table 3 simulate the received signal based on the results of tests performed server application. The simulated RSSI values were randomly generated in <−70, −90> range.

Analysing the data in Table 3, it can be concluded that the system tried to include samples 1, 4 in the calculation of the number of stops driven by the user. Samples 2, 3, 5 were not considered. By calling the endpoint responsible for counting the number

Fig. 4. Simulated route entered into Be-in/Be-out system for 3rd test.

Table 3. Samples of user readings entered into Be-in/Be-out system for 3rd test.

Sample number	iBeacon device ID	RSSI [dBm]	Coordinates (latitude, longitude)
1	dc02f682-82ad-439e-973a-566970c899c3	−70	51.7622445686098, 19.456697308306012
2	dc02f682-82ad-439e-973a-566970c899c3	−71	51.76226656478569, 19.45693602488649
3	24578b5f-3c4c-4c78-9435-b303542d9317	−75	51.762321000733586, 19.45777177903929
4	dc02f682-82ad-439e-973a-566970c899c3	−70	51.76237405071485, 19.458387199365486
5	24578b5f-3c4c-4c78-9435-b303542d9317	−74	51.76242922262921, 19.459078047252543

of stops travelled for the test user, it can be concluded that the algorithm does not work correctly. The prototype of the system qualified one stop. A detailed analysis of the problem shows that the condition that checks the strength of the received signal is particularly important in the algorithm. Repeating the experiment with lower RSSI values, the system does not correctly register the presence of system user walking parallel to the vehicle. Based on the above results, the better way is to place more iBeacons in Be-in/Be-out vehicles and limit the received signal strength condition to −70 dBm.

Based on conducted experiments, the original concept of Be-in/Be-out system correctly classifies the presence of an user in vehicle, except for the case when the user moves in parallel with the vehicle. IoT devices subjected to an analysis of the average signal strength, show similar characteristics of transmitting the Bluetooth signal. Both types of devices can be used in this type of systems.

7   Conclusions

The paper presented the proposal of approach of Be-in/Be-out model using wireless technologies to user detection in the vehicle, which eliminates errors in already created solutions. The experiments were carried out on the prototype of the system, which was supported by iBeacon devices. The particular attention was paid to the study of operation of the algorithm that counts the number of stops travelled for individual users of the system. This algorithm uses RSSI readings, GPS coordinates, and metadata from IoT devices in its calculations.

In analysed existing studies, too little attention was paid to the issue of user detection in the vehicle. In addition, it can be said that most of the existing prototypes performed calculations regarding the presence of a passenger in the vehicle using mobile devices, without taking into account the protection of sensitive data. Additionally, portable devices have insignificant amounts of computing resources that can significantly impact the performance and accuracy of a Be-in/Be-out system. The analysed works did not take into account anomalies that may occur on mobile devices in the context of operation of the devices themselves and the signals they receive. On the basis of the analysed works, it can be concluded that too little attention has been paid to research in the context of checking the operation of the system in realistic conditions. Analysed works do not provide information on characteristics of devices using wireless technologies, in particular strength of propagated signal in relation to the distance.

The new concept of Be-in/Be-out system was proposed, which focuses on simplifying the computational complexity involved in charging users for the number of stops travelled. This idea is based on iBeacon devices that propagate unique identifiers that are assigned to vehicles. The role of mobile devices is to provide information about the current position of the user and RSSI measurement of detected iBeacon devices. The server software having a historical record of RSSI measurements, coordinates of the user's position and the vehicle's route is able to calculate the number of routes travelled by the system user. The made analyses show that the use of iBeacon devices in Be-in/Be-out system is promising. These devices can play their part well in terms of propagating additional metadata. It is worth noting that the information emitted can significantly optimize the calculation processes of the Be-in/Be-out system. In the conducted study on the propagation of signal by two separate IoT devices, similar values were obtained over the tested distance. Experiments show that the greatest difference in signal strength can be read on a 2 m distance from the device propagating the signal. At a distance greater than 2 m, the signal showed a downward trend and tended towards noise.

References

1. Eremia, M., Toma, L. and Sanduleac, M.: The smart city concept in the 21st century. Procedia Eng. **181**, 12–19 (2017)
2. Vakula, D., Raviteja, B.: Smart public transport for smart cities. In: Proceedings of 2017 International Conference on Intelligent Sustainable Systems (ICISS), Palladam, India, pp. 805–810 (2017)
3. Matseliukh, Y., Bublyk, M., Vysotska, V.: Development of intelligent system for visual passenger flows simulation of public transport in smart city based on neural. In: Proceedings of COLINS-2021, 5th International Conference on Computational Linguistics and Intelligent Systems, Kharkiv, Ukraine (2021)
4. Narzt, W., Mayerhofer, S., Weichselbaum, O., Haselbock, S., Hofler, N.: Be-in/be-out with bluetooth low energy: implicit ticketing for public transportation systems. In: Proceedings of 2015 IEEE 18th International Conference on Intelligent Transportation Systems, Gran Canaria, Spain, pp. 1551–1556 (2015)
5. Bitew, M.A., Muhammad, A., Fandiantoro, D.H., Boedinoegroho, H., Kurniawan, A.: E-payment for public transportation using BIBO method based on bluetooth low energy beacon. In: 2020 International Conference on Computer Engineering, Network, and Intelligent Multimedia (CENIM), pp. 199–204 (2020)
6. Tuveri, G., et al.: Automating ticket validation: a key strategy for fare clearing and service planning. In: 2019 6th International Conference on Models and Technologies for Intelligent Transportation Systems (MT-ITS), Cracow, Poland, pp. 1–10 (2019)
7. Narzt, W., Mayerhofer, S., Weichselbaum, O., Haselbock, S., Hofler, N.: bluetooth low energy as enabling technology for be-in/be-out systems. In: Proceedings of 13th Annual IEEE Consumer Communications & Networking Conference (IEEE CNCC), Las Vegas, USA (2016)
8. Liu, Q., Yang, X., Deng, L.: An IBeacon-based location system for smart home control. Sensors **18**, 1897 (2018)

9. Ferreira, M.C., Dias, T.G., Falcao J.: Is bluetooth low energy feasible for mobile ticketing in urban passenger transport? Transp. Res. Interdiscip. Perspect. **5**, 100120 (2020). ISSN 2590–1982

10. Martín, F.A., Castro-Gonzalez, A., Malfaz, M., Castillo, J.C., Salichs, M.A.: Identification and distance estimation of users and objects by means of electronic beacons in social robotics. Expert Syst. Appl. **86**, 247–257 (2017)

11. Ferreira, M.C., Dias, T.G., Cunha, J.F.: An in-depth study of mobile ticketing services in urban passenger transport: State of the art and future perspectives. Smart Syst. Des. Appl. Challenges 145–165 (2020)

12. Poniszewska-Maranda, A., Kubiak, M.: Be-in/Be-out system for a smart city using iBeacon devices. In: Proceedings of 29th Annual International Conference on Mobile Computing and Networking (MobiCom 2023), Spain (2023)

13. Choi, M., Lee, J., Kim, S., Jeong, Y.S., Park, Y.H.: Location based authentication scheme using BLE for high performance digital content management system. Neurocomputing **209**, 25–38 (2016)

14. Huang, C.-J., Chi, C.-J., Hung, W.-T.: Hybrid-AI-based iBeacon indoor positioning cybersecurity. Attacks and defenses. Sensors **23**(4), 2159 (2023)

Towards a Systematic Comparison Framework for Cloud Services Customer Agreements

Elena Molino-Peña[1]([⊠])[iD] and José María García[1,2][iD]

[1] Smart Computer Systems Research and Engineering Laboratory (SCORE),
Universidad de Sevilla, Seville, Spain
{mmolino,josemgarcia}@us.es
[2] Research Institute of Informatics Engineering (I3US), Universidad de Sevilla,
Seville, Spain

Abstract. The growing need to understand and compare elements in service agreements has generated strong interest in the industry. Although there are projects and tools for the automatic detection of information in contracts, automatic analysis is still a developing area of research. This becomes even more relevant with the rise of cloud service organizations, which highlights the need for tools for comparing contractual agreements. In this paper, we present a framework designed to automate contract analysis and comparison. In order to demonstrate the effectiveness of this approach, we created a prototype that uses language models to automatically detect obligations, rights, and parties involved in contracts. In addition, we applied an initial metric to determine the extent to which the customer benefits compared to the provider. The results of the evaluation support the effectiveness of the system by facilitating the understanding and reasoning of both parties regarding the terms of the agreement.

Keywords: Services Agreements · Automatically analyse ·
Comparison Framework

1 Introduction

In today's digital age, most companies often outsource some of their infrastructure management and storage to cloud services, which exposes them to a whole range of risks in terms of security, loss of data property, business continuity disruptions and other associated challenges. To mitigate these risks, it is crucial to understand the terms and conditions offered by providers and to ensure

This work has been partially supported by the following grants: PID2021-126227NB-C21, PID2021-126227NB-C22, TED2021-131023B-C21, and PDC2022-133521-I00 which are funded by MCIN/AEI/10.13039/501100011033 and "ERDF a way of making Europe"; and grant PYC20 RE 084 US, which is funded by Junta de Andalucia/ERDF, UE.

F. Monti et al. (Eds.): ICSOC 2023 Workshops, LNCS 14518, pp. 241–252, 2024.
https://doi.org/10.1007/978-981-97-0989-2_19

that they fulfill the clauses stipulated in the service agreement (also known as Customer Agreement or CA) that governs cloud services. CAs are composed of a set of legal documents that contain the terms and conditions concerning the acquisition and use of the provided cloud service [15]. They are the basis for protecting the interests of the parties and are an essential resource for bringing legal actions, for obtaining compensation or for termination of the contract, among other possible scenarios.

In spite of the importance of the agreement in the cloud computing ecosystem, there is currently no effective mechanism to clearly comprehend the terms and conditions and compare the services offered by different providers. This entails additional costs for companies, as they need a higher number of professionals to analyse and ensure both the successful evolution of their contracts and new subscriptions. Moreover, since this is a manual task and considering the heterogeneity of the content within each supplier's contract, the analysis is frequently tedious, time-consuming, and prone to error. Therefore, the lack of a tool that allows for the extraction and analysis of the information contained in the agreement, as well as the need for a set of general metrics that facilitate the evaluation and comparison across services, are two of the primary challenges limiting the automated analysis of CAs.

To address this issue, a solution is needed that is able to reason about terms and conditions defined in the agreements, providing answers to a set of analysis operations that allows customers to compare between CAs. In other words, we refer to a system capable of identifying the relevant information in the agreement, giving answer to questions that may arise for both parties throughout the entire lifecycle of the agreement [5], spanning from before, during, and after the subscription process. From these answers, we can derive the value of various indicators applicable to all agreements, providing an effective way to compare the characteristics of the agreement. In this article, we present the following contributions:

- A framework to automatically analyse and compare CAs. We define the functionality of the system and the components necessary for its development.
- A preliminary solution that applies the previous approach to partially address the analysis of Service Level Agreements (SLAs). It allows automatic extraction of obligations and rights of the parties and execution of an analysis operation.

The remainder of the article is organized as follows. Section 2 describes our motivating scenario. Then, Sect. 3 introduces the proposed framework, while Sect. 4 describes our initial solution for detecting obligations, rights and actor in SLAs. Section 5 discusses some related work and finally in Sect. 6 we discuss our conclusions and future work.

2   Motivating Scenario

The increasing number of available cloud service providers presents a challenge for IT organizations when selecting the most suitable one for their business goals.

Most cloud providers offer services with similar features but differ in the terms and conditions outlined in their agreements and the associated costs. At this point, the analysis and comparison of individual providers' agreements can be a complex task due to the lack of uniformity and the absence of a set of measurable general characteristics. Therefore, having a system that allows customers to ask questions about any doubts they may have about the terms and conditions of services becomes even more crucial in this context.

To better motivate the need for a CA comparative framework, let us examine the following example represented in Fig. 1, which provides a general overview of the situation a customer faces when they need to subscribe to a new service. Consider the case where the company *Acme* would like to host some of their systems on a cloud infrastructure, so that its personnel could search for the different Infrastructure-as-a-Service (IaaS) alternatives available. Moreover, they have to assess which of them best suits their needs. Of all the possibilities, imagine that they only select Amazon Web Services, Microsoft Azure and Google Cloud for simplicity, as exemplified in the figure. Each of these selected organisations structures their agreements differently, possibly including some vendor-specific policies. In addition, they have a multitude of documents that need to be analysed because they may contain information that can directly affect the services to be contracted. In this situation, comparing the terms and conditions established by each provider and selecting the one that most closely aligns with the customer's requirements is often costly, particularly when properly managing potential operational risks that may arise.

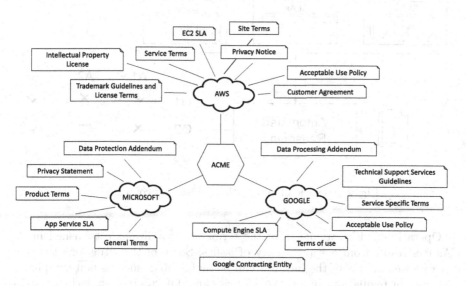

Fig. 1. Essential topics covered by each provider's CA

This scenario motivates the definition of a CAs comparative framework to effectively and efficiently support customers in these decisions, by automatically extracting and reasoning about the information contained in each of these agreements.

3   Systematic Comparison Framework

This section aims to outline the minimum requirements necessary for building a framework that automates the CA analysis and facilitates comparisons between different providers. The main objective of this system is to accurately process agreements, enabling automated analysis operations. This analysis culminates in the calculation of various quantitative and qualitative metrics, allowing for an evaluation of the agreement from the perspective of operational risks and its impact on the client's business. This provides an efficient means of comparing agreements from different providers.

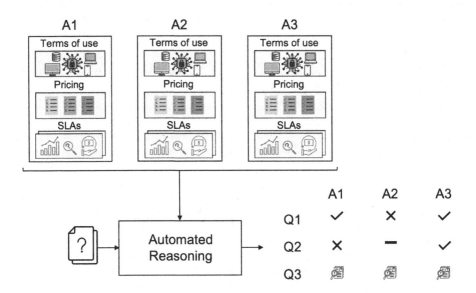

Fig. 2. Scenario of automatic analysis and comparison

Operational risks arising from the terms and conditions established in the CAs can result from a wide variety of issues. Some of the situations that can generate weaknesses in the business can be highlighted, such as non-compliance with current regulations in terms of security and data protection, lack of responsibilities defined for certain participants in the contract, non-existent or ineffective clauses and inconsistencies between various conditions, among other possible aspects. Trying to mitigate and be aware in time of the scope of these potential losses and the rights granted can help the client to realise the actual coverage offered by each provider, to understand the responsibilities of the parties, to take legal action if deemed necessary, and in general to get the most out of the contracted service.

Figure 2 shows the general workflow of our proposed systematic CA comparison framework. The system can take as input the CAs from different providers and, in addition, a set of analysis operations that need to be solved. The automatic reasoner must obtain responses to each of the analysis operations using the information contained in the agreements to be evaluated, represented as Qi and Ai, respectively. This response must be able to be affirmative, negative, without sufficient information, or with detailed explanations. The ultimate goal is to facilitate the understanding of the differences between providers with respect to these analysed characteristics, as represented in the bottom-right part of Fig. 2.

For this process to be effective, the automatic reasoner will need at least two critical and necessary components to automate CA analysis. The first of this is the information extractor, which in general should be responsible for processing the text in natural language and identifying those clauses that contain relevant information based on the query to be performed. There are several techniques that can be applied to solve this task, such as tokenization, Part-Of-Speech (POS) tagging and other preprocessing possibilities to analyse text. In addition, patterns, traditional Natural Language Processing (NLP) models and Large Language Models (LLMs) can be used to obtain the information.

The second component is the engine responsible for enabling reasoning about the content of the agreement. This engine applies analysis operations to the structured information previously extracted. This allows obtaining simple answers, such as "yes" or "no", as well as more complex answers, including detailed explanations of the answer provided. One of the ways to reason about the identified information is to interpret it and translate it into a formal language or structure that allows the application of a resolution or optimization algorithm to obtain a solution based on the defined constraint functions [4]. Another alternative is to use LLMs to process the detected clauses and answer the questions provided. Finally, another approach could involve establishing quantitative and qualitative metrics to derive conclusions from the information extracted.

4   Use Case Validation

Cloud services are used to deliver value to customers by simplifying the management and maintenance of IT resources. It is important to keep in mind that the provider will make every effort to minimize its own losses. At this point, it is particularly interesting to understand the obligations and rights of each party involved to ensure that all parties are fulfilling their responsibilities. Furthermore, a comprehension of these clauses can help both parties to understand critical aspects such as who benefits the most, potential impacts on the business resulting from subscribing to the services, and whether both parties have fair and sufficient rights and responsibilities. Hence, it is essential to have a set of analysis operations that, through various metrics, provide a comprehensive representation of the agreement to be evaluated.

In order to translate this idea into practice using our systematic comparison framework approach, we developed a prototype solution that can automatically extract from the SLA part of CAs their obligations and rights, together with the actors involved. On the other hand, we propose a first simple metric that allows to assess the risk or benefits of the parties, taking into account the relationship between the obligations and the rights of the parties involved in the agreement. Figure 3 shows the workflow that the developed system follows. Its architecture is divided into two proposed components for the automatic reasoner, which are the information extractor and the analysis engine. These components will be explained in detail below.

In general terms, the figure aims to show the different activities and elements necessary to achieve the expected results. First, we process the agreement by dividing the SLA text into sentences that are then evaluated by an LLM which is able to decide whether any of the clauses is an obligation, a right or a simple condition of the contract. Once we obtain these propositions, we use the Open AI GPT-3.5 turbo model to identify who is the actor involved in each of these clauses. Finally, using all of this information we can calculate the ratio of clauses that benefit each party.

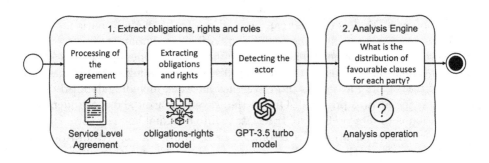

Fig. 3. Prototype solution workflow

4.1   Information Extractor

The important advances in NLP and deep learning techniques lead us to consider that an excellent alternative to extract information from SLAs is to apply LLMs. Most of these models are prepared to address a variety of tasks, such as text classification, translation, question-answering, or text summarising. These models have been trained with a large corpus, which allows them to be flexible solutions for different domains. However, their main limitation is that they are not specifically designed to solve a particular problem. Therefore, it is usual to perform a fine-tuning process of a pre-trained model with a specific data set to address the required task [2].

Given the diversity of options, we decided to fine-tune a model specifically for classifying statements into the categories of *obligation, right,* or *neither*. In this context, due to the limited amount of labeled data in the agreement domain, we had to generate a corpus[1] of SLA sentences from various providers, classified into the categories mentioned above. Despite performing a manual tagging of 52 SLAs from 18 leading cloud providers, it is important to note that the available data set is still quite limited.

Therefore, we decided to use an innovative approach known as SetFit for training a variety of models, getting the best results with the *paraphrase-mpnet-base-v2 model*[2], a modification of the Bert model [14]. SetFit is a framework that has proven to be highly effective for fitting pre-trained models, even when a limited number of examples are available, by applying contractive learning techniques [16]. The result is the *paraphrase-mpnet-base-v2-sla-obligations-rights model*[3] specially trained to detect obligations and rights in the SLA domain. The values obtained for the model evaluation metrics are as follows: Accuracy: 0.83, F1-macro: 0.829, Precision-macro: 0.8309, and Recall-macro: 0.83.

After having a model that can extract a catalog of sentences indicating an obligation or right from any SLA, we query the OpenAI API to detect the actor using the *gpt-3.5-turbo model*[4]. The process consists of generating a prompt with the extracted obligations or rights, and as a result the model generates a list with the actors involved in the corresponding clause.

We have developed an initial prototype[5] following this approach. The system has an API that allows interacting with all the previously defined functions. The proposed solution for information extraction automatically assigns the phrase type based on the semantics of the input data, avoiding the dependency on specific patterns. However, it is important to note that this assignment may be affected by the knowledge and possible biases of the classifier. In addition, one of the most robust models for actor detection is used, reducing possible problems produced by previous techniques used in other approaches. Although we need to further validate this solution, we have obtained promising early results, as outlined in Sect. 4.3.

4.2   Analysis Engine

The information extracted allows us to reason about the terms of the agreement. Based on a set of metrics, we can, for instance, analyse whether the agreement is beneficial to the customer or the provider, as well as the risks involved in subscribing to the cloud service, among other analysis operations. Currently,

---

[1] Dataset available at https://huggingface.co/datasets/marmolpen3/slas-obligations-rights-sentences.

[2] https://huggingface.co/sentence-transformers/paraphrase-mpnet-base-v2.

[3] https://huggingface.co/marmolpen3/paraphrase-mpnet-base-v2-sla-obligations-rights.

[4] https://platform.openai.com/docs/models/gpt-3-5.

[5] Prototype available at https://github.com/isa-group/iContracts.

there are limitations regarding the impact that the detected clauses can have on the reasoning process. This is because the system is unable to identify the meaning of the clause.

For the identification of a meaningful metric, we use the Goal Question Metric (GQM) method. Our metric seek to understand the balance of obligations and rights between parties involved in the agreement, through a quantitative analysis. In other words, it is about assessing the extent to which the contract could provide protection against potential risks.

- **Goal**: The degree to which the terms and conditions are favourable to the parties.
- **Question**: What is the distribution of favourable clauses for each party?
- **Client benefit**: $benefit_{client} = \frac{\frac{Ob_p}{Ob_p+Ob_c} + \frac{R_c}{R_p+R_c}}{2}$
- **Explanation**: The customer's benefits are represented by the sum of the percentage of the provider's obligations and the percentage of the customer's rights, where a higher number of obligations on the provider's side leads to a higher coverage and consequently to a more significant benefit for the customer.
- **Provider benefit**: $benefit_{provider} = \frac{\frac{Ob_c}{Ob_p+Ob_c} + \frac{R_p}{R_p+R_c}}{2}$
- **Explanation**: The provider's benefit is represented by the sum of the percentage of the customer's obligations and the percentage of the provider's rights, where a higher number of obligations on the part of the customer leads to a higher benefit for the provider.

In the formulas, Ob_p represents the number of obligations on the provider's side, and R_p represents the number of rights. Conversely, Ob_c denotes the number of obligations on the customer's side, while R_c signifies the number of rights. To calculate the ratio between the customer's and provider's percentage of benefit, we divide the customer's percentage by the provider's percentage. This determines whether the provider's responsibilities are greater than those of the customer.

4.3   Initial Evaluation

In order to perform an initial validation of the developed system, we propose to answer the following evaluation objectives:

- **Goal 1**: *How does the system behave in a real use case?* We intend to evaluate the performance of the system against a real scenario, such as the one described in the motivation section (Fig. 1).
- **Goal 2**: *What are the results if an agreement is analysed with different tools?* Our objective is to evaluate the performance of the system compared to other tools available for the automatic analysis of obligations and rights in SLAs. We will compare the results obtained when evaluating an SLA using the Chat GPT language model, the framework developed by Natalona et al. [12], and our solution approach.

Sentence	Type	Actor
During the Term of the agreement under which Google has agreed to provide Google Cloud Platform to Customer (as applicable, the Agreement), the Covered Service will provide a Monthly Uptime Percentage to Customer as follows (the Service Level Objective or SLO).	Obligation	provider
Customer Must Request Financial Credit	Obligation	customer
In order to receive any of the Financial Credits described above, Customer must notify Google technical support within 60 days from the time Customer becomes eligible to receive a Financial Credit.	Obligation	customer
Customer must also provide Google with log files showing Downtime Periods and the date and time they occurred.	Obligation	customer
If Customer does not comply with these requirements, Customer will forfeit its right to receive a Financial Credit.	Obligation	customer
Financial Credits will be in the form of a monetary credit applied to future use of the Covered Service and will be applied within 60 days after the Financial Credit was requested.	Obligation	provider
If Google does not meet the SLO, and if Customer meets its obligations under this SLA, Customer will be eligible to receive the Financial Credits described below.	Right	customer
This SLA states Customer's sole and exclusive remedy for any failure by Google to meet the SLO.	Right	customer
As applicable, Customer will only be entitled to Financial Credit for Downtime of a particular virtual machine instance as either a Single Instance or Instances in Multiple Zones, but not both.	Right	customer

Fig. 4. Excerpt of Google Compute Engine obligations, rights and actors detected by our proposal

Table 1. Results obtained for each SLA

SLA	EC2	Compute Engine	App Service
Ob_p	3	2	6
Ob_c	2	4	5
R_p	3	0	0
R_c	4	3	4
Metric 1	0.586	0.667	0.773
Metric 2	0.414	0.333	0.227
Ratio	1.415	2	3.4

Experiment 1: Analysis of Cloud Computing SLAs. In this experiment, we aim to answer the first goal by evaluating the obligations, rights and actors detected by our approach. We analyse the SLAs of the companies mentioned in the motivation scenario, which are AWS' EC2 SLA, Microsoft's App Service SLA and Google's Compute Engine SLA. Figure 4 showcases an excerpt of the information that our system can extract from the agreement. The global results are presented in Table 1, which shows a summary of the information extracted by the system. According to these results, the customer benefits more than the provider in all SLAs analysed, with the biggest difference in the Microsoft App Service SLA. Specifically, in this case, the customer's benefit is 3.4 times higher than the provider or, in other words, the provider's responsibilities are greater than those of the customer. The experimental study confirms the system's ability to extract information from the SLA, helping the customer to better understand the responsibilities and rights of the parties, as well as the most supportive agreement.

Experiment 2: Comparison Between Tools that Automate SLA Analysis. In this experiment, our aim is to answer the second goal by comparing the results obtained by three different tools, including our prototype, when automatically analysing the SLA of Digital Realty. Among the tools compared is Chat GPT, the most representative chatbot based on large language models at present. Despite being more robust than our system, the main difference is that it is not specifically trained to extract obligations and rights from legal texts. We also use Natolana's framework [12], whose approach focuses on extracting knowledge from the SLA, in fact part of this information is the obligations, rights and actors involved. However, its technique has limitations as it is based on patterns, as we discussed in a previous work [9].

To study the results, we compared the outputs obtained by each of the systems evaluated with the manual analysis of the agreement. According to our manual study, the SLA is composed of 12 obligations and 4 rights, which are represented in the Fig. 5 as the blue dashed line. These graphs summarises the results of our study, in which our approach has a higher precision and recall than the other tools. In comparison with the rest of systems we correctly detect a greater number of clauses representing obligations and rights. More information on this experiment can be found in a previous work [8].

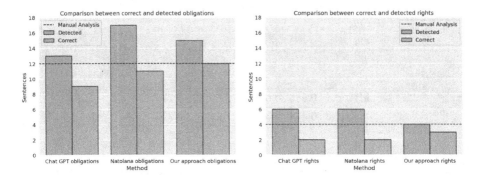

Fig. 5. Comparison between correct positives and detected values

5   Related Work

The automation of contract analysis has been studied from a variety of perspectives. Some approaches have focused specifically on the analysis of terms of service (TOS), while others have addressed the automation of pricing plans or the management of SLAs. Marco Lippi et al. [7] propose Claudette, a solution designed to evaluate abusive clauses found in TOS. In automatic SLA analysis, several approaches have been developed. For example, Lucia De Marco et al. [1] have as main objective the automatic extraction of service level objectives.

Efforts have also been made to automatically detect inconsistencies between the conditions defined in the SLA [10, 11]. One of the most novel works is the one by Natolana et al. [12]. In this work, they present a comprehensive framework for SLA knowledge extraction, combining text mining, semantic web, and traditional NLP techniques.

There are also community efforts, such as the project Terms of Service; Didn't Read (ToS;DR) [6], which aims to analyse and grade the TOS and privacy policies, though this evaluation is carried out manually. Within this line of work, the commercial platform Term Scout [13] is highlighted from an industrial perspective. It employs a hybrid approach, combining legal expert analysis with the use of artificial intelligence. This tool focuses on facilitating the review of agreements, especially TOS. It works as an extensive database that hosts public contracts previously analysed through a set of questions related to the terms of the agreement. Based on the answers to these questions and supported by the 22 WorldCC Contracting Principles [3], which are fundamental to ensure balanced commercial contracts, the platform provides a set of conclusions about the agreements.

6   Conclusions and Future Work

This article presents a common approach for the development of systems that aim to automate some parts of the analysis of CAs and facilitate comparisons between agreements. We have also developed a first prototype that following this approximation, allowing users to automatically extract the obligations, rights and actors involved in those clauses. This system can be valuable to ensure transparency and responsibilities in the agreement, allowing users to better comprehend the commitments and operational risk involved in subscribing to a cloud service.

Many challenges remain for future work, one of the most important being to improve the extraction of current knowledge. In order to not only identify the clauses that indicate obligation or right, but also the meaning of these clauses, allowing us to develop metrics that perform a more complete reasoning of CAs. Currently, we are trying to improve the developed system to increase its efficiency, defining also a more exhaustive experimental evaluation.

Acknowledgements. The authors would like to thank Antonio Ruiz Cortés for his constant support, help and valuable comments.

References

1. De Marco, L., Ferrucci, F., Kechadi, T., Napoli, G., Salza, P.: Towards automatic service level agreements information extraction, pp. 59–66, April 2016. https://doi.org/10.5220/0005873100590066
2. Face, H.: The hugging face course (2022). https://huggingface.co/course. Accessed 18 Apr 2023

3. Commerce & Contracting Foundation, W.: World Commerce and Contracting Principles (2022). https://www.worldcc.com/Resources/Tools/Contracting-Principles. Accessed 15 June 2023

4. García, J.M., Ruiz, D., Cortés, A.R., Martín-Díaz, O., Resinas, M.: An hybrid, QoS-aware discovery of semantic web services using constraint programming. In: Kramer, B.J., Lin, K.J., Narasimhan, P. (eds.) Service-Oriented Computing – ICSOC 2007. ICSOC 2007. LNCS, vol. 4749, pp. 69–80. Springer, Berlin, Heidelberg (2007). https://doi.org/10.1007/978-3-540-74974-5_6

5. García, J.M., Martín-Díaz, O., Fernandez, P., Müller, C., Ruiz-Cortés, A.: A flexible billing life cycle for cloud services using augmented customer agreements. IEEE Access **9**, 44374–44389 (2021). https://doi.org/10.1109/ACCESS.2021.3066443

6. Hugo Roy: Terms of Services (2023). https://tosdr.org/en/frontpage#ratings. Accessed 07 May 2023

7. Lippi, M., Palka, P., Contissa, G., Lagioia, F., Micklitz, H.W., Sartor, G., Torroni, P.: Claudette: an automated detector of potentially unfair clauses in online terms of service. Artif. Intell. Law **27**, 117–139 (2019). https://doi.org/10.1007/s10506-019-09243-2

8. Molino-Peña, E.: Automatic analysis of obligations and rights in customer agreements. https://hdl.handle.net/11441/149944

9. Molino-Peña, E., García, J.M., Ruiz-Cortés, A.: Limitations of current techniques to detect Obligations and Rights in SLA. Sistedes (2023). https://hdl.handle.net/11705/JCIS/2023/3589

10. Müller, C., Gutierrez, A.M., Fernandez, P., Martín-Díaz, O., Resinas, M., Ruiz-Cortés, A.: Automated validation of compensable SLAs. IEEE Trans. Serv. Comput. **14**(5), 1306–1319 (2021)

11. Müller, C., Resinas, M., Ruiz-Cortés, A.: Automated analysis of conflicts in WS-agreement. IEEE Trans. Serv. Comput. **7**(4), 530–544 (2014)

12. Natolana Ganapathy, D., Pande Joshi, K.: A semantically rich framework to automate cloud service level agreements. IEEE Trans. Serv. Comput. **16**(1), 53–64 (2023). https://doi.org/10.1109/TSC.2022.3140585

13. Otto Hanson, J.: Termscout (2023). https://www.termscout.com/. Accessed 17 July 2023

14. Reimers, N., Gurevych, I.: Sentence-Bert: sentence embeddings using Siamese Bert-networks. In: Proceedings of the 2019 Conference on Empirical Methods in Natural Language Processing. Association for Computational Linguistics (2019). http://arxiv.org/abs/1908.10084

15. Technical-Committee: Information technology-cloud computing-service level agreement (SLA) framework-Part 1: Overview and concepts. Technical report 19086-1:2016(E), ISO/IEC, Geneva, Switzerland (2016)

16. Tunstall, L., et al.: Efficient few-shot learning without prompts. arXiv preprint arXiv:2209.11055 (2022)

Formalizing Microservices Patterns with Event-B: The Case of Service Registry

Sebastián Vergara, Laura González$^{(\boxtimes)}$, and Raúl Ruggia

Instituto de Computación, Facultad de Ingeniería, Universidad de la República,
Montevideo, Uruguay
{svergara,lauragon,ruggia}@fing.edu.uy

Abstract. Microservices have emerged as an architectural style in which applications are composed of small and focused services. Several patterns have been proposed to guide the construction of microservices applications. However, they are usually stated in natural-language, which may lead to ambiguity and erroneous application. This paper addresses these issues by advancing in the formalization of microservices patterns using the Event-B method. An Event-B model for the Service Registry pattern is proposed, which is then leveraged for verification/validation purposes. The overall goal is to contribute to the comprehension of microservices patterns and the quality of microservices applications.

Keywords: microservices patterns · event-b · service registry

1 Introduction

Microservices have emerged as an architectural style in which applications are composed of small and focused services [24]. Several patterns have been proposed to guide the construction of microservices applications, document knowledge and address recurring situations. Particularly, the list of patterns compiled by Richardson covers areas such as service discovery (e.g. Service Registry), reliability (e.g. Circuit Breaker) and data management (e.g. Saga) [24].

Microservices patterns are frequently stated in natural-language, which may lead to ambiguity and erroneous application. Indeed, different implementations for the same pattern have variations in behavior.

A broadly applied strategy to eliminate ambiguity in prose descriptions is applying formalization techniques. Particularly, the Event-B method has been used to formalize different types of systems [1] (e.g. architectural patterns [30]).

In this line, our previous work leveraged this method to formalize integration and policy-based solutions [13,18]. We have recently focused on formalizing microservices patterns, such as the Circuit Breaker [33].

This paper continues advancing in this area by proposing an Event-B formalization for the Service Registry (SR) pattern and using the resulting model

F. Monti et al. (Eds.): ICSOC 2023 Workshops, LNCS 14518, pp. 253–264, 2024.
https://doi.org/10.1007/978-981-97-0989-2_20

for verification and validation (V&V) purposes. The overall goal is to contribute to the comprehension of microservices patterns, aiming to facilitate the development of microservices applications and positively impact their quality.

The paper is organized as follows. Section 2 presents the background. Section 3 describes the SR Event-B model, and Sect. 4 shows its use for V&V. Section 5 analyzes related work. Section 6 presents conclusions and future work.

2 Background

This section provides background on Event-B and related tools, as well as on the Service Registry pattern.

2.1 Event-B and Rodin Tool

The Event-B method enables the formalization of systems that can be modelled as discrete transition systems [26]. It is centered around the notion of events (i.e. transitions) and its main purpose is to aid the development of correct by construction systems [2]. It is based on first-order logic and a typed set theory.

Event-B models comprise contexts (static part of the system) and machines (dynamic part of the system) [3]. The Event-B method enables the incremental development of models by context extension and machine refinement.

Contexts may contain carrier sets (user-defined types), constants, axioms and theorems [26]. Machines specify behavioural properties of Event-B models and may be related to several contexts [26]. Machines may contain variables (state of a machine), invariants (constraining variables), theorems, a variant (to prove convergence properties) and events. Events describe the dynamics of machines [26] and may contain parameters, guards (conditions under which an event is enabled) and actions (how the state variables evolve when the event occurs).

Proof obligations (POs) specify what is to be proved for an Event-B model [1]. They verify a model's properties, demonstrate that a model is sound, analyse a model, and guide the user while building a model [15]. Proof obligations may focus on invariant preservation, numeric variant, variant and well-definedness, among others [1].

The Rodin tool is intended to support the construction and verification of Event-B models [3]. It automatically generates proof obligations and transmit them to provers, which support automatic and interactive proofs within the tool.

2.2 Service Registry Pattern

When a client needs to communicate with microservices, it requires their network locations which are unknown beforehand. Indeed, many microservice instances may be running simultaneously, with locations set at runtime [28].

In this context, the Service Registry (SR) pattern aims to provide a database that can be queried and containing the network locations of available microservices' instances, so that clients can communicate with them [24]. Optionally, the

SR may have information on each microservice health check API (i.e. an API that returns the health of the service), in favor of keeping registry data updated.

In summary, a SR stores the location of each service instance. Service instances are registered with the SR on startup and deregistered on shutdown. Lastly, the SR can be queried to retrieve all the available instances of a service. Moreover, the SR might invoke the health check API of its registered service instances to verify that they are ready to handle requests.

3 Service Registry Formalization

The first step in modeling a system with Event-B is identifying its requirements [1]. Within this work, the scope of the system to be modeled consists of the SR per se, a mechanism for registering/unregistering services and their instance endpoints, and a way to query the endpoints of registered services. Table 1 shows these requirements gathered for the SR pattern, as described in Sect. 2.2.

Table 1. Reference Text for Service Registry Requirements.

Req.	Description
FUN-1	A SR stores the location of each service instance
FUN-2	Instances are registered with the SR on startup and deregistered on shutdown
FUN-3	The SR can be queried to retrieve all the available instances of a service

The SR Event-B model, developed with the Rodin tool and available online [34], comprises one context and one machine. Listing 1.1 presents the context named *c0_service_registry*.

Listing 1.1. SR Event-B Context

```
CONTEXT
    c0_service_registry
SETS
    S // set of all possible services
    E // set of all possible instance endpoints to assign to the different services
CONSTANTS
    S1
    ..
    S5
    E1
    ..
    E6
AXIOMS
    ax1 : partition(S,{S1},{S2},{S3},{S4},{S5})
    ax2 : partition(E,{E1},{E2},{E3},{E4},{E5},{E6})
END
```

In order to address FUN-1, the context defines a set (S) containing all possible services to be registered and a set (E) containing all possible instance endpoints to be stored (as Event-B handles finite sets). Services (S1..S5) and endpoints (E1..E6) are defined as constants. The context also defines two axioms (ax1, ax2) using the predicate *partition(P, p1, .. , pn)*, which indicates that sets p1...pn constitute a partition of P (the union of p1..pn is P and p1..pn are disjoint).

Listing 1.2 shows part of the SR Event-B machine, named *m0_service_registry*.

Listing 1.2. SR Event-B Machine: Variables and Invariants

```
MACHINE
    m0_service_registry
SEES
    c0_service_registry
VARIABLES
    services // represent the set of microservices in the registry
    endpoints // represent the endpoints of microservices in the registry
    last_endpoint_query_result // last response obtained from querying a service endpoints
INVARIANTS
    inv1 : services ⊆ S
    inv2 : endpoints ∈ services → ℙ(E)
    inv3 : last_endpoint_query_result ∈ ℙ(E)
```

The machine sees the *c0_service_registry* context and defines three variables: *services* (representing the set of registered services in the SR), *endpoints* (representing the endpoints of microservices), and the *last_endpoint_query_result* (representing the last response obtained from querying the endpoints of a service).

One invariant per variable is used to designate its type. First, *services* are a subset of all possible services to be registered in the SR (inv1). Second, *endpoints* are functions whose domain is *services* and their range is the power set of all possible endpoints to be stored in the SR (inv2). Lastly, the *last_endpoint_query_result* belongs to the power set of all possible endpoints to be stored in the SR (inv3).

Listing 1.3 presents the events identified for the SR Event-B machine.

The *INITIALISATION* event sets all machine variables to empty sets (init1, init2, init3).

The *register* event receives *a_service* belonging to the set of all possible services minus the services set (grd1), so that only new services are registered. The *register* event adds *a_service* to *services* and initializes its endpoints to an empty set (act1 and act2).

The *unregister* event receives *a_service* belonging to *services* so that only registered services can be unregistered (grd1). This event removes all endpoints of the service and the service from the set of services (act1 and act2).

The *add_endpoint* event receives: *a_service* belonging to the registered services (grd1), and *an_endpoint* belonging to the set of all possible endpoints minus all the registered ones (grd2), so that services cannot share endpoints. This event adds *an_endpoint* to the registered endpoints of *a_service* (act1).

Listing 1.3. SR Event-B Machine: Events

```
EVENTS

INITIALISATION ≙
BEGIN
    init1 : services := ∅
    init2 : endpoints := ∅
    init3 : last_endpoint_query_result := ∅
END

register ≙
ANY
    a_service
WHERE
    grd1 : a_service ∈ S\services // can only register a new service
THEN
    act1 : services := services ∪ {a_service}
    act2 : endpoints(a_service) := ∅
END

unregister ≙
ANY
    a_service
WHERE
    grd1 : a_service ∈ services // can only unregister existing services
THEN
    act1 : endpoints := {a_service} ⩤ endpoints // domain substraction
    act2 : services := services\{a_service}
END

add_endpoint ≙
ANY
    a_service
    an_endpoint
WHERE
    // can only add endpoints to registered services
    grd1 : a_service ∈ services
    // two services can not share endpoints
    grd2 : an_endpoint ∈ E\union(ran(endpoints))
THEN
    act1 : endpoints(a_service) := endpoints(a_service) ∪ {an_endpoint}
END

remove_endpoint ≙
ANY
    a_service
    an_endpoint
WHERE
    // can only remove an endpoint from a previously registered service
    grd1 : a_service ∈ services
    // can only remove a registered endpoint of a service
    grd2 : an_endpoint ∈ endpoints(a_service)
THEN
    act1 : endpoints(a_service) := endpoints(a_service)\{an_endpoint}
END

query_endpoints ≙
ANY
    a_service
    result
WHERE
    grd1 : a_service ∈ S
    grd2 : result ⊆ E
    grd3 : a_service ∈ services ⇒ result = endpoints(a_service)
    grd4 : a_service ∉ services ⇒ result = ∅
THEN
    act1 : last_endpoint_query_result := result
END
```

The *remove_ endpoint* event receives *a_ service* and *an_ endpoint*, both of which must be registered in the SR (grd1 and grd2). This event removes *an_ endpoint* from the registered endpoints of *a_ service* (act1).

The *query_ endpoints* receives *a_ service* to query the endpoints for and a guard-defined argument *result*. While *a_ service* belongs to the set of all possible services, *result* is a subset of all possible endpoints. Particularly, *result* is defined as empty when *a_ service* is not registered and as the registered endpoints of *a_ service* otherwise. This event sets the variable *last_ endpoint_ query_ result* to the value of *result*.

4   Verification and Validation Using the Event-B Model

This section presents how the SR Event-B model was used for verification and validation purposes by leveraging tools such as Rodin, ProB and BMotionWeb.

4.1   Proof Obligations

The PO generator of Rodin did not produce POs for the context, but it produced nine POs for the machine. Five POs are related to invariant preservation, which ensures that each invariant in a machine is preserved by each event [1]. The rest are related to well-definedness, which ensures that a potentially ill-defined axiom, theorem, invariant, guard or action is indeed well-defined [1]. Five POs were discharged automatically by the auto provers included in Rodin. The rest were interactively discharged. Figure 1 shows elements of the proving view of Rodin. In particular, the Event-B Explorer shows the generated POs, indicating if they are discharged (the ones in green) and how (the "A" stands for automatically). Also, the Goal and the Proof Tree are shown for the selected PO.

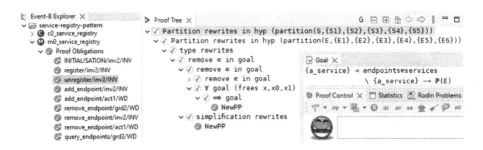

Fig. 1. Rodin Proving View Elements. (Color figure online)

4.2   Event-B Model Animations

Model animation complements modeling/proving, by enabling users to validate that the modelled system operates as expected (according to requirements) [1].

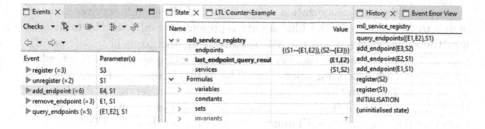

Fig. 2. SR Event-B Model Animation with ProB plugin.

Animations of the SR Event-B model were performed using ProB [17]. As shown in Fig. 2, the ProB plugin for Rodin was used to animate the model. A video showing this animation is available online [34].

The ProB view enables the user to select the next event to be executed and indicate its parameters' values (left). It also shows the history of executed events (right) and the state of the machine (i.e. values of its variables) (middle). In this case, after the *INITIALISATION* event, the following events were executed: two *register* events, receiving S1 and S2; three *add_endpoint* events, receiving (E1, S1), (E2, S1) and (E3, S2); and a *query_endpoints* event, receiving S1. As shown in the machine's state, the result of the last event is {E1, E2}.

BMotionWeb was used to create a formal prototype (i.e. an animation of a model that provides a lightweight formal validation of a system using an interactive mockup and model execution) [16]. BMotionWeb is built on top of ProB, leverages web technologies (e.g. HTML, SVG), and comprises a visual editor and a simulation engine. The editor aims to facilitate the development of mockups and their bindings to the formal model, using observers and events. The engine enables users to interact with the formal prototype and explore its behavior. Figure 3 presents the formal prototype of the SR (developed and animated with BMotionWeb). The code of the animation and a video are available online [34].

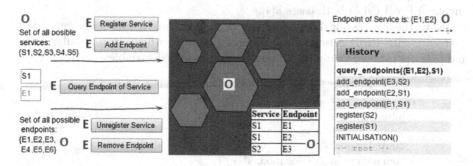

Fig. 3. BMotionWeb Animation of SR Formal Prototype. (Color figure online)

In particular, the visualization shows the set of all possible services and end-points to be registered. The blue square represents the SR and the table on it lists the stored data. When the SR has any data, the green hexagons are displayed. Two inputs enable the user to indicate a service and an endpoint, which are used as parameters for operations. The available operations are presented as buttons. The result of querying the endpoints of a service is displayed on the right side between braces. The animation comprises five events (E) and five observers (O), associated with animation elements, as shown in Fig. 3.

4.3   Test Cases Automatic Generation

Model-based Testing (MBT) is an extensively used approach to validate a system under test (SUT). The idea behind MBT is to depart from an abstract model of the SUT, and from it generate test cases automatically by means of tooling [27]. In this context, MBT can be leveraged to determine the compliance of an implementation with respect to a formal model of a system.

ProB offers two algorithms to generate test cases [23]: model-checking-based (MCM) and constraint-based (CBC). MCM test case generation builds the state space of the model and traverse it in breath-first manner until the coverage condition specified is met. Feasible coverage criteria for this approach are: (i) depth of the state space graph, (ii) have passed through a maximum number of states, (iii) the satisfaction of an end predicate by the final state, and (iv) have covered at least a set of operations. On the other hand, the CBC algorithm makes use of the constraint solver to build feasible sequences of events in a breadth-first manner and stops when the coverage condition is met. In this approach, constants and parameters of the operations are instantiated as required by the target sequence. As a drawback, this alternative cannot detect cycles, so it might get caught in an infinite loop.

By using the ProB Cli, a command-line interface for ProB, abstract test cases were generated for the SR Event-B model using both algorithms: MCM and CBC. Due to space limitations, the set of abstract test cases are not included in this paper, but they are available online as well as the parameters used for invoking ProB Cli in both cases [34].

Nevertheless, Listing 1.4 presents an example of an automatically generated test case with ProB comprising a sequence of steps which, in particular, may indicate operations, values of parameters and modified variables.

Listing 1.4. Automatically Generated Test Cases

```
<test_case>
 <initialisation>
   .....
 </initialisation>
 <step name="query_endpoints">
   <value name="result">{}</value>
   <value name="a_service">S1</value>
 </step>
</test_case>
```

In this example the test case comprises two steps: an *initialisation* step, where all variables are set, and a *query_ endpoints* step, representing a query to the SR for the network locations of microservice *S1* and whose result should be the empty set.

The XML-based abstract test cases are the basis for generating concrete test cases targeting specific pattern implementations. In the context of this work and as shown in Listing 1.5, the generation of concrete test cases from abstract test cases was performed manually leveraging JUnit. However, it is important to note that the automation potential of this task is remarkable.

Listing 1.5. Manually Generated JUnit Test Case

```
public void testCase_1(){

    // case setup
    Endpoints endpoints = Endpoints.parse("{}");
    SetString last_endpoint_active_query_result = SetString.parse("{}");
    SetString services = SetString.parse("{}");

    // case execution
    Wrapper app = new Wrapper();
    app.initialisation(endpoints, last_endpoint_active_query_result,
        services);
    assertTrue(app.isValid(endpoints, last_endpoint_active_query_result,
        services));

    a_service = "S1";
    app.query_endpoints(a_service);
    assertTrue(app.isValid(endpoints, last_endpoint_active_query_result,
        services));
    ......

}
```

5   Related Work

Many authors have worked on design patterns formalization resulting in different approaches to fulfill this gap. These approaches can be characterized as being based on: an existing language or the combination of many [12,21,22], extending a specification language [7], interactive theorem proving [8], formalization of temporal logic [6,20], developing a new language [19,29], and formal methods [14,25,31].

In the particular context of microservices, there are also formalization proposals based on time-basic Petri nets for specifying and verifying microservices-based process flows [11], and formal approaches for reasoning on microservices applications deployment aspects [9].

In addition, the Event-B method has been used in related contexts for developing formal specifications of patterns and systems. In particular, it was leveraged for the formal modeling of web service compositions [5], service-oriented architecture design patterns [30] and BPMN models [10]. More recently, the method has also been used for the modeling and verification of cyber-physical systems [4] and Internet of Things (IoT) design patterns [32].

However, to the best of our knowledge, Event-B models have not been used to formalize microservices patterns nor have been leveraged for V&V of such patterns in the way that we propose.

6   Conclusions and Future Work

This paper presented advances in the formalization of microservices patterns with Event-B, aiming to contribute to their precise comprehension. We proposed an Event-B model for the Service Registry (SR) pattern and leveraged it for V&V purposes. This enabled us to confirm the potential that these models may have to: eliminate ambiguity of natural-language descriptions of patterns, facilitate their comprehension (e.g. by using animations), and determine the degree of compliance of concrete implementations (e.g. by using MBT). The main contribution of this paper is the SR Event-B model and related developments for V&V (e.g. formal prototype), which constitutes a step forward in formalizing microservices patterns.

We are currently enhancing the SR Event-B model, by context extension and machine refinement, in order to consider other aspects such as Health Check APIs. We are also improving the formal prototype and advancing on MBT to automatically generate concrete test cases for specific pattern implementations.

Future work includes addressing the formalization of other microservices patterns (e.g. Saga), evaluating the degree of compliance of patterns' implementations, and providing an integrated environment for the formalization and V&V of these patterns. In addition, we are planning to apply this approach within other areas such as complex event processing and blockchain.

References

1. Abrial, J.R.: Modeling in Event-B: System and Software Engineering, 1st edn. Cambridge University Press, Cambridge (2010)
2. Abrial, J.R.: On B and Event-B: principles, success and challenges. In: Butler, M., Raschke, A., Hoang, T., Reichl, K. (eds.) Abstract State Machines, Alloy, B, TLA, VDM, and Z. ABZ 2018. LNCS, vol. 10817, pp. 31–35. Springer, Cham (2018). https://doi.org/10.1007/978-3-319-91271-4_3
3. Abrial, J.R., Butler, M., Hallerstede, S., Hoang, T.S., Mehta, F., Voisin, L.: Rodin: an open toolset for modelling and reasoning in Event-B. Int. J. Softw. Tools Technol. Transfer 12(6), 447–466 (2010). https://doi.org/10.1007/s10009-010-0145-y
4. Afendi, M.: A correct by construction approach for the modeling and the verification of cyber-physical systems in Event-B. In: Raschke, A., Méry, D., Houdek, F. (eds.) ABZ 2020. LNCS, vol. 12071, pp. 401–404. Springer, Cham (2020). https://doi.org/10.1007/978-3-030-48077-6_31

5. Ait-Sadoune, I., Ait-Ameur, Y.: Formal modelling and verification of transactional web service composition: a refinement and proof approach with Event-B. In: Thalheim, B., Schewe, K.D., Prinz, A., Buchberger, B. (eds.) Correct Software in Web Applications and Web Services. TEXTSMONOGR, pp. 1–27. Springer, Cham (2015). https://doi.org/10.1007/978-3-319-17112-8_1

6. Alencar, P.S.C., Cowan, D.D., de Lucena, C.J.P.: A formal approach to architectural design patterns. In: Gaudel, M.C., Woodcock, J. (eds.) FME 1996. LNCS, vol. 1051, pp. 576–594. Springer, Heidelberg (1996). https://doi.org/10.1007/3-540-60973-3_108

7. Bayley, I., Zhu, H.: Formal specification of the variants and behavioural features of design patterns. J. Syst. Softw. **83**(2), 209–221 (2010)

8. Bergner, K.: Specification of Large ß Object Networks with Component Diagrams. CS-Press (1997)

9. Bravetti, M., Giallorenzo, S., Mauro, J., Talevi, I., Zavattaro, G.: A formal approach to microservice architecture deployment. In: Bucchiarone, A., et al. (eds.) Microservices, pp. 183–208. Springer, Cham (2020). https://doi.org/10.1007/978-3-030-31646-4_8

10. Bryans, J.W., Wei, W.: Formal analysis of BPMN models using Event-B. In: Kowalewski, S., Roveri, M. (eds.) FMICS 2010. LNCS, vol. 6371, pp. 33–49. Springer, Cham (2010). https://doi.org/10.1007/978-3-642-15898-8_3

11. Camilli, M., Bellettini, C., Capra, L., Monga, M.: A formal framework for specifying and verifying microservices based process flows. In: Cerone, A., Roveri, M. (eds.) SEFM 2017. LNCS, vol. 10729, pp. 187–202. Springer, Cham (2018). https://doi.org/10.1007/978-3-319-74781-1_14

12. Dwivedi, A.K., Rath, S.K., Chakravarthy, S.L.: Formalization of SOA design patterns using model-based specification technique. In: Chaki, N., Devarakonda, N., Sarkar, A., Debnath, N. (eds.) ICCIDE 2018. LNDECT, vol. 28, pp. 95–101. Springer, Singapore (2019). https://doi.org/10.1007/978-981-13-6459-4_11

13. González, L., Ruggia, R.: Formalizing a policy-based compliance control solution with Event-B. In: Proceedings of the 14th International Conference on Software Technologies. SCITEPRESS (2019)

14. Hachicha, M., Dammak, E., Halima, R.B., Kacem, A.H.: A correct by construction approach for modeling and formalizing self-adaptive systems. In: 2016 17th IEEE/ACIS International Conference on Software Engineering, Artificial Intelligence, Networking and Parallel/Distributed Computing (SNPD), pp. 379–384. IEEE (2016)

15. Hallerstede, S.: On the purpose of Event-B proof obligations. Formal Aspects Comput. **23**, 133–150 (2011). https://doi.org/10.1007/s00165-009-0138-3

16. Ladenberger, L., Leuschel, M.: BMotionWeb: a tool for rapid creation of formal prototypes. In: De Nicola, R., Kühn, E. (eds.) SEFM 2016. LNCS, vol. 9763, pp. 403–417. Springer, Cham (2016). https://doi.org/10.1007/978-3-319-41591-8_27

17. Leuschel, M., Butler, M.: PROB: an automated analysis toolset for the B method. Int. J. Softw. Tools Technol. Transfer **10**(2), 185–203 (2008). https://doi.org/10.1007/s10009-007-0063-9

18. Llambías, G., Ruggia, R.: A middleware-based platform for the integration of bioinformatic services. CLEI Electron. J. **18** (2015)

19. Marmsoler, D.: A framework for interactive verification of architectural design patterns in Isabelle/HOL. In: Sun, J., Sun, M. (eds.) ICFEM 2018. LNCS, vol. 11232, pp. 251–269. Springer, Cham (2018). https://doi.org/10.1007/978-3-030-02450-5_15

20. Mikkonen, T.: Formalizing design patterns. In: Proceedings of the 20th International Conference on Software Engineering, pp. 115–124. IEEE (1998)
21. Montero, S., Díaz, P., Aedo, I.: Formalization of web design patterns using ontologies. In: Menasalvas, E., Segovia, J., Szczepaniak, P.S. (eds.) AWIC 2003. LNCS, vol. 2663, pp. 179–188. Springer, Cham (2003). https://doi.org/10.1007/3-540-44831-4_19
22. Nicholson, J., Eden, A.H., Gasparis, E., Kazman, R.: Automated verification of design patterns: a case study. Sci. Comput. Program. **80**, 211–222 (2014)
23. ProB: Test case generation - ProB documentation (2023). https://prob.hhu.de/w/index.php?title=Test_Case_Generation
24. Richardson, C.: Microservices Patterns: With Examples in Java, 1st edn. Manning Publications (2018)
25. Ritter, D., Rinderle-Ma, S., Montali, M., Rivkin, A., Sinha, A.: Formalizing application integration patterns. In: 2018 IEEE 22nd International Enterprise Distributed Object Computing Conference (EDOC), pp. 11–20. IEEE (2018)
26. Romanovsky, A., Thomas, M. (eds.): Industrial Deployment of System Engineering Methods. Springer, Heidelberg (2013). https://doi.org/10.1007/978-3-642-33170-1
27. Schieferdecker, I.: Model-based testing. IEEE Softw. **29**(1), 14–18 (2012). https://doi.org/10.1109/MS.2012.13
28. Taibi, D., Lenarduzzi, V., Pahl, C.: Architectural patterns for microservices: a systematic mapping study. In: Proceedings of the 8th International Conference on Cloud Computing and Services Science, Portugal. SCITEPRESS (2018)
29. Taibi, T., Ngo, D.C.L.: Formal specification of design patterns - a balanced approach. J. Object Technol. **2**(4), 127–140 (2003)
30. Tounsi, I., Hadj Kacem, M., Hadj Kacem, A.: Building correct by construction SOA design patterns: modeling and refinement. In: Drira, K. (ed.) ECSA 2013. LNCS, vol. 7957, pp. 33–44. Springer, Cham (2013). https://doi.org/10.1007/978-3-642-39031-9_4
31. Tounsi, I., Hadj Kacem, M., Hadj Kacem, A., Drira, K.: A refinement-based approach for building valid SOA design patterns. Int. J. Cloud Comput. **4**(1), 78–104 (2015)
32. Tounsi, I., Saidi, A., Hadj Kacem, M., Hadj Kacem, A.: Internet of Things design patterns modeling proven correct by construction: application to aged care solution. Future Gener. Comput. Syst. **148**, 395–407 (2023)
33. Vergara, S., González, L., Ruggia, R.: Towards formalizing microservices architectural patterns with Event-B. In: 2020 IEEE International Conference on Software Architecture Companion (ICSA-C), pp. 71–74 (2020)
34. Vergara, S., González, L., Ruggia, R.: Complementary material (2023). https://www.fing.edu.uy/owncloud/index.php/s/9Vs9rDde1wYpQxt

Privacy Engineering in the Data Mesh: Towards a Decentralized Data Privacy Governance Framework

Nemania Borovits[1(✉)], Indika Kumara[2], Damian A. Tamburri[1], and Willem-Jan Van Den Heuvel[2]

[1] Jheronimus Academy of Data Science, TU/e, Eindhoven, The Netherlands
n.borovits@tue.nl
[2] Jheronimus Academy of Data Science, Tilburg University, Tilburg, The Netherlands

Abstract. Privacy engineering, emphasizing data protection during the design, build, and maintenance of software systems, faces new challenges and opportunities in the emerging decentralized data architectures, namely data mesh. By decentralizing data product ownership across domains, data mesh offers a novel paradigm to rethink how privacy principles are incorporated and maintained in modern system architectures. This paper introduces a conceptual framework that integrates privacy engineering principles with the decentralized nature of data mesh. Our approach provides a holistic view, capturing essential dimensions from both domains. We explore the intersections of privacy engineering and data mesh dimensions and provide guidelines for the stakeholders of a data mesh initiative to embed better data privacy controls. Our framework aims to offer a blueprint to ensure robust privacy practices are inherent, not just additive, during the adoption of data mesh.

Keywords: Privacy engineering · Data mesh · Privacy by design

1 Introduction

Privacy Engineering (PE), as a discipline, concerns itself with integrating privacy principles into software and system development, right from design to deployment [9,19]. This discipline arises from a need to protect data subjects and to ensure that software, systems, and processes comply with established privacy laws and regulations. The concept of Privacy by Design (PbD), enshrined in Article 25 of the General Data Protection Regulation (GDPR), emphasizes proactive privacy measures that aim to prevent data privacy violations from occurring [4]. Such legal mandates have increased attention to PE in research and practice. At the heart of PE's practical application are Privacy Enhancing Technologies (PETs) which facilitate the collection, processing, and sharing of data in a privacy-preserving manner [18].

F. Monti et al. (Eds.): ICSOC 2023 Workshops, LNCS 14518, pp. 265–276, 2024.
https://doi.org/10.1007/978-981-97-0989-2_21

The data mesh is an emerging decentralized and domain-driven architecture for managing enterprise data at scale [11]. Although efficient in many ways, traditional centralized data platforms and architectures can become bottlenecks when scaling and adapting to the dynamic nature of modern businesses [11,16]. Data mesh addresses this by promoting domain-oriented ownership of data, product thinking, and self-serve platforms. In this paradigm, teams or domains treat their data as a product, offering it to consumers within and outside the organization. The decentralized nature of this approach promises scalability, flexibility, and democratization of data.

The data mesh principles of domain ownership of data and computational federated governance can facilitate applying PbD principles for enterprise data [20]. While PE provides a robust framework for building privacy-preserving systems, its application in a decentralized, domain-centric architecture like data mesh has yet to be investigated [34]. This paper aims to bridge this research gap, introducing a framework that integrates the strengths of PE with the agility and scalability of data mesh architecture.

This paper presents a conceptual framework that can guide the integration of PE principles into data mesh architectures. Our framework aims to serve both practitioners at the forefront of building next-generation data systems and researchers, who provide the theoretical foundations for these systems. In terms of scope, this paper restricts itself to conceptual guidelines and foundational principles. While practical implementations can vary based on specific use cases, industries, and regulatory landscapes, the framework provides a versatile blueprint that can be adapted and expanded upon.

This paper is organized as follows. Section 2 introduces PE and data mesh and reviews the related studies. Section 3 presents our framework in detail, including dimensions of data mesh and PE and their interconnections. Section 4 concludes the paper while providing the directions for further research.

2   Background and Related Work

2.1   Privacy Engineering

The inception of Privacy Engineering (PE) is deeply rooted in society's growing concern about individual privacy in the digital age. With the emergence of digital platforms and the Internet in the 1990s, the vast data generated posed new threats to individual privacy. Early endeavors in the domain, such as Cranor's P3P [6], aimed to grant users increased control over their sensitive information. Yet, as technology advanced, so did the techniques and methods to compromise privacy. This escalating threat made the establishment of a structured discipline essential. Legislative responses like the GDPR [28] and the California Consumer Privacy Act (CCPA) [27] emphasized the importance of integrating privacy considerations from the outset.

Central to PE is the principle PbD [4], which emphasizes the integration of privacy rights from the conceptual phase of software development. This proactive approach dictates that privacy should be considered throughout the entire life cycle of software systems and business processes. PETs [18] have been the primary technical solution. Over the years, they have matured from basic anonymization techniques to sophisticated strategies tailored for complex software systems and service architectures. Other crucial principles include Data Minimization (DM), which aims to ensure that only the essential data for a particular process is collected and Purpose Limitation (PL), which restricts the use of data to its intended purpose [3].

Despite its importance, implementing privacy in modern software engineering environments is challenging. The agility and speed of contemporary development processes, such as DevOps, sometimes appear to be at odds with the thorough, proactive approach required by PE [31]. The surge in interconnected devices, thanks to the Internet of Things (IoT), exponentially expands the landscape of potential vulnerabilities. Additionally, distributed architectures, like microservices and cloud-native platforms, introduce data management and control complexities, often straining traditional privacy-preserving techniques [17,24]. These systems' dynamic and evolving nature calls for a reconceptualization of how we view and implement privacy.

2.2   Data Mesh

Data mesh emerged as a response to the challenges posed by traditional centralized data architectures [11,16]. In a typical enterprise, business domains generate data. The centralized collection and management of domain data hinders domain teams from transforming domain data into valuable assets for the enterprise. Data mesh aims to unlock this bottleneck. At the heart of the data mesh paradigm is treating data as a product, owned and maintained by cross-functional domain teams, who intimately know the data. These teams are responsible for the entire data product lifecycle, from creation to distribution and use. The domain teams are equipped with a self-serve platform technology.

The decentralized nature of data ownership in a data mesh introduces challenges and advantages. On the one hand, it democratizes data access, enabling more rapid and domain-specific insights. It also facilitates better scalability, as data solutions can be designed and scaled at the domain level, rather than being hindered by a centralized platform team [16]. However, this decentralization also brings challenges, especially regarding data consistency, interoperability, and governance. Ensuring that data products from various domains seamlessly interoperate and adhere to organizational standards requires robust governance mechanisms and possibly new tooling [11,23].

The implications of data mesh for privacy are multifaceted. Decentralized data ownership can allow for tighter control over data, as domain teams may have a clearer understanding of the specific privacy concerns related to their data. However, the distributed nature of the architecture can also pose challenges in uniformly enforcing privacy regulations and standards. The inherently open and accessible ethos of data mesh might conflict with stringent data protection measures unless privacy is embedded as a core tenet from the outset [10].

2.3   Related Work and Research Gaps

The transition from centralized architectures to decentralized ones, notably from monolithic systems to microservices in software engineering, mirrors the evolution in the data realm from centralized data architectures to data meshes [25]. While fostering adaptability and modular design, this paradigm shift brings intricate challenges, especially concerning governance and traceability [29,34]. Historically, centralized governance, with its single-point control, allowed for relatively straightforward privacy protocol enforcement, such as adherence to GDPR [33]. However, this enforcement becomes significantly more complex in the dispersed landscape of data meshes. One of the pioneering methods to address these challenges is the k-anonymity approach, which has been crucial for understanding and identifying data attributes that could potentially compromise privacy in centralized databases [32]. However, when applied to decentralized systems, this method's time complexity and other limitations become accentuated, revealing its constraints in such environments.

Data meshes, with their modular and decentralized structure, are fraught with complexities. While allowing for quick iterations and deployment, their flexible nature also introduces challenges in tracing data lineage and ensuring consistent governance [11,16]. The issue of quasi-identifiers (i.e., indirect identifiers of individuals such as area code or date of birth) exemplifies these challenges. While these have always been a potential threat to data privacy, in a decentralized context, the risk is amplified. The fragmented nature of data meshes makes tracking and managing quasi-identifiers across various domains an arduous task [13]. Another notable gap lies in scalability. As data grows and more instances are integrated into the mesh, there is a marked increase in execution times, highlighting the inefficiencies that can emerge in such setups [30]. Crucially, the tools and methodologies tailored for centralized systems can become inefficient in the decentralized landscape. Accurate and efficient data lineage remains a significant challenge [8]. Furthermore, the distributed quasi-identifiers problem within data meshes is a pressing issue. This problem is not just a scaled version of existing challenges but presents unique complexities. Identifying Personally Identifiable Information (PII) scattered across multiple database instances in a data mesh complicates the task manifold.

3   A Framework for Decentralized Data Privacy Governance

This section presents our framework for incorporating PE into data mesh architecture. First, we present the dimensions of our framework and then discuss the manifestation of those dimensions within the data mesh architecture.

3.1   Dimensions of Decentralized Data Privacy Governance

We divide the elements of decentralized data privacy governance into two overarching themes: data mesh dimensions and PE dimensions. Figure 1 visualizes these dimensions.

Privacy Engineering Dimensions

		Modeling & Specification	Privacy Metrics	User-centric Privacy	PETs	Privacy Verification & Testing	Lifelong Privacy Management	DM & PL
Data Mesh Dimensions	RSPGs							
	Organization							
	Processes							
	Data Products							
	Computational Federated Governance							
	Self-serve Data Platform							
	Infrastructure							

Fig. 1. Data Mesh and Privacy Engineering Dimensions

Data Mesh Dimensions. The data mesh is a decentralized data architecture that adheres to four principles: data as a product, domain ownership of data, self-serve data platform, and federated computational governance. Based on the previous studies on PE [17,35], we identify seven conceptual dimensions of data mesh that any PE approach for data mesh should consider.

Regulations, Standards, Policies, and Goals (RSPGs). The elements of the data mesh (e.g., data products, platform services, and governance applications [11,16]) should comply with common data privacy regulatory frameworks such as GDPR [28] and CCPA [27]. In addition, the standards adopted by the organization (e.g., security standards, metadata management standards, and data quality assessment standards), organizational policies, goals, and expectations of the internal and external stakeholders of the organization can also contribute to the compliance and privacy requirements for the data mesh of an organization.

Organization. The data mesh introduces a set of new roles and responsibilities for teams and individuals in an organization, which change the existing operational and governance structures in the organization [11,16,34]. For example, autonomous domain teams own the domain data and are responsible for turning their data into privacy-compliant data products. The central platform team builds and manages platform services, including self-serve PE tools. The federated governance team is responsible for defining and enforcing policies for privacy-preserving integration and interoperability of data products. These teams define the roles and responsibilities of various actors involved with the governance and management of data in an organization [21,22].

Processes. An organization needs to establish processes and guidelines to ensure various teams across (and outside of) the organization can effectively communicate and collaborate in managing data and supporting infrastructure in a consistent and privacy-compliant manner [21]. Some examples are a procedure for assessing the trustworthiness of data sources used by data products or processes for reviewing business rules and requesting and making changes. Some of these processes may be automated through services/tools the self-serve platform provides.

A data mesh architecture comprises four main building blocks: data products, self-serve platform, operating infrastructure, and computational federated governance.

Data Products. The data mesh applies product thinking to process and consume analytical data in an organization. The data owners offer their data as valuable assets to potential data consumers within and outside of the organization. To become a valuable asset, a data product should possess attributes such as discoverable, interoperable, trustworthy, and secure [11,16].

Computational Federated Governance. The data mesh adopts a computational federated governance model [34] where data products' compliance with policies and regulations is automated using software code and associated tools (i.e., *policy-as-code* and *compliance-as-code* [1]).

Self-serve Data Platform. Self-serve platforms offer a set of platform services/tools to data owners (from data domains) to build and manage data products efficiently, including embedding privacy by design principles into data products.

Infrastructure. Data products, self-serve data platforms, and data source systems are deployed and hosted using fundamental resources such as computing, storage, and networks. An organization can acquire these resources from public and private clouds, and may also adopt a hybrid or multi-cloud strategy. The data privacy requirements of an organization can significantly influence the selection of the cloud strategy [5].

Privacy Engineering Dimensions. This section discusses the key dimensions of PE, which are fundamental to ensuring comprehensive privacy practices in the data mesh.

Modeling and Specification. This PE dimension elicits and represents privacy requirements for the data mesh, including data products and self-serve data platforms. The privacy requirements help bridge the gap between high-level privacy goals and their tangible realization in technical architectures. They can be derived from various sources, including regulations, standards, policies, and stakeholders' expectations (e.g., data product owners, data product consumers, and platform and governance teams). For instance, when dealing with a healthcare data product, privacy requirements might be modeled to ensure compliance with regulations such as the Health Insurance Portability and Accountability Act (HIPAA) and to specify the permissible data access and sharing mechanisms among various medical stakeholders. The modeling approaches, such as goal modeling and ontologies, can be used to specify the privacy requirements formally [26].

Privacy Metrics. In the context of the data mesh, metrics play an integral role in assessing the privacy attributes of distributed data products and self-serve data platform services. Privacy metrics (e.g., amount of leaked information, system anonymity level, and maximum information leakage) quantitatively measure the level of privacy protection, providing insights into how well privacy requirements are met across various data domains and zones within the mesh. For example, in a retail data product scenario, metrics might measure the proportion of customer data that remains unidentified in aggregated sales reports, ensuring that no single customer's purchase behavior can be easily discerned. These metrics facilitate evaluating and comparing privacy implementations across different data products, thereby driving alignment with privacy standards and best practices throughout the data mesh ecosystem [12].

User-centric Privacy. In the decentralized data mesh, emphasizing user-centric privacy is crucial. Prioritizing consumers and stakeholders in privacy decisions ensures that protections are robust and contextually appropriate. For example, a healthcare data product might offer clear privacy controls, letting users share specific medical data while withholding sensitive details. As data products get developed and consumed across the mesh, a user-centric approach ensures that privacy is seamlessly integrated, empowering users and fostering trust throughout the data ecosystem [14].

Privacy-Enhancing Technologies (PETs). In the data mesh, where data is distributed across various data products and infrastructures, PETs play an instrumental role. These tools and protocols protect users' sensitive data across the mesh, particularly when data products are shared and consumed across different teams and domains. For example, when dealing with geolocation data within a transportation data product, differential privacy techniques might be employed to ensure that individual users' locations are obfuscated to prevent potential misuse or identification. As the data mesh promotes decentralized data ownership and autonomy, PETs, integrated into the self-serve platform, can help maintain a consistent and robust privacy protection layer across this dispersed ecosystem [36].

Privacy Verification and Testing. In the data mesh, where data products are autonomously developed and managed by diverse domain teams, privacy verification and testing become paramount. For instance, after introducing a new anonymization technique in a healthcare data product, one might employ privacy penetration testing to ascertain if the anonymized data can be re-identified or if any other privacy breaches are feasible. These methodologies and tools ensure that privacy requirements are uniformly and correctly implemented across the entire mesh despite the decentralized ownership and management of data. As data products continually evolve and interact, regular assessments validate that they consistently uphold their privacy guarantees, thus fostering trust and compliance in the mesh ecosystem [2].

Lifelong Privacy Management. In the data mesh, continuous privacy management is vital due to the dynamic nature of data products and their interactions. Take, for instance, a data product focused on users' shopping behaviors. As it evolves to incorporate location-based promotions, fresh privacy issues like users' geolocation arise. This evolution demands updated privacy controls, possibly employing geo-obfuscation methods. This dimension emphasizes the need for ongoing privacy evaluations, from a product's creation to its retirement or adaptation. It ensures that privacy measures keep pace with shifting data dynamics, usage trends, and emerging vulnerabilities, bolstering trust and resilience in the data mesh [15].

Data Minimization and Purpose Limitation (DM & PL). Within the data mesh, it is essential to ensure data products gather and utilize data strictly relevant to their set goals. For example, a data product targeting users' reading choices in an online bookstore should not collect data on their physical whereabouts, as it's unnecessary and might pose privacy risks. DM & PL serve to mitigate dangers from superfluous data and amplify the transparency and reliability of each product's role in the mesh. Matching data practices with defined purposes is key to safeguarding individual privacy and upholding the data mesh's integrity [7].

3.2 Responsibilities of Actors in Privacy-Compliant Data Mesh

This section discusses the roles of the key stakeholders in a data mesh regarding adopting PE when creating and managing a data mesh. Figure 2 shows the four primary teams in a data mesh architecture [11,16] and their responsibilities.

Governance Team. This team develops and operationalizes data governance policies using the tools provided by the governance plane and self-serve platform. For example, the governance team can use a regulatory compliance management system to monitor the compliance of the data mesh interactively. Such a tool can actively illuminate adherence levels, preemptively indicate potential non-conformities, and facilitate instantaneous rectifications, maintaining perpetual congruence with legal injunctions and organizational directives.

Domain Teams. These teams are responsible for embedding privacy directly at the heart of every data product. Recognizing each data product's unique characteristics and requirements, they can adopt specialized PETs tailored to each dataset's nuances. For example, while differential privacy might be applied to datasets prone to re-identification risks during analytics, homomorphic encryption could be chosen for data products requiring computations on encrypted data without decryption. This product-centric privacy approach ensures that from the moment data is created to when it is consumed, every step of its journey is transparent, controlled, and infused with privacy-preserving measures. In doing so, the domain team can ensure the

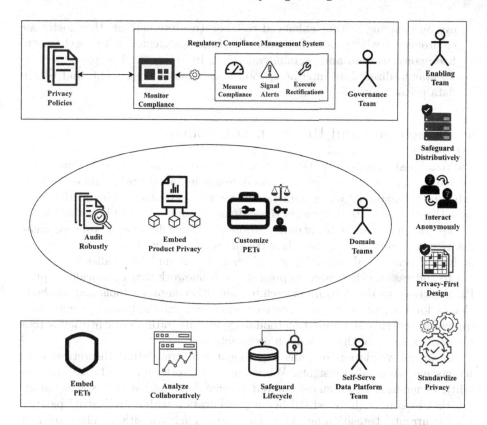

Fig. 2. Roles and Responsibilities of Actors in Privacy-Compliant Data Mesh Architectures

data products' reliability and integrity and consistently generate audit trails that can be tangible evidence of privacy-preserving practices, bolstering trust and confidence in decentralized data ecosystems.

Platform Team. The self-serve data platform team is instrumental in adopting foundational, privacy-centric infrastructures. Key to their responsibilities is the endorsement and implementation of PETs, such as secure multi-party computation protocols and advanced cryptographic solutions. These technologies ensure the protection and confidentiality of data across its entire lifecycle and enforce privacy standards and policies of the data mesh. Additionally, their adoption streamlines collaborative analytics, guaranteeing data confidentiality and reinforcing the rigorous data privacy standards.

Enabling Team. This team is pivotal in ushering in technological advancements and championing the cause of data democratization. Embracing principles of PbD, the enabling team is entrusted with the inception of decentralized storage solutions that accentuate data sovereignty and prioritize DM and PL by instituting efficacious data ownership protocols. They ensure that data remains an asset without unwarranted privacy risks. Moreover, with a keen eye on enabling privacy-enhanced collaborative interactions, they foster an environment where data discoverability is supplemented with mechanisms like anonymization and pseudonymization. In doing so, they pave the way for standardized data interfaces, robust metadata management, and better data privacy controls.

4 Conclusion and Research Directions

The data mesh aims to solve the deficiencies in the centralized data architectures related to sharing data across business domains in an enterprise and extracting value from domain data. It grants data ownership to business domains that produce the data and also empowers those domain teams by providing a self-serve data platform and automating data governance. While data mesh positions organizations to capitalize on their data resources effectively, ensuring data privacy under a decentralized ownership model remains a formidable challenge.

To address this challenge, we presented a framework that holistically applies PE principles to the data mesh architecture. PE comprises tools and methodologies for integrating privacy controls seamlessly into software systems. Our framework offers a structured methodology for integrating data privacy across the various facets of the data mesh architecture.

Empirical validation remains instrumental in translating theoretical constructs into actionable insights. While our framework aims for broad applicability, understanding its nuances about specific data mesh domains is essential. For that reason, we have established a collaboration with an industrial partner who is currently transitioning to the data mesh. Their transitional phase offers a fertile ground, providing a rich context for both the application and refinement of our framework.

Our collaborative action plan is outlined as follows:

1. *Integration within the Ongoing Transition:* Initially, a deep dive into the current transition state of our industrial partner to identify areas apt for our framework's integration.
2. *Continuous Feedback Loop:* After integration, institute regular checkpoints to amass feedback from domain teams, enabling timely resolution of challenges.
3. *Calibration and Refinement:* Use the accumulated feedback to iteratively refine the framework, ensuring it resonates with the real-world intricacies faced during the data mesh transition.
4. *Documentation and Case Study:* Post refinement cycles, draft a detailed case study that encapsulates the framework's efficacy and offers a beacon for enterprises on a similar trajectory.

In conclusion, our framework sets the stage for a landscape where the pillars of data collaboration and individual privacy stand together, supporting a future where they harmoniously coexist.

References

1. Agarwal, V., et al.: Compliance-as-code for cybersecurity automation in hybrid cloud. In: 2022 IEEE 15th International Conference on Cloud Computing (CLOUD), pp. 427–437 (2022)
2. Antignac, T., Sands, D., Schneider, G.: Data minimisation: a language-based approach. In: De Capitani di Vimercati, S., Martinelli, F. (eds.) SEC 2017. IAICT, vol. 502, pp. 442–456. Springer, Cham (2017). https://doi.org/10.1007/978-3-319-58469-0_30
3. Bier, C., Birnstill, P., Krempel, E., Vagts, H., Beyerer, J.: Enhancing privacy by design from a developer's perspective. In: Preneel, B., Ikonomou, D. (eds.) APF 2012. LNCS, vol. 8319, pp. 73–85. Springer, Heidelberg (2014). https://doi.org/10.1007/978-3-642-54069-1_5
4. Cavoukian, A., et al.: Privacy by design: the 7 foundational principles. Information and privacy commissioner of Ontario, Canada 5, 12 (2009)
5. Chen, D., Zhao, H.: Data security and privacy protection issues in cloud computing. In: 2012 International Conference on Computer Science and Electronics Engineering, vol. 1, pp. 647–651 (2012)
6. Cranor, L.: Web Privacy with P3P. O'Reilly Media Inc., Sebastopol (2002)
7. Cranor, L.F.: Necessary but not sufficient: standardized mechanisms for privacy notice and choice. J. Telecommun. High Technol. Law 10, 273 (2012)
8. Crosby, M., Pattanayak, P., Verma, S., Kalyanaraman, V., et al.: Blockchain technology: beyond bitcoin. Appl. Innov. 2(6–10), 71 (2016)
9. Danezis, G., et al.: Privacy and data protection by design-from policy to engineering. arXiv preprint arXiv:1501.03726 (2015)
10. De Montjoye, Y.A., Rocher, L., Pentland, A.S.: bandicoot: a python toolbox for mobile phone metadata. J. Mach. Learn. Res. 17(1), 6100–6104 (2016)
11. Dehghani, Z.: Data Mesh Delivering Data-Driven Value at Scale. O'Reilly Media, Sebastopol (2022)
12. Díaz, C., Seys, S., Claessens, J., Preneel, B.: Towards measuring anonymity. In: Dingledine, R., Syverson, P. (eds.) PET 2002. LNCS, vol. 2482, pp. 54–68. Springer, Heidelberg (2003). https://doi.org/10.1007/3-540-36467-6_5
13. El Emam, K., Dankar, F.K.: Protecting privacy using k-anonymity. J. Am. Med. Inform. Assoc. 15(5), 627–637 (2008)
14. Fang, L., LeFevre, K.: Privacy wizards for social networking sites. In: Proceedings of the 19th International Conference on World Wide Web, pp. 351–360 (2010)
15. Friedland, G., Sommer, R.: Cybercasing the joint: on the privacy implications of geo-tagging. In: 5th USENIX Workshop on Hot Topics in Security (HotSec 2010) (2010)
16. Goedegebuure, A., et al.: Data mesh: a systematic gray literature review. arXiv preprint arXiv:2304.01062 (2023)
17. Grünewald, E.: Cloud native privacy engineering through DevPrivOps. In: Friedewald, M., Krenn, S., Schiering, I., Schiffner, S. (eds.) Privacy and Identity 2021. IAICT, vol. 644, pp. 122–141. Springer, Cham (2022). https://doi.org/10.1007/978-3-030-99100-5_10
18. Heurix, J., Zimmermann, P., Neubauer, T., Fenz, S.: A taxonomy for privacy enhancing technologies. Comput. Secur. 53, 1–17 (2015)
19. Hoepman, J.-H.: Privacy design strategies. In: Cuppens-Boulahia, N., Cuppens, F., Jajodia, S., Abou El Kalam, A., Sans, T. (eds.) SEC 2014. IAICT, vol. 428, pp. 446–459. Springer, Heidelberg (2014). https://doi.org/10.1007/978-3-642-55415-5_38

20. Jarmul, K.: Privacy-first data via data mesh (2022). https://www.thoughtworks. com/insights/articles/privacy-first-data-via-data-mesh
21. Khatri, V., Brown, C.V.: Designing data governance. Commun. ACM **53**(1), 148–152 (2010)
22. Kumara, I., Kayes, A.S.M., Mundt, P., Schneider, R.: Data governance. In: Liebregts, W., van den Heuvel, W.-J., van den Born, A. (eds.) Data Science for Entrepreneurship. CCB, pp. 37–62. Springer, Cham (2023). https://doi.org/10. 1007/978-3-031-19554-9_3
23. Lăzăroiu, G., Kovacova, M., Kliestikova, J., Kubala, P., Valaskova, K., Dengov, V.V.: Data governance and automated individual decision-making in the digital privacy general data protection regulation. Administratie si Manag. Public **31**, 132–142 (2018)
24. de Montjoye, Y.A., Hidalgo, C.A., Verleysen, M., Blondel, V.D.: Unique in the crowd: the privacy bounds of human mobility. Sci. Rep. **3**(1), 1376 (2013)
25. Newman, S.: Building Microservices. O'Reilly Media Inc., Sebastopol (2021)
26. Otto, P.N., Antón, A.I.: Addressing legal requirements in requirements engineering: a systematic literature review. IEEE Trans. Softw. Eng. **43**(2), 158–171 (2017)
27. Pardau, S.L.: The California consumer privacy act: towards a European-style privacy regime in the United States. J. Tech. L. & Pol'y **23**, 68 (2018)
28. General Data Protection Regulation: Regulation (EU) 2016/679 of the European parliament and of the council. Regulation (EU) 679/2016 (2016)
29. Richards, M.: Microservices vs. Service-Oriented Architecture. O'Reilly Media, Sebastopol (2015)
30. Schneider, S., Sunyaev, A.: Determinant factors of cloud-sourcing decisions: reflecting on the IT outsourcing literature in the era of cloud computing. J. Inf. Technol. **31**, 1–31 (2016). https://doi.org/10.1057/jit.2014.25
31. Spiekermann, S., Korunovska, J., Langheinrich, M.: Inside the organization: why privacy and security engineering is a challenge for engineers. Proc. IEEE **107**(3), 600–615 (2018)
32. Sweeney, L.: k-anonymity: a model for protecting privacy. Int. J. Uncertainty Fuzziness Knowl.-Based Syst. **10**(5), 557–570 (2002)
33. Voigt, P., von dem Bussche, A.: Enforcement and fines under the GDPR. In: Voigt, P., von dem Bussche, A. (eds.) The EU General Data Protection Regulation (GDPR), pp. 201–217. Springer, Cham (2017). https://doi.org/10.1007/978-3-319-57959-7_7
34. Wider, A., Verma, S., Akhtar, A.: Decentralized data governance as part of a data mesh platform: concepts and approaches. In: 2023 IEEE International Conference on Web Services (ICWS), pp. 746–754 (2023)
35. Williams, J., Nee, L.: Privacy engineering. Computer **55**(10), 113–118 (2022)
36. Xu, R., Baracaldo, N., Joshi, J.: Privacy-preserving machine learning: methods, challenges and directions. arXiv preprint arXiv:2108.04417 (2021)

Ph.D. Symposium

Towards a Taxonomy and Software Architecture for Data Processing and Contextualization for the Internet of Things

Adrian Bazan-Muñoz[1]([⊠]) [iD], Guadalupe Ortiz[1] [iD], and Alfonso Garcia-de-Prado[2] [iD]

[1] Department of Computer Science, University of Cádiz, Puerto Real, Spain
{adrian.bazan,guadalupe.ortiz}@uca.es
[2] Department of Computer Architecture and Technology, University of Cádiz, Puerto Real, Spain
alfonso.garciadeprado@uca.es

Abstract. Nowadays, the Internet of Things (IoT) and intelligent decision-making systems are growing exponentially, rising new needs to be addressed. Although we can currently find a large number of IoT applications that can process huge amounts of data in real time, it is difficult to find solutions that integrate data from different application domains for further contextualization and personalization of the offered services. To address this gap, we propose a taxonomy and a context-aware software architecture. The taxonomy will allow the description of data from different domains according to current needs and their use for further contextualization of smart applications. Through the software architecture it will be possible to easily integrate and correlate, thanks to the use of taxonomy, data from different application domains, processing large amounts of data in real time, and enabling the development of smarter decision making systems.

Keywords: Context Awareness · Taxonomy · Smart Everything · Collaborative Internet of Things · Complex-Event Processing

1 Motivation and Problem Statement

In recent years the Internet of Things (IoT) has evolved to a large extent due to the exponential growth of Smart Everything [1] applications. Smart Everything refers to heterogeneous application domains in which real-time data processing enables improved decision making, by enriching the context of smart applications, smart cities, etc.

Over the years, research related to data processing in Smart Everything applications have focused on processing and monitoring data from a specific application domain, providing intelligent actions for that domain, without taking into consideration data from other domains (context). Furthermore, there is currently no consensus or standard on the definition of the specific data of a Smart Everything domain. This situation makes it difficult to integrate and correlate data from different systems. However, increasing

---

G. Ortiz and A. Garcia-de-Prado—This authors are Supervised.

F. Monti et al. (Eds.): ICSOC 2023 Workshops, LNCS 14518, pp. 279–284, 2024.
https://doi.org/10.1007/978-981-97-0989-2_22

the contextualization of smart devices, through a software architecture that facilitates the integration and correlation of data from heterogeneous domains, would benefit society. We therefore seek to pave the way towards the Collaborative Internet of Things (C-IoT) [2, 3], which would require agreeing on a common criterion for successfully sharing data from heterogeneous domains.

These are two of the gaps that we aim to solve in this PhD thesis: firstly, we intend to fill the existing gap in the IoT and Smart Everything domain with respect to a standard description of data from different application domains. For this purpose, we intend to define a taxonomy to facilitate the description of IoT and Smart Everything data in a homogeneous way for different application domains. This taxonomy will provide a set of common attributes for IoT and Smart Everything domains, but at the same time, it will be extensible with other attributes that might be specific to a given domain. Secondly, we seek to achieve the integration and correlation of data from different application domains to enrich the context in Smart Everything applications. To this end, we propose a software architecture for the acquisition, processing and correlation of domain and contextual data, defined according to the previously mentioned taxonomy, and using Complex Event Processing (CEP) technologies for real-time data processing and decision making.

The rest of the paper is organized as follows. Section 2 presents the research challenges. Section 3 presents the proposal. Section 4 presents the research plan, while Sect. 5 presents related work. Finally, Sect. 6 presents the conclusions.

2   Research Challenges

In this PhD, we will face the following research challenges:

1. First of all, to define a taxonomy generic enough to be useful across multiple Smart Everything application domains, but at the same time providing the appropriate mechanisms to tailor the elements of the taxonomy to be useful in each particular domain. In addition, we seek to address the lack of consensus on the definition of data specific to a Smart Everything domain, which makes it difficult to integrate and correlate data from different systems. Furthermore, although some standards focused on streaming data processing have been defined [4], these standards are too generic and their use practically requires a redesign of the standards in order to adequately represent the different domains.
2. Secondly, to define different types of events that allow us to represent data from different Smart Everything application domains using the defined taxonomy. To do so, we consider that we need to classify events into three types according to the domain they come from: domain events, local context events, and remote context events, as explained in Sect. 3.
3. Thirdly, to design a software architecture with a processing system that facilitates the integration and real time processing of data from different application domains. Therefore, integration of the different application domains will be facilitated by using the three previously mentioned event types, which will be defined according to a data structure that makes use of the taxonomy. Then, the different type of events will be processed together according to a series of previously defined event patterns through the use of the CEP engine incorporated in the software architecture proposed.

4. Finally, since the software architecture can handle data from a very wide range of Smart Everything application domains, including many critical user data, security and privacy must be a priority. This includes ensuring secure communications, data encryption, and accessibility to the various storage and processing systems.

3 Proposed Solution

The proposed software architecture can be seen in Fig. 1; in the following lines we explain and motivate its components.

As mentioned in the introduction, one of our aims is to define a taxonomy (in the left-hand side of Fig. 1) to facilitate the description of IoT and Smart Everything data in a homogeneous way for different application domains. We evaluated whether to use a taxonomy or an ontology. Although ontologies have some advantages, such as allowing a better description of the relationships between attributes and defining rules of action, their use also has some limitations, such as the complexity of their use, the few available languages, etc. Taxonomies, however, allow defining the context but not the rules associated to it. But, although this may be a limitation, it has the advantage of allowing us to be more flexible in describing the information. For these reasons we decided to make use of a taxonomy, considering that they are more adapted to our needs and complement them with CEP to address the lack of taxonomy rules. We are currently in the process of defining a taxonomy based on the most common attributes and classes present in other approaches and in IoT and Smart Everything domains.

On the other hand, the proposed taxonomy will be accompanied by a data structure that will facilitate the description of IoT data according to the taxonomy, in order to facilitate data processing. Although there are currently some standards focused on streaming data processing such as XES [4], this standard is too generic and based on the use of XML. The reality is that many datasets are offered in JSON, for example many more JSON datasets than XML datasets can be found on the European Union's data portal [5]: 112 047 JSON datasets are currently available compared to 33 313 XML datasets, which is why we strongly consider that a JSON structure should be used.

Furthermore, we consider necessary the categorisation of events into three types, domain events, local context events and remote context events, also represented in Fig. 1. We believe this categorisation is necessary to clearly distinguish whether the events are exclusively related to the domain in question (domain event), for example if a person opens a door inside his/her house, that interaction will be a domain event, whether the event is generated by the interaction of our user with another domain (local context event), for example if a person leaves his/her house and makes a card payment in a shop, that interaction would be a local context event, and whether our event is not related to any local user of the system (remote context event), for example information from a temperature sensor in the street, would be a remote context event.. This classification will facilitate dealing with the sharing polices more easily. Particularly, domain events will not be shared with other domains, in order to preserve the privacy of domain-specific data; local context events will be shared if we consider they might be relevant to other domains; remote context events will be publicly available.

Therefore, the data sources will generate the different types of events as JSON structured events and according to the defined taxonomy. These events will be sent to a message broker, which will allow us sharing domain and contextual data from different application domains. This data will be integrated and processed together in the processing system (in the right-hand side of the Figure), which in our proposal will be a CEP engine; other approaches could replace it by other processing system. Finally, the processing system will generate notifications or actions as output.

This way, the architecture allows facilitate data correlation and a better knowledge of the context of the system.

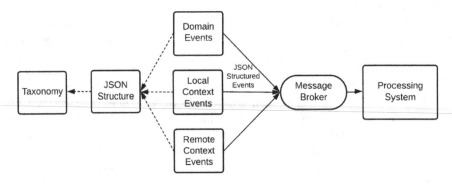

Fig. 1. Proposed software architecture

4   Research Plan

In this section we will explain the current status of the doctoral thesis one year after its start in November 2022.

The PhD thesis started with an extensive study of the state of the art of the problem, as well as an analysis of a possible solution. After that we decided that it was necessary to make use of some kind of element for the definition of the data. Therefore, a detailed study of the different ontologies and taxonomies existing in the literature was carried out, looking for the advantages and disadvantages of using each of them, as well as the most common elements in each of them. After carrying out this analysis, taking into account the attributes and classes most commonly found in the different approaches, we proceeded to define a taxonomy. Once the taxonomy was defined, we analyzed the situation of the context and domain data, and proceeded to make a division of the different types of events that our domain could receive according to their relationship with the user. This led us to the need to make use of a JSON data structure based on the taxonomy to send the data to the processing system.

Currently, after designing a prospective software architecture, we are in the phase of developing it for the integration of the different domain and contextual events. Once the architecture has been developed, it will be essential to implement security and privacy measures in accordance with the critical data that the system is expected to process. Finally, we will carry out the implementation of a case study to evaluate the functioning of the whole system, to finally write and defend the PhD thesis.

5   Related Work

Over the years, the approaches proposed for the definition of context data have been based on the use of ontologies or taxonomies. On the one hand, we find well-known ontologies such as the one proposed by Chen et al. [6], where a first approach to context-aware ontologies was made. Later, this proposal was extended with SOUPA [7] extending the previously general use ontology to be used for a specific application domain. Also Gu et al. [8] propose an ontology for IoT domains in which cross-domain data sharing was provided.

Regarding taxonomies, we find different proposals such as the one from Hemmati et al. [9], where firstly an assessment of the state of the art for the applications of autonomous things is made, subsequently a taxonomy to fill the existing gap in this field is presented. Mountrouidou et al. [10], propose a taxonomy that considers categorisation as an abstraction of the network of things, being a very specific taxonomy. Also, Iftikhar et al. [11] proposed a taxonomy focused on edge and cloud computing based on artificial intelligence. On the other hand, Islam et al. [12] make a proposal focused on fog computing that allows linking the IoT layer with the cloud layer; based on an initial study of different context parameters and fog computing practical cases they provide a context-aware taxonomy for fog computing.

The main drawback we found in the existent related work is that the proposed taxonomies are only applicable to specific application domains, and do not facilitate the correlation of data from different domains of IoT and Smart everything.

6   Conclusion

We have proposed a PhD focused on providing a system for the integration and correlation of data from different application domains, with the aim of enriching the context of smart applications. We envision a solution based on the definition of a taxonomy and structure for the description of data from different application domains for IoT and Smart Everything. Furthermore, we envision the creation of a software architecture for the integration and correlation of these heterogeneous domain data using the previously defined taxonomy. This proposal is an evolution of the a first approach presented last year [13]. We have currently advanced in the definition of the taxonomy, the categorization of the events into domain, local context and remote context events, and the design of the software architecture to facilitate the sharing, correlation and contextualization of several domains data to enrich the smart decision making.

Acknowledgments. This work was supported by AwESOMe Project PID2021-122215NB-C33 funded by MCIN/AEI /10.13039/501100011033/ and by ERDF A way to do Europe.

References

1. Streitz, N.: Beyond smart-only cities: redefining the 'smart-everything' paradigm. J. Ambient. Intell. Humaniz. Comput. **10**(2), 791–812 (2018). https://doi.org/10.1007/s12652-018-0824-1

2. Behmann, F., Wu, K.: Collaborative Internet of Things (C-IoT): For Future Smart Connected Life and Business. John Wiley and Sons Inc., Hoboken (2015)

3. Garcia-de-Prado, A., Ortiz, G., Boubeta-Puig, J.: COLLECT: COLLaborativE ConText-aware service oriented architecture for intelligent decision-making in the Internet of Things. Expert Syst. Appl. **85**, 231–248 (2017). https://doi.org/10.1016/j.eswa.2017.05.034

4. Günther, W.C., Verbeek, E.: XES (2014). http://www.xes-standard.org/_media/xes/xesstanda rddefinition-2.0.pdf,

5. Open EU Datasets | Official Portal for EU Data | data.europa.eu. https://data.europa.eu/data/datasets?locale=en. Accessed 03 Aug 2023

6. Chen, H., Finin, T., Joshi, A.: An ontology for context-aware pervasive computing environments. Knowl. Eng. Rev. **18** (2003). https://doi.org/10.1017/S0269888904000025

7. Chen, H., Perich, F., Finin, T., Joshi, A.: SOUPA: standard ontology for ubiquitous and pervasive applications. Presented at the September 22 (2004). https://doi.org/10.1109/MOBIQ. 2004.1331732

8. Gu, T., Wang, X.H., Pung, H.K., Zhang, D.Q.: An Ontology-based Context Model in Intelligent Environments (2020). https://doi.org/10.48550/arXiv.2003.05055, http://arxiv.org/abs/2003.05055

9. Hemmati, A., Rahmani, A.M.: The internet of autonomous things applications: a taxonomy, technologies, and future directions. Internet Things **20**, 100635 (2022). https://doi.org/10. 1016/j.iot.2022.100635

10. Mountrouidou, X., Billings, B., Mejia-Ricart, L.: Not just another Internet of Things taxonomy: a method for validation of taxonomies. Internet Things. **6**, 100049 (2019). https://doi. org/10.1016/j.iot.2019.03.003

11. Iftikhar, S., et al.: AI-based fog and edge computing: a systematic review, taxonomy and future directions. Internet Things **21**, 100674 (2023). https://doi.org/10.1016/j.iot.2022.100674

12. Islam, M.S.U., Kumar, A., Hu, Y.-C.: Context-aware scheduling in fog computing: a survey, taxonomy, challenges and future directions. J. Netw. Comput. Appl. **180**, 103008 (2021). https://doi.org/10.1016/j.jnca.2021.103008

13. Bazan-Muñoz, A.: Towards a context-aware framework for internet of things and smart everything. In: Troya, J., et al. (eds.) Service-Oriented Computing – ICSOC 2022 Workshops. ICSOC 2022. LNCS, vol. 13821, pp. 308–313. Springer, Cham (2023). https://doi.org/10. 1007/978-3-031-26507-5_25

Advanced Serverless Edge Computing

Inacio Gaspar Ticongolo[1,2]([✉]), Luciano Baresi[1], and Giovanni Quattrocchi[1]

[1] Politecnico di Milano, Dipartimento di Elettronica, Informazione e Bioingegneria, Milan, Italy
inaciogaspar.ticongolo@polimi.it
[2] Departamento de Matematica e Informatica, Universidade Eduardo Mondlane, Maputo, Mozambique

Abstract. Serverless computing is becoming an attractive means to implement applications on top of edge infrastructures. Developers break applications into small components (functions), and this modularity allows one to cope with the limited resources of edge nodes and meet the stringent response times typical of edge applications. Different frameworks already support serverless edge computing, that is, the management and operation of serverless applications on top of edge infrastructures, but they usually cope with the different problems in isolation: for example, function placement, dependency management, cold starts, data management, and resource allocation. In contrast, we claim that these aspects must be dealt with all together. This work borrows from NEPTUNE and aims to fill the gap. We plan to complement NEPTUNE with dependency-aware function placement and resource allocation, to tackle image instantiation and cold start mitigation, and to address data management. The first results on the use of function dependencies to ameliorate resource allocation indicate significant improvements with respect to the state of the art.

Keywords: serverless · edge computing · function dependencies · resource allocation · placement · image instantiation · cold start · data management

1 Introduction

Serverless computing provides suitable means to properly deploy, manage, and operate applications on top of edge infrastructures. Serverless applications are usually developed and deployed as cooperating isolated components (functions). The granularity imposed by serverless computing fits perfectly the needs of edge applications: it helps manage the efficient placement of functions on edge nodes, the allocation of limited resources [7], and fluctuating workloads. Functions' modularity and isolation produce applications that are more flexible and can quickly be scaled to meet contingent needs.

Supervised by Luciano Baresi and Giovanni Quattrocchi.

Serverless edge computing, that is, serverless applications on top of edge infrastructures, has already been widely studied [8]. Function isolation can foster flexibility and adaptation, but dependencies, instance creation, and data management may complicate application management. All these (advanced) aspects pose new challenges that an *advanced* infrastructure must deal with. Existing solutions [7,12,13] tend to approach the different problems in isolation, and thus they are not complete. For example, some solutions focus on placement [8], resource allocation [7], or cold start mitigation [12]. To the best of our knowledge, only NEPTUNE [1] addresses placement, routing, resource allocation, and GPU support all together, but it does not consider function dependencies, and does not support instance allocation, cold start mitigation, dynamic node assemblies, and data management.

This work aims to borrow from and complement NEPTUNE to design, implement, and assess an *advanced* serverless edge infrastructure that: (i) exploits function dependencies to allocate computations on nodes and to provision them with suitable resources, (ii) resorts to dynamic slicing of node topologies to cope with their sizes, (iii) addresses the problem of function instantiation and cold start mitigation, and (iv) manages computation and data in a coherent way.

The rest of the paper is structured as follows. Section 2 briefly describes NEPTUNE, that is, the starting point of this work. Section 3 frames the problem. Section 4 introduces envisioned contributions, while Sect. 5 summarises some preliminary results. Section 6 concludes the paper and introduces some deadlines.

2   NEPTUNE in a Nutshell

NEPTUNE is a state of the art serverless edge infrastructure [1]. It requires users to upload the source code of functions as container images and to specify, for each function, a threshold on the response time (also known as a service level agreement or SLA), and the memory necessary for their execution. It employs a three-tier management architecture consisting of topology, community, and node levels. At the topology-level, the edge network is divided into independent *communities*, each containing edge nodes with low network latency between them. These communities are only changed periodically in case of node failures.

At the community-level, a controlled based on Mixed-Integer Programming determines the optimal function placement and routing policies that minimize network latency within the community. Function placement entails selecting the optimal number of function instances and their corresponding hosting nodes. Due to the limited resources available on nodes, NEPTUNE calculates routing policies to distribute the workload across the community when the receiving node cannot handle it in its entirety. The workload that can benefit from GPU acceleration is managed first and placed on GPU-equipped nodes (if possible); the remaining workload is then tackled using nodes with standard CPUs.

A node-level controller focuses on ensuring that CPU-based executions comply with the expected SLA. Each function instance is equipped with a lightweight Proportional Integral (PI) controller to maintain response times close to a predefined set point that is equal to or lower than the corresponding SLA. In the short term, these controllers manage the workload fluctuations typical of edge computing.

3   Problem Formulation

Serverless edge computing is an open research topic already tackled by diverse solutions. For example, Wang et al. [11] propose LaSS to cope with the response time of serverless functions by means of careful *resource allocation*. LaSS scales resources up and down given the actual workload; weights associated with functions are used to allocate resources when they are not enough to serve all requests.

Resource allocation is not enough. One should also consider *function placement* and exploit their dependencies to improve it. For example, He et al. [6] exploit dependencies to properly deploy microservice applications onto edge nodes and optimize their response times. They also manage function instances, but do not consider resource allocation and GPU management. Deng et al. [3] address placement and minimize response times by considering network bandwidth and the computational power of the different nodes. They do not consider load balancing, GPUs, dynamic instance management, and cold starts. Similar limitations can be identified in [13].

Edge infrastructures are *live* entities where nodes crash, users may move, and workloads fluctuate significantly. This means that the sub-network of interest can change over time, and the whole infrastructure must be organized in *groups dynamically* to cope with the aforementioned problems. Sinaeepourfard et al. [9] partition the network into static sub-groups to simplify network management but they cannot handle dynamic changes.

Cold start in serverless computing refers to the latency incurred when deploying a new function instance, and it is particularly critical in edge environments where low latency is a primary requirement. While numerous studies address the cold start problem [10], they do not consider function dependencies. NEPTUNE and others [6] assume that function images are always stored onto nodes properly, but this might not be true in practice and remote and time-consuming downloads are required.

Data management [13] means allocating computation and data close to each other to mitigate network latency during data access, while also tackling data consistency in a geographically distributed setup. Consequently, optimizing the placement of both computation and data is crucial, alongside designing strategies for data replication and sharding at the edge. This research is still in its infancy and requires further investigation [4].

Advanced serverless infrastructures should assemble all these aspects into a single integrated solution. They should take into account function dependencies, network delays, workload routing and balancing, dynamic instance management (given the current workload), and cold start mitigation. In addition, the use of GPUs could speed up the performance of computation-intensive applications, but complicates the placement problem that must deal with heterogeneous executors —no existing solutions can handle them. NEPTUNE is a good starting point that supports the wider set of characteristics we are aware of, but it is not complete and can be improved significantly.

4   Foreseen Contributions

The main goal of this work is to extend NEPTUNE and make it provide additional capabilities in addition to those summarized in Sect. 2. The plan is to mix extensions to already identified solutions and novel problems (contributions) that were not previously considered. The first part of the work [2], whose first results are summarized in Sect. 5, extends the solution implemented in NEPTUNE by considering function dependencies when allocating resources. For example, let us consider two functions f_1 and f_2, where the former depends on the latter, and f_2 experiences a workload peak that increases the response time of both f_2 and f_1. Increasing the resources provisioned to both functions —as existing solutions would do— is useless since the dependency implies that the slowdown of f_1 is due to f_2, and thus one should only add resources to the second function.

In a similar way, we are also working on exploiting dependencies to ameliorate function placement on nodes. Serverless functions are isolated, but they are not independent and thus a placement that eases cooperation would positively impact the overall performance of the different applications. Dependent functions should stay as close as possible: being on the same node would be the ideal solution, but two adjacent nodes could become a reasonable compromise if a single node cannot host all related functions. Again, we are working on constraining how NEPTUNE places function instances to always minimize the delay between dependent functions. The idea is to start from endpoint functions and create clusters of related functions, which must be allocated one near the others.

The third aspect for which dependencies can help is for mitigating the cold restart problem of newly created instances. Being aware of who does what can help foresee which instances must be activated and when. While existing solutions mostly address cloud applications and use learned models [10] to anticipate the activation of the instances of interest, we would like to adapt the solution proposed by Gunasekaran et al. [5] to predict future workloads for entry-point functions, and then create, reuse, or kill instances based on when they were or will be used. We want to exploit the workload of entrypoint functions, the last time they were called, and their dependencies to decide where and when we run, pause, or kill function instances.

As said above, NEPTUNE partitions the edge infrastructure into sub-nets to slice the global problem into manageable chunks, called communities. Unfortunately, the highest level control manages communities periodically —and with periods in the order of hours— and thus it cannot cope with exceptions and unforeseen spikes in incoming workload. The plan is to extend the overall control embedded in NEPTUNE and conceive a two-step process: a first solution that can react to emergencies quickly, and then exploit NEPTUNE to re-balance the different communities properly. We can envision two types of exceptions: node crashes and then they are not part of a community anymore, and communities that become overloaded and they cannot manage (properly) the workload they should. Note that the former case may imply the latter. In the former case, it is mainly a matter of removing crashed nodes from the routing tables and replicating lost function instances properly. In the latter case, we are working on migration rules to move nodes from one community to another. For example, one could think of suspending instances running on a node N, migrate them to another node of the same community, and then move N to the new community. We could also think of isolating N, wait till all its computations end, and then move it. In case of strict emergencies, the computations on N could even be killed and the node moved immediately.

The last open problem we would like to address refers to data management and to the symbiosis between data and computation in edge computing, that is, every time we want to keep latency under control. The problem is manyfold since one must work on where data are generated with respect to where the computation takes place. Given moving data can easily become a bottleneck, one should move the computation, and thus the placement of function instances must also take into account the data they are supposed to exploit. The last dimension refers to the possible partitioning and replication of data elements, which must be considered very carefully to avoid useless delays and to not waste too many resources with this activity. Currently, we are more aware of the problem and of what we would like to have, but we are still studying the state of the art to identify and frame our contribution properly.

All contributions will be formulated properly, assessed by means of dedicated simulators, and then implemented and embedded in our framework for serverless edge computing. All solutions will also be assessed through known and real case studies, and released as open-source software to support the replicability of experiments.

5   First Results

The first part of the envisioned work focused on the use of dependencies to ameliorate resource provisioning, without changing the way NEPTUNE allocates function instances to nodes.

The set F of dependent functions is represented as a $DAG(F, E)$, where vertices are function instances and edges are invocations between functions. The response time of a function $f_i \in F$ is the sum of local response time, that is, the time needed to execute the code of f_i without considering function invocations, and external response time, which is the time spent interacting with other functions. Invocations can be either *sequential* (synchronous) or *parallel* (asynchronous).

Given a DAG and the SLA for each user-invoked function, we measured the nominal response time and nominal local response time by profiling each function. We then used such metrics to compute local set points for the node-level controllers so that they were aware of how long they had to wait for external calls.

We implemented the new provisioning strategy in a special-purpose simulator[1] and tested it with three different applications, simulated 10 times for

---

[1] Source code available at https://github.com/deib-polimi/RAS.

20 min each. *Hotel reservation*[2] comprises four functions and two entry points, *shock shop*[3] has seven functions and five entry points, and *complex* is a complex application, we generated randomly, that embeds twenty five functions and six entry points.

Since Baresi et al. [1] had already highlighted NEPTUNE's advantages over industrial solutions such as K3S, Knative, and OpenFaaS, we compared our solution against NEPTUNE in terms of response time, SLA violations, and core allocation with and without bottlenecks. Obtained results witness that the new solution saves more than 42% of CPU cores, and the more complex the application is, the more cores are saved. Detailed results are available in Baresi et al. [2].

6   Conclusions

A PhD program lasts three years in Italy. We used the first half to identify the problem, survey the state of the art, and work on the first sub-problem. We plan now to speed up the development and cover the other sub-problems described above in the second half. We are confident we should be able to address all the features, but we might decide to skip data management in the end given its intrinsic complexity.

References

1. Baresi, L., Hu, D.Y.X., Quattrocchi, G., Terracciano, L.: NEPTUNE: network- and GPU-aware management of serverless functions at the edge. In: Proceedings of the 17th Symposium on Software Engineering for Adaptive and Self-Managing Systems, pp. 144–155. ACM (2022)
2. Baresi, L., Quattrocchi, G., Ticongolo, I.G.: Dependency-aware resource allocation for serverless functions at the edge. In: Monti, F., Rinderle-Ma, S., Ruiz Cortes, A., Zheng, Z., Mecella, M. (eds.) Service-Oriented Computing. ICSOC 2023. LNCS, vol. 14419, pp. 347–362. Springer, Cham (2023). https://doi.org/10.1007/978-3-031-48421-6_24
3. Deng, S., et al.: Dependent function embedding for distributed serverless edge computing. IEEE Trans. Parallel Distrib. Syst. **33**(10), 2346–2357 (2022)
4. de Assuncao, M.D., da Silva Veith, A., Buyya, R.: Distributed data stream processing and edge computing: a survey on resource elasticity and future directions. J. Netw. Comput. Appl. **103**, 1–17 (2018)
5. Gunasekaran, J.R., Thinakaran, P., Nachiappan, N.C., Kandemir, M.T., Das, C.R.: Fifer: tackling resource underutilization in the serverless era. In: Proceedings of the 21st International Middleware Conference, pp. 280–295. ACM (2020)
6. He, X., Zhiying, T., Wagner, M., Xiaofei, X., Wang, Z.: Online deployment algorithms for microservice systems with complex dependencies. IEEE Trans. Cloud Comput. **11**(2), 1746–1763 (2023)

---

[2] https://github.com/vhive-serverless/vSwarm/tree/main/benchmarks/hotel-app.
[3] https://github.com/microservices-demo/microservices-demo.

7. Pinto, D., Dias, J.P., Ferreira, H.S.: Dynamic allocation of serverless functions in IoT environments. In: Proceedings of the 16th International Conference on Embedded and Ubiquitous Computing, pp. 1–8. IEEE (2018)

8. Cassel, G.A.S., et al.: Serverless computing for internet of things: a systematic literature review. Futur. Gener. Comput. Syst. **128**, 299–316 (2022)

9. Sinaeepourfard, A., Garcia, J., Masip-Bruin, X., Marin-Tordera, E.: Data preservation through Fog-to-Cloud (F2C) data management in smart cities. In: Proceedings of the 2nd International Conference on Fog and Edge Computing, pp. 1–9. IEEE (2018)

10. Vahidinia, P., Farahani, B., Aliee, F.S.: Mitigating cold start problem in serverless computing: a reinforcement learning approach. IEEE Internet Things J. **10**(5), 3917–3927 (2023)

11. Wang, B., Ali-Eldin, A., Shenoy, P.: LaSS: running latency sensitive serverless computations at the edge. In: Proceedings of the 30th International Symposium on High-Performance Parallel and Distributed Computing, pp. 239–251. ACM (2021)

12. Wang, L., Li, M., Zhang, Y., Ristenpart, T., Swift, M.: Peeking behind the curtains of serverless platforms. In: Proceedings of the USENIX Annual Technical Conference, pp. 133–145. USENIX Association (2018)

13. Zichuan, X., et al.: Stateful serverless application placement in MEC with function and state dependencies. IEEE Trans. Comput. **72**(9), 2701–2716 (2023)

Demos and Resources Introduction

Demos and Resources Track

Devis Bianchini[1] and Damian A. Tamburri[2]

[1]University of Brescia, Italy
devis.bianchini@unibs.it
[2]TU/e JADS, Politecnico di Milano, Italy
d.a.tamburri@tue.nl

The Demo and Resources track at the 21st International Conference on Service-Oriented Computing (ICSOC 2023) provided a platform to showcase innovative works in progress, late-breaking research, and impactful contributions across various domains related to Service-Oriented Computing. This encompassed submissions on pioneering applications influencing Data Science, Artificial Intelligence (AI)-enabled services, process automation, crowdsourcing and social services, Internet of Things (IoT)-enabled services, cloud and edge services, quantum services, and virtual and augmented reality. In a noteworthy addition this year, the track invited presentations and sharing of resources stemming from academic initiatives or industrial experiences. These resources included datasets, taxonomies, labeled and annotated logs, corpora, and both quantitative and qualitative benchmarks.

From a pool of submissions, we meticulously selected four high-quality demo papers, maintaining an acceptance rate of 50%. Each paper underwent a thorough single-blind review process by three Program Committee members, with final decisions made by a meta-reviewer, who been engaged in a discussion phase following the initial reviews. The accepted demo papers explored diverse yet interconnected topics. These included a 3D simulator tailored for the Drone-as-a-Service framework, a tool for automating API Gateway configurations, a tool suite facilitating dependency management in web APIs, and an open-source tool designed to detect instances of security concerns, known as "security smells," in microservice applications deployed with Kubernetes.

All accepted demos were effectively presented during the conference, utilizing demonstration videos, live sessions, leaflets, and presentation slides. Engaging discussions unfolded among demo speakers and participants, adding value to the overall conference experience.

We extend our gratitude to our authors, Program Committee members, and the ICSOC Organizing Committee for their invaluable support, contributing to the success of the Demo and Resources track at ICSOC 2023!

November 2023   Demos and Resources track Organizers

Organization

Demos and Resources track Chairs

Devis Bianchini   University of Brescia, Italy
Damian A. Tamburri   TU/e - JADS, The Netherlands &
     Politecnico di Milano, Italy

Program Committee members

Simone Agostinelli   Sapienza University of Roma, Italy
Hernan Humberto Alvarez Valera   University of Pau and the Pays de l'Adour,
     France

Martina De Sanctis   Gran Sasso Science Institute, Italy
Martin Grambow   Technical University of Berlin, Germany
Reza Poorzare   Karlsruhe University of Applied Sciences,
     Germany

Giovanni Quattrocchi   Politecnico di Milano, Italy

Immersive 3D Simulator
for Drone-as-a-Service

Jiamin Lin, Balsam Alkouz$^{(\boxtimes)}$ [ID], Athman Bouguettaya [ID],
and Amani Abusafia [ID]

University of Sydney, Sydney, Australia
jlin6645@uni.sydney.edu.au,
{balsam.alkouz,athman.bouguettaya,amani.abusafia}@sydney.edu.au

Abstract. We propose a 3D simulator tailored for the Drone-as-a-Service framework. The simulator enables employing dynamic algorithms for addressing realistic delivery scenarios. We present the simulator's architectural design and its use of an energy consumption model for drone deliveries. We introduce two primary operational modes within the simulator: the edit mode and the runtime mode. Beyond its simulation capabilities, our simulator serves as a valuable data collection resource, facilitating the creation of datasets through simulated scenarios. Our simulator empowers researchers by providing an intuitive platform to visualize and interact with delivery environments. Moreover, it enables rigorous algorithm testing in a safe simulation setting, thus obviating the need for real-world drone deployments. Demo: https://youtu.be/HOLfo1JiFJ0.

Keywords: Unmanned Aerial Vehicles · Drones · Drone Delivery · Simulator

1 Introduction

The rapid proliferation of Unmanned Aerial Vehicles (UAVs), also known as drones, has transformed many industries, including logistics and transportation [1]. The potential for drone delivery systems to enhance the efficiency and speed of last-mile deliveries has captured the attention of both researchers and industry leaders [1,2]. In parallel, the concept of *skyway networks*, i.e., aerial corridors designated for autonomous drone traffic, has gained traction as a solution to the challenges of managing and regulating drone operations in urban environments [3]. Consequently, several drone service approaches have been proposed to achieve efficient delivery [3,4]. However, testing these approaches by deploying them on physical drones is challenging due to the potential safety risks [3]. Thus, there is a pressing need for *advanced simulators* to harness the full potential of drone delivery within skyway networks. These tools should be capable of modeling, analyzing, and optimizing these complex systems, especially within the framework of *Drone-as-a-Service (DaaS)*.

Traditional simulations often rely on numerical tracking and data-driven modeling [5–7]. However, these may fall short of replicating the dynamics of

F. Monti et al. (Eds.): ICSOC 2023 Workshops, LNCS 14518, pp. 297–303, 2024.
https://doi.org/10.1007/978-981-97-0989-2_24

real-world urban drone operations. 3D simulation, on the other hand, provides a holistic and *immersive* environment that replicates the physical aspects of the skyway network. This offers a more accurate representation of how drones interact with their surroundings. Moreover, it allows for the evaluation of spatial relationships, environmental factors, and dynamic obstacles, all of which are critical in urban airspace management [8]. In a 3D simulation, researchers and stakeholders may visualize complex scenarios, observe emergent behaviors, and validate the feasibility of their solutions.

The existing drone simulation tools often focus on specific aspects of drone operations, e.g., obstacle avoidance [9]. However, they lack the integration required for comprehensive urban delivery system evaluation. Notable tools include AirSim [10], Gazebo [9], and PX4 [9]. These tools focus on modeling drone flight dynamics and sensor simulations. However, they primarily serve the needs of the drone development community and *are hardly useful in addressing the unique challenges of urban drone delivery within a skyway network.*

We propose a 3D simulator that distinguishes itself by offering a comprehensive analytical and visual framework. Our simulator is *tailored to the DaaS framework within urban environments* [11]. It encompasses *route planning, real-world data integration, airspace management, and scalability analysis*, all in a 3D environment that replicates the complexities of skyway networks. This comprehensive approach aligns with the growing demand for seamless, end-to-end solutions. It enables researchers, businesses, city planners, and drone operators to evaluate and optimize their operations from a service-oriented perspective.

2 Demo Setup

Drone-as-a-Service (DaaS) for delivery refers to the concept of providing delivery services within a skyway environment [3,12]. The skyway network comprises building rooftops equipped with charging and landing pads, functioning as nodes in the system. Any segment of the network that is served by a delivery drone is categorized as a DaaS service. The concept of Swarm-based Drone-as-a-Service (SDaaS) extends this idea to encompass delivery services provided by a swarm of drones [13,14]. In this context, a segment in the network serviced by a drone swarm carrying multiple packages is referred to as an SDaaS segment [15,16]. Figure 2 provides a visual representation of the skyway arrangement.

This demo paper showcases a simulation system specifically designed for evaluating DaaS and SDaaS within a 3D simulated skyway environment. In this section, we will delve into the key components that constitute this simulator.

2.1 System Architecture

The system architecture comprises two primary modules that collaborate closely. These modules consist of a front end (client side) and a back end (server side) (See Fig. 1). The front end, implemented in Unity[1], serves as the visual and

---

[1] https://unity.com/.

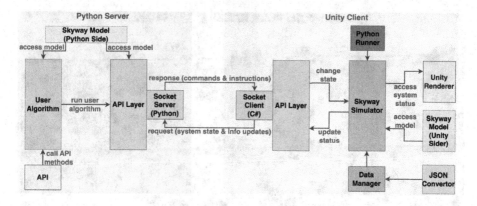

Fig. 1. System Architecture

simulation hub where users interact with the system. Meanwhile, the back end is a Python script environment, chosen due to its popularity among researchers [3,17]. Users may incorporate their Python code to implement their algorithms in the back end and visualize the simulation at the front end.

Within the Unity-based front end, users engage with the Skyway Simulator and Skyway Model, allowing them to interact with the system's simulation. Changes made in the front end are transmitted to the back end as drones traverse the network. At each node, the Unity client updates the Python server, providing the algorithm with real-time information about the Skyway's status. The algorithm reacts dynamically to any changes, composing services as necessary. It is essential to emphasize that this architecture operates non-deterministically, and updates are regularly exchanged to trigger actions between the client and server sides.

2.2 Energy Consumption Model

We employ the Kirchstein energy consumption model to simulate the drones energy usage [18]. This model offers a distinct advantage as it accounts for drone flight's ascent and descent phases. Given that our simulation involves connecting various buildings of varying heights with skyway segments, it becomes crucial to factor in the flight angle as drones navigate this terrain. The model accounts for vertical movements and hovering This is essential for accurately depicting the drones' actions during takeoff and landing at designated recharging pads. Furthermore, it is important to highlight that this model is theoretical, which makes it more suitable for simulations and adaptable to various drone types. This sets it apart from regression models that depend on empirical data from actual drones [19].

2.3 Simulation Environment

For the simulation environment, we incorporated a 3D city model in Unity to represent the buildings. Our simulator offers two primary modes of operation.

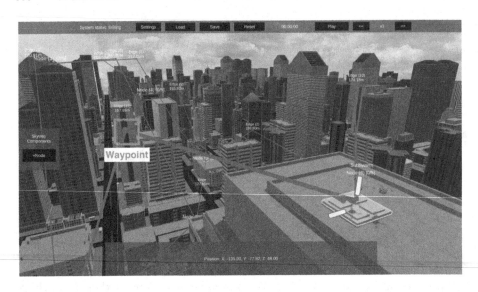

Fig. 2. Edit Mode

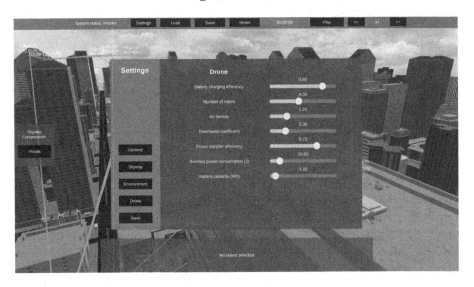

Fig. 3. Settings in Edit Mode

The first is the *Edit Mode*, which allows users to customize the skyway environment and edit the experimental variables according to their preferences. The second mode is the *Runtime Mode*, during which drones initiate flights based on the Python algorithm provided, facilitating data exchange between the client and server sides at each node. Below, we provide an overview of the specifics for each mode:

Edit Mode: Illustrated in Fig. 2, the edit mode provides users with the ability to perform various actions such as adding or removing nodes, connecting or disconnecting segments, and resizing the skyway network to suit the requirements of their experiments. This functionality proves invaluable for modeling both densely interconnected and sparsely connected networks. Additionally, users can reposition nodes through intuitive mouse controls within this mode. The "Load" button facilitates the importation of a JSON file containing essential network setup details. This includes node configurations, their positions, and segment specifications. Conversely, the "Save" button empowers users to preserve the current network configuration as a JSON file for future reference and utilization.

Furthermore, we introduce the concept of *waypoints*, as depicted in Fig. 2. Waypoints connect segments that cannot be directly linked to two nodes due to disparities in elevation or challenging terrain. This concept adds a layer of realism by acknowledging that drones cannot always establish a direct, unobstructed flight path between nodes [20]. Lastly, when the settings button is pressed, users can specify attributes related to the energy consumption model, payload capacity, and drone speed (Fig. 3).

Runtime Mode: Once the play button is hit in the Edit mode, the Runtime mode starts (Fig. 4). In the runtime mode, the drones become visible and begin traversing according to the provided algorithm. As previously mentioned, this tool operates in a non-deterministic manner. Consequently, if a segment (a service) becomes inaccessible from the originally composed path, the algorithm promptly adapts to this change, redirecting the drones accordingly.

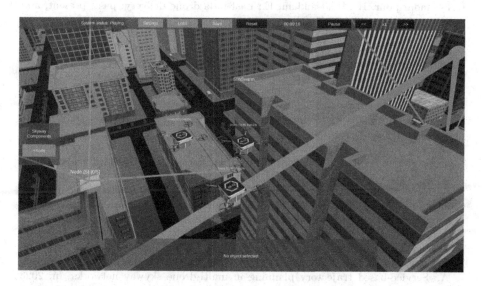

Fig. 4. Runtime Mode

The camera tracks the drones during their journey automatically. However, users also have the option to take control using the WASD buttons for manual camera adjustments. To provide users with an enriched experience, double-clicking on any item in the environment offers a close-up view. Each object within the simulation is thoughtfully labeled to convey its relevant attributes, such as segment length or drone battery percentage. The timer displays the simulation time elapsed since the commencement of the trip and permits users to adjust the simulation speed, enabling the drones to move at varying rates.

2.4 Data Collection

This tool serves a dual purpose: not only it assists users in visualizing potential scenarios in drone deliveries under the DaaS model but also functions as a valuable data collection tool for environmental interactions. Following each trip, users may export a CSV file containing comprehensive data regarding the status of every drone in the network. This data encompasses crucial information such as drone energy consumption, battery levels, time spent at each node, and travel times for each segment at each time frame. Such data can be leveraged to refine and improve DaaS composition algorithms.

Acknowledgements. This research was partly made possible by LE220100078 and DP220101823 grants from the Australian Research Council. The statements made herein are solely the responsibility of the authors.

References

1. Eskandaripour, H., Boldsaikhan, E.: Last-mile drone delivery: past, present, and future. Drones **7**(2), 77 (2023)
2. Alkouz, B., Bouguettaya, A.: Formation-based selection of drone swarm services. In: MobiQuitous 2020-17th EAI International Conference on Mobile and Ubiquitous Systems: Computing, Networking and Services, pp. 386–394 (2020)
3. Shahzaad, B., Alkouz, B., Janszen, J., Bouguettaya, A.: Optimizing drone delivery in smart cities. IEEE Internet Computing (2023)
4. Alkouz, B., Bouguettaya, A., Mistry, S.: Swarm-based drone-as-a-service (SDaaS) for delivery. In: 2020 IEEE International Conference on Web Services (ICWS), pp. 441–448. IEEE (2020)
5. Alkouz, B., Bouguettaya, A.: A reinforcement learning approach for re-allocating drone swarm services. In: Hacid, H., Kao, O., Mecella, M., Moha, N., Paik, H.Y. (eds.) Service-Oriented Computing. ICSOC 2021. LNCS, vol. 13121, pp. 643–651. Springer, Cham (2021). https://doi.org/10.1007/978-3-030-91431-8_40
6. Janszen, J., Shahzaad, B., Alkouz, B., Bouguettaya, A.: Constraint-aware trajectory for drone delivery services. In: Hacid, H., et al. (eds.) Service-Oriented Computing – ICSOC 2021 Workshops. ICSOC 2021. LNCS, vol. 13236, pp. 306–310. Springer, Cham (2022). https://doi.org/10.1007/978-3-031-14135-5_26
7. Bradley, S., Janitra, A.A., Shahzaad, B., Alkouz, B., Bouguettaya, A., Lakhdari, A.: Service-based trajectory planning in multi-drone skyway networks. In: 2023 IEEE International Conference on Pervasive Computing and Communications Workshops and other Affiliated Events (PerCom Workshops), pp. 334–336. IEEE (2023)

8. Alkouz, B., Shahzaad, B., Bouguettaya, A.: Service-based drone delivery. In: 2021 IEEE 7th International Conference on Collaboration and Internet Computing (CIC), pp. 68–76. IEEE (2021)
9. García, J., Molina, J.M.: Simulation in real conditions of navigation and obstacle avoidance with px4/gazebo platform. Pers. Ubiquit. Comput. **26**(4), 1171–1191 (2022)
10. Shah, S., Dey, D., Lovett, C., Kapoor, A.: AirSim: high-fidelity visual and physical simulation for autonomous vehicles. In: Hutter, M., Siegwart, R. (eds.) Field and Service Robotics. LNCS, SPAR, vol. 5, pp. 621–635. Springer, Cham (2018). https://doi.org/10.1007/978-3-319-67361-5_40
11. Lee, S., Shahzaad, B., Alkouz, B., Lakhdari, A., Bouguettaya, A.: Autonomous delivery of multiple packages using single drone in urban airspace. In: Adjunct Proceedings of the 2022 ACM International Joint Conference on Pervasive and Ubiquitous Computing and the 2022 ACM International Symposium on Wearable Computers, pp. 72–74 (2022)
12. Lee, W., Alkouz, B., Shahzaad, B., Bouguettaya, A.: Package delivery using autonomous drones in skyways. In: Adjunct Proceedings of the 2021 ACM International Joint Conference on Pervasive and Ubiquitous Computing and Proceedings of the 2021 ACM International Symposium on Wearable Computers, pp. 48–50 (2021)
13. Guo, S., Alkouz, B., Shahzaad, B., Lakhdari, A., Bouguettaya, A.: Drone formation for efficient swarm energy consumption. In: 2023 IEEE International Conference on Pervasive Computing and Communications Workshops and other Affiliated Events (PerCom Workshops), pp. 294–296. IEEE (2023)
14. Alkouz, B., Bouguettaya, A., Lakhdari, A.: Density-based pruning of drone swarm services. In: 2022 IEEE International Conference on Web Services (ICWS), pp. 302–311. IEEE (2022)
15. Liu, X., Lam, K., Alkouz, B., Shahzaad, B., Bouguettaya, A.: Constraint-based formation of drone swarms. In: 2022 IEEE International Conference on Pervasive Computing and Communications Workshops and other Affiliated Events (PerCom Workshops), pp. 73–75. IEEE (2022)
16. Alkouz, B., Bouguettaya, A.: Provider-centric allocation of drone swarm services. In: 2021 IEEE International Conference on Web Services (ICWS), pp. 230–239. IEEE (2021)
17. Alkouz, B., Bouguettaya, A., Lakhdari, A.: Failure-sentient composition for swarm-based drone services. In: 2023 IEEE International Conference on Web Services (ICWS). IEEE (2023)
18. Kirschstein, T.: Comparison of energy demands of drone-based and ground-based parcel delivery services. Transp. Res. Part D: Transp. Environ. **78**, 102209 (2020)
19. Dorling, K., Heinrichs, J., Messier, G.G., Magierowski, S.: Vehicle routing problems for drone delivery. IEEE Trans. Syst. Man Cybern. Syst. **47**(1), 70–85 (2016)
20. Alkouz, B., Abusafia, A., Lakhdari, A., Bouguettaya, A.: In-flight energy-driven composition of drone swarm services. IEEE Trans. Serv. Comput. (2022)

SLA-Wizard - Automated Configuration of RESTful API Gateways Based on SLAs

Ignacio Peluaga Lozada⬥, Pablo Fernandez⬥, and José María García(✉)⬥

SCORE Lab, I3US Institute, Universidad de Sevilla, Seville, Spain
{ipeluaga,pablofm,josemgarcia}@us.es

Abstract. In the digital age, the API Economy, fueled by microservice architectures, is revolutionizing software development. Crucial to this transition is the Open API Specification (OAS) that standardizes API description of functional elements and has been complemented with extensions like SLA4OAI to define limitations for the API users, like qoutas or rates in a standard way. Building on this, the paper presents SLA-Wizard, a tool designed to automate API Gateway configurations; it supports four, widely used, proxies that are used in the Industry as API Gateways (Envoy, Nginx, HAProxy and Traefik). This paper presents the tool and highlights its effectiveness in managing API Proxy configuration and how it paves the way for enhancing their capabilities and systematic benchmarking.

Tool demonstration video available at: http://tiny.cc/sla-wizard.

1 Introduction and Motivation

In today's digital era, the rise of the API Economy is driving innovation and modern software development. The rise of microservice architectures, which boost cloud-native SaaS applications, has propelled this shift, emphasizing the deployment and integration of microservices via RESTful Web APIs (APIs from now on). These architectures are critical to connect external APIs and enable organizations to position themselves as service providers in the market.

A key milestone in this evolution is the standardization brought about by the Open API Specification (OAS), focusing on defining the functional elements of APIs. It has encouraged the development of a diverse ecosystem of tools, evidenced by its acceptance by the academy (e.g. [2] or [3]) and the extensive industry tool catalog available (e.g. the portal https://openapi.tools/, featuring more than 350 tools).

Furthermore, formulating business models incorporating API limitations, such as quotas or rates (e.g., restricting API calls to 300 requests per second), is crucial to regulating user behavior and ensuring service quality. Addressing the

This work has been partially supported by the following grants: PID2021-126227NB-C22, TED2021-131023B-C21, and PDC2022-133521-I00 which are funded by MCIN/AEI/10.13039/501100011033 and "ERDF a way of making Europe"; and grant PYC20 RE 084 US, which is funded by Junta de Andalucia/ERDF,UE.

need for standardized information on API limitations, SLA4OAI [1] is introduced as an extension to OAS, offering a structured approach to describing API limitations and fostering the automation of API operations to enhance interaction efficiency and reliability.

In this context, we present SLA-Wizard[1], a tool developed to take advantage of the SLA4OAI extension. Specifically, SLA-Wizard is engineered with the capability to automate the configuration of the most used proxies in API Gateways. This means that the tool can efficiently set up the correct quota for each consumer API key based on a comprehensive set of SLA4OAI specifications. This functionality is particularly vital, as it ensures that API consumers are allocated appropriate quotas, thereby maintaining a balanced and equitable API ecosystem.

Using the SLA4OAI extension in conjunction with tools like SLA-Wizard, developers and organizations can improve the manageability and operability of their APIs. This approach not only helps to the precise allocation of resources to each API consumer, but also fosters a more structured and standardized environment for API development and utilization, thereby contributing to the evolution of the API Economy.

The remainder of the paper is organized as follows. In Sect. 2, we outline the main elements of SLA-Wizard, detail its main elements, and explain the principles that guide its functionality. In Sect. 3, we develop a practical use case involving proxy analysis to explore and compare different alternatives. Lastly, Sect. 4 is dedicated to presenting some conclusions and potential directions for future research and development.

2   Usage

The SLA-Wizard tool is available for use in various environments, and its architecture is modularized to be able to configure different types of proxies in an extensible manner. Currently, support is provided for the following proxies: Envoy (envoyproxy.io), HAProxy (haproxy.com), Nginx (nginx.org) and Traefik (traefik.io). These proxies are widely used independently or integrated within commercial API gateways.

To install the tool, users can use the npm package manager with the command `npm install sla-wizard` or by cloning the repository from its GitHub page. The SLA Wizard command line interface includes two main commands: configuration, used to generate a proxy configuration file with specified rate limiting, and runTest, which validates the rate limiting defined on a proxy. The tool provides a variety of options and arguments that allow customization, such as specifying the proxy type, output file, service level agreement (SLA) path, and authentication parameters.

The SLA Wizard operates with a set of SLAs and validates them against the SLA4OAI-Specification JSON schema. It is crucial that SLAs are valid and

---

[1] https://github.com/isa-group/sla-wizard.

duplicated SLAs are ignored. The tool requires the indication of the API server in the OAS document, considering only the first server if multiple servers are listed. Although the SLA can be referenced directly in the OAS document, the tool requires the use of the -sla option to locate the SLA document(s).

The tool supports various API authentication methods, such as API keys in headers, query parameters, or parts of the URL. The tool's config command offers the -authLocation option to set the location of the API key, with a default value set as header. The SLA should include the property context.apikeys, which lists all valid API keys for authenticating API calls.

The tool is adept at creating new configuration files or modifying existing ones for four distinct proxy technologies. After generating the proxy configuration file and initiating it, the tool's behavior can be validated using specific npm commands.

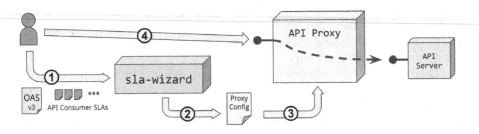

Fig. 1. SLA-Wizard standard workflow.

2.1 Workflow

In order to utilize the SLA Wizard tool effectively, users are expected to adhere to the workflow outlined below (as depicted in Fig. 1):

1. **Providing Specifications and Agreements.** The initial step involves the user supplying the SLA Wizard with a functional description of the API in OpenAPI Specification v3, alongside one or more SLA agreements using SLA4OAI extension; these documents include the necessary information regarding the API structure, endpoints, and the corresponding service level agreements that detail the expected levels of service.
2. **Generation of Proxy Configuration File.** Upon receiving the required specifications and SLA agreements, the SLA Wizard proceeds to generate a proxy configuration file. This file defines the rate-limiting parameters derived from the provided SLA(s). For further details, please refer to the section titled "Creating proxy configurations" in the tool documentation.
3. **Configuring the Proxy Server.** Subsequent to the generation of the configuration file, this file is then deployed to the proxy server during its initialization. Users can select from the range of supported proxies. This versatility ensures adaptability to varying user requirements and system architectures.

4. **Rate limit testing.** The final stage of the workflow sees the implementation of the rate limitation on API requests. This limitation is aligned with the statements set forth in the proxy configuration file, thereby ensuring congruence with the initial SLA(s) indicated by the user. Consequently, this step guarantees that API interaction with API consumers adheres strictly to predefined service levels, thus mitigating the risks of overuse and maintaining system integrity.

3   Use Case Application

The main purpose of SLA-Wizard is to automatically generate the necessary proxy configuration to provide an API gateway that manages accesses to those APIs with respect to the limitations stated in the associated SLAs. After this configuration process, proxy implementations are responsible for actually enforce the desired quotas and rates. However, there are several factors that can affect the correct application of these limitations, such as the number of API keys that the proxy has to manage, the scalability of proxy solutions to support concurrent API users, or even the configuration capabilities they offer. In this scenario, we can introduce a benchmark to measure the performance and capabilities of different proxy solutions [4], allowing us to compare them and choose the most appropriate one to support the workflow described in Sect. 2.1.

To this extent, we used SLA-Wizard to systematically generate benchmarks for a series of proxy implementations. Our use case focuses on benchmarking the rate limiting capabilities of the different supported proxies. Specifically for this use case, we generated the configuration for the four proxies reported in Sect. 2 according to a test bed that contains several SLAs defined using the SLA4OAI schema. Then, SLA-Wizard generates HTTP requests to the corresponding API endpoints above the limitations specified, so that we can check if those limitations are properly enforced when using each proxy implementation.

Table 1. Excerpt of benchmarking results

Rate limit	Expected	Nginx	HAproxy	Traefik	Envoy
1/second	90	93	81	93	✓
2/minute	18	21	✓	✓	✓
3/second	270	273	269	✓	✓
4/minute	36	39	✓	✓	39
5/second	450	453	✓	✓	✓
10/second	900	903	897	✓	894
20/minute	180	183	✓	✓	183
30/second	2700	2699	2691	2693	2646
40/minute	360	363	✓	✓	✓
50/second	4500	4497	4488	4487	4470

Table 1 presents some preliminary results obtained from our experimental use case. We carried out the benchmarking experiment by deploying each proxy and configuring them so that for each endpoint tested, we simulated three API keys under the same subscribed SLA, and then we ran the experiment for 30 s or 3 min, depending on the temporal unit used to define the rate limit we wanted to test. SLA-Wizard is configured to perform requests above the expected number shown in the table for each endpoint, considering the temporal unit and the limit stated. The other numbers in the table represent the actual requests that were allowed by each proxy. These results show that Nginx usually allows for a few more requests than allowed, while the other proxies in most cases either allow the expected number of requests or a few less, with Traefik being the most accurate one in terms of rate limiting. However, benchmarking results change substantially when adding more API keys. Figure 2 shows our experimental results obtained with different combinations of SLAs and API keys.

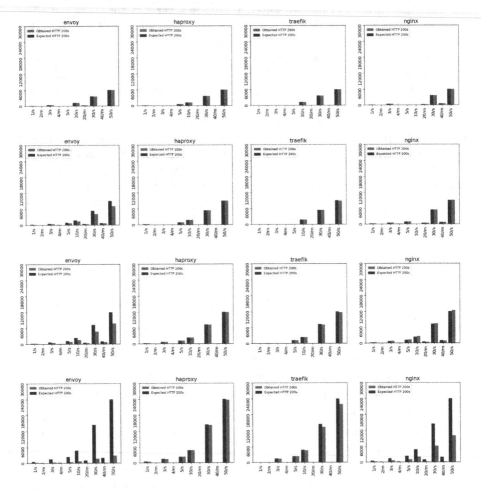

Fig. 2. Results variation based on number of API keys.

The first row of the figure presents the results for 4 SLAs subscriptions, each with 2 API keys, totaling 8 API keys. This configuration simulates 8 users sending requests in parallel. Correspondingly, the second row shows the results for 6 SLAs with 2 API keys each (12 API keys in total), the third row for 8 SLAs with 2 API keys each (16 API keys in total); and the fourth row for 8 SLAs with 4 API keys each (32 API keys in total). For all plots showcased in the figure the y-axis represents the number of HTTP requests, while the x-axis represents the different endpoints that the API offers (10 in total) identified by the rate limiting that applies to each as described in the SLA plan. There is a clear conclusion to take away from the plots: the more API keys, the worse the results obtained in Envoy and Nginx are. Conversely, in the case of HAProxy and Traefik, the results stay acceptable.

4   Conclusions

API gateways are a common facility in microservices architectures that are responsible for managing access to the available APIs according to their business models. SLA-Wizard helps with the configuration of proxies acting as API gateways, automatizing their configuration with respect to the limitations associated with APIs and their concrete consumers. With our proposed tool, APIs specified in OAS v3 along with SLA detailed using the SLA4OAI extension can be directly configured in the proxy API so that the quotas and rates can be automatically enforced. SLA-Wizard is a modularized tool that currently supports four major commercial API proxies (Envoy, HAProxy, Nginx, and Traefik), allowing the user not only to generate the configurations for them, but also to test the accuracy of the rate limitations stated for each endpoint and consumer using different approaches. We plan to extend the capabilities of SLA-Wizard by supporting additional API proxies, such as Caddy (caddyserver.com), as well as means of configuring and testing the quota specified in the SLAs. Furthermore, we are currently performing a more comprehensive benchmarking of the supported tools to investigate the reasons behind the incongruencies detected in our use case since SLA-Wizard greatly facilitates the task of running different benchmarks and perform comparative analysis.

References

1. Gamez-Diaz, A., Fernandez, P., Ruiz-Cortes, A.: Automating SLA-driven API development with SLA4OAI. In: Yangui, S., Bouassida Rodriguez, I., Drira, K., Tari, Z. (eds.) ICSOC 2019. LNCS, vol. 11895, pp. 20–35. Springer, Cham (2019). https://doi.org/10.1007/978-3-030-33702-5_2
2. González-Mora, C., Barros, C., Garrigós, I., Zubcoff, J., Lloret, E., Mazón, J.N.: Improving open data web API documentation through interactivity and natural language generation. Comput. Stand. Interfaces 83, 103657 (2023)

3. Martin-Lopez, A., Segura, S., Müller, C., Ruiz-Cortés, A.: Specification and automated analysis of inter-parameter dependencies in web APIs. IEEE Trans. Serv. Comput. **15**(4), 2342–2355 (2021)
4. Peluaga, I., Fernandez, P., Garcia, J.M.: Towards a systematic approach to proxy benchmarking for API Rate Limiting management. In: Berrocal, J. (ed.) Actas de las XVIII Jornadas de Ingeniería de Ciencia e Ingeniería de Servicios (JCIS 2023). SISTEDES (2023). https://hdl.handle.net/11705/JCIS/2023/8443

The IDL Tool Suite: Inter-parameter Dependency Management in Web APIs

Saman Barakat[1]([✉]) [iD], Alberto Martin-Lopez[2] [iD], Carlos Müller[1] [iD],
and Sergio Segura[1] [iD]

[1] SCORE Lab, I3US Institute, Universidad de Sevilla, Seville, Spain
{salias,cmuller,sergiosegura}@us.es
[2] SEART @ Software Institute, Universitá della Svizzera Italiana, Lugano,
Switzerland
alberto.martin@usi.ch

Abstract. Web APIs contain inter-parameter dependencies that restrict the way in which input parameters can be combined to form valid calls to the service. Inter-parameter dependencies are extremely common and pervasive: they appear in 4 out of every 5 APIs across all application domains and types of operations. In this demonstration paper, we present the IDL tool suite, a comprehensive collection of tools designed to facilitate dependency management in web APIs. The IDL tool suite includes a specification language for inter-parameter dependencies (IDL), and OAS extension (IDL4OAS), a web editor for IDL specifications, an analysis engine (IDLReasoner), a web API for the analysis of IDL, and a website with detailed information about the tool suite and a playground. In addition to these tools, we present a catalog of applications where the IDL tool suite has already proven useful, including automated testing, code generation, and dependency-aware API gateways. We trust that the IDL tool suite will enable promising new research and applications in the area of web API management. The demo video of the IDL tool suite is available at https://www.youtube.com/watch?v=Hy5HYGK8Yn4.

Keywords: Web API · REST · OpenAPI Specification · IDL

1 Introduction

Web Application Programming Interfaces (APIs) facilitate communication between software systems over the Internet, which makes them ideal for software integration. Modern web APIs typically adhere to the Representational State Transfer (REST) architectural style [3], and are often described using the OpenAPI Specification (OAS) [9], which provides a human- and machine-readable description of the API's supported operations, parameters and responses. OAS documents are a valuable asset for automating tasks in the API lifecycle such as testing, code generation, and documentation. Despite this, OAS (and other specification languages) currently lack official support for describing *inter-parameter*

F. Monti et al. (Eds.): ICSOC 2023 Workshops, LNCS 14518, pp. 311–316, 2024.
https://doi.org/10.1007/978-981-97-0989-2_26

dependencies, i.e., restrictions between parameters that must be satisfied to form a valid API request [5,6]. For instance, when searching for businesses in the Yelp API [11], the parameter `location` is "required if either `latitude` or `longitude` is not provided". A recent study on 40 industrial APIs revealed that inter-parameter dependencies are extremely common and pervasive, as they appear in 4 out of every 5 APIs across all application domains and types of operations [6].

In previous work [5], we introduced the Inter-parameter Dependency Language (IDL) and IDLReasoner as a first step to specify and automatically analyze dependencies, respectively. We also created IDL4OAS, an OAS extension to integrate our approach in this language. Built upon this foundation, in this demonstration paper we present the IDL tool suite, a comprehensive collection of tools designed to facilitate dependency management in web APIs. The IDL tool suite extends IDL and IDL4OAS with the following novel contributions: 1) a web editor for IDL specifications, 2) an enhanced version of IDLReasoner, 3) a new analysis operation (explanation), 4) a web API for automated analysis of IDL with interactive documentation, and 5) a website with detailed information about the tool suite and a playground. In the rest of the paper, we provide an overview of the tools included in the IDL tool suite and the applications that these have already enabled, as well as future promising applications.

2   The IDL Tool Suite

All our tools are publicly available on the IDL website [4]. The tool suite includes the IDL language, the IDL4OAS extension, an enhanced version of IDLReasoner, an IDLReasoner web API, and a web-based editor for IDL specifications. In the following sections, we provide an overview of each of these tools (Fig. 1).

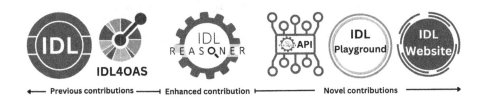

Fig. 1. IDL tool suite contributions.

2.1   Inter-parameter Dependency Language (IDL)

IDL is a textual domain-specific language (DSL) that allows to formally specify all the seven patterns of dependencies identified in our previous study [6]. Listing 1 shows some real-world examples of inter-parameter dependencies from the Google Maps Places API. For instance, line 3 shows a REQUIRES dependency: if parameter `rankby` is set to `'distance'`, then either `keyword`, `name` or `type` must be present in the API request. Similarly, line 4 defines an ARITHMETIC dependency, which states that parameter `maxprice` must be greater than or equal to `minprice`. IDL supports five other dependency patterns, namely, OR, ZeroOrOne, OnlyOne, AllOrNone and Complex dependencies. We refer the reader to our previous work for a detailed description of these dependencies, the IDL language and its grammar [5].

```
1   // Operation: Search for places within specified area:
2   ZeroOrOne(radius, rankby=='distance');
3   IF rankby=='distance' THEN keyword OR name OR type;
4   maxprice >= minprice;
5
6   // Operation: Query information about places:
7   AllOrNone(location, radius);
8   Or(query, type);
9   maxprice >= minprice;
10
11  // Operation: Get photo of place:
12  OnlyOne(maxheight, maxwidth);
13
14  // Operation: Automcomplete place name:
15  IF strictbounds THEN location AND radius;
```

Listing 1. IDL specification of the Google Maps Places API.

2.2 IDL4OAS

IDL4OAS is an OAS extension that allows to describe inter-parameter dependencies within an OAS document, as shown in Listing 2, which depicts the specification of the search operation of the Google Maps Places API. As illustrated, the property `x-dependencies` is added at the operation level, allowing to specify dependencies among its parameters with IDL. An IDL4OAS document can serve as the basis for automated dependency-aware testing, code generation and monitoring, as will be shown in Sect. 3.

```
1  paths:
2    /search:
3      get:
4        [...]
5        x-dependencies:
6        - ZeroOrOne(radius, rankby=='distance');
7        - IF rankby=='distance' THEN radius OR name OR type;
8        - maxprice >= minprice;
```

Listing 2. OAS document extended with IDL4OAS.

2.3 IDLReasoner

IDLReasoner is a Java library for automatically analyzing IDL specifications [5]. It supports analysis operations for multiple purposes, for example, to check if an IDL specification is consistent, or to detect dead parameters (i.e., parameters that can never be used in API requests due to contradictory constraints). For instance, the IDL4OAS document shown in Listing 2 actually contains a mistake, since the first dependency (line 6) states that `radius` and `rankby=='distance'` cannot be used together, while the second dependency states that if `rankby=='distance'`, parameter `radius` may be included in the API request. IDLReasoner can detect these inconsistencies automatically.

In this paper, we introduce a completely refactored version of IDLReasoner that leverages Choco [10]—a popular Java library for constraint programming—as the default constraint solver, making it more time- and memory-efficient. In addition, we implement a novel *explanation* analysis operation, which returns a human-readable explanation of the output of any of the existing analysis operations. For example, for the previous error, the explanation message would indicate the presence of two contradictory dependencies in lines 6 and 7.

2.4 Web API

One of our novel contributions to the IDL tool suite is the IDLReasoner API.[1] It consists in a RESTful API described in OAS, complemented with a Swagger documentation portal. The API supports all IDLReasoner analysis operations via simple HTTP requests. It is a key asset for integrating IDLReasoner into external projects such as test case generators or documentation portals. As a matter of fact, the IDLReasoner API is integrated into the IDL web editor.

2.5 IDL Web Editor

Our last novel contribution for the IDL tool suite is a web-based editor for IDL.[2] This editor acts as a playground for external users to learn and understand the capabilities of IDL, IDLReasoner and IDL4OAS, but also to analyze their own APIs on the fly, without the need of installing additional software.

3 Applications

In this section, we outline some of the useful applications that the IDL tool suite has enabled in varied domains, including automated testing, code generation, and API gateways.

3.1 Automated Testing

API specifications enhanced with IDL4OAS can be automatically analyzed with IDLReasoner. Testing tools for web APIs generally derive test cases automatically from the API specification. Thus, given an OAS document enriched with IDL4OAS, the IDL tool suite can support the automated generation of valid test cases (i.e., those satisfying all inter-parameter dependencies). This is the case of RESTest [7], a constraint-based testing tool which has automatically found over 200 bugs in industrial APIs such as Spotify and YouTube [8].

---

[1] http://idl-reasonerapi.tech/swagger-ui/index.html.

[2] http://idl-playground.tech.

3.2   Code Generation

An OAS document can drive the generation of source code for API client libraries or server stubs in a variety of programming languages [9]. Recently, we proposed IDLGen [1], an approach to automatically generate code to handle inter-parameter dependencies in servers written in Java and Python. Based on an OAS document extended with IDL4OAS, IDLGen generates assertions to validate the inter-parameter dependencies of incoming API requests, as well as code to handle invalid requests that violate one or more dependencies. Our results show that IDLGen can generate up to 10 times more code than current generators, and it can save up to 25 min of development time per API operation [1], potentially avoiding input validation failures in production [8].

3.3   Smart API Gateway

When deployed in an API gateway, IDLReasoner can be used to detect and block invalid requests that violate inter-parameter dependencies as well as to automatically generate explanations for such violations. In a recent study [2], we found that a dependency-aware API gateway could reduce response times of invalid requests by up to 80%, while incurring a negligible overhead in terms of latency and throughput for valid requests.

4   Conclusion and Future Work

The IDL tool suite is a comprehensive solution for inter-parameter dependency management in web APIs. These assets have already proven useful for the development of dependency-aware approaches for automated testing of web APIs, code generation for client and server applications, and API gateways. We envision new promising applications of the IDL tool suite in the future, including enhanced documentation portals, monitoring solutions, and API design tools.

Acknowledgements. This work has been partially supported by grants PID2021-126 227NB-C22 and TED2021-131023B-C21, funded by MCIN/AEI/10.13039/501100 011033 and by European Union "NextGenerationEU"/PRTR».

References

1. Barakat, S., Sanchez, A.B., Segura, S.: IDLGen: automated code generation for inter-parameter dependencies in web APIs. In: Monti, F., Rinderle-Ma, S., Ruiz Cortés, A., Zheng, Z., Mecella, M. (eds.) ICSOC 2023. LNCS, vol. 14419, pp. 153–168. Springer, Cham (2023). https://doi.org/10.1007/978-3-031-48421-6_11
2. Barakat, S., Sanchez, A.B., Segura, S.: Toward dependency-aware API gateways. In: JCIS (2023)
3. Fielding, R.T.: REST: architectural styles and the design of network-based software architectures. Doctoral dissertation, University of California (2000)
4. The IDL Tool Suite. https://isa-group.github.io/IDL/. Accessed July 2023

5. Martin-Lopez, A., Segura, S., Müller, C., Ruiz-Cortés, A.: Specification and automated analysis of inter-parameter dependencies in web APIs. IEEE Trans. Serv. Comput. **15**(4), 2342–2355 (2021)

6. Martin-Lopez, A., Segura, S., Ruiz-Cortés, A.: A catalogue of inter-parameter dependencies in RESTful web APIs. In: Yangui, S., Bouassida Rodriguez, I., Drira, K., Tari, Z. (eds.) ICSOC 2019. LNCS, vol. 11895, pp. 399–414. Springer, Cham (2019). https://doi.org/10.1007/978-3-030-33702-5_31

7. Martin-Lopez, A., Segura, S., Ruiz-Cortés, A.: RESTest: black-box constraint-based testing of RESTful web APIs. In: Kafeza, E., Benatallah, B., Martinelli, F., Hacid, H., Bouguettaya, A., Motahari, H. (eds.) ICSOC 2020. LNCS, vol. 12571, pp. 459–475. Springer, Cham (2020). https://doi.org/10.1007/978-3-030-65310-1_33

8. Martin-Lopez, A., Segura, S., Ruiz-Cortés, A.: Online testing of RESTful APIs: promises and challenges. In: ESEC/FSE, pp. 408–420 (2022)

9. OpenAPI Specification. https://www.openapis.org/. Accessed July 2023

10. Prud'homme, C., Fages, J.G.: Choco-solver: a Java library for constraint programming. J. Open Source Softw. **7**(78), 4708 (2022)

11. Yelp API. https://docs.developer.yelp.com/reference. Accessed July 2023

Smelling Homemade Crypto Code in Microservices, with KubeHound

Thomas Howard-Grubb[1], Jacopo Soldani[2(✉)] ⓘ, Giorgio Dell'Immagine[2],
Francesca Arcelli Fontana[1] ⓘ, and Antonio Brogi[2] ⓘ

[1] Universitá di Milano-Bicocca, Milan, Italy
[2] Universitá di Pisa, Pisa, Italy
jacopo.soldani@unipi.it

Abstract. Microservices are pervading enterprise IT, and securing microservices hence became crucial. KUBEHOUND is an open-source tool devised for this purpose, as it enables detecting instances of so-called *security smells* in microservice applications deployed with Kubernetes. KUBEHOUND features a plugin-based extensibility, meaning that its smell detection capabilities can be extended by developing plugins implementing additional smell detection techniques. In this demo paper, we illustrate how to extend KUBEHOUND with plugins enabling to detect two different instances of the *own crypto code* security smell, whose detection was not yet featured by KUBEHOUND. We also show the practical use of the newly added plugins by applying them to case studies, two of which are based on existing, third-party microservice applications.

Keywords: microservices · security smell · smell detection · Kubernetes

1 Introduction

Microservices enable obtaining cloud-native applications, namely applications that can fully exploit the potentials of cloud computing [3]. This is one of the main reasons why microservices are pervading enterprise IT [19].

Securing microservices is, therefore, crucial, and microservices raise new security challenges [4,5]. These include the so-called microservice *security smells*, which were recently proposed by Ponce et al. [14]. A security smell is defined as a possible symptom of a bad (though often unintentional) decision while designing a microservice application, which can negatively affect its security. Examples of security smells are *non-secured service-to-service communications* and *unauthenticated traffic*, which occur when the interactions among the microservices forming an application are not encrypted nor authenticated. Another example is given by *own crypto code* security smell, which occurs when the encryption solutions used for securing a microservice are (re-)implemented by the developers of the microservice, rather than by reusing established and widely assessed encryption technologies.

F. Monti et al. (Eds.): ICSOC 2023 Workshops, LNCS 14518, pp. 317–324, 2024.
https://doi.org/10.1007/978-981-97-0989-2_27

KUBEHOUND [8] is an open-source tool that allows to detect security smells in microservice applications deployed with Kubernetes. KUBEHOUND – in its original version [8] – featured the implementation of techniques for detecting instances of a selected subset of the security smells in [14]. Such detection techniques were all based on the static analysis of the specification of an application's deployment in Kubernetes, or on dynamically interacting with the Kubernetes cluster where an application is running.

KUBEHOUND is designed to be modular and extensible. New functionalities can indeed be included by developing and integrating custom plugins, e.g., implementing the detection of other security smell instances. We retake this feature in this demo paper, with a twofold objective. One the one hand, we aim at extending KUBEHOUND to enable analysing the source code of an application source code and to detect instances of the *own crypto code* security smell for microservices (as per its definition in [14]). At the same time, we aim at demonstrating the extensibility of KUBEHOUND itself, by showing how we developed the plugins implementing the extension mentioned above.

The main contributions of this demo paper are, therefore, the following.

- We first illustrate how we extended KUBEHOUND with plugins enabling to parse the source code of an application's microservices and to detect instances of the *own crypto code* security smell therein, if any.
- We then report on the practical assessment of the newly proposed plugins, which we applied in three case studies. The first case study is based on a mock application, while the other two case studies are based on two existing, third-party applications, i.e., Sock Shop [21] and Online Boutique [11].[1]

The rest of this paper is organized as follows. Section 2 provides some background on KUBEHOUND. Section 3 introduces the plugins added to KUBEHOUND to detect the instances of the *own crypto code* security smell. Section 4 reports on a case study practically assessing the newly introduced plugins. Finally, Sect. 5 draws some concluding remarks and sheds light on planned future work.

This paper builds on our previous work [8], where we already discussed the positioning of KUBEHOUND with respect to state-of-the-art solutions for securing microservices, e.g., [6,16,18,23], and with respect to the existing tools that can be used for identifying security vulnerabilities/weaknesses in microservice applications, e.g., [1,2,7,10,15,20,22]. For space limitations, we here piggyback on the related work discussion in our previous work [8] and we only discuss the novelty with respect to our previous work [8], which resides in adding the support for statically analysing the source code of the microservices forming an application, and in exploiting such a new feature to run static analyses enabling to detect two possible instances of the *own crypto code* security smell.

---

[1] A video showing how to run KUBEHOUND with the newly added plugins is publicly available online: https://youtu.be/3lSC7pO2vmQ.

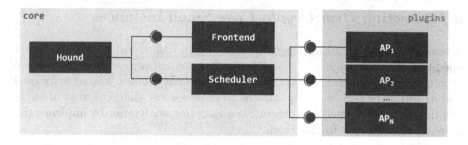

Fig. 1. Plugin architecture of KUBEHOUND.

2   Background: KUBEHOUND

To detect security smell instances, KUBEHOUND can analyse the sources and deployment specification of the microservices forming an application, when available. The information on where to find such files is given in an input configuration file, which is used by KUBEHOUND to retrieve the sources and deployment specification, which are then analysed by the set of featured plugins.

KUBEHOUND implements the plugin architecture pattern [17] as displayed in Fig. 1. The tool is composed of three core components, namely Hound, Frontend, and Scheduler, and a set of analysis plugins (sketched as $AP_1, AP_2, \ldots AP_n$ in the figure). Each analysis plugin is responsible for implementing one or more techniques for detecting instances of security smells for microservices. Prior to this work, KUBEHOUND already featured plugins for detecting instances of a subset of the security smells defined in [14], details on which can be found in [8].

The core components are responsible for acquiring the configuration files specifying an application deployment, parsing them, scheduling the analysis plugins implementing the featured smell detection techniques, and collecting their results. More precisely, Hound takes the input files and orchestrates the smell detection on the microservice application specified therein. It first passes the input files to the Frontend, which is responsible for application data acquisition and parsing. Frontend then returns to Hound a collection of application objects, each representing a resource in the application's sources, together with some metadata about them. Application objects and metadata are then passed to the Scheduler, which is responsible for invoking the plugins to run the analyses they implement. The Scheduler adopts a "best effort" approach, in the sense that it schedules an analysis plugin only if all the inputs required by such plugin are available. The results returned by the invoked plugins are merged by the Scheduler and then passed to Hound. Finally, Hound returns the overall analysis results to the end-user, by displaying them with a structured textual format on the command line.

3   Detecting *Own Crypto Code* Smell Instances

To enable KUBEHOUND to detect the *own crypto code* security smell, we developed two different plugins for two different instances of such smells, i.e., *usage of cryptographic primitives* and *suspicious cryptographic names*. The security smell and its instances were carefully selected to showcase two different ways of implementing a plugin, namely by integrating an existing analyser or by implementing an analysis technique from scratch.[2]

3.1   Detecting the *Usage of Cryptographic Primitives*

The occurrence of a cryptographic primitive [13] in the source code of a microservice may possibly denote the symptom of a cryptography solution being reimplemented, instead of reusing established and trusted technologies [9]. Therefore, the *usage of cryptographic primitives* is considered to be an instance of the *own crypto code* security smell [14], which we wish to enable getting detected by KUBEHOUND.

The detection of cryptographic primitives is already featured in production-ready code analysis tools, like SonarQube [20], which can be configured to detect "security hotspots" denoting the presence of custom crypto code, e.g., definition or invocation of custom cryptographic functions. Therefore, we decided to reuse a suitably configure instance of SonarQube to develop a plugin implementing the detection of the *usage of cryptographic primitives*. More precisely, we developed a plugin that spawns a Docker container running an instance of SonarQube configured to analyse the security hotspots in the source code of the target application's microservices. The plugin waits for the SonarQube instance to complete the analysis, and it then retrieves all the detected security hotspots. These are filtered to keep only the security hotspots denoting the use of non-standard cryptographic algorithms, e.g., the creation of `BasePasswordHasher` subclasses in Python applications, or that of `java.security.MessageDigest` subclasses in Java applications. Indeed, according to SonarQube documentation [20], such a type of security hotspots denotes the use of custom cryptographic primitives.

3.2   Detecting *Suspicious Cryptographic Names*

The occurence of a name related to some cryptography technology may possibly denote a symptom that such technology is being re-implemented, instead of relying on established libraries [12]. Therefore, the occurrence of *suspicious cryptographic names* is considered to be an instance of the *own crypto code* security smell [14], and our aim here is to extend KUBEHOUND to enable detecting one such smell instance.

In this case, to showcase the from-scratch implementation of a plugin (rather than integrating an existing tools), we decided to directly implement the static

---

[2] The implementation of the plugins is publicly available on GitHub: https://github.com/di-unipi-socc/kube-hound/tree/master/kube_hound/builtin_analyses.

analysis of the source code of the microservices forming an application. In particular, for Java, JavaScript, and Python, the plugin exploit the existing libraries to parse the source code files and obtain their representation in the form of abstract syntax trees. For any other type of source file, the plugin instead relies on regular expressions to tokenize the lists of words therein. Then, the plugin processes the obtained abstract syntax trees and/or lists of words, and it searches for suspicious cryptographic names therein, namely for words including suspicious keywords, e.g., RSA, IV, or AES. The detected suspicious cryptographic names – which might be multiple within a same source file, if some own cryptography solution is being implemented – are clustered by file when returned by the plugin. More precisely, the plugin returns information on which files contain suspicious cryptographic names and it lists, for each file, the numbers of the lines where each suspicious keywords appear.

4   Case Study

We assessed the practical applicability of the proposed detection of *own crypto code* smell instances by running three different case studies based on three applications, viz., a mock microservice application, Sock Shop [21], and Online Boutique [11]. The source code for repeating such analyses with all the three applications is publicly available on GitHub.[3] In all the three cases, we were able to detect instances of the *own crypto code* smell. For reasons of space limitations, and with the purpose of demonstrating both plugins, we here describe the case of the mock application, since Sock Shop [21] and Online Boutique [11] only included *suspicious cryptographic names*.

The mock application was configured so that its microservices include both the considered instances of the *own crypto code* security smell, i.e., *usage of cryptographic primitives* and *suspicious cryptographic names*. This was done by placing the microservices' source code in a single remote repository,[4] which includes multiple different files, among which

- the files customCrypto.py, customCrypto.java, customCryptoPython.py, and customCryptoJava.java include the *usage of cryptographic primitives*, while
- test_ucp.java, test_ucp.php, test_ucp.py, test_ucp.js, test_ucp.kt, test_ ucp.ts, test_ucp.vb include *suspicious cryptographic names*.

The files were organized in different folders and sub-folders, to also check whether the implemented plugins can suitably navigate through the organization of a remote repository. They were also of different types – denoted by their file extensions – to check the effectiveness of the plugin searching for *suspicious cryptographic names* with different file types.

---

[3] https://github.com/di-unipi-socc/kube-hound/tree/master/data/examples.
[4] https://github.com/di-unipi-socc/kube-hound/tree/master/data/examples/sourcecode_mock.

We then run KUBEHOUND with the newly included plugins, by feeding it with a configuration file[5] specifying where to find the source code of the microservices forming the mock application. As a result, KUBEHOUND successfully identified all the injected smell instances, by displaying them as sketched in Fig. 2.

```
Usage of Cryptographic Primitives Analysis-detected smells {OCC}
  Sonarqube found potential problems in customCrypto.java at
  line 4
  > public class MyCustomHashAlgorithm extends MessageDigest {
  reason: Make sure using a non-standard cryptographic algorithm
  is safe here
```

(a)

```
Suspicious Cryptographic Names Analysis-detected smells {OCC}
  Potential usage of custom crypto code in test_ucp.py
  - 'AES' at lines: 1, 5, 7, 12, 36, 37, 47, 48.
  - 'RSA' at lines: 2, 16, 18, 24, 29, 41, 49, 50.
  ...
  - 'cyphertext_rsa' at lines: 43, 44, 49.
  - 'decrypted_text_rsa' at lines: 44, 50.
  reason: Suspicious names found in the file, which may indicate
  the implementation of custom crypto code. Check for custom
  code implementation.
```

(b)

Fig. 2. Examples of (a) *usage of cryptographic primitives* and (b) *suspicious cryptographic names* detected by KUBEHOUND when running our case study.

5   Conclusions

We have extended KUBEHOUND with two plugins detecting two different instances of the *own crypto code* security smell, by also showing how they effectively enabled detecting such smell instances when injected in the application considered in our case study. This allowed us to not only demonstrate that the instances of the *own cripto code* security smell can be detected in microservice applications, but also to demonstrate the extensibility of KUBEHOUND's functionalities by developing and integrating novel plugins.

KUBEHOUND is an ongoing research project. We recently integrated three other plugins, all based on reusing Checkov [15] for detecting two different instances of the *hardcoded secrets* security smell, and an instance of the *non-encrypted sensitive data* smell. These are also available in the GitHub repository

---

[5] https://github.com/di-unipi-socc/kube-hound/blob/master/data/examples/ sourcecode_mock/config.yaml.

of KUBEHOUND, along with examples for showcasing their use. We plan to further extend KUBEHOUND by developing other plugins for detecting different instances of the microservice security smells described in [14].

We also plan to further extend the applicability of KUBEHOUND and to enhance its performances. As for KUBEHOUND's applicability, we plan to exploit its plugin-based extensibility to introduce a support for other container-orchestration frameworks than Kubernetes. As for KUBEHOUND's performances, instead, we plan to enable a parallel execution of the plugins, so as to run multiple different smell detection techniques in parallel, when possible.

Acknowledgments. This work has been partly supported by the research project FREEDA (CUP: I53D23003550006), funded by MUR (Italy) under the framework PRIN 2022.

References

1. Aqua Security Software: Kube Bench. https://github.com/aquasecurity/kube-bench
2. Aqua Security Software: Kube Hunter. https://github.com/aquasecurity/kube-hunter/
3. Balalaie, A., Heydarnoori, A., Jamshidi, P.: Microservices architecture enables devops: migration to a cloud-native architecture. IEEE Softw. **33**(3), 42–52 (2016). https://doi.org/10.1109/MS.2016.64
4. Berardi, D., Giallorenzo, S., Mauro, J., Melis, A., Montesi, F., Prandini, M.: Microservice security: a systematic literature review. PeerJ Comput. Sci. **8** (2022). https://doi.org/10.7717/peerj-cs.779
5. Bocci, A., Forti, S., Ferrari, G.L., Brogi, A.: Secure FaaS orchestration in the fog: how far are we? Computing **103**, 1025–1056 (2021). https://doi.org/10.1007/s00607-021-00924-y
6. Chondamrongkul, N., Sun, J., Warren, I.: Automated security analysis for microservice architecture. In: 2020 IEEE International Conference on Software Architecture Companion (ICSA-C), pp. 79–82 (2020). https://doi.org/10.1109/ICSA-C50368.2020.00024
7. Control Plane: KubeSec - Security risk analysis for Kubernetes resources. https://kubesec.io/
8. DellImmagine, G., Soldani, J., Brogi, A.: KubeHound: detecting microservices' security smells in Kubernetes deployments. Future Internet **15**(7) (2023). https://doi.org/10.3390/fi15070228
9. Fehrer, T., Lozoya, R., Sabetta, A., Di Nucci, D., Tamburri, D.: Detecting security fixes in open-source repositories using static code analyzers. CoRR abs/2105.03346 (2021)
10. Ferech, M., de Bruijn, T., Ponsard, N.: OpenAPI fuzzer. https://github.com/matusf/openapi-fuzzer
11. Google Cloud Platform: Online Boutique. https://github.com/GoogleCloudPlatform/microservices-demo
12. Khan, A.: How to secure your microservices: shopify case study. Dzone (2018)
13. NIST: Guideline for using cryptographic standards in the federal government: cryptographic mechanisms. NIST Special Publication 800-175B, Revision 1 (2020)

14. Ponce, F., Soldani, J., Astudillo, H., Brogi, A.: Smells and refactorings for microservices security: a multivocal literature review. J. Syst. Softw. **192**, 111393 (2022). https://doi.org/10.1016/j.jss.2022.111393
15. Prisma Cloud: Checkov. https://www.checkov.io
16. Rahman, A., Parnin, C., Williams, L.: The seven sins: security smells in infrastructure as code scripts. In: Bultan, T., Whittle, J. (eds.) 2019 IEEE/ACM 41st International Conference on Software Engineering (ICSE 2019), pp. 164–175. IEEE Computer Society (2019). https://doi.org/10.1109/ICSE.2019.00033
17. Richards, M.: Software Architecture Patterns, 1st edn. O'Reilly Media Inc., Newton (2015)
18. Schneider, S., Scandariato, R.: Automatic extraction of security-rich dataflow diagrams for microservice applications written in Java. J. Syst. Softw. **202**, 111722 (2023). https://doi.org/10.1016/j.jss.2023.111722
19. Soldani, J., Tamburri, D.A., Van Den Heuvel, W.J.: The pains and gains of microservices: a systematic grey literature review. J. Syst. Softw. **146**, 215–232 (2018). https://doi.org/10.1016/j.jss.2018.09.082
20. Sonar Solutions: SonarQube: Documentation. https://docs.sonarsource.com/sonarqube/
21. Weaveworks, Container Solutions: Sock Shop. https://microservices-demo.github.io/
22. ZAP Dev Team: Zed Attack Proxy. https://www.zaproxy.org/
23. Zdun, U., et al.: Microservice security metrics for secure communication, identity management, and observability. ACM Trans. Softw. Eng. Methodol. **32**(1) (2023). https://doi.org/10.1145/3532183

Tutorials

What is Blockchain and How Can it Help My Business? (Extended Tutorial Summary)

Marco Comuzzi[1]([⊠])(iD), Paul Grefen[2](iD), and Giovanni Meroni[3](iD)

[1] Ulsan National Institute of Science and Technology, Ulsan, Korea
mcomuzzi@unist.ac.kr
[2] Eindhoven University of Technology and Eviden Digital Transformation
Consulting, Eindhoven, The Netherlands
p.w.p.j.grefen@tue.nl
[3] Technical University of Denmark, Kgs. Lyngby, Denmark
giom@dtu.dk

Abstract. The content of this tutorial is drawn from a recent textbook that the authors have published. The book aims at introducing blockchain from scratch, providing first an implementation-agnostic view of the mechanisms underpinning blockchain, like immutable databases, consensus mechanisms, and smart contracts. Then, it moves to presenting the most prominent blockchain systems and platforms currently available. These range from widely known public blockchains and cryptocurrencies like Bitcoin and Ethereum, to platforms for building private blockchain network systems, such as Hyperledger Fabric. Next, the book introduces a set of tools to support decision making regarding the suitability of blockchain for a given business scenario. The book explains how business models can be used to analyze blockchain-based business scenarios. The book ends with illustrating how a blockchain system can be part of an innovative business application landscape.

Keywords: Blockchain · platform · business scenario · teaching · textbook

1 Introduction

While most people may know about blockchain from Bitcoin and news about its price in the financial markets, blockchain is a technology that increasingly permeates the way in which modern businesses operate. However, its dynamics and functioning remain obscure for most people. This tutorial, the content of which is entirely drawn from a textbook recently published by the authors [1], provides the tools to understand the full extent to which blockchain technology is or can be used in business.

First, we focus on the functioning of blockchain systems, introducing basic concepts such as transactions, consensus mechanisms and smart contracts, as

F. Monti et al. (Eds.): ICSOC 2023 Workshops, LNCS 14518, pp. 327–334, 2024.
https://doi.org/10.1007/978-981-97-0989-2_28

well as giving a smooth introduction to the basic features of cryptography that underpin blockchain technology, e.g., digital signatures and hashing. Then, we shift to specific blockchain platforms (Bitcoin, Ethereum, private blockchain platforms) currently used for the implementation of cryptocurrencies and other blockchain systems. Finally, we introduce a set of tools to understand and analyse the suitability of blockchain technology in different business scenarios from the software architecture, business model, and business operation perspectives.

The book associated with this tutorial provides the basis for readers to understand (i) the conceptual essence of blockchain technology, (ii) the design and functioning of Bitcoin, Ethereum, and other private blockchain platforms for the implementation of cryptocurrencies and smart contract-enabled blockchain systems, (iii) the applicability of blockchain as an enabling and/or transformative technology in different business scenarios from both an economic and an IT system perspective.

These goals are achieved through a modular structure of content. The tutorial is, like the book, organised into three parts. Part 1 (see Sect. 2) introduces the basic concepts of blockchain at a conceptual level, providing a solid basis to understand any concrete implementation of blockchain platforms. Part 2 (see Sect. 3) discusses prominent examples of concrete public and private blockchain systems, such as Bitcoin, Ethereum, and Hyperledger Fabric, and provides also an in-depth discussion of the potential role of blockchain in implementing IoT systems. Part 3 (see Sect. 4) provides the conceptual background, knowledge and tools to assess the applicability of blockchain technology in various business scenarios using decision trees and business models. It also illustrates the use of blockchain in a complex business application and technology context.

This tutorial and its associated book target students and educators with an interest in blockchain technology providing a one-stop shop to obtain a deep and complete insight in blockchain technology and its applicability in different business scenarios. The textbook is designed primarily for undergraduate students in industrial engineering, business and management, and information systems. However, it can be adopted also in the computer science majors, since it does not strictly require any specific pre-requisite knowledge. At the graduate level, this book can be used in courses for industrial engineering, information systems and management students. Finally, the book is also of interest to practitioners, like business analysts, process analysts and information system architects, to understand the enabling and transformative potential of blockchain in a given business scenario.

2 Part 1: Defining Blockchain in an Implementation-Agnostic Way

The first part of the tutorial faces the challenge of introducing blockchain. Because of its novelty and multidisciplinary aspects, introducing blockchain to students is challenging, no matter their background, whether more technical or more business-oriented. We decided to tackle this challenge in this book and

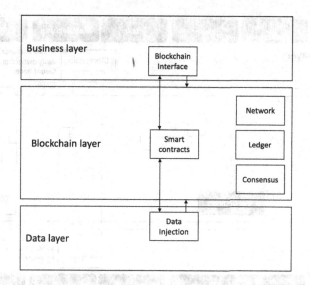

Fig. 1. A general architecture for blockchain systems. Reprinted from [1], Chapter 4.

tutorial by (i) first presenting blockchain as a general mechanism, abstracting from any specific implementation of it, and (ii) separating the presentation of the blockchain mechanism from the technical details of the core technology enabling it, i.e., cryptographic tools.

One of the main outcomes of Part 1 is the general architecture of blockchain systems shown in Fig. 1. According to the model proposed in Part 1, blockchain is a combination of a P2P network of computational nodes, an immutable database, i.e., a distributed ledger, replicated at each node, and a set of rules, i.e., a consensus mechanism, for nodes to agree on the content of the database at any time. Blockchain can be enhanced with smart contracts, that is immutable business logic that can be triggered by transactions, and comprises two types of users: data injectors, who provide the data, in the form of blockchain transactions, and business users, who use the data stored in the blockchain application to fulfil some business objective. Note that, in many business scenarios, the same entity can play both the role of data injector and business user simultaneously.

3   Part 2: Blockchain Platforms

Blockchain is a mechanism that creates trust among a set of business partners who face the need to exchange valuable assets and information, while not necessarily trusting each other. This mechanism is enabled by a set of cryptographic tools, which are presented avoiding as much as possible the more technical details. In all the discussions of Part 1, we have been careful in maintaining an implementation-agnostic standpoint.

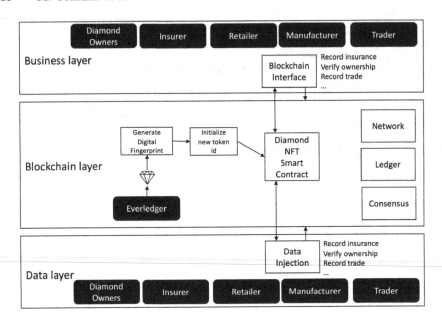

Fig. 2. Architecture of an Ethereum-based Distributed Application. Reprinted from [1], Chapter 6.

In Part 2, we look at how the blockchain mechanism is implemented into real-world blockchain systems. To this aim, we must abandon the implementation-agnostic standpoint and we must look at the implementation details of different blockchain technologies. We begin by discussing the most famous examples of (public) blockchain systems, of which most of you probably have heard already in the news: Bitcoin and Ethereum. Then, we discuss the peculiarities of private blockchain and how we can build private blockchain systems. Specifically, we discuss how Ethereum can also be used for private blockchain, and we additionally present two frameworks for building private blockchains: Corda and Hyperledger Fabric. Finally, we look in detail at the relationship between blockchain and IoT technology. In this context, we introduce another blockchain framework, IOTA, which has been created specifically to implement blockchain systems handling IoT data.

This part presents extensive examples of the application of blockchain in different scenarios. For instance, Fig. 2 and Fig. 3 show two instantiations of the architecture of Fig. 1 to the case of tracking and tracing the provenance of diamonds in the diamond trade and distribution market and the case of a general IoT scenario, respectively.

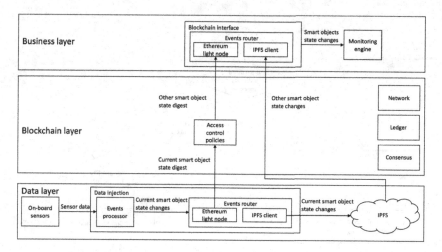

Fig. 3. Architecture of a blockchain-supported IoT application. Reprinted from [1], Chapter 8.

4 Part 3: Blockchain Suitability for Business

The first two parts of this tutorial (and the book) focus on blockchain as a mechanism and a technology. The blockchain mechanism can be exploited to create the trust required to exchange valuable information and assets in a trustless network of business partners. In Part 2, we have then presented different types of blockchain technology that implement the mechanisms introduced in Part 1. In doing so, we have also introduced many concrete applications of blockchain in the real world.

Blockchain is a technology that can support a wide range of business scenarios, but certainly not all of them. So, in which situations or under which conditions does the use of blockchain make sense? And if it makes sense, what would a blockchain application look like from the business perspective? Answering these questions is the focus of Part 3. We begin by presenting a set of decision-making tools that help structuring the decision on whether to use blockchain in a given business scenario. Then, we look at blockchain from the standpoint of business models, with the aim of understanding how blockchain can transform existing business models and even enable new ones. Finally, we discuss the application of blockchain in a novel class of business scenarios, i.e., scenarios for outcome management.

The first main outcome of this part of the tutorial and the book consists of decision making tools to assess the suitability of blockchain. Figure 4 shows the tool that we designed for assessing the features of a business scenario and their fit with blockchain, while Fig. 5 shows the tool that can be used to assess the more technical characteristics of a blockchain system implementation. The second outcome is the demonstration of the use of business models for the analysis of blockchain-based business scenarios. The final outcome is the demonstration

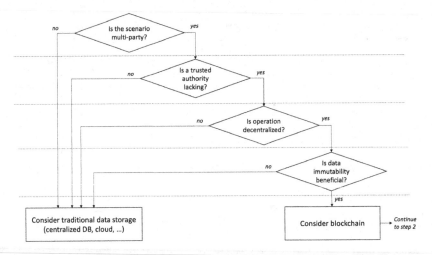

Fig. 4. Assessing the suitability of blockchain for a business scenario. Reprinted from [1], Chapter 9.

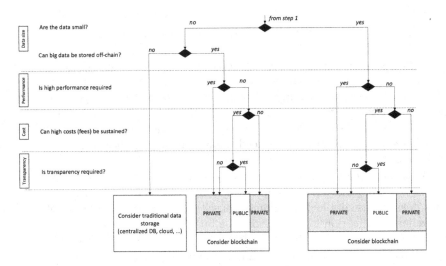

Fig. 5. Technical assessment of blockchain suitability. Reprinted from [1], Chapter 9.

that blockchain needs to be combined with other technologies in most real-world business application scenarios. We show an example in business outcome management in which blockchain technology is combined with IoT technology, federated learning (as a sub-domain of artificial intelligence), wide-area network technology, enterprise information system technology and software process management technology. This is illustrated in Fig. 6.

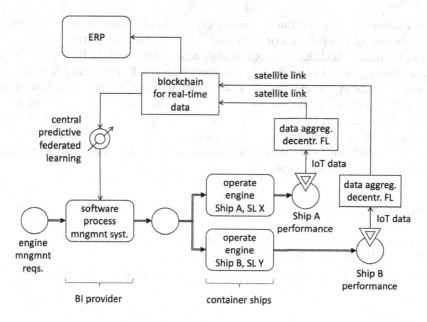

Fig. 6. Combining blockchain and other technology in a complex business scenario. Reprinted from [1], Chapter 11.

5 Conclusion

This tutorial and the book associated with it fulfill a primary need of the authors: finding an appropriate textbook for our courses on digital transformation using blockchain. While there are excellent books focusing on the technical implementation aspects of specific blockchains, like Bitcoin or Ethereum, or looking at blockchain from a software engineering or financial engineering perspective, we have struggled to find a book taking a 'design science' standpoint on blockchain: providing sufficient explanation of the technical details in order to understand how blockchain can be used to address specific business needs in the real world.

For students, we hope that this tutorial and this book serve a twofold objective. First, helping you to shed some light on the inner functioning of a new technology like blockchain, in its different forms. Second, allowing you to critically assess whether blockchain is an appropriate solution for a (new or existing) business scenario.

For professionals, depending on your background, this tutorial and this book will also serve diverse needs. If you come from a business-oriented background, then this book helps you to understand the technical details behind a technology that is increasingly adopted in the corporate world. If your background concerns more the software design and implementation, this book helps you finding suitable business applications for a technology that you may know deeply only from a technical standpoint, but for which you have struggled to grasp the usefulness in the practical world.

No matter your background, our objective is to give you the tools to evaluate the potential of blockchain critically and fairly. In fact, while the world is populated by many blockchain 'maximalists', who think blockchain is the solution to everything, and blockchain 'minimalists', who think blockchain is only cryptocurrency, and cryptocurrency is only a global scam, we take a balanced and critical perspective on the impact of blockchain on modern, digitally-supported and digitally-enabled business. Our Latin ancestors, unsurprisingly, used to say that "in medio stat virtus", or more precisely, "virtus est medium vitiorum et utrimque reductum" ("virtue is the middle between two vices, and is equally removed from either extreme", Horace, Epistole, I, 18, 9).

Reference

1. Comuzzi, M., Grefen, P., Meroni, G.: Blockchain for Business: IT Principles into Practice. Routledge, Milton Park (2023)

Quantum Services: A Tutorial on the Technology and the Process

Javier Romero-Álvarez(✉) , Jaime Alvarado-Valiente , Enrique Moguel ,
José Garcia-Alonso , and Juan M. Murillo

Quercus Software Engineering Group, Universidad de Extremadura, Cáceres, Spain
{jromero,jaimeav,enrique,jgaralo,juanmamu}@unex.es

Abstract. The emergence of quantum computing has introduced a new paradigm in the realm of computer science and software engineering, expanding the frontiers of computer applications designed for problem-solving. The transformation of quantum algorithms into services is a promising avenue to address this new paradigm, as it allows them to be integrated into conventional distributed applications. This tutorial provides an overview of the process of transforming quantum algorithms into quantum services. It explains how these quantum services can be effectively deployed, specifically using the Amazon Braket platform for quantum computing, and how they can be invoked through classical service endpoints. This tutorial not only presents the step-by-step methodology but also provides insight into best practices for successful implementation through a development process. It highlights the use of an extended version of the OpenAPI Specification and the automation capabilities offered by GitHub Actions, which play a key role in improving efficiency throughout the development and deployment phases.

Keywords: Quantum Computing · Service-Oriented Computing · Quantum Programming · OpenAPI · Continuous Deployment

1 Introduction

The advent of quantum computing has marked the beginning of a new era in the fields of computer science and software engineering, opening new horizons in the field of computational problem-solving applications [1]. This cutting-edge technology has proven to be especially valuable in tasks that until now remained beyond the reach of the most powerful classical computers within reasonable time frames [2]. These tasks include the discovery of new materials or pharmaceutical compounds and the analysis of vast data sets and applications in, for example, the field of health care [3].

Several large computer companies have already successfully built functional quantum computers, and have developed several programming languages and quantum simulators that are accessible to the general population [4,5]. The implications of this emerging paradigm are changing not only the landscape of

F. Monti et al. (Eds.): ICSOC 2023 Workshops, LNCS 14518, pp. 335–342, 2024.
https://doi.org/10.1007/978-981-97-0989-2_29

computing but also the landscape of areas in which it can be effectively applied. However, it is essential to recognize that, at present, and probably soon, quantum computing must coexist with classical computing. Therefore, a coexistence encapsulated in the concept of hybrid classical-quantum architectures is necessary [6]. A solid guiding framework for navigating this landscape of hybrid architectures lies in leveraging the fundamental principles service-oriented computing provides, given the rich history of classical service engineering [7].

Therefore, from the point of view of Service-Oriented Computing, the integration of quantum software is not much different from that of classical services. However, the current lack of software engineering techniques specific to quantum services poses a challenge for performing quantum service-related activities [8]. In response to these problems, new approaches are emerging that simplify the translation of conventional processes to the realm of quantum computing [9,10].

Hence, the main objective of this tutorial is to clarify the details of implementing and deploying quantum services adapted to hybrid classical-quantum architectures. The tutorial aims to provide developers with a thorough understanding of the process involved in transforming quantum algorithms into services, hosting them in cloud environments, and seamlessly integrating them into distributed applications. To this end, specific examples of real-world problem-solving using quantum computing on the Amazon Braket platform service will be presented.

Furthermore, we will outline a procedure for generating quantum services employing the OpenAPI Specification[1], allowing developers to follow a familiar methodology similar to that of conventional services [11]. This approach not only streamlines the definition of input and output parameters for quantum services but also facilitates understanding and usability for other developers. In addition, a continuous deployment approach will be presented by automating the deployment of quantum services through GitHub Actions[2], which streamlines the process of integrating quantum computing capabilities into software development workflows.

2   Intended Audience

This tutorial is aimed at people from academia and industry who share an interest in the world of Quantum Service-Oriented Computing. While some previous experience in quantum software development is desirable, it is by no means a strict prerequisite for understanding the tutorial content. However, a basic understanding of microservices, JSON file structures, and the Python programming language is indispensable to actively participate in the practical aspects of the tutorial. This background knowledge is necessary especially to be able to follow the hands-on demonstrations.

---

[1] https://www.openapis.org/.

[2] https://github.com/features/actions.

To facilitate the learning process, comprehensive resources are provided, such as the source code of all examples used throughout the tutorial[3]. In addition, a short introductory section on the fundamentals of quantum computing will be provided as part of the tutorial to ensure that attendees have the necessary background knowledge.

Those who wish to participate in the hands-on section of the tutorial should have a laptop equipped with a text editor, a working Python installation, and an active Amazon Web Services (AWS) account. The inclusion of these tools allows attendees to actively participate in the hands-on exercises, thus consolidating their understanding of quantum services.

Detailed instructions for setting up the required environment will be provided before attending the tutorial. These guidelines include the initial steps involved in running quantum code on the attendee's local machine, simulating quantum processes using the Amazon Braket SDK, and advanced techniques for individuals wanting to use real quantum machines. It is important to note that these advanced steps, while valuable, are not obligatory for participation in the tutorial.

For the convenience of attendees, the tutorial slides, in addition to the aforementioned environment setup instructions, and supplementary resources, will be available online (see Footnote 3), ensuring easy and convenient access to the materials needed to fully benefit from the tutorial.

3   Outline of the Tutorial

This section provides a comprehensive outline of the tutorial—Fig. 1—, designed to last a half-day duration, encompassing approximately three hours, during which both informative lectures and hands-on practical activities will be featured.

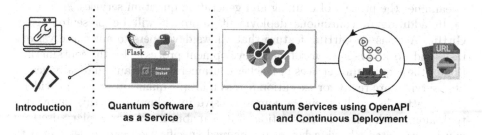

Fig. 1. Outline of the Tutorial

Introduction
The tutorial begins with a brief but informative presentation that delves into the concept of servitization within the realm of quantum software. This segment

---
[3] https://uex.be/tutorial.

clarifies the transformation of pre-existing quantum algorithms into traditional services, providing insight into the conceptual framework.

Following the presentation, attendees will experience a hands-on demonstration of how these quantum services can be deployed and executed. The hands-on aspect will leverage Python libraries tailored to classic services and Postman to test the deployed services. This pragmatic demonstration is intended to bridge the gap between theoretical concepts and real-world applications. To illustrate these principles, quantum algorithms will be used as a practical example. These algorithms will be adapted to the Amazon Braket platform and its associated programming language, demonstrating the versatility of the platform and serving as a template for similar adaptations on alternative quantum platforms.

Quantum Software as a Service

The second segment of the tutorial offers a hands-on experience for attendees. Participants will actively deploy and invoke their initial quantum service during this practical session. Two pivotal quantum algorithms will take center stage: 1) Shor's algorithm for factoring large numbers, representing gate-based quantum computing, and 2) a solution to the Traveling Salesman Problem, symbolizing annealing-based quantum computing.

The implementation of these quantum algorithms, customized for compatibility with Amazon Braket, will be provided to attendees. Their primary focus will be deploying and utilizing these algorithms as traditional services. This practical exercise empowers participants to gain firsthand experience in transitioning quantum algorithms into practical services, thereby consolidating their understanding of the conversion process.

Quantum Services using OpenAPI and Continuous Deployment

Given the current limitations arising from the need to use different software development kits (SDKs) depending on the quantum machine provider, a solution is presented in this part of the tutorial. This solution involves the generation of quantum services by using an extension of the OpenAPI Specification, which streamlines the process of defining and generating quantum services.

In addition, a continuous deployment approach will be presented using GitHub Actions—a GitHub feature that allows developers to automate various tasks and workflows in their software development process—for the containerization of these quantum services in Docker containers. These automatically generated services are ready for execution across multiple quantum service providers.

So, attendees will receive a comprehensive introduction to this innovative tool, along with a live demonstration of its capabilities. An exemplary use case will be presented, showing how a pre-defined specification can be leveraged to automatically generate, deploy, and test quantum services.

The tutorial ends with a detailed presentation and practical demonstration of the tool. The automation of quantum service definition, generation, deployment, and execution will be explained with real examples, emphasizing the efficiency and effectiveness of incorporating quantum computing into software development workflows.

In summary, the modular structure ensures that both beginners and experts in the field can benefit from the session. Hence the delivery of a more theoretical part and a practical part to allow participants to perform their experimentation with the quantum software.

4   Learning Objectives and Outcomes

At the end of the tutorial, participants will have acquired a thorough understanding of the following key learning objectives and outcomes:

- *Servitization of Quantum Algorithms:* attendees will have gained an in-depth understanding of the concept of servitization as it relates to quantum algorithms. They will understand the principles of transforming quantum algorithms into practical services, effectively bridging the theoretical and practical aspects of this process.
- *Hybrid classical-quantum service architectures:* The tutorial will allow participants to think and conceptualize in the realm of hybrid classical-quantum service architectures. This new perspective will enable them to better understand the current paradigms of classical and quantum computing.
- *Extension of the OpenAPI specification for quantum services*: Presentation of the OpenAPI specification extension for quantum services. This knowledge enables participants to define and generate quantum services efficiently. It provides them with the necessary skills to streamline the integration of quantum computing into software development workflows, increasing the level of abstraction in the development of quantum services.
- *Continuous development and deployment of quantum service:* An essential outcome of the tutorial is the ability to automate the deployment of quantum services tailored to various service providers using GitHub Actions. The proposal's deployment approach will thus streamline the continuous development and deployment of quantum solutions in various quantum computing ecosystems.

In essence, the tutorial's learning objectives and outcomes encompass not only theoretical knowledge but also the practical skills necessary to navigate the complex and evolving landscape of quantum computing and Quantum Service-Oriented software development. This knowledge empowers attendees to actively engage with quantum technology and implement it in real-world scenarios.

5   Biographies of Presenters

In recent years, the expertise of the presenters in the field of software engineering has culminated in several noteworthy contributions and innovative approaches. These contributions cover innovative Service-Based Computing models aimed at realizing the vision of the "Internet of People" [12]. Moreover, their work has extended to pioneering the concept of "People as a Service" (PeaaS) [13], which reflects their dedication to redefining the paradigms of digital interaction.

In the realm of quantum computing, the presenters have delved into hybrid models that seamlessly blend classical computing techniques with the emerging quantum paradigm [7]. Their endeavors have also shed light on the nuances and challenges inherent in developing high-quality quantum services [14] and in the management of these services [15], and also have made various advances in the field of Quantum OpenAPI [11,16]. These insights are pivotal in enabling the effective integration of quantum computing within various applications.

In addition to their work, the presenters are actively engaged in cutting-edge projects within the domain of quantum computing. These projects include *"QSalud: Quantum Pharmacogenetics Applied to Ageing"* and *"QServ: Quantum Service Engineering development, quality, testing & security of quantum microservices"*. These projects show their involvement in pushing the limits of quantum computing and exploring its potential applications in a variety of fields.

Below, a brief biography of the presenters can be found:

Javier Romero-Álvarez is a PhD student and research scientist fellow at the University of Extremadura, Spain. He obtained his degree in Computer Science from the University of Extremadura in 2020. His research interests include Web Engineering, Quantum Computing, Service-Oriented Computing, Mobile Computing, and Chatbot Development.

Jaime Alvarado-Valiente is a PhD student and research scientist fellow at the University of Extremadura, Spain. He obtained his degree in Computer Science from the University of Extremadura in 2020. His research interests include Web Engineering, Quantum Computing, Quantum Software Engineering, and Service-Oriented Computing.

Enrique Moguel is an Assistant Professor at the University of Extremadura (Spain). He completed his MSc in Computer Science at the University Carlos III (Spain) in 2010 and a Ph.D. in Computer Science at the University of Extremadura in 2018. His research interests include Software Engineering, Smart Systems, eHealth, and Quantum Computing.

Jose Garcia-Alonso is an Associate Professor at the University of Extremadura, Spain, where he completed his PhD in software engineering in 2014. He is the co-founder of Gloin, a software consulting company, and Health and Aging Tech, an eHealth company. His interests include Web Engineering, Quantum Software Engineering, Pervasive Computing, eHealth, and Gerontechnology.

Juan M. Murillo is Full Professor at the University of Extremadura, Spain, and co-founder of the start-up Gloin. His research interests include software architectures, Pervasive and Mobile Computing, and Quantum Computing. Murillo holds a PhD in computer science from the University of Extremadura.

Acknowledgements. This work has been partially funded by the European Union "Next GenerationEU /PRTR", by the Ministry of Science, Innovation and Universities (projects PID2021-1240454OB-C31, TED2021-130913B-I00, and PDC2022-133465-I00). It is also supported by QSERV: Quantum Service Engineering: Development Quality, Testing and Security of Quantum Microservices project funded by the Spanish Ministry of Science and Innovation and ERDF; by the Regional Ministry of

Economy, Science and Digital Agenda of the Regional Government of Extremadura (GR21133); and by European Union under the Agreement - 101083667 of the Project "TECH4E -Tech4effiencyEDlH" regarding the Call: DIGITAL-2021-EDlH-01 supported by the European Commission through the Digital Europe Program. It is also supported by the QSALUD project (EXP 00135977/MIG-20201059) in the lines of action of the Center for the Development of Industrial Technology (CDTI). And by grant PRE2022-102070, funded by MCIN/AEI/10.13039/501100011033 and by FSE+.

References

1. Gill, S.S., et al.: Quantum computing: a taxonomy, systematic review and future directions. Softw. Pract. Exp. **52**(1), 66–114 (2022). https://doi.org/10.1002/spe.3039
2. Zhao, J.: Quantum software engineering: landscapes and horizons. arXiv (2020). arXiv:2007.07047
3. Rasool, R.U., Ahmad, H.F., Rafique, W., Qayyum, A., Qadir, J.: Quantum computing for healthcare: a review. Future Internet (2022). https://doi.org/10.36227/TECHRXIV.17198702.V3
4. Tacchino, F., Chiesa, A., Carretta, S., Gerace, D.: Quantum computers as universal quantum simulators: state-of-the-art and perspectives. Adv. Quantum Technol. **3**(3), 1900052 (2020)
5. Alvarado-Valiente, J., Romero-Álvarez, J., Moguel, E., García-Alonso, J., Murillo, J.M.: Technological diversity of quantum computing providers: a comparative study and a proposal for API gateway integration. Softw. Qual. J. 1–21 (2023). https://doi.org/10.1007/s11219-023-09633-5
6. Pérez-Castillo, R., Serrano, M.A., Piattini, M.: Software modernization to embrace quantum technology. Adv. Eng. Softw. **151**, 102933 (2021)
7. Moguel, E., Rojo, J., Valencia, D., Berrocal, J., Garcia-Alonso, J., Murillo, J.M.: Quantum service-oriented computing: current landscape and challenges. Softw. Qual. J. **30**(4), 983–1002 (2022)
8. Serrano, M.A., Perez-Castillo, R., Piattini, M.: Quantum Software Engineering. Springer, Cham (2022)
9. Weder, B., Barzen, J., Leymann, F., Vietz, D.: Quantum software development lifecycle. In: Serrano, M.A., Pérez-Castillo, R., Piattini, M. (eds.) Quantum Software Engineering, pp. 61–83. Springer, Cham (2022). https://doi.org/10.1007/978-3-031-05324-5_4
10. McCaskey, A., Dumitrescu, E., Liakh, D., Humble, T.: Hybrid programming for near-term quantum computing systems. In: 2018 IEEE international conference on rebooting computing (ICRC), pp. 1–12. IEEE (2018). https://doi.org/10.1109/ICRC.2018.8638598
11. Romero-Álvarez, J., Alvarado-Valiente, J., Moguel, E., García-Alonso, J., Murillo, J.M.: Using open API for the development of hybrid classical-quantum services. In: Troya, J., et al. (eds.) ICSOC 2022. LNCS, vol. 13821, pp. 364–368. Springer, Cham (2023). https://doi.org/10.1007/978-3-031-26507-5_34
12. Miranda, J., et al.: From the internet of things to the internet of people. IEEE Internet Comput. **19**(2), 40–47 (2015)
13. Guillen, J., Miranda, J., Berrocal, J., Garcia-Alonso, J., Murillo, J.M., Canal, C.: People as a service: a mobile-centric model for providing collective sociological profiles. IEEE Softw. **31**(2), 48–53 (2013)

14. Alvarado-Valiente, J., et al.: Quantum services generation and deployment process: a quality-oriented approach. In: Fernandes, J.M., Travassos, G.H., Lenarduzzi, V., Li, X. (eds.) QUATIC 2023. CCIS, vol. 1871, pp. 200–214. Springer, Cham (2023). https://doi.org/10.1007/978-3-031-43703-8_15

15. Alvarado-Valiente, J., Romero-Álvarez, J., Moguel, E., García-Alonso, J.: Quantum web services orchestration and management using DevOps techniques. In: Garrigós, I., Murillo Rodríguez, J.M., Wimmer, M. (eds.) ICWE 2023. LNCS, vol. 13893, pp. 389–394. Springer, Cham (2023). https://doi.org/10.1007/978-3-031-34444-2_33

16. Romero-Álvarez, J., Alvarado-Valiente, J., Moguel, E., García-Alonso, J., Murillo, J.M.: Enabling continuous deployment techniques for quantum services. Authorea Preprints (2023). https://doi.org/10.22541/au.168998413.35984731/v1

Satellite Computing: From Space to Your Screen

Qing Li[(✉)] and Daliang Xu

Peking University, Beijing 1000871, China
{liqingpostdoc,xudaliang}@pku.edu.cn

Abstract. The space industry is undergoing a transformative shift driven by the rapid growth of LEO satellite mega-constellations. These constellations cater to growing demands in various sectors, from intelligent transportation and smart cities to maritime surveillance and disaster response. Satellite computing emerges as a pivotal foundation in this evolution. In our tutorial lecture, we embark on a journey into the realm of satellite computing, a burgeoning field with immense potential. We begin by addressing a fundamental question: What is satellite computing? We delve into core concepts, revealing how satellites can function as computational powerhouses orbiting our planet. As we progress, we explore diverse scenarios where satellite computing shines. We also confront the unique challenges it faces in space's harsh environment, featuring deep vacuum conditions, radiation exposure, strong vibrations, and extreme temperature ranges. Our tutorial offers insights into our research in satellite computing. We share practical experiences from deploying the Tiansuan constellation, showcasing the real-world applications of these cutting-edge technologies. Our vision is to democratize satellite computing access. By transforming satellites into servers "with wings", we envision a future where every corner of the globe reaps the benefits of satellite computing's vast potential.

Keywords: Satellite computing · Tiansuan constellation · LEO satellite

1 Introduction

In the ever-evolving landscape of space technology, the resurgence of low-earth orbit (LEO) satellites has emerged as a transformative force, fueled by advancements in miniaturization, cost reduction, and an increasing demand for versatile satellite capabilities. This tutorial embarks on a journey through the fascinating realm of satellite computing, unraveling the intricacies of LEO satellites and their pivotal role in shaping the future of communication, earth observation, and beyond.

As we delve into the satellite industry's resurgence, the spotlight shines on the Tiansuan constellation - an open research platform at the forefront of satellite innovation [9]. Established with a vision to bridge global connectivity divides,

Tiansuan represents a paradigm shift in satellite experimentation, contributing to real-world advancements in satellite technology and computing.

This tutorial is designed to provide a comprehensive understanding of the driving forces behind the satellite renaissance, the diverse applications of LEO satellites, and the compelling need for satellite computing in the face of complex on-orbit tasks. Together, we will explore the goals, achievements, and ongoing experiments on the Tiansuan constellation, offering participants a hands-on experience in the realm of space technology.

From the deployment of 6G core networks [7] to the optimization of satellite energy systems [5], Tiansuan serves as a beacon for cutting-edge research and experimentation. Participants will gain practical insights into real-world satellite advancements, exploring open-source codebases and unraveling the potential future trends that could shape the landscape of satellite computing.

Join us in this tutorial to unravel the mysteries of LEO satellites, witness the innovation behind the Tiansuan constellation, and gain a deeper appreciation for the transformative potential of satellite computing in addressing global challenges and propelling us toward an interconnected future.

2   Intended Audience

This tutorial is crafted for professionals, researchers, and enthusiasts eager to explore the dynamic intersection of space technology, satellite computing, and the transformative applications reshaping our connected world. The content is designed to cater to individuals with diverse backgrounds, including:

Communication and Networking Professionals: Professionals interested in the role of satellites in global communication networks, exploring the evolution of satellite-based technologies and their impact on connectivity.

Researchers and Academia: Scholars and researchers in the fields of space science, telecommunications, and computer science looking to deepen their understanding of real-world satellite experiments and the potential implications for future research.

Space Enthusiasts and Hobbyists: Individuals fascinated by space exploration and technology, regardless of their technical background, who wish to grasp the fundamentals of satellite computing and its practical applications.

Students in Relevant Disciplines: Undergraduate and graduate students studying engineering, computer science, telecommunications, or related fields, interested in gaining a practical understanding of satellite computing and its applications.

By catering to a broad audience with varied expertise levels, this tutorial aims to create an inclusive learning environment that fosters curiosity and enables participants to navigate the intricate landscape of satellite technology and computing.

3 Part 1: Satellite Computing: Concepts, Applications, Challenges, and Visions

The recent surge in LEO satellite constellations has transformed the satellite industry, with advancements in miniaturization technology and reduced launch costs driving this renewed interest. This section explores the factors contributing to the resurgence of LEO satellites, with a focus on the diverse applications of satellite computing. Additionally, the section delves into the challenges faced by satellite computing, such as space radiation, orbital characteristics, and inherent system limitations. Finally, the potential of satellite computing to revolutionize space missions, wide area real-time communication, and space-based data centers is discussed.

3.1 Advancements in LEO Satellites

The cost-effectiveness of satellite manufacturing and launch has significantly increased, paving the way for the rise of small satellites. These satellites, defined by NASA as those with a mass less than 500 kg [10], are becoming instrumental in various applications, including communication, earth observation, global navigation, and space exploration. Notably, the miniaturization trend enables more agile and cost-effective solutions for space exploration and communication.

Satellites are evolving from single-function entities to sophisticated systems requiring on-board computation. The complexity of on-orbit tasks, the demand for on-orbit data processing, and the scalability challenges of ground control systems are driving the need for satellite computing. On-board computation becomes crucial for tasks like space autonomous control, dynamic calculations of target positions, and alleviating pressure on space-to-ground communication.

3.2 Applications of Satellite Computing

Earth Observation. Satellite computing enhances the performance of earth observation satellites by enabling on-board processing using deep learning models. This facilitates real-time data analysis, reducing the need for transmitting large volumes of raw data to Earth.

Wide Area Real-Time Communication. Satellite computing addresses latency issues in wide area real-time communication systems, particularly in remote or underdeveloped areas. By optimizing communication paths and reducing round-trip times, satellite computing enhances user experience in real-time communication [3].

Space Content Delivery Networks (CDNs). CDNs integrated with satellites significantly reduce content access times for users by deploying CDN nodes in space. Simulation experiments in [2] demonstrate the potential of satellite computing in improving CDN performance.

3.3   Challenges in Satellite Computing

Space Radiation. The industry is transitioning towards using low-cost, high-performance Commercial Off-The-Shelf (COTS) products to replace radiation-hardened components. The space environment poses challenges to satellite computing, with space radiation affecting electronic components.

Orbital Characteristics. The dynamic nature of satellite constellations and limited contact with the ground present challenges in maintaining collaboration between satellites. Frequent switching of connections adds complexity to ensuring a high-quality user experience.

Inherent System Characteristics. Satellite computation faces challenges from the satellite's primary mission of maintaining normal operation in orbit. Energy and thermal control systems influence the performance of on-board computation, with miniaturization trends impacting power collection and storage capacities.

3.4   Innovations and Future Prospects

Despite challenges, innovations such as the use of COTS components in space, advancements in radiation tolerance, and reliability design at both hardware and software levels present opportunities for the continued development of satellite computing. Additionally, the potential for satellite computing in supporting space missions, improving communication systems, and establishing space-based data centers highlights a promising future for this technology.

4   Part 2: Tiansuan Constellation: The Cutting-Edge Technologies

This section explores the Tiansuan constellation, an open research platform aimed at revolutionizing satellite computing and addressing global connectivity challenges. With a focus on the deployment, experimentation, and optimization of services, the Tiansuan project contributes to advancing space technology and promoting universal connectivity. This section discusses the motivation, development, goals, and achievements of the Tiansuan constellation, covering a range of research topics and innovative experiments conducted on real satellites. The presented work includes the deployment of 6G core networks, energy optimization strategies, and the development of a specialized operating system for satellites. Future research directions and the vision for a unified public platform are also outlined.

4.1   The Genesis of Tiansuan

As human society faces development bottlenecks and envisions interstellar voyages, the role of satellite networks becomes crucial. However, most of land and ocean remain unconnected to the internet. Tiansuan Constellation is introduced as an open research platform, addressing the connectivity divide through real satellite experiments.

Established in June 2020, SNIC LAB in Shenzhen embarked on a mission involving interstellar civilization, satellite networks, and distributed AI computing. After extensive experimentation on experimental satellites, Tiansuan Constellation was initiated in October 2021, with goals spanning three phases and a completion timeline by 2024 [8].

4.2   Experiments Conducted on Tiansuan

The Tiansuan constellation serves as a versatile research platform, supporting experiments at various layers, including the physical, network, transport, and application layers. It enables computing services in LEO satellites, offering real-time earth observation, AI in space, new satellite operating system tests, security and reliability technology, and hardware testing [9]. On the five launched satellites, a series of innovative experiments were conducted, including the implementation of a 5G Core Network with 5G gNB software, a cognitive service architecture for 6G Core Network, a cloud-native satellite system, QUIC protocol testing, and network measurement experiments. The satellite images and related codebase are open-sourced on GitHub[1].

4.3   Research Work Based on Tiansuan

Space Service Computing Architecture [1]. This work introduced the Space Service Computing architecture, addressing challenges in space networking. The architecture divides into three layers: Satellite Network, Aerial Network, and Terrestrial Network, catering to spatial-temporal connectivity, efficient resource utilization, and diverse user demands.

Dynamic Service Deployment and Optimization [4]. A Lyapunov optimization technique and Gibbs sampling method were employed to dynamically deploy services on Tiansuan. The focus was on achieving global on-demand service coverage while ensuring robustness by balancing deployment costs and redundancy.

Energy System Optimization [6]. The integration of satellite computing posed challenges to the energy system due to volume and weight constraints. A battery-aware power management strategy was developed, leveraging online convex optimization frameworks. This optimization aims to improve satellite lifespan by 1.32 times.

6G Core Networks on Tiansuan [7]. With the explosive growth of satellite constellations, managing them becomes challenging. Deploying lightweight core networks on satellites, Tiansuan verified a cognitive service architecture for

---

[1] https://github.com/TiansuanConstellation/TiansuanExperimentPlatform

6G Core Networks. The edge core deployment on Tiansuan aims to enhance flexibility in constellation management.

Ongoing research on Tiansuan includes collaborative tasks, privacy in shared learning, and machine learning efficiency. The project aims to create an upgraded satellite computer system, offering advanced functions and a distributed computing solution using System on Chip (SOC) clusters. The ultimate vision of Tiansuan is to establish a public, web-based unified platform offering services to third-party researchers and practitioners. This involves launching satellites, building ground stations, and integrating with cloud data centers.

Tiansuan Constellation stands as a pioneering initiative in the satellite computing domain, contributing to the evolution of space technology and the realization of global connectivity. Through experimentation, optimization, and a commitment to open research, Tiansuan paves the way for a future where satellites play a central role in addressing societal challenges and advancing human exploration beyond Earth.

5   Learning Objectives

By the end of this tutorial, participants will have a comprehensive understanding of the recent developments in satellite computing. We expect the participants:

Understanding Satellite Resurgence. Gain insights into the factors driving the resurgence of LEO satellites, including reduced costs, miniaturization, and increased capabilities.

Exploring Satellite Applications. Explore the diverse applications of LEO satellites, focusing on communication, earth observation, global navigation, space exploration, and the emerging role of satellite computing.

Recognizing the Need for Satellite Computing. Understand the evolving role of satellites from single-function entities to computing platforms, driven by the increasing complexity of on-orbit tasks and the demand for on-orbit data processing.

Hands-On Satellite Experimentation. Gain practical insights into satellite experimentation by exploring the open-sourced codebase of Tiansuan on GitHub and understanding its applications in real-world scenarios.

6   Biographies of Presenters

Qing Li is a postdoctoral fellow at Peking University. She received her Ph.D. from Beijing University of Posts and Telecommunications and currently serves as a core technical member of the Tiansuan Constellation. Her research interests includes edge computing, satellite computing, and resource scheduling and optimization. She has contributed to publications in top conferences and journals in computer science, including MobiCom, TMC, and IoTJ. She has received the Outstanding Ph.D. Award from the Service Computing Committee of the China

Computer Society. She has also been honored with the IEEE EDGE'21 Best Paper Award and the ICSOC'23 Distinguished Paper Award.

Daliang Xu is a third-year Ph.D. student in Peking University of China. His research interest is in mobile computing and system software. He has contributed to publications in top conferences and journals in computer science, including MobiCom, ASPLOS, TMC.

References

1. Guo, Y., Li, Q., Li, Y., Zhang, N., Wang, S.: Service coordination in the space-air-ground integrated network. IEEE Netw. **35**(5), 168–173 (2021). https://doi.org/10.1109/MNET.111.2100153
2. Lai, Z., Li, H., Zhang, Q., Wu, Q., Wu, J.: : Cooperatively constructing pervasive and low-latency CDNs upon emerging LEO satellites and clouds. IEEE/ACM Trans. Netw. 1–16 (2023). https://doi.org/10.1109/TNET.2023.3260166
3. Lai, Z., Liu, W., Wu, Q., Li, H., Xu, J., Wu, J.: SpaceRTC: unleashing the low-latency potential of mega-constellations for real-time communications. In: IEEE INFOCOM 2022-IEEE Conference on Computer Communications, pp. 1339–1348. IEEE (2022)
4. Li, Q., et al.: Service coverage for satellite edge computing. IEEE Internet Things J. **9**(1), 695–705 (2021)
5. Li, Q., Wang, S., Ma, X., Zhou, A., Yang, F.: Towards sustainable satellite edge computing. In: 2021 IEEE International Conference on Edge Computing (EDGE), pp. 1–8 (2021). https://doi.org/10.1109/EDGE53862.2021.00010
6. Li, Q., Wang, S., Ma, X., Zhou, A., Yang, F.: Towards sustainable satellite edge computing. In: 2021 IEEE International Conference on Edge Computing (EDGE), pp. 1–8. IEEE (2021)
7. Li, Y., Huang, J., Sun, Q., Sun, T., Wang, S.: Cognitive service architecture for 6g core network. IEEE Trans. Industr. Inf. **17**(10), 7193–7203 (2021). https://doi.org/10.1109/TII.2021.3063697
8. Wang, S., Li, Q.: Satellite computing: vision and challenges. IEEE Internet Things J. **10**(24), 22514–22529 (2023). https://doi.org/10.1109/JIOT.2023.3303346
9. Wang, S., Li, Q., Xu, M., Ma, X., Zhou, A., Sun, Q.: Tiansuan constellation: an open research platform. In: 2021 IEEE International Conference on Edge Computing (EDGE), pp. 94–101 (2021). https://doi.org/10.1109/EDGE53862.2021.00022
10. Yost, B., et al.: State-of-the-art small spacecraft technology (2021)

Services in Industry 4.0. Modeling and Composition for Agile Supply Chains

Francesco Leotta$^{(\boxtimes)}$ ⓘ, Flavia Monti ⓘ, and Luciana Silo ⓘ

Sapienza Università di Roma, 00185 Rome, Italy
{leotta,monti,silo}@diag.uniroma1.it

Abstract. In recent years, there has been a growing interest in employing intelligent techniques for managing manufacturing processes in smart manufacturing. These processes often involve tens of resources distributed across several different companies that make up the supply chain. The status of these various resources evolves over time in terms of cost, quality, and the likelihood of failure, necessitating an adaptive process that is resilient to disruptions. The tutorial explores the modeling of Industry 4.0 systems as services and their composition. We discuss how these systems are designed, integrated, and orchestrated to create an interconnected manufacturing environment. The potential and limitations of automated reasoning techniques in enabling decision-making and process optimization in the modeled systems are then analyzed. Finally, a case study and a demonstration (Adaptive Industrial APIs - AIDA) will be presented to illustrate the practical application of intelligent techniques in a real manufacturing environment.

Keywords: Industry 4.0 · Smart Manufacturing · Agile supply chains · Artificial Intelligence · Digital Services

1 Introduction

Industry 4.0 represents the latest evolution in industrial automation. In contrast to Industry 3.0, which introduced the use of interconnection technologies such as EtherCAT, Industry 4.0 brings the incorporation of the Internet of Things (IoT). Like every stage of industrial automation evolution, starting from the so-called Industry 1.0 (characterized by the introduction of the steam engine), the objectives are to enhance productivity and the quality of finished products, simplify workers' tasks, and create new business opportunities [5].

The term Industry 4.0 is often used in conjunction to other trends such as Zero Defect Manufacturing [12] and Mass Customization [14].

Compared to the past, the novelty of Industry 4.0 lies in the vast amount of data that can be provided by the Internet of Things (IoT), which is supposed to simplify prediction and estimation. However, data alone is not sufficient. It is expected that this enormous volume of data will be fed into algorithms, such

F. Monti et al. (Eds.): ICSOC 2023 Workshops, LNCS 14518, pp. 350–357, 2024.
https://doi.org/10.1007/978-981-97-0989-2_31

as Artificial Intelligence techniques, to introduce "smartness" into the manufacturing process. For this reason, the term *smart manufacturing* is often used synonymously with Industry 4.0, although it can also be applicable, in principle, to Industry 3.0.

This tutorial focuses on a specific aspect of Industry 4.0: providing agility to industrial supply chains [2], which consist of so-called manufacturing networks [11], by utilizing symbolic artificial intelligence [10]. While many conclusions from this study may apply to Industry 3.0 as well, the type of information required to model services necessitates the use of the Internet of Things (IoT) and machine learning. These technologies are considered fundamental in Industry 4.0

An agile supply chain is particularly resilient to disruptions (e.g., when a machine is unavailable) and consistently chooses the solution that most likely provides the best (most rewarding) outcome. Specifically, the common goal is to develop what is known as the *triple-A* supply chain [8], which involves the simultaneous implementation of three distinct concepts: agility - responding quickly to short-term changes in demand or supply; adaptability - adjusting the supply chain design to accommodate market changes; and alignment - creating incentives for partners to enhance the performance of the entire chain. We expand this definition to include *resilience* as the ability to react to disruptions along the chain. While adaptivity and the flexibility of processes are discussed in general terms [13], the focus is typically on processes without specific reference to industrial processes and supply chains, which is instead the focus of this tutorial.

2 Intended Audience

This tutorial targets individuals from both academia and industry who have an interest in Industry 4.0 and, more broadly, in smart manufacturing.

While we strive to make the tutorial as self-contained as possible within the constraints of the allotted time, a prior understanding of concepts from the artificial intelligence domain (such as automated planning and Markov Decision Processes) is beneficial.

Participants have the option to either conduct the experiments autonomously during the tutorial or to carry them out later at their own pace by accessing the materials on the GitHub repository.

3 Outline of the Tutorial

The tutorial consists of four sections. After a brief introduction to smart manufacturing (see Sect. 1), the idea of modeling Industry 4.0 systems in terms of digital services is introduced aimed at their composition to obtain complex resilient industrial processes (see Sect. 3.1). In the third section, possible techniques from the (symbolic) artificial intelligence world to obtain this goal are described (see Sect. 3.2). Finally, the last section, introduces the AIDA tool, which implements some of these techniques (see Sect. 3.3).

3.1 Modeling and Composing Industry 4.0 Systems as Services

An Industry 4.0 supply chain encompasses a variety of actors, including humans, machines, and information systems, often from different organizations [3]. In certain situations, entire organizations may be treated as actors within the supply chain if more detailed information is not available. Additionally, the products being manufactured can also be considered as actors in their own right.

Each actor in the supply chain has a range of possible actions, each defined by specific preconditions and effects on the actor's state. The formalism used to describe these actions and state influences impacts (i) the accuracy of the actual behavior of the actor, (ii) the specific reasoning techniques that can be employed for resilience, and (iii) the methods required to keep the model current.

Actions can be classified as deterministic, non-deterministic, or probabilistic. In deterministic modeling, an action leads the actor from one state to another in a predictable manner. Non-deterministic actions, on the other hand, could result in any one of a set of possible states. Probabilistic actions are similar to non-deterministic ones, but they assign probabilities to each potential outcome.

When probabilistic actions are used, their probabilities can be determined using prediction techniques, like estimating the Remaining Useful Life of components.

Another important distinction is whether actions have associated costs or rewards. The presence of these financial factors can influence the preference for executing one action over another, or choosing one actor over another.

For instance, the wear of specific machine components might reduce the reward from using that machine compared to a newer one, indicating the need for maintenance to optimize the overall process reward.

These examples illustrate various ways to model actor behavior, and additional elements, such as precondition modeling, can be incorporated.

Representing actors by their available actions is akin to treating them as services that can be invoked to achieve specific manufacturing goals. Moreover, as most of these actions are accessible through digital interfaces, these services are essentially digital services. This applies to humans as well, whose involvement can be requested indirectly through devices like smartphones or advanced interfaces like augmented reality.

From this discussion, it is evident that modeling actors as services demands an abstraction effort that goes beyond just defining actions. It involves data refinement, often favoring discrete or discretized attributes over continuous ones, as continuous data can significantly increase the complexity of symbolic artificial intelligence methods used for control.

3.2 Approaches to Agile Supply Chain

All adaptive approaches found in the literature can be modeled as black boxes (*controllers*) taking as input the specification of the involved resources (in our case a set of services) and the final target (in our case a manufacturing goal) and providing as output an adaptive process (see Fig. 1). A conceptual classification

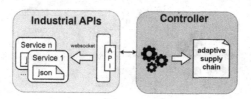

Fig. 1. Service-based adaptive framework

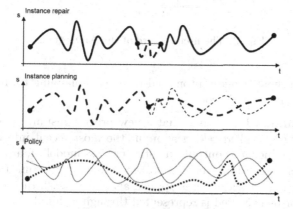

Fig. 2. Schematizing adaptive strategies.

of the possible alternatives can be defined by considering the different options for inputs and outputs. Concerning the input, we can distinguish between the deterministic and non-deterministic (or probabilistic) behaviors of manufacturing resources, and between fully specified and under-specified manufacturing goal.

Figure 2 shows an intuitive representation of the three possible strategies generated as output [10]. For each of them, the horizontal axis represents the evolution over time, whereas the vertical axis is an intuitive representation of the overall state of the resources (a tuple) in some numeric form. Each action performed in a supply chain is actually a couple $<a, r>$ where a is an action and r is the resource executing the action. The chosen sequence of actions and manufacturing resources change the state of the resources from an initial state, to a final one representing the end of the manufacturing process and possibly fulfilling the manufacturing goal(s). In the following the three different types of strategies are described.

Instance Repair. The supply chain process is precisely defined. If an unexpected exception happens (e.g., a machine breaks), automated reasoning is employed to restore the state of resources to the expected one. Adaptivity is applied locally, but the overall forthcoming process remains unchanged. In Fig. 2, the process model is represented using a solid line, whereas adaptation is represented using a dashed line. A noticeable example of instance repair is represented

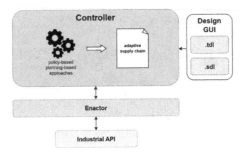

Fig. 3. The architecture of the AIDA tool.

by [9], where authors applies automated (classical) planning to "fix" the execution of a manually defined process.

Instance Planning. Every time that a new process instance is needed, automated reasoning is applied taking as input the most recent information about resources and producing as output an entire process model. If, at a certain point of the execution, something (e.g., a broken resource) prevents the plan to be completed, automated reasoning is applied again. In Fig. 2, the part of the process that cannot be executed is represented through a thin dashed line, whereas the thick dashed line represents the process actually executed. An example is presented in [4], where authors implements a mechanism based on cascading non-deterministic planning domains to find a solution which takes into account failures.

Policy-Based. Automated reasoning is employed to obtain a policy, i.e., a function that for each state proposes the next action. Differently from the *instance planning* case, here if something unexpected happens, there is no need to reapply planning, as all the possibilities have been already computed. In Fig. 2, all the possible legal executions of the process are represented through dashed lines. Among these, according to the state of the different resources, a specific one (represented as a thick dashed line) is chosen. Authors in [7], for example, model services as markov decision processes, taking into account probabilities and costs. At this point they define a composition MDP, which integrates the process definition, which produces a policy maximixing the probability of success which minimizing the cost of execution.

3.3   AIDA - Adaptive InDustrial APIs: Case Study and Demo

Figure 3 shows the architecture of the AIDA tool [6], which is used during the tutorial. The tool is freely available on the GitHub repository[1]

The tool is composed by three modules. The *Design GUI* allows to model services (in the form of SDL - Service Definition Language files) and manufacturing supply chains (in the form of TDL - Target Definition Language files). These

---

[1] cf. https://github.com/iaiamomo/icsoc2023_tutorial.

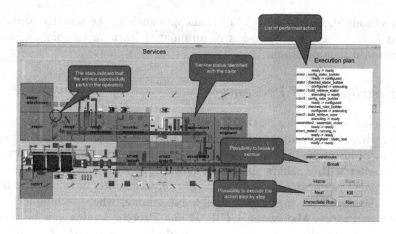

Fig. 4. The monitoring tool.

files are load by the controller, which is in charge of finding the best solution to the manufacturing process, i.e., to create an adaptive supply chain. At this point the plan/policy is passed to the enactor that calls the actual actors through the exposed Industrial APIs. The Design GUI can also be used to monitor the execution of the process as shown in Fig. 4.

At the actual stage the tool implements *(i)* an instance planning solution based on (classical) automated plannnig, *(ii)* a policy based solution with a rigid manufacturing process, and *(iii)* a policy based solution with a loosely defined manufacturing process (defined as an LTL - Linear Temporal Logic formula).

The tutorial shows the employment of the tool in the case of an electric motor manufacturing case study.

4   Learning Objectives and Outcomes

Researchers participating in this tutorial will learn how to model Industry 4.0 actors as services and how to combine them to achieve an agile manufacturing process. Additionally, attendees will explore the use of the AIDA tool (referenced in Sect. 3.3) to experiment with a range of artificial intelligence techniques that enhance supply chain agility.

Experimental results indicate that while the direct application of automated planning and Markov decision processes to complex supply chains is promising, it results in computationally intensive, albeit exact, solutions. Future research should therefore focus on simplifying the problem formulation of service composition.

Moreover, this tutorial primarily concentrates on symbolic artificial intelligence techniques for composing Industry 4.0 services. However, machine learning, particularly deep learning and Large Language Models (LLM), present compelling alternative approaches in the near future [1]. Researchers considering these methods should be mindful of challenges such as the scarcity of training data and the inherent imprecision of automated learning techniques, such as LLM-induced hallucinations.

5   Biographies of Presenters

Francesco Leotta got his PhD in Engineering in Computer Science at Sapienza in 2014, where he currently covers the position of Assistant Professor. Since the beginning of his research activity, he addressed several challenges related to how users interact with a smart space and how the environment senses the users and reactively perform actions to meet user requirements. In this research context, he developed an approach, called habit mining, where techniques typical of Business Process Management (BPM) and Process Mining can be adapted to user habit modelling and discovery. Beside this main research activity, his research interests cover advanced user interfaces, service-oriented architectures (SOA), matchmaking applied to entrepreneurship, and e-Government. He regularly serves as a reviewer for international conferences and journals in the fields of smart spaces and information systems engineering.

Flavia Monti is a PhD student in Engineering in Computer Science at the Department of Computer, Control and Management Engineerign Antonio Ruberti at Sapienza University of Rome. She got the bachelor's degree in Computer and System Engineering in 2018 at Sapienza Unversity of Rome, where she also got a master's degree in Engineering in Computer Science in 2021. Her research interests mainly concern Smart Manufacturing and Industry 4.0. Particularly the augmentation of industrial machinery through the application of innovative technologies such as digital twin, computer vision and artificial intelligence. The goal of her research is to improve production quality, reduce costs, increase machinery uptime, analyze failures and defects towards zero defect manufacturing.

Luciana Silo is a PhD student in Artificial Intelligence (National Program) at the Department of Computer, Control and Management Engineering Antonio Ruberti at Sapienza University of Rome. She obtained the bachelor's degree in Computer and System Engineering in 2017 at Sapienza Unversity of Rome, and a master's degree in Engineering in Computer Science in 2021. Currently she is also working as a software engineer at Camera Dei Deputati in Rome. Her research activity focuses on the study of Artificial Intelligence and Service Composition techniques applied to industrial processes, in the field of Smart Manufacturing and Industry 4.0. Particularly her main goal is to create an intelligent production plan minimizing failure risks and costs and optimizing the production, by making use of Digital Twins.

Acknowledgments. This work is partially funded by the ERC project WhiteMech (no. 834228), the PRIN project RIPER (no. 20203FFYLK), the Electrospindle 4.0 project (funded by MISE, Italy, no. F/160038/01-04/X41). This study was carried out within the PE1 (CUP B53C22003980006) - FAIR (Future Artificial Intelligence Research) and PE11 (CUP B53C22004130001) - MICS (Made in Italy - Circular and

Sustainable) - European Union Next-Generation-EU (Piano Nazionale di Ripresa e Resilienza - PNRR). The work of Flavia Monti is supported by the MISE agreement on "Agile&Secure Digital Twins (A&S-DT)".

References

1. Aiello, M., Georgievski, I.: Service composition in the ChatGPT era. Serv. Oriented Comput. Appl. 1–6 (2023)
2. Bicocchi, N., Cabri, G., Mandreoli, F., Mecella, M.: Dynamic digital factories for agile supply chains: an architectural approach. J. Ind. Inf. Integr. **15**, 111–121 (2019)
3. Catarci, T., Firmani, D., Leotta, F., Mandreoli, F., Mecella, M., Sapio, F.: A conceptual architecture and model for smart manufacturing relying on service-based digital twins. In: 2019 IEEE international conference on web services (ICWS), pp. 229–236. IEEE (2019)
4. Ciolek, D., D'Ippolito, N., Pozanco, A., Sardina, S.: Multi-tier automated planning for adaptive behavior. In: Proceedings of the International Conference on Automated Planning and Scheduling, vol. 30, pp. 66–74 (2020)
5. Dalenogare, L.S., Benitez, G.B., Ayala, N.F., Frank, A.G.: The expected contribution of industry 4.0 technologies for industrial performance. Int. J. Prod. Econ. **204**, 383–394 (2018)
6. De Giacomo, G., Favorito, M., Leotta, F., Mecella, M., Monti, F., Silo, L.: AIDA: a tool for resiliency in smart manufacturing. In: Cabanillas, C., Pérez, F. (eds.) CAiSE 2023. LNBIP, vol. 477, pp. 112–120. Springer, Cham (2023). https://doi.org/10.1007/978-3-031-34674-3_14
7. De Giacomo, G., Favorito, M., Leotta, F., Mecella, M., Silo, L.: Digital twins composition in smart manufacturing via Markov decision processes. Comput. Ind. **149**, 103916 (2023)
8. Lee, H.L., et al.: The triple-a supply chain. Harv. Bus. Rev. (2004)
9. Marrella, A., Mecella, M., Sardina, S.: Intelligent process adaptation in the SmartPM system. ACM Trans. Intell. Syst. Technol. (TIST) **8**(2), 1–43 (2016)
10. Monti, F., Silo, L., Leotta, F., Mecella, M.: On the suitability of AI for service-based adaptive supply chains in smart manufacturing. In: 2023 IEEE International Conference on Web Services (ICWS), pp. 704–706. IEEE (2023)
11. Papazoglou, M.P., van den Heuvel, W.J., Mascolo, J.E.: A reference architecture and knowledge-based structures for smart manufacturing networks. IEEE Softw. **32**(3), 61–69 (2015)
12. Powell, D., Magnanini, M.C., Colledani, M., Myklebust, O.: Advancing zero defect manufacturing: a state-of-the-art perspective and future research directions. Comput. Ind. **136**, 103596 (2022)
13. Reichert, M., Weber, B.: Enabling Flexibility in Process-aware Information Systems: Challenges, Methods, Technologies. Springer, Heidelberg (2012). https://doi.org/10.1007/978-3-642-30409-5
14. Tseng, M.M., Jiao, J.: Mass customization. Handb. Ind. Eng. **3**, 684–709 (2001)

Author Index

A

Abusafia, Amani 297
Ahmed, Noor 119
Aiello, Marco 39
Alibasa, Muhammad Johan 5
Alkouz, Balsam 297
Alvarado-Valiente, Jaime 335
Anaissi, Ali 5

B

Barakat, Saman 311
Baresi, Luciano 285
Barzen, Johanna 150
Bazan-Muñoz, Adrian 279
Bechtold, Marvin 150
Beckert, Bernhard 137
Borovits, Nemania 265
Bouguettaya, Athman 297
Brogi, Antonio 317

C

Cameron, Ian 27, 49
Chang, Ya-Yuan 5
Chomątek, Lukasz 229
Claßen, Henrik 213
Comuzzi, Marco 327
Craig, Ashley 27, 49

D

Dell'Immagine, Giorgio 317

F

Farhood, Helia 72
Fernandez, Pablo 304
Fontana, Francesca Arcelli 317
Fürntratt, Hermann 162

G

García, José María 241, 304
Garcia-Alonso, Jose 197

G (cont.)

Garcia-Alonso, José 335
Garcia-de-Prado, Alfonso 279
Georgievski, Ilche 39
Ghodratnama, Samira 17, 62
González, Laura 253
Grefen, Paul 327

H

Howard-Grubb, Thomas 317

J

Jeffar, Farouk 107

K

Kao, Odej 213
Keckeisen, Michael 150
Klamroth, Jonas 137
Krebs, Florian 162
Kubiak, Mateusz 229
Kumara, Indika 265

L

Leotta, Francesco 350
Leymann, Frank 150
Li, Qing 343
Lin, Jiamin 297
Ling, Xiaojun 91

M

Maldonado-Romo, A. 185
Mandl, Alexander 150
Martínez-Felipe, M. 185
Martin-Lopez, Alberto 311
McMahon, John E. 27, 49
Meroni, Giovanni 327
Moguel, Enrique 335
Molino-Peña, Elena 241
Monti, Flavia 350
Montiel-Pérez, J. 185

F. Monti et al. (Eds.): ICSOC 2023 Workshops, LNCS 14518, pp. 359–360, 2024.
https://doi.org/10.1007/978-981-97-0989-2

Müller, Carlos   311
Murillo, Juan Manuel   197, 335

N
Najafi, Mohammad   72

O
Onofre, Victor   185
Ortiz, Guadalupe   279

P
Peluaga Lozada, Ignacio   304
Pesl, Robin D.   39
Plebani, Pierluigi   107
Poniszewska-Marańda, Aneta   229

Q
Quattrocchi, Giovanni   285

R
Raibulet, Claudia   91
Romero-Álvarez, Javier   335
Roozegar, Rasool   27
Ruggia, Raúl   253
Ruiz-Cortés, Antonio   197

S
Saberi, Morteza   72
Sanchez-Rivero, Javier   197
Schnabl, Paul   162
Segura, Sergio   311
Silo, Luciana   350
Soldani, Jacopo   317

Störl, Uta   174
Stötzner, Miles   39
Suleiman, Basem   5

T
Talaván, Daniel   197
Tamburri, Damian A.   265
Thierfeldt, Jonas   213
Ticongolo, Inacio Gaspar   285
Tochman-Szewc, Julian   213

U
Unterberger, Roland   162

V
Van Den Heuvel, Willem-Jan   265
Vaudrevange, Patrick K. S.   150
Vergara, Sebastián   253

W
Wiesner, Philipp   213

X
Xu, Daliang   343

Y
Young, Ricky   185

Z
Zajac, Markus   174
Zakershahrak, Mehrdad   17, 62
Zeiner, Herwig   162

Printed in the United States
by Baker & Taylor Publisher Services

Printed in the United States
by Baker & Taylor Publisher Services